Taxation Policy & Practice

1997/98 edition

Dora Hancock

The Business School, Leeds Metropolitan University, UK

INTERNATIONAL THOMSON BUSINESS PRESS
I(T)P® An International Thomson Publishing Company

London · Bonn · Boston · Johannesburg · Madrid · Melbourne · Mexico City · New York · Paris
Singapore · Tokyo · Toronto · Albany, NY · Belmont, CA · Cincinnati, OH · Detroit, MI

Taxation Policy & Practice 1997/98, 5th edition
Copyright © 1997 Dora Hancock

I(T)P® A division of International Thomson Publishing Inc.
The ITP logo is a trademark under licence

Produced by Gray Publishing, Tunbridge Wells
Printed in the UK by the Alden Press, Oxford

British Library Cataloguing-in-Publication Data
A catalogue record for this book is available from the British Library

Published by Chapman & Hall
First edition 1993
Second edition 1994
Third edition 1995
Fourth edition International Thomson Business Press 1996

ISBN 1-8615-2105-7

International Thomson Business Press   International Thomson Business Press
Berkshire House   20 Park Plaza
168–173 High Holborn   13th Floor
London WC1V 7AA   Boston MA 02116
UK   USA

http://www.itbp.com

For Kathy and Michael, who should know why.

Contents

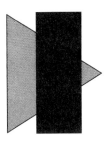

Preface

The fifth edition of this book has been fully updated to take account of the measures introduced in the Finance Act 1997. Some new questions have been included in this edition. Once again, apart from a reduction in the basic rate of tax there were relatively few changes introduced in the budget although the move to reduce tax avoidance will inevitably make the law more complex in the future.

Once again model answers to many of the end of chapter questions have been included at the end of the book.

I hope that readers of the text find it useful and thought-provoking. Any comments on the text should be sent to the publishers and will be taken into account when preparing future editions of the book.

Dora Hancock

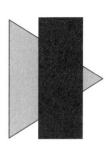

Preface to the first edition

I have felt for some time there has been a need for a text for accounting students studying taxation. This book has been written to meet that need.

There are a number of texts for students preparing for professional exams as well as texts for students studying the legal aspects of taxation. There are also texts which focus on the economics of tax.

Accounting students need to have some practical appreciation of tax which the latter two groups of books do not provide nor do the professional texts offer the theoretical framework which academic students need.

This text offers basic coverage of current tax law together with practical questions taken from the professional accounting examining bodies set in the context of the economics of taxation.

The book is designed to enable students to undertake independent study and has a large number of activities which will help a student to evaluate his/her progress. Wherever possible the impact of taxation on the behaviour of individuals and businesses has been discussed and the way in which taxation sometimes reflects social change has also been illustrated. For example, the taxation of the family unit since the Second World War is set in the context of the change in the family that has taken place during that time.

Each chapter is intended to be dealt with during one lecture and one seminar, although some chapters, particularly those on business tax and capital gains tax, could profitably be dealt with in two sessions rather than one.

The book is suitable for a one-year course. The one-semester courses taught by the author omits the chapters on group tax and inheritance tax as well as much of the detail of the chapters on income tax, corporation tax and VAT.

It would also be appropriate for students to be asked to read some of the early chapters as preparation for the course. Many references to these early chapters are made throughout the book thus encouraging students to undertake such preparation. Finally taxation offers a rich source of topics for project work. There are suggestions for suitable areas throughout the book.

I hope that readers will find the book useful and stimulating. Any comments about the text should be sent to the publishers and will be taken into account when preparing the next edition of the book.

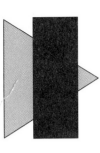

Acknowledgments

I would like to thank all the people at International Thomson Publishing and Gray Publishing, especially Sarah Henderson, Sophie Durlacher, Linda Yelverton and Robert Gray for all their hard work in publishing the text in record time this year. I would also like to thank CIMA and ACCA who allowed me to use past examination questions. I have prepared the answers to past examination questions. As always I am grateful to Tony Underhill who has reviewed the text and corrected many of my mistakes and has, as always, made many useful suggestions. I could not have updated the text this year without the help of my mother, my husband and Kathy who have looked after Jamie once again while I was locked in the study.

The legislative framework of taxation

Introduction

Ever since people started to gather together in groups and provide resources for the community such as defence, taxes had to be raised to pay for such services. In the latter part of the 20th century taxes are used to achieve a number of government objectives as well as raise revenue to fund Parliament's spending. In 20th-century Britain we largely accept taxation as a necessary part of our society. However, it has not always been so.

At the end of this chapter you will be able to:

- discuss the historical background of taxation, particularly in the UK
- describe the main features of the UK tax system today, including the systems for collecting taxes, the legal framework of taxation and the administration of taxation
- discuss the impact of taxation on the behaviour of individuals and organisations
- define fiscal neutrality
- identify progressive and regressive taxes and discuss their characteristics
- compare and contrast tax evasion, tax avoidance and tax mitigation
- discuss the main points of the Finance Act 1997.

A brief history of taxation

Before we study the history of tax we must first determine what a tax is. All taxes have some features in common. They are a compulsory levy, imposed by government, on either income, expenditure or capital assets, for which the taxpayer receives nothing specific in return. The primary purpose of imposing a tax is to raise money for public purposes.

Taxation in Roman times

In the time of Julius Caesar Roman citizens did not pay tax. All the revenue required by the empire, including the cost of the military operations, was requisitioned from the people who lived in territories which had been occupied by the Romans. Only indirect taxes were raised in Rome itself because direct taxes were seen to be humiliating and undignified.

Indirect taxes, such as customs duties, are paid by an individual through purchasing goods and services, and are not directly related to the personal circumstances of the taxpayer. On the other hand, direct taxes, such as income tax, can directly reduce the taxpayer's income and can be directly related to the taxpayer's personal circumstances. Romans resisted direct taxes, not so much because of an unwillingness to pay them, but because of the loss of privacy which such taxes necessitated.

Requisitioning required every citizen to assist the Roman state with his labour and property. The system had a number of serious disadvantages, principally its lack of certainty. This led to tax demands being levied in an unpredictable and arbitrary way.

Think about the system of tax which operates in the UK today. Employers are required to collect the taxes due from their employees under the PAYE system. This is really a form of compulsory service imposed on employers. If they don't comply they are potentially liable to fines and interest on tax unpaid. In addition businesses are required to operate as unpaid tax collectors under the systems for collecting VAT and once again failure to comply can lead to punitive fines and penalties.

Some commentators may also argue that there is a lack of certainty about the tax liability which a transaction may attract because the Inland Revenue refuses to advise taxpayers of their attitude towards activities in advance of submitting accounts or computations. Even if the taxpayer believed that he would ultimately succeed in an action against the Revenue the cost is such as to be a deterrent and so the attitude of the Revenue to a transaction can be crucial.

The Romans introduced a system of collective responsibility so that members of the taxpayer's family, neighbours and community could be called upon to pay any taxes which the taxpayer defaulted on. Tax collection was undertaken by publican companies under contract to the emperor and there was a considerable amount of corruption by both the emperors and the publican companies.

Occasionally it was necessary to raise a direct tax, called a *tributum*, on the citizens of Rome, leading to the necessity of a census. Often the *tributum* was repaid by the state after the need for it passed. In addition some indirect taxes were raised by charging import and export duties. There are a number of references to the tax system of the day in the New Testament, particularly in Matthew's Gospel, which you may find interesting to read.

Augustus realised that a fairer system of tax would have to be introduced and created a civil service to administer the tax. He introduced a 5% inheritance tax, which was payable on the death of a taxpayer from his estate, a 1% sales tax on public auctions and a 4% tax on the sale of slaves.

Tiberius, when encouraged to increase the direct taxation from the provinces, refused saying 'A good shepherd should shear his flock, not skin it.' Indeed this offered wisdom is hung prominently inside No. 11 Downing Street.

Chancellors today seem to agree with Tiberius, operating as they do with a top rate of tax of 40%, but in the 1970s some taxpayers paid tax at a top rate of 98% on their investment income.

The Romans also introduced a rudimentary system of social security by paying a form of family allowance nearly 2,000 years ago.

Between the 2nd and 3rd centuries AD inflation was extremely high and the taxes described above were allowed to lapse. Instead taxes were raised in the form of goods rather than money.

At the beginning of the 4th century AD Diocletian introduced *capitatio*, a poll tax, and *jugatio*, a tax on landed property. The land was divided into four classes: vines, olive trees, arable land and pasture land, each class with further sub-classes. Land of a higher quality fell into a higher class leading to greater taxes than land of a lower quality, regardless of the way in which the land was actually used. This is the first example of the capacity to generate wealth being taxed rather than taxing the wealth generated.

An individual paid poll tax for himself and all his employees. The tax on women was a fraction of the tax for a man. The fraction varied across the empire. A man was taken as being a unit of tax with all other taxes, including land taxes expressed as a fraction of a man.

The Empire decided how much tax should be raised in total and allocated this to regions, which then calculated the tax which must be levied on a man. From this all tax liabilities were calculated and collected from the citizens. Taxes were still based on payment in kind rather than cash and the majority of the taxes were collected at source. Hence landowners with tenants were required to pay taxes for themselves and their tenants. Individuals who were not wealthy landowners or tenants paid their taxes directly to the local municipal council. In practice the tax tied citizens to their land, limiting prospects for advancement and was extremely progressive.

Under a progressive tax system a taxpayer who is better off pays a higher proportion of his income in tax than a less well off individual. In contrast the burden of tax falls heavily on the poorest in a regressive tax system. The direct tax system in the UK is progressive because taxpayers on relatively low incomes pay a relatively low proportion of their income in income tax while better off taxpayers pay a higher proportion. For a tax system to be progressive it is not enough for better off taxpayers to pay more tax than the less well off: the better off must pay proportionately more in tax than the less well off.

In fact the system in Diocletian's time was so progressive that the higher a taxpayer's income before tax the lower his income after tax. That is the tax paid on an extra unit of income was greater than 100%. This tax system was blamed for the decline in both economic prosperity and personal freedom and ultimately contributed to the downfall of the Roman Empire.

The introduction of taxation in the UK

In medieval times kings had access to revenue from three sources. They received income from Crown property and from feudal rights, which were considered to provide the kings with sufficient revenue to meet their normal expenditure. In addition kings could raise customs duties and grants in times of emergency, provided that Parliament approved. In practice Parliament usually did not grant the king the right to raise all the revenue he asked for.

The role of Parliament was to act as a brake on public expenditure. Ironically, with the large budget deficit which exists today, it is more likely to be Parliament which is restrained by the Treasury than the other way round.

The customs duties were levied on both imports and exports. Initially the funds raised were used for naval purposes and offered some protection to merchants against piracy. Merchants consequently saw the tax as something of an insurance premium. However, in much the same way as with the road fund licence today, the revenue raised was soon diverted to other uses. Most of the goods which were imported were luxury goods and so the tax was ultimately suffered by wealthy people who probably gained most benefit from the money raised. The peasants would have been largely unaffected by the taxes.

The feudal services and the right to a payment in lieu of such services are examples of direct taxes, while customs duties are indirect taxes. The indirect taxes proved to be both easy and economical to collect while the direct taxes were difficult and expensive to collect. Citizens were able to challenge an assessment to tax in the courts and case law is still an important source of law today. There were, and are, a number of advantages of customs taxes. Firstly, during this time there was a large volume of overseas trade, primarily with Europe, so that a relatively large amount of tax could be raised from a relatively low rate of tax. Secondly the tax was relatively cheap and easy to collect although tax evasion, through smuggling, was widespread.

As you have already seen, kings could raise money from a variety of feudal services, or payments in lieu of services, and from their income-generating assets, which were primarily land. However, income from both these sources was expensive to collect and evasion and avoidance was widespread. Tax evasion, unlike tax avoidance, is illegal. For instance, if a trader conceals some of his revenue from the authorities in order to reduce his burden of taxation he is evading tax, but if he legally arranges his affairs so as to reduce the amount of tax payable this is tax avoidance and is permissible. For example, a man may transfer investments to his non-working wife in order for the income from them to escape tax. However, as we shall see, the courts are taking an increasingly tough line on tax avoidance and artificial schemes which have no business purpose other than to reduce a tax liability are open to challenge by the Inland Revenue.

In times of war the king was unable to raise enough revenue to fund the military effort. The king had no absolute right to raise additional funds and so had to negotiate with his wealthier subjects. These subjects usually insisted that the king follow the formal procedures which meant that Parliament had to be convened for the king to request either increases in customs duties or to raise a lay subsidy, called the system of the fifteenths and tenths, which was a tax on all movable property and income. Some personal goods such as clothes and armour were exempt from the tax. The members of Parliament were the country's wealthiest citizens, who were also the people most likely to be affected by an increase in the king's tax raising power. However, these members were also the people with the most to lose if the king was unsuccessful in the war, and so Parliament usually granted the king his request. In fact increases in these taxes had the effect of redistributing wealth from the king's wealthier subjects to the peasants who became soldiers. However, there was a great power struggle between the monarchy and Parliament, which of course was eventually won by Parliament.

In 1377 Parliament gave the king permission to levy a poll tax of four old pence on all his adult male subjects. Two years later the king was granted permission to raise a graduated poll tax. Peasants still paid four old pence but subjects with positions were taxed at higher rates depending on their status: up to £4 for barons, earls and mayors. In real terms the tax represented about 2% of income. The amount which was levied varied according to the income of the individual but there were no mechanisms for determining fluctuating incomes and so only fixed incomes were taxed.

On both occasions the general populace rebelled and evasion was widespread. Two years later Parliament once again, and with reluctance, granted the king the right to levy a poll tax, this time at one shilling (12 pence) a head. Because the tax was not graduated by reference to the taxpayer's wealth it was regressive, that is the burden of tax fell most heavily on the poorest members of society, and was once again widely evaded. In fact the peasants revolted and nearly brought about the downfall of the king. (Perhaps if Margaret Thatcher had read her history she might have survived the challenge to her leadership in 1990.) Interestingly the evidence suggests that the revolt was not so much due to an inability to pay as to an unwillingness to pay this new tax which was set at a relatively high level.

In 1435 and 1450 a graduated income tax was introduced as a temporary measure. The tax was levied at a rate of 2.5% on small incomes and 10% on large incomes. Once again only fixed incomes were taxed.

By Henry VIII's reign a mixture of the two systems was operating. Individuals whose income could easily be ascertained, such as the clergy, wage-earners and landowners, were subject to income tax while individuals whose income fluctuated, such as merchants, professional men and tenant farmers, were subject to tax on their movable property. During the reign of Elizabeth the income tax rate was 20% while movables were taxed at a rate of two-fifteenths. Movables included coins, plate, merchandise, household goods and debts owed to the taxpayer less debts owed by him. Even the poor were subject to these taxes as exemption limits were set very low. As before both these taxes were only raised during times of financial urgency. However, by the middle of the 16th century the exemption limits had been raised and only the upper and middle classes paid taxes.

Taxation became a contentious issue between the king and Parliament during the reign of the Stuarts primarily because, as is now generally agreed, the Stuarts had insufficient revenue to fulfil their royal functions. This led to King James applying to Parliament for financing the ordinary expenses of government which caused bitter quarrels. King Charles I, James's son, also suffered from this problem and Parliament refused to grant him the right to raise revenue through customs duties for life, as had been done in the past, but granted the duties for 12 months. Eventually Charles levied the duties without the consent of Parliament. The differences between the monarch and Parliament became insurmountable and finally there was a civil war and Charles was executed. From that day until the present, Parliament has ruled in the UK, although a limited monarchy was restored with Charles II. One interesting result of this struggle is that the Board of the Inland Revenue receive their commission to act from the Crown rather than from Parliament. Thus the Board is deemed to have inherited some of the qualities of the Crown, in particular justice, equity and mercy. We will not have the opportunity to evaluate the performance of the Inland Revenue against these criteria in this book but you might like to consider the matter during your working life.

Excise duties on food, drink and other essentials were introduced in 1643. They were unpopular as the burden of the tax fell on everyone including the poor but had the advantage of being easy to collect. Like the poll taxes before them, excise duties on the necessities of life are regressionary, that is, the poor pay a larger proportion of their income in duty than the better off.

Parliament attempted to reform the personal tax system after Charles's execution but was largely unsuccessful. The country was divided into regions who were required to raise a set amount of revenue with little guidance about the way in which the tax should be levied and little supervision. The tax soon became a tax on land rather than on income or other assets.

In 1662 a hearth tax was introduced which was readily avoided by the simple expedient of blocking up hearths.

In 1688 a graduated poll tax and the General Aid system was introduced. Individuals paid poll tax according to their rank. Under the General Aid system three types of tax were levied. Individuals with property in goods, merchandise, money and debts were required to pay 5% on their annual profits which were deemed to equal 6% of their net capital. Employees paid 5% of their salary in tax. Finally a tax of 5% was levied on the true yearly value of all lands, tenements, tithes and mines. By 1692 the rate had increased to 20%. Initially the General Aid tax was successful but the revenue raised fell over the years and in 1698 the poll tax was abandoned and a fixed quota system for each region was reintroduced, although this time the basis for assessment to tax was clearly laid down together with the rates at which tax should be paid. Salaries were taxed at 15% and the balance of the quota was to be raised from the Land Tax which was a rate on land, tenements, tithes and mines in the district. Over time the tax on income proved to be largely uncollectable and the Land Tax became the sole source of direct tax for Parliament. The Land Tax was finally repealed in 1949. One of the reasons for the longevity of the Land Tax is the ease of collecting the tax and the virtual impossibility of tax evasion. These advantages outweighed the many disadvantages of the Land Tax. The Council Tax introduced in April 1993 is a form of land tax, with reliefs for low income groups and single occupancy accommodation. Despite its many disadvantages it is already proving to be easier to collect than the Community Charge was.

In 1747 a window tax was introduced in an attempt to make taxes less regressive. It was argued that the rich had larger houses and more windows and so would pay more tax than poorer citizens. Like the hearth tax before, avoidance was easy and evasion was widespread. In 1851 the window tax was abolished on the grounds of public health.

Today governments often use the tax legislation to influence individuals' behaviour in order to achieve their objectives as well as to raise revenue. For instance, the UK government offers tax incentives to individuals who provide for a pension for themselves, thus reducing the financial burden on the state of an ageing population.

Modern-day income tax has its roots in the tax introduced by William Pitt in 1799. When the Napoleonic Wars started William Pitt borrowed money against future excise revenue, in order to finance the war. This was the first budget deficit. However, it became apparent that the war was going to last too long to enable this method of financing to be sustained. Pitt needed to find a new way to raise taxes. He introduced an income tax at a rate of 10% which was targeted on the rich middle and upper classes, the people with the most to lose if the war was lost. There was massive evasion of the tax and only £6m was raised in the first year rather than the £10m anticipated.

Although the poorest people were not subject to income tax it is estimated that by 1810 a labourer earning £22 a year paid £11 in indirect tax, a truly colossal proportion of his income. It did not seem possible to fund the war by increasing indirect taxes. Taxpayers earning over £60 per annum were required to make a return listing all their sources of income and calculating the amount of tax which was due on that income.

The law did not allow for any control over the correctness of the return. In an attempt to reduce evasion, which was widespread, withholding taxes were introduced by the Bank of England. For example, the Bank paid dividends net of tax. Pitt resigned in 1801 and his income tax was repealed in 1802 by Addington because it was seen as a wartime tax only. In 1803 Addington introduced a new income tax which introduced the five Schedules, A to E, which have survived, apart from Schedule B which was abolished in 1988, until today. Addington was also responsible for 'taxation at the source'. Rent, salaries, pensions and interest were all paid net of basic rate tax. Because of this innovation it is probably fair to say that Addington is the true father of income tax rather than Pitt who has generally been awarded the honour. Addington's income tax was progressive and ranged from 1% on an income of £60 to 10% on an income of over £200. Income tax was repealed once again in 1816.

In 1842 Peel reintroduced income tax as a temporary measure, at a very low level, to deal with an inherited budget deficit of £5 million. Peel drew on Addington's Act of 1803 for his legislation making only minor amendments. Peel rejected proposals to impose high rates of tax on the wealthy arguing that it would lead to them closing their businesses or even leaving the country. A second major criticism of income tax was the need to undertake an annual investigation, or as Peel put it: 'A certain degree of inquisitorial scrutiny is, therefore, inseparable from an income tax.' It was this rather than the actual rate of the tax which was generally opposed. It seems that income tax was as unwelcome in the 19th century as it was in Roman times.

Income below £150 was exempted and income above this figure was taxed at 3% regardless of the amount of the income. At the same time indirect taxes were reduced in order to help the country's manufacturing, trading and commercial sectors.

The income tax was supported, despite its drawbacks, because not only was it seen to be temporary and set at a low level but also industrialists believed that for the government to raise all its revenue by means of indirect taxation was cutting consumer spending and increasing inflation. Ironically these measures received more approval from the opposition than from Peel's own party. Not all income was taxed in full: for example, farmers were taxed on the rental value of their land rather than their farming profits. Farmers were not taxed on their income until 1941.

Peel also created a system of Special Commissioners, who were experts in taxation, with whom businessmen could deal rather than the General Commissioners, who were local businessmen, from whom the taxpayer might want privacy. In addition, if the taxpayer disputed the amount of tax which was deemed to be payable he could choose to appeal to either the Special

Commissioners or the General Commissioners. This system remains in force today.

Peel also introduced a fixed penalty of £50 for any taxpayer who was found to be 'neglectful in connection with his return of income'. The penalty was abolished in 1923 but today the Inland Revenue can impose interest charges as well as penalties on taxpayers who fail to pay the full amount of tax due.

William Gladstone introduced 13 budgets during the last half of the 19th century. At the time of his first budget in 1853 public expenditure was over £50 million a year and nearly £30 million of the total was used to pay interest on the National Debt. Gladstone claimed that the cause of the deficit was the prevailing level of income tax. Less tax was raised in 1853 from income tax than was collected in each of the years from 1806 to 1815. Gladstone was aware of the limitations of the system of income tax, especially self-assessment which led to widespread fraud. To start to redress the balance Gladstone extended legacy duty so that land and businesses were subject to tax on the death of their owner. He reduced the rates of indirect taxation, believing that this would stimulate consumption and thus not actually reduce the net receipts to the government. This, together with the reforms introduced by Peel, helped to free the restrictions on trade by encouraging imports and enabling exports to be sold as cheaply as possible. However, Gladstone has been criticised for failing to reduce the National Debt or spend money on social issues such as public health and housing.

Gladstone intended to phase income tax out by 1860 but for a number of reasons this did not prove to be possible and the rate of income tax had to rise. Public expenditure was already growing rapidly, much to Gladstone's regret, and this made it impossible ever again to consider abolishing income tax.

Harcourt introduced Estate Duty, referred to as Death Duties, in 1894. The Estate Duty removed many of the injustices of the old legacy duties which had evolved over many centuries and so suffered from inconsistencies. The origin of the present-day inheritance tax can be traced to 1694 and probate duties. This new tax fell most heavily on the landowners. Harcourt justified this bias by claiming that property values had been greatly increased since the railways were built. The duty was at the rate of 1% on estates worth between £100 and £500 with estates worth more than £1 million taxed at 8%. The money raised was largely used to fund the expansion of the Navy. The new tax was highly unpopular with the families who were affected by it. They argued that an individual who chose to spend his money could avoid paying the tax which would be levied on the estate of the careful man who accumulated assets to pass on to the next generation. Others argued that future Chancellors would be unable to resist the temptation to increase both the rate of the tax and its scope. The question of tax avoidance was also raised, commentators arguing that by simply giving the estate away during the lifetime of the testator the tax could be completely avoided. Harcourt defended his tax, arguing that estate duty was the only opportunity to tax non-income-generating assets such as the taxpayer's main residence.

Harcourt next turned his attention to income tax, considering the possibility of making it progressive. Harcourt was strongly in favour of the system of deduction of tax at source, which applied to about three-quarters of all income tax collected, arguing that it meant that there was no 'inquisitorial prying' into the affairs of individuals. The Revenue argued that were it not for the system of deduction at source the investigations that they would have to make and the penalties which they would have to impose for mis-declarations would 'render the collection of the Income Tax so odious as to imperil its existence and in all probability make it impossible to maintain the tax.' He concluded that the system of deduction at source, which he approved of, made a progressive income tax system impossible.

Taxation in the 20th century

Until this century tax was paid on earned income by less than a million people. Hence tax was still paid only by the better off. However, during the 20th century public expenditure has increased phenomenally. In 1907 Asquith introduced personal allowances, which exempted a proportion of earned income from income tax. In 1908 old-age pensions were introduced. This, together with a need to increase spending on the Navy, necessitated an increase in taxation. In 1909 Lloyd George introduced the first progressive tax on income in the so-called 'People's Budget'. The budget was not generally accepted and was rejected by the House of Lords in November 1909 but eventually became law in 1910. The power of the House of Lords to veto budgets was removed in 1911. Lloyd George believed that everyone should contribute taxes no matter how poor they were. He also believed that taxes should be so constructed that they did not inflict injury on trade and commerce. This is an idea which we will consider later in this chapter and in some detail in Chapters 2 and 3.

The First World War led to increases in tax including a top rate of 15%. However, the tax raised was insufficient to fund the war and the deficit was funded by borrowing. The new tax was called supertax and caused the rate of income tax to be doubled. In 1928 supertax was renamed surtax and income over £5,000 (over £150,000 stated in today's values) was taxed at 8%. In addition motor car licences were introduced and a new tax on petrol was imposed. By 1939 fewer than one in five of the working population was liable to income tax and so people of average earnings did not pay tax. However, the Second World War tripled the number of taxpayers to 12 million as well as tripling the amount of tax raised. One of the reasons for this increase was a substantial increase in inflation during the Second World War.

A system termed 'pay-as-you-earn' (PAYE) was introduced in 1944 where tax was deducted from individuals' pay before they received it. Until the introduction of PAYE only individuals paid by central or local government had tax deducted at source from their salaries. The PAYE system had a number of advantages. The government's cash flow was improved, as there was no more waiting until the end of the tax year for the collection of tax. Bad debts were reduced, the government became the ultimate preferential creditor, receiving its cut even before the individual. It was also easier for individuals to pay tax weekly rather than facing a large bill at the end of the tax year.

There was an explosion in government expenditure and this was matched by the increase in taxes raised, with the top rate of tax on incomes of over £20,000 per annum standing at 52.5% in 1946. However, taxation is also used as an economic regulator as well as to modify individuals' behaviour.

By 1946 the limit for estate duty purposes increased from £100 to £3,000, the first increase for 50 years. The increase had the effect of exempting many smaller estates from the duty. However, the highest rates of tax were also increased to a maximum of 75% on estates of over £2 million.

After the war the National Health Service was formed and national insurance contributions were introduced to provide for health care, retirement pensions and sickness benefit.

Purchase tax was used to tax spending. There were a large number of rates of tax and many inconsistencies in the rates applied to various expenditure. For example, pianos and organs were exempt but other musical instruments were taxed at 27.5%; records were taxed at 50% while books were exempt from the tax. Purchase tax was replaced in 1973 by VAT.

In 1965 two new taxes were introduced, corporation tax and capital gains tax. Until 1965 companies were subject to income tax and there are still many similarities between the two systems. We will consider corporation tax in Chapters 8 and 9. Capital gains tax, which is discussed in Chapter 7, was intended to reduce tax avoidance and increase the equity of the tax system rather than to raise significant revenue.

In 1975 capital transfer tax was introduced only to be replaced by inheritance tax in 1984. Estate duty only taxed the value of the taxpayer's estate at death. Lifetime gifts were completely exempt. Capital transfer tax introduced tax on lifetime transfers for the first time. However, over the next few years the impact of capital transfer tax was limited by the introduction of a seven-year cycle and was finally replaced by inheritance tax in 1984.

In 1979 the top rate of tax on earned income in the UK was 83% and unearned income over £5,500 such as rents received and dividends was subject to an investment income surcharge of 15% giving a top rate of tax of 98% for some taxpayers.

The administration of taxation today

As with many other public sector institutions the 1980s and 1990s have led to many changes in the organisation of the Inland Revenue.

The Chancellor of the Exchequer, Kenneth Clarke, is responsible for the Treasury. The Treasury appoints the Board of Inland Revenue, also termed the Commissioners of Inland Revenue (CIR). The Board of Inland Revenue receive their authority from the Crown, not from Parliament, and this imposes a requirement that they adopt, among others, the qualities of justice, equity and mercy. In *Sebel Products Ltd* v *Commissioners of Customs and Excise* (1949) Mr Justice Vaisey stated that the Commissioners were 'an emanation of the Crown, which is the source and fountain of justice' and so were bound to maintain the highest standards of probity and fair dealing. The Board of Inland Revenue is staffed by civil servants who administer income tax, corporation tax and capital gains tax. The administration of these taxes is governed by the Taxes Management Act 1970 (TMA 1970).

The Board of Inland Revenue divides the UK into a number of autonomous Executives each run by a Regional Chief Executive. Each region is then subdivided into districts which are the responsibility of a district inspector. Each district inspector has a number of other inspectors (called HM Inspectors of Taxes, HMITs) and clerical staff working for him. The districts are responsible for calculating the amount of tax which is due from individuals, businesses and companies and raising a notice of assessment. They use information sent to them by taxpayers, the main sources being tax returns and sets of accounts.

The Collectors of Taxes are also appointed by the Board of Inland Revenue. Collectors are responsible for collecting the amount of tax which is assessed to be payable by the Inspectors. Collectors have powers to apply through the courts to seize taxpayers' assets to satisfy the debt. The collection of taxes is largely undertaken on a national rather than a regional basis.

The Lord Chancellor appoints special and general commissioners. Both general and special commissioners hear taxpayers' appeals against the assessment of the inspectors. General commissioners are part time and unpaid. They are appointed for a division and appoint a clerk, usually an accountant or a lawyer, who is paid by the Board of Inland Revenue.

On the other hand, special commissioners are full time and are paid for their services. They must have been legally qualified for at least ten years and hear more complex appeals.

Because income tax was reintroduced as a temporary tax it is necessary to pass a law each year to enable the tax to continue to be collected.

Like much of the rest of English law there are a series of Acts of Parliament, which form the legislative framework within which to operate, together with a substantial number of cases which have been used both to clarify the law and, in recent years, to extend it.

Until the mid-18th century the government used an accounting year which ended on Lady day, which was 25th March, the first quarter day in the calendar year. In 1752 the government adopted the Gregorian calendar which necessitated the loss of 11 days between the 2nd and 14th of September to bring the calendar year back into line with the solar year. However, the government was unwilling to have an accounting period which did not run for 365 days and so moved their year end forward by 11 days to 5th April. Hence today a fiscal year runs from 6th April to the following 5th April: the fiscal year 1997/98 runs from 6th April 1997 to 5th April 1998. At the beginning of each fiscal year the Inland Revenue sends out a 'Tax Return' to many taxpayers. If a taxpayer receives a return it must be completed and returned to the inspector within 30 days of receipt. The taxpayer must include details about his or her income for the previous fiscal year as well as claiming allowances and reliefs for the coming year. For instance, in a return for the fiscal year 1997/98 a taxpayer will include details of income for the fiscal year 1996/97 and information about personal circumstances for 1997/98. If the taxpayer runs a business he or she must also submit accounts to the revenue unless the business turnover (or rental income) is less than £15,000, in which case a statement of turnover, total expenses and profit is sufficient, although the Inland Revenue still may request the full accounts.

The Inland Revenue has the right to impose penalties if the tax return is late, although in practice it often does not enforce them. Not every taxpayer receives a tax return each year but if a taxpayer becomes chargeable to either income tax or capital gains tax he or she must notify the Inland Revenue within one year of the end of the year of assessment for which he or she is chargeable.

In 1996/97 a system of self-assessment was introduced which was intended to make it easier for taxpayers to complete their own tax returns.

Income taxed at source

Another key feature of our tax system is the extent to which income is taxed at source. For example, if a taxpayer receives interest or dividends tax will have already been deducted. An individual who is not liable to income tax can reclaim the tax deducted at source. The amount of tax deducted at source is independent of the taxpayer's personal circumstances. Taxpayers who are employed pay tax under the PAYE scheme. Although tax is clearly deducted at source it is somewhat different to the other examples because the amount of tax deducted is dependent on the taxpayer's personal circumstances.

The income tax schedules and corporation tax

Until 1965 individuals and companies were taxed under the same rules. In 1965 corporation tax was introduced but there are still many similarities between the taxation of the two groups.

Income is taxed with reference to a number of Schedules and Cases. For example, income from employment, including pensions, is taxed under Schedule E. Income from a trade or profession is taxed under Schedule D Case I. Each source of income received by a taxpayer is assessed under a Schedule. Schedule D Case VI is used to tax annual profits or gains not falling under any other Case of Schedule D and not charged by virtue of Schedules A, C or E (ICTA 1988 s18(3)). Each Schedule has its own rules which determine how much income should be assessed, what deductions are allowed and when the tax should be paid. We will study these rules in detail in Chapters 4, 5 and 6. Corporate income is taxed under the same Schedules and Cases as income tax. The principal difference is that for a company tax is due to be paid nine months after the end of the accounting period whereas individuals will make interim payments on 1st January in the tax year and 31st July following the tax year and a final payment on 31st January following the tax year.

Direct and indirect taxation

Direct tax is tax which is suffered directly by the taxpayer, for instance income tax. Indirect tax is a tax which is passed on to the final consumer, for instance VAT and customs duties. Hence direct tax is a tax on income and indirect tax is a tax on expenditure. We have seen that expenditure taxes can be recessionary and regressionary rather than progressive. The Conservative Party tends to favour indirect tax; note that VAT has risen from 8% to 17.5% since 1979. In the past the Labour Party has tended to favour direct taxation because of its progressive nature.

The current tax legislation

There are a number of sources of tax law today. Income tax and corporation tax is legislated for in the Income and Corporation Taxes Act 1988 (ICTA 1988) together with subsequent Finance Acts. Capital allowances are regulated by the Capital Allowances Act 1990 (CAA 1990) together with subsequent

Finance Acts. Capital gains tax is legislated for in the Taxation of Chargeable Gains Act 1992 (TCGA 1992) together with subsequent Finance Acts. Value Added Tax is dealt with in the Value Added Tax Act 1994 (VATA 1994) together with subsequent Finance Acts. Finally inheritance tax is legislated for in the Inheritance Tax Act 1984 (IHTA 1984) together with subsequent Finance Acts.

In addition the Taxes Management Act 1970 (TMA 1970) deals with the administration of taxes. This text does not include a detailed consideration of the administration of taxation.

Current issues in taxation

The first part of this chapter was intended both to set taxation today in its historical context and to explore the history of tax to see if it is possible to learn lessons which can be applied today. We also briefly considered the administration of taxation today. In this section we will discuss other ideas and concepts which are relevant to taxation today.

Hypothecated taxes

Taxes which are raised to provide particular benefits are termed hypothecated taxes. They are unpopular with the Treasury who see these taxes as undermining its control of public expenditure.

The Treasury argues that the revenue raised by hypothecated taxes oscillates in line with the economic cycle. That is when the economy is strong a relatively large amount of revenue is raised but relatively little revenue is raised when the economy is weak.

However, there are a number of examples of hypothecated taxes: vehicle excise duties were originally intended to fund highway construction and maintenance and the television licence fee was intended to fund the BBC. In practice the vehicle excise duties are used for general expenditure but the television licence fee is still used exclusively to finance the BBC.

The British Medical Association considered a proposal for the National Health Service to be funded by way of a hypothecated tax because it believed that taxpayers would be willing to pay more taxes if a clear link between the tax and health care could be established. A new hypothecated tax was proposed by the Chancellor, Kenneth Clarke, in his November 1993 budget. As soon as it is technically possible electronic road pricing will be introduced to raise revenue from the use of motorways to finance motorways.

Equitable taxes

Some taxes raise very little money but are seen to be equitable. The main example of this is capital gains tax which is often subject to rumour about its abolition in a budget because so little revenue is raised but remains in place because it is seen to be a 'fair' tax.

Fiscal neutrality

Like the window tax of the 18th century many of these taxes affected the behaviour of individuals and companies. It is argued by many that the introduction of road-pricing for motorways will encourage drivers to use other roads, particularly A roads. This potential transfer of traffic is generally seen as an unwelcome consequence of charging for motorway use. The accident rate per mile driven is higher on roads which are not motorways, leading to fears of an increase in road traffic accidents after the scheme is introduced. It also seems likely that congestion will increase on roads which do not carry a charge. This might increase journey times and fuel consumption for all road users and the accident rate might rise still further. To minimise these effects the Chancellor will have to set the cost per mile travelled at such a level that relatively few road users are deterred from using motorways.

Tax systems which do not distort the decisions made by individuals and companies are termed fiscally neutral. We will discuss this further in Chapter 2.

During the 1980s there was a move towards the reformation of tax throughout the world. There were moves to limit the level of public expenditure, particularly in the UK and the USA. Then the assessment of taxation was reformed. Tax rates were reduced throughout the world but the tax base was broadened. That is, more of a taxpayer's income is taxed but the tax rate applied is lower. In 1979 the highest rate of tax in the UK was 98%. This was rightly seen as undesirable, if only because the incentives to avoid or even evade tax were so large. Today the highest rate of tax in the UK is a mere 40%, and in the USA it is only 28%. The tax base was broadened by decreasing the range of allowances which taxpayers could use to reduce their taxable income. The reduction in the relief available for interest paid on mortgages and the steadily decreasing benefit of the married couple's allowances are examples of the broadening of the tax base.

In addition the 100% first-year allowances on capital expenditure on plant and machinery which had been available to businesses were phased out leaving only a 25% writing down allowance to be claimed. At the same time the rate of corporation tax was reduced from 52% to 35%. This has subsequently been reduced to 33%, the lowest rate in Europe.

This is not to say that the Conservative government is committed to fiscal neutrality to the extent of never introducing policies which are intended to distort the economic decisions made by individuals and businesses. Tax advantageous treatment has been bestowed on new forms of investments, particularly pensions, but also TESSAs (Tax Exempt Special Saving Accounts) and on items of expenditure like health insurance for individuals over 60 years of age.

The tax implications of the single European market

Now a new challenge faces Chancellors. As Europe draws remorselessly closer and companies become more sophisticated the harmonisation of tax rates becomes more important. Efforts were initially concentrated on VAT and customs and excise duties. After years of work it has proved possible to reach some agreement about the ranges at which VAT will be charged in member states, although problems such as the UK's zero rate for food and children's clothing are still to be resolved. Attention is now being turned to the harmonisation of direct taxes, particularly corporation tax. This process of harmonisation also raises questions about sovereignty. The UK government, among others, believes that the right to raise taxes is one of the fundamental rights of a government and is reluctant to cede power to the EU.

Progressivity

In the UK there is a generally accepted principle that tax should be progressive, that is that better off taxpayers should pay a higher proportion of their income in tax than less well off taxpayers. In fact a detailed analysis of tax paid and benefits received shows that the net tax paid as a proportion of income is not always progressive.

A tax can still be progressive if it only has two rates of tax. Consider two taxpayers, one earning £10,000 per annum and the other earning twice that, £20,000 per annum. Let both taxpayers have personal allowances of £5,000. This means that the first £5,000 of income is not subject to income tax. The rest of the income is taxed at 25%. The taxpayer earning £10,000 per annum will pay £1,250 ((£10,000 − 5,000) × 25%) tax, 12.5% of their income, while the higher earning taxpayer will pay £3,750 ((£20,000 − 5,000) × 25%) tax, 18.75% of their income.

This example is extremely simple. When other factors are taken into account, for example tax relief on interest paid on a loan to purchase a taxpayer's main residence and tax relief on contributions paid into a pension fund, the analysis may not give the same results. We will study this further in Chapter 2.

VAT, on the other hand, is not a progressive tax. Wealthy individuals save proportionally more of their income than poorer taxpayers who consequently suffer a higher proportion of their income being paid in VAT. This problem is ameliorated to some extent by the zero rate of tax on food. The poorest people spend much of their income on food and so pay relatively little VAT. The poorest people also spend proportionately more on fuel than the better off which has led to a political outcry about the introduction of VAT on domestic fuel.

The relationship between statute and case law and anti-avoidance legislation in the UK today

As we have already seen, people throughout the ages have found ways of circumventing a liability to tax. Some evade tax, for instance by smuggling. Tax evasion is illegal and is punishable by fines and/or imprisonment. Tax avoidance on the other hand is legal. Some avoidance is simple and completely acceptable. For instance, saving money in a TESSA has the disadvantage of requiring the taxpayer to tie his or her money up for five years. In return income from the scheme is paid without deduction of tax. This therefore is a scheme which enables taxpayers to avoid paying tax on interest received. Individuals may also attempt to avoid paying tax by using a scheme devised by tax planning experts who try to exploit loopholes in the tax legislation. Many of the schemes were incredibly complicated and completely artificial, that is they served no business purpose, and their sole objective was to avoid or postpone paying tax.

In the past the Inland Revenue took a very reactive role. They simply plugged any loopholes which the experts exposed. There were three main problems with this approach. Firstly legislation is not retrospective. Hence the Inland Revenue can stop the scheme being used again but legislation cannot be used to foil a scheme which has already been executed. Secondly the anti-avoidance legislation which was needed created increasingly complex Finance Acts. During the 1980s accountants lobbied the Chancellor of the Exchequer, not to give tax reliefs, but to simplify the legislation. The more complex legislation is the more likely there are to be anomalies which were not detected when the legislation was drafted but which cause endless difficulties for those people who have to deal with the consequences of the legislation. The third disadvantage of anti-avoidance legislation is that it often creates new loopholes which can be exploited by the increasingly sophisticated tax avoidance industry.

The other avenue of attack open to the Revenue is to challenge the legitimacy of any scheme in the courts. Certainly the Inland Revenue have the resources to do this but until recently the courts were unwilling to be seen to be creating new law. That is they chose merely to interpret the law as it stood and so would only consider the legal nature of the scheme, as in the case of IRC v *Duke of Westminster* (1936). In this case servants were not paid wages but received an income from a deed of covenant. A deed of covenant is valid only if no valuable consideration is provided by the recipient in return. However, the Duke of Westminster and his servants had an understanding that so long as the deed of covenant operated the servants would not claim the wages due to them. The scheme enabled the Duke to claim tax relief for the amounts paid to his servants whereas payment of wages to servants would not be an allowable deduction from income tax. Today such a scheme could not be used because deeds of covenant are no longer tax effective when paid to individuals. The House of Lords found for the Duke, declaring that they would only consider the legal nature of the transaction. Until the mid-1980s this case remained a precedent and the Inland Revenue were rarely successful in challenging tax avoidance schemes in the courts.

Before you read about the details of these schemes it would be useful if you knew a little about capital gains tax. As you might have expected, transactions of a capital nature rather than a revenue nature are subject to capital gains tax. A capital gains tax liability only arises when an asset is disposed of. Hence a taxpayer may defer a capital gains tax liability simply by refraining from selling an asset.

In 1981 in *W T Ramsay Ltd* v IRC the House of Lords took a completely different view of an anti-avoidance scheme.

The case involved an 'artificial scheme' which was used to create a large capital loss. The company had realised a capital gain and intended to set the artificial loss against a chargeable gain to avoid paying tax on the gain. The scheme was artificial because it was made up of a series of preordained steps which were to be carried out in rapid succession. The scheme required that all steps be completed once the first one had been made. At the end of the series of steps the taxpayers would be in the same position as they had been at the beginning and any loss created would not be a real loss. In fact the only losses which had been suffered were the professional fees which were paid for the scheme's operation. The House of Lords decided that although each step in the scheme was a separate legal transaction it was possible to view the scheme, not as a series of separate legal transactions, but as a whole, by comparing the position of the taxpayer in real terms at the start and finish of the scheme. When this was done no real loss was incurred and the scheme was self-cancelling.

Lord Wilberforce explained the decision thus:

> While obliging the court to accept documents or transactions, found to be genuine, as such, it does not compel the court to look at a document or a transaction in blinkers, isolated from any context to which it properly belongs. If it can be seen that a document or transaction was intended to have effect as part of a nexus or series of transactions, or as an ingredient of a wider transaction intended as a whole, there is nothing in the doctrine to prevent it being so regarded; to do so is not to prefer form to substance, or substance to form. It is the task of the court to ascertain the legal nature of any transaction to which it is sought to attach a tax, or a tax consequence, and if that emerges from a series, or combination of trans actions, intended to operate as such, it is that series or combination which may be regarded.

The *Ramsay* principle was extended in *Furniss v Dawson* (1984). This time the objective was to defer capital gains tax by using an intermediary company based in the Isle of Man. The scheme was not circular or self-cancelling. The House of Lords decided that the scheme should still be set aside for tax purposes because once again the scheme required a series of steps to be carried out in quick succession.

The case of *Craven v White* (1989) was used by the House of Lords to limit the application of the *Ramsay* principle. Once again an intermediary company in the Isle of Man was used to defer a capital gains tax liability. The key difference between *Craven v White* and *Furniss v Dawson* was that when the shares were transferred to the Isle of Man company the final disposal of the shares had not been agreed. Hence no preordained series of steps existed at the time that the first transaction was undertaken. Consequently the House of Lords refused to view the series of transactions as a whole and the scheme was successful. This case has great significance for anti-avoidance schemes generally. It makes planning well in advance critical. If transactions are undertaken before the final step is known with certainty there is a greater likelihood of the scheme being successful.

In the early part of 1993 it became public knowledge that John Birt, the new Director General of the BBC, was not on the payroll as an employee of the BBC but was employed, through his own company, as a consultant to the organisation. In this capacity John Birt was able to arrange his affairs so that his tax liability was much less than it would have been had he been an employee. The details of his financial arrangements were published in virtually all the national newspapers and widely discussed on television and radio. Although there was no suggestion that such an arrangement was illegal — indeed it was claimed that for some groups of staff within the BBC it was normal — there was widespread condemnation of the situation. It was soon announced that

John Birt would become an employee of the BBC and pay tax under the PAYE system. It seems to be clear that tax avoidance schemes which are substantially artificial in nature have become less acceptable as well as being less useful because of the case law described above. Today taxpayers are more likely to try to mitigate their tax liabilities.

Now that you have a basic understanding of the system of taxation operating in the UK today we will finish this chapter by considering the main points in the 1996 budget. Once again we will concentrate on the principles rather than the detailed changes introduced in the budget.

The November 1996 budget

On 26th November 1996 Chancellor Kenneth Clarke presented what was almost certainly a pre-election budget. Despite the undoubted pressure on him to present a 'vote winning' budget by reducing taxes substantially the budget was substantially neutral, that is the measures introduced will not significantly affect the total amount of tax raised in 1997/98. After the budget the *Financial Times* described the Chancellor as 'neither Santa nor Scrooge' although some commentators questioned the reliability of many of his forecasts, especially of the growth in the economy next year. The Chancellor stated that his aim was to ensure that the right amount of tax should be paid by the right people. In order to achieve this he intends to introduce anti-avoidance measures to further restrict the avoidance of tax. These measures will be discussed in detail later in the book. In addition the Chancellor reduced the number of reliefs available to taxpayers. Specifically he announced that profit-related pay relief will be phased out by 1st January 2000 and the reduction of capital allowances on much plant and machinery which has an estimated useful life of more than 25 years. All of these moves have the effect of broadening the tax base, that is the amount of income which is subjected to tax is increased. The broader the tax base the lower the rate of tax that is needed in order to raise the same amount of tax.

The continued progress towards a basic rate of income tax of 20% was probably the centrepiece of the Chancellor's proposals. This progress was achieved by an increase in the threshold below which all income is taxed at 20% by £200 which was more than was required to compensate for inflation and a reduction in the basic rate of tax from 24% to 23%.

In addition the Chancellor increased most personal allowances by more than was needed to compensate for inflation. Every individual who lives in the UK is entitled to at least a single personal allowance. Chapter 4 contains a complete list of personal allowances and the conditions which must be satisfied to claim them. In recent years there have been several budgets in which the personal allowances have not been raised. In addition earnings have consistently increased by more than the rate of inflation. This leads to more individuals being liable to pay income tax and increases the proportion of income which is paid in tax for all taxpayers. Any increase in personal allowances benefits individuals with lower incomes proportionately more than better-off individuals. Hence increases in personal allowances help to increase the progressivity of an income tax system. The next activity illustrates this point.

Average earnings increase by 20% during a period in which personal allowances increase by only 10%. The personal allowance was worth one quarter of average earnings at the beginning of the period and the basic rate of tax is 25%. Find the increase in the tax paid by the following taxpayers expressed as a percentage of total earnings:

- Ben who has an income equal to half average earnings
- Laura who has an income equal to average earnings
- Ashley who has an income equal to twice average earnings.

Feedback

Let A = average earnings at the beginning of the period.

First calculate the proportion of income paid in tax at the beginning of the period.

	Ben	Laura	Ashley
Income	0.5A	A	2A
Less personal allowances	0.25A	0.25A	0.25A
Taxable income	0.25A	0.75A	1.75A
Tax paid	0.0625A	0.1875A	0.4375A
Proportion of income paid in tax	12.5%	18.75%	21.875%

Next calculate the proportion of income paid in tax at the end of the period.

	Ben	Laura	Ashley
Income	0.6A	1.2A	2.4A
Less personal allowances	0.275A	0.275A	0.275A
Taxable income	0.325A	0.925A	2.125A
Tax paid	0.08125A	0.23125A	0.53125A
Proportion of income paid in tax	13.5%	19.3%	22.1%

This result may surprise you. However, a little thought may help to explain your results. Because incomes have risen faster than personal allowances each of the taxpayers has paid tax on a higher proportion of their income at the end of the period than they did at the beginning. Hence you should expect the proportion of tax paid to increase for all the taxpayers.

You might have expected the proportion of tax paid to increase by more for the lower income taxpayer than the other taxpayers because the personal allowance forms a greater proportion of his income and hence the impact of its falling value as a proportion of his income is relatively greater relative than for the other taxpayers.

Of course the tax system is still progressive but it is less progressive than it was.

In addition to these changes the Chancellor increased the inheritance tax threshold by £15,000, again far more than needed to compensate for inflation. This measure is designed to increase the amount of money which can be transferred from one generation to the next without a tax liability arising.

In line with the reduction in the basic rate of income tax the Chancellor reduced the small companies tax rate from 24% to 23%. Companies with profits below £300,000 pay tax at the small companies rate.

In this section we have considered some of the most important measures introduced in the budget of 1996. Some of the legislation relates to matters which are beyond the scope of this book and so has not been considered in this chapter. Other legislation is dealt with in later chapters.

Progressivity revisited

Throughout this chapter we have considered the progressive nature of many taxes. You have seen how successive budgets in the 1980s and 1990s have reduced the progressive nature of the UK tax system with the move to indirect taxation and the reduction in the marginal rates of taxation for high-income taxpayers. As you have seen, although tax systems were progressive in the past they were also proportional to the expenses incurred by the kings on behalf of the taxpayer and to the benefits received by the taxpayer. That is, only relatively wealthy individuals paid tax and these were also the people with most to lose if the kings were unsuccessful in their defence of the realm.

In the 19th and 20th centuries the principle of progressivity became entrenched in the fiscal system. Socialists espoused the concept as part of their belief in the redistribution of wealth. Economists developed the law of diminishing marginal utility which states that the amount of satisfaction which is derived from the consumption of successive units of the same good or service will decline. It was argued that for there to be equality of sacrifice the better off would have to pay proportionately more of their income in tax. However, many economists challenged the validity of this law. Seligman in *Progressive Taxation in Theory and Practice* concluded that 'The imposition of "equal sacrifices" on all taxpayers must always remain an ideal impossible of actual realisation. Sacrifice denotes something psychical, something psychological. A tax takes away commodities, which are something material, something tangible. To ascertain the exact relations between something psychical and something material is impossible. No calculus of pains and pleasures can suffice.'

It is argued by many today that it is the better off who accumulate capital and invest in resources to generate wealth in the future. A progressive system of tax interferes with these activities and may impair a nation's ability to invest in its future.

You have been presented with the arguments for and against progressivity and must make up your own mind. However, when the electorate was invited to vote for a top rate of tax of 50%, against the 40% in force, in 1992 there was a convincing rejection of the proposal. Since the general election in 1992 in the UK the electorates in the USA and Australia have also rejected proposals to increase taxation.

Summary

In this chapter we have laid the foundations which you will need to study taxation. We have drawn on the lessons of history to try to understand how taxation affects all of us today. You are now able to trace the history of taxation over more than 2000 years. The difficulties facing Parliament today have been faced by leaders through out the centuries. Governments must raise revenues in ways which are seen by the electorate as being fair and equitable.

A modern Chancellor is likely to have many conflicting objectives when setting out his tax proposals in the annual budget. He must decide how much tax he wishes to raise and then determine exactly how that tax should be raised. To do this a Chancellor must be aware of the potential consequences of his legislation on individuals and businesses. For example, a large increase in taxation may lead to a reduction in the economic activity in the private sector which is not compensated for by an increase in the economic activity in the public sector. A Chancellor is also likely to have an opinion about where the burden of tax should fall. In recent years the UK tax system has become less progressive, suggesting that Chancellors do not consider the redistribution of wealth to be an objective of our tax system.

In this chapter we have been able to explore the complex relationship between legislation and case law and understand the limitations of each.

Finally we have thought a little about the nature of taxation and we are now in a position to define a successful tax. For a tax to be successful it should be difficult to avoid or evade in order to increase the equitable nature of tax and to maximise the revenue raised. In Chapters 2 and 3 we will consider in more detail the nature of a 'good' tax if indeed any tax can be considered to be good.

In the remaining chapters of the book we will study current taxation in some detail.

Project areas

There are a number of areas covered in this chapter which would provide good material for projects. These include the following:

- a comparison of the progressive nature of the tax systems of a number of countries
- surveys of taxpayers to determine current attitudes to taxation, for example a study of the effect of phasing out MIRAS on the attitude to home ownership
- an evaluation of the impact of self-assessment on either compliance costs or collection rates.

Discussion questions

Question 1. Road fund licences were originally introduced to pay for road building and maintenance. This is a tax based not on an ability to pay but according to use. In practice much of the road fund licence fee is used for other purposes. Is this a good way to raise taxes?

Question 2. Do you think that the decision in *W T Ramsay v IRC* was the right one?

2 The impact of the UK tax system

Introduction

As we have already seen in Chapter 1 tax can affect the economic decisions made by taxpayers. When the window tax was introduced in 1747 homeowners blocked up their windows, leading to health problems. Today the government uses taxpayers' eagerness to avoid tax to influence their behaviour. For example, in the Finance Act 1991 the Chancellor introduced tax relief for the payer of health insurance premiums on individuals aged 60 and over. This was done to encourage older people, who are expensive to provide medical facilities for, to provide for themselves. When making this relief available the Chancellor must have undertaken some sort of cost benefit analysis. For example, if the only people who took advantage of the scheme were those who were already subscribers to private medical insurance the Chancellor would have lost some revenue without encouraging anyone to reduce the costs of the National Health Service by investing in health insurance. In this chapter we will look at a number of other ways in which the tax system in the UK affects the decisions made by taxable persons.

At the end of this chapter you will be able to discuss the:

- concept of fiscal neutrality
- distorting effects of UK taxation on the decisions made by individuals, businesses and companies
- impact of tax on the personal investment decision
- impact of tax on the business investment decision
- problems of moving towards fiscal neutrality.

Fiscal neutrality

A tax system can be said to be fiscally neutral if it does not discriminate between economic choices. That is, the introduction of the system does not change the economic choices made by taxpayers. Hence a fiscally neutral system seeks to raise revenue in ways which avoid distortionary substitution effects.

A tax has a distortionary substitution effect if it changes the relative cost of goods and services. For example VAT is levied on chocolate biscuits like Hobnobs because they are a luxury good but not on Jaffa Cakes which are deemed to be cakes and therefore an item of food. The law of supply and demand tells us that an increase in the price of Hobnobs without a corresponding increase in the price of Jaffa Cakes will lead to a decline in the number of boxes of Hobnobs sold compared to the number of boxes of Jaffa Cakes sold. This will cause a reduction in demand for Hobnobs because of the increase in price. Indeed some individuals may purchase Jaffa Cakes rather than Hobnobs because of the price differential. This switch from one product to another, because of taxation, is called a distortionary substitution effect.

Until the autumn of 1993 there was a similar distortion between freshly squeezed fruit juice, which was not subject to VAT, and long-life fruit juice which was taxed at 17.5% as a luxury good. This tax treatment had the effect of making freshly squeezed juice relatively more attractive than long-life juice. In the autumn of 1993 the government announced that freshly squeezed juice would also be taxed at 17.5%, thus removing the substitution distortion between the two products.

We can say that VAT would be fiscally neutral if all goods and services were taxed at the same rate. If this was so the marginal rate of substitution of one product for another will be the same including and excluding VAT.

If a tax system is not fiscally neutral the economic loss to the community is greater than the revenue raised by the tax. The difference between the economic loss and the revenue raised is termed the economic, or excess, burden of taxation. While you are reading this chapter and the next one try to decide if there is an excess burden of taxation in each case.

Since VAT is charged only when money is spent VAT makes saving relatively more attractive than spending money on consumer products. This is another example of the inefficiencies in our tax system and explains why turnover taxes are considered to be recessionary because they encourage saving at the expense of consumption.

If investments are taxed neutrally the amount of tax paid will be related to the returns earned and will be independent of the particular investment vehicle used.

Hence in a fiscally neutral environment all forms of income and all types of savings would be subject to the same taxation.

You may feel that tax systems should be fiscally neutral. In practice this is almost certainly impossible and most governments and businesses do not demand fiscal neutrality from their tax systems. It can be argued that it is the discrepancies in the tax systems, and in particular the loopholes and anomalies, which cause people to behave in particular ways. Certainly many, if not most, of the financial investment instruments available in the UK today have been devised to exploit the lack of fiscal neutrality in the existing tax system.

Decisions about work and leisure activities

Many individuals have the opportunity to choose whether to earn more money by working harder. Some people may be able to work overtime, others may choose to do jobs which have longer basic working hours in order to earn more money and still others may work many extra hours in the hope of gaining promotion. Of course many people also make decisions which reduce their income, for instance taking early retirement, working part time or taking unpaid holidays.

A UK company recently offered unpaid leave to some of its employees in order to avoid redundancies and was surprised by the large number of people applying for the scheme.

We will spend a little time considering the factors which influence an individual when making a decision about how hard to work and then briefly consider the effect of their decisions on wealth creation and the revenues collected by governments.

Marginal rates of taxation

When considering the role that tax plays in the decision to work harder or not it is the marginal rate of tax which is important, rather than the average rate of tax. Remember that the marginal rate of tax is the amount of tax which is due if the taxpayer earns £1 more. One of the reasons given for the reduction in the top rate of tax is that lower marginal rates of tax encourage individuals to work harder. Another supposed benefit is that people will be less reluctant to pay tax if the tax rate is low, thus reducing the attractiveness of tax evasion and avoidance.

The detail of national insurance contributions and income tax rates is contained in Chapter 4. However, in order to understand the table in this section you need only to know that:

- individuals are entitled to a personal allowance
- employees' national insurance contributions are a percentage of earnings up to a limit of £465 per week. Income over this limit does not incur a further liability to national insurance contributions
- income tax is levied at four marginal rates which increase as the taxpayer's income increases.

We will start by determining the marginal rates of tax which are in force in the UK in 1997/98. The effective rate of tax on earned income is surely the combined rate of income tax and national insurance contributions since they are both compulsory.

It is not possible to list the marginal rates absolutely because they depend, to some extent, on the personal circumstances of the taxpayer. Let us consider a single person, without investment income, who does not contribute to a pension scheme. His marginal rates of tax are:

Annual income £	Tax rate %	NI rate %	Effective marginal tax rate %
0–3,224	0	0	0
3,225–4,045	0	10	10
4,046–8,146	20	10	30
8,147–24,180	23	10	33
24,181–30,145	23	0	23
30,146 onwards	40	0	40

This table may surprise you. You may find it hard to justify a tax system which levies a marginal rate of tax of 33% on an individual with income of £9,000 per annum, 23% on an individual with income of £25,000 and 40% on an individual with income of £31,000. Note that individuals who earn more than £3,224 must pay national insurance contributions of 2% of £3,224 as well as 10% on earnings over £3,224 up to the annual limit of £24,180. This gives a marginal rate of tax of over 100% on income between £3,223 and £3,224 per annum. We will ignore this rather strange result in the rest of this chapter as in practice it rarely causes a problem. Read the section on national insurance contributions in Chapter 4 to find out how the system has evolved to become what it is today.

Our tax system is still progressive because the marginal rate of tax exceeds the average rate of tax at all times. However, you may like to reflect on the 'fairness' of a system which incorporates a drop in the marginal rate of tax as income increases. When offered the opportunity to change this in the general election in 1992 when the Labour Party manifesto included a commitment to remove the upper limit on national insurance contributions the electorate rejected the plan.

To work or play?

As already suggested, many taxpayers are able to decide whether or not to increase their income by increasing their work effort. Let us take a simple example where an employee is offered the opportunity to work for an extra hour one evening. When making the decision an individual is likely to weigh the benefit of any extra money he might earn against the cost of working an extra hour.

Some individuals will be offered pay at a higher hourly rate to encourage them to undertake overtime. In a recent interview on television individuals explained that they did not object to working on Sundays in the retail sector because they could earn twice as much money as working on any other day.

Employers offer their employees the opportunity to work overtime because they believe that the marginal cost is less than the marginal benefit to be gained from the work which the employee will do.

In addition to the extra money being earned an employee should also consider the tax consequences of the decision. An employee who undertakes overtime will pay tax at his or her marginal rate. There may also be some cost savings; for example, the employee might have gone out for a drink with friends if he or she had not worked overtime and thus saved the cost of the drinks.

There may also be some benefits from working overtime which are difficult to express in monetary terms. For example, if some kind of emergency has brought about the need for overtime, there may be an enjoyable sense of camaraderie among the individuals who undertook extra work.

Now let us consider the costs of working overtime. These may be zero but other employees may incur significant costs if they work for an extra hour including any of the following:

- child care
- transport
- eating out.

In addition there may be many other costs which cannot be assigned a monetary value, for example, missing a planned activity such as a walk.

Now that we have identified some of the costs and benefits of making the decision to work overtime we can consider the marginal utility of an extra £1 to a taxpayer. For example, an individual may be willing to work more overtime in the month before she goes on holiday than at other times. Try and think of some more circumstances in which either an employee would rather work more hours at one time than another or one employee might choose to work overtime and another might decline the offer.

We have now identified one reason for the employer to offer extra work: the marginal benefit is greater than the marginal cost. For the employee the decision will be based on the same criteria, that is the marginal benefit is greater than the marginal cost, although identifying the marginal benefits and the marginal costs is likely to be difficult sometimes.

Now let us extend our argument to consider the effect of taxation on the decision to work overtime. Once again we will only consider marginal rates of taxation rather than the total tax paid or the average rates of tax. Suppose an employee habitually works overtime. If his marginal rate of tax is increased he may choose to work more hours to maintain his net income. Alternatively he may decline to work overtime because his net income per hour is such that the marginal costs exceed the marginal benefits. We can illustrate this with two examples. The first is an individual with a large mortgage who has to earn a given amount in overtime each month to sustain his lifestyle. The second is an individual with children who has to pay a childminder an hourly rate to look after the children. The first taxpayer may choose to increase his hours of overtime to maintain his level of income because his marginal rate of tax has increased. The second taxpayer may conclude that the net benefit of working overtime, that is the extra gross income less the tax and the costs of childcare, are too low to be worthwhile.

Similarly a drop in the marginal rate of tax may provide an incentive to work extra hours to some taxpayers while others may limit the hours they work so as to maintain their previous net income. However, if we return to our original hypothesis, that the work would be undertaken so long as the marginal costs are less than the marginal benefits, then the lower the marginal rate of tax the higher the marginal benefits and the more likely it is that individuals will undertake the extra work.

So far we have only considered individuals who are already working and are deciding whether or not to accept overtime. Let us consider the situation of those who do not currently work but would be able to obtain work if they chose to. One of the biggest groups here are single-parent families, usually mothers, of whom some 90% are to some extent dependent on state benefits. If these women work their benefits are reduced once they earn over a relatively low limit. Once single parents start to work their effective marginal rate of tax is extremely high. Not only do they pay tax and national insurance contributions but they lose state benefits and may incur travelling and child care costs. The Chancellor went some way towards addressing these problems recently when he provided single parents with some relief for the cost of child care. There are many important issues here which are beyond the scope of this text but we can conclude that the lower the marginal rate of tax the more likely it is that single parents will choose to work.

Do-it-yourself or subcontract?

So far we have considered the marginal costs and benefits without looking in detail at the alternatives to working overtime.

Activity

Suppose that a taxpayer can choose to work overtime regularly on Saturday morning. If the overtime is worked the taxpayer will employ a sole trader to maintain his garden. Let us assume that the taxpayer does not enjoy gardening any more than he enjoys work and that he works less efficiently in the garden than in his normal job. We will also assume that the gardener, who has special skills and equipment, works more efficiently in the garden than our taxpayer.

List the tax implications of the two situations. You may assume that all the transactions are recorded and tax is not evaded.

Feedback

If the taxpayer chooses to reject the opportunity of overtime and maintains his own garden there are the following tax consequences:

- his direct taxation is unchanged
- his employer does not benefit from his work and so his profits are not increased and the corporation tax payable is unchanged
- the taxpayer is likely to be working less efficiently than an experienced gardener and the economic value of the work he produces is likely to be less valuable than the economic value of the work which he would have undertaken during the period of overtime he has declined.

If the taxpayer chooses to work the overtime and employ a gardener there are the following tax consequences:

- his direct taxation increases as his earnings increase
- his employer's profits increase and so the corporation tax payable increases
- the gardener receives an income
- the amount of direct tax paid by the gardener increases
- if the gardener's turnover is over £48,000 per annum he will also account for VAT on his taxable supplies

- the employer and the gardener have increased their net income which enables them to spend more money and thus potentially pay more tax in the future, perhaps in the form of VAT.

As you can see, from the government's point of view there is an increase in tax revenues and an increase in the income generating activity of the economy if the individual chooses to work overtime and employ a gardener.

Now let us turn our attention to the monetary factors which would increase an employee's desire to undertake additional hours at work and employ others to work for him.

The gardener will decide how much to charge for his services by deciding how much money he wants for himself and then adding on the cost of any tax, direct and indirect, which he must pay. Indeed some tradesmen will quote two prices to potential customers, one price if an invoice is required or payment will be made by cheque, and a lower price if the job is done for cash. The difference in the two quotes will be related to the amount of tax which the trader will have to pay on the transaction if it is recorded in his accounting system.

Hence the amount that our gardener will charge for his services will depend on the money which he wants for himself and the amount of tax, both income tax and VAT, which he must pay.

The greater the difference between the after-tax income which the employee can earn and the gross cost of employing the gardener the more likely it is that the employee will undertake the overtime.

The after-tax income of the employee will be increased if his marginal rate of tax is reduced. Similarly the gross cost of employing the gardener will be reduced if either his marginal rate of tax is reduced or the rate of VAT he must charge is reduced.

In conclusion then:

- the lower the rate of corporation tax the more likely the employer is to increase his level of economic activity
- the lower the rate of income tax the more likely it is that the employee will undertake extra work and employ others himself
- the lower the level of VAT the more likely it is that an individual will purchase services from registered traders.

In this example we have considered the situation of employing a gardener. You may feel that in practice many people working in this way do not declare all of their income to the Inland Revenue and the Customs and Excise. However, there are many other situations which illustrate the point in which tax evasion is unlikely. The decision to eat at home or go out for a meal is a good example as is the decision to service the car at home or take it to a garage. Given a little thought you will be able to think of other examples yourself.

The personal investment decision

The financial services sector has proved to be very creative and there is a huge choice of investment vehicles for individuals who wish to save money rather than spend it. In this section we will consider some of the most common, tax-efficient methods of saving. In particular we will consider TESSAs, PEPs, pensions and housing.

Tax-exempt special savings accounts

Tax-exempt special savings accounts (TESSAs) were introduced in the Finance Act 1990 in order to encourage individuals to save. TESSAs could be opened on or after 1st January 1991 by an individual aged 18 or more (ICTA 1988 s326A(3)). Any interest or bonus payable in respect of a TESSA is exempt from income tax (ICTA 1988 s326A(1)). Only institutions, including building societies, authorised in the Banking Act 1987 can offer TESSAs (ICTA 1988 s326A(4)). Each TESSA must be owned by one individual, that is the account cannot be a joint account, and an individual may hold only one TESSA at a time (ICTA 1988 s326A (5) & (6)). The individual holding the account must be the beneficial owner of the account (ICTA 1988 s326A(7)).

An account ceases to be a tax-exempt special savings account on the earliest of the following:

- the date when any of the conditions listed above cease to be fulfilled (ICTA 1988 s326B(1))
- the date of the death of the account-holder
- five years after the day on which the account was opened (ICTA 1988 s326A(2)).

The maximum amount which can be deposited in a TESSA is £3,000 during the first 12 months in which it is open and £1,800 in any 12-month period after the initial 12-month period. The maximum which can be deposited throughout the life of a TESSA is £9,000. An account will cease to be a TESSA if the total withdrawals from the account exceed the total interest, net of basic rate, which has been credited to the account on the date of the withdrawal (ICTA 1988 s326B(2)).

If the account ceases to be a TESSA all the interest and bonuses which accrued during the period in which the account was a TESSA are deemed to be credited to the account immediately after it ceases to be a TESSA (ICTA 1988 s326B(3)). Hence any interest, net of basic rate tax, can be withdrawn without penalty. However, if an amount in excess of this is withdrawn all interest credited to date becomes liable to tax immediately at the rate then in force. This could be disadvantageous if the rate of tax has increased. In addition the interest taxed could be enough to put the taxpayer into a higher tax bracket and so more tax could be due.

It should be noted that the potential tax savings are not high. A basic rate taxpayer with £9,000 invested in the final year at an interest rate of 5% will save $£9,000 \times 5\% \times 20\% = £90$ in tax, and savings in earlier years will be much less than this. Against this should be weighed the potential opportunity costs. We have already considered the risk that the taxpayer's marginal rate of tax may increase so that if funds are withdrawn from the TESSA he or she may incur a greater tax liability than if he or she had deposited the money in a building society deposit account. In recent years interest rates have fluctuated and there is evidence that some building societies are not passing on the benefit of interest rate increases to existing savings account holders. This could lead to investors having to accept lower interest rates or incur penalties when transferring the account.

Once an account has been maintained for five years the capital invested, but not the interest accrued, can be transferred to a new TESSA. This means that investors are able to transfer their capital invested so as to continue to receive interest tax free for a further five years. To take advantage of the scheme the second account must be opened within six months of the first account maturing.

While TESSAs have proved very popular initial evidence suggests that most of the money invested in them has been transferred from other deposit accounts. This implies that the tax forgone by the Treasury may have been wasted in that the total amount saved has not been significantly increased.

Personal equity plans

Personal equity plans (PEPs) enable individuals to invest in equities, either directly or using unit trusts. An individual can invest up to £6,000 each year in a general PEP and a further £3,000 in a single company PEP (PEP Regulations 1989 s4(4)). All dividends and capital gains received from securities held in a PEP are free of tax. This tax saving must be balanced against the charges levied by PEP managers.

A PEP may be a general plan or a single company plan.

Only individuals aged 18 or over who are resident and ordinarily resident in the UK are eligible to invest in a PEP and an individual may subscribe to only one general plan and one single plan during a fiscal year (PEP Regulations 1989 s7(1) & (2)). A plan cannot be subscribed to by more than one individual. Within the conditions outlined above an individual can transfer shares obtained by way of an application for shares in a public offer to either a general or single company PEP provided they are transferred within 42 days of allotment (PEP Regulations 1989 s4(2) & (3)).

A single company plan is a plan in which the securities of only one company are invested in. A general plan is a plan which is not a single company plan (PEP Regulations 1989 s2(1)).

Qualifying investments for general plans are:

- ordinary shares, other than shares in an investment trust, issued by a quoted company which is incorporated in the EU
- units in an authorised unit trust of a fund or funds or shares in an investment trust
- cash which a plan manager holds for the purpose of investing in qualifying investments of general plans as described above (PEP Regulations 1989 s6(2))
- UK corporate bonds and convertibles and UK and EU preference shares in quoted companies. To qualify corporate bonds must have fixed interest rates and at least five years to maturity.

If these conditions are met no tax is chargeable on the plan manager or the managers nominee or the plan investor in respect of interest, dividends or gains in respect of plan investments. In addition losses in respect of plan investments shall be disregarded for the purposes of capital gains tax (PEP Regulations 1989 s17(1)).

Clearly the higher a taxpayer's marginal rate of tax the more advantageous a personal equity plan would be. An individual who does not pay capital gains tax because his or her net chargeable gains for the year are less than £6,000 will not benefit from the capital gains tax exemption of a personal equity plan. Equally a higher rate taxpayer will benefit from the income tax relief of a PEP at 40% while basic rate taxpayers will only receive relief at the basic rate on savings of 20%.

Like TESSAs, PEPs have proved to be popular, with 1,380,000 general plans taken out in 1993/94, nearly twice as many as in 1992/93.

Personal pensions

Saving via a personal pension plan, particularly if it is a scheme to which a taxpayer's employer contributes, is extremely tax efficient. Contributions to an approved pension fund are eligible for tax relief at the taxpayer's marginal rate of tax and employer contributions are also eligible for tax relief. Investments in the pension fund are free of income tax and capital gains tax. However, apart from a tax-free lump sum, income from a pension is taxed as earned income.

A detailed consideration of pension schemes is contained in Chapter 6.

Home ownership

Finally, I would like to consider the privileged tax incentives available for home owners. For 1997/98 the interest paid on the first £30,000 borrowed to buy the taxpayer's main or only residence attracts tax relief at 15%.

This is a reduction in the rate from 20% in 1994/95 and 25% in 1993/94. During the 1980s homeowners could obtain relief at their marginal rate of tax but the real tax advantage of housing was that capital growth did not give rise to a capital gains tax liability. Imagine the attitude of home owners to increases in house prices if a quarter or more of the increase had to be paid in tax when moving. A detailed consideration of the taxation of the capital gains of living accommodation is contained in Chapter 7.

Because of the privileged tax position of housing people have often been persuaded to commit more of their wealth to their main residence than would otherwise be the case. Remember products A and B in the section on fiscal neutrality. The distorting effects of taxing A and not B made buying units of B relatively more attractive. Hence the tax advantages of owning a house over other forms of investment create a propensity to hold wealth in property.

The tax legislation may also encourage some individuals to move house or to borrow more when they move house.

If a loan is raised, perhaps to buy a car, no tax relief is available on the interest paid on the loan. But if an individual moves house and retains capital from the sale of the house to buy a car, thus increasing the amount of the mortgage needed to purchase the new house the same total amount will have been borrowed but, provided it is less than £30,000, all of it will be eligible for tax relief.

The Conservative governments of the late 1980s and early 1990s have interfered in the operation of the housing market on a number of occasions by amending the tax laws.

In the 1988 budget the Chancellor announced a change from mortgage interest relief being applicable to the individuals buying the property to its being applied to the property. If two individuals, who were not married, bought a house before this change they were each eligible for relief on interest on a mortgage up to a maximum of £30,000. Hence two people who were not married could claim relief on a loan of up to £60,000 compared to a married couple who could get maximum relief of only £30,000. The Chancellor could have made the change in the law immediate, perhaps by only allowing the higher relief if the contract had been signed by the end of that day. However, he allowed a delay of nearly six months and so fuelled an already buoyant housing market by providing an incentive for multiple purchasers to complete quickly thus increasing demand. This delay has been blamed for some of the increase in house prices in 1988, thus making the subsequent slump worse.

In 1992 the government attempted to exploit this behaviour by abolishing stamp duty on house purchases under £250,000 for a limited period of eight months in an attempt to boost the failing housing market.

Problems of moving towards fiscal neutrality

Suppose an investment receives concessionary tax relief. The best example of this in practice is the tax relief available on the interest paid on the first £30,000 of any loan used to purchase an individual's main residence. Consider for the moment investments which offer a nominal return of 12%, with tax charged at 20%. Now suppose a new investment is introduced which also offers a nominal return of 12%, but is free of basic rate income tax. If the investments are traded on a market initially one offers a net return of 9.6% while the other offers one of 12%. Investors will sell the first investment and buy the second investment to increase their return. This will have the effect of pushing up the price of the second investment until equilibrium is reached when both the investments offer a return of 9.6% net of tax. At this point £300, nominal, of the second stock will be trading at £375. If the tax relief were now removed from the second stock the value of the stock would simply fall to £300, causing a loss of 20% in the value of the investment to the investors holding it. The only investors who gain from the above scenario are those who held the second investment on the date that the tax concession was announced. All other holders of the investment suffer a capital loss due to the withdrawal of the concession. Apart from the original investors nobody benefits from the tax concession available.

It is easy to extrapolate this example into other areas, particularly housing, where, if the income tax and capital gains tax concessions on home ownership were removed, a reduction in the value of houses might follow in which every home owner would suffer a loss in the capital value of his or her home.

Tax and the business investment decision

Businesses invest by incurring expenditure now in order to increase revenue in the future. There are a number of ways in which this investment can be undertaken. A business might invest in fixed assets or in training costs to prepare its workforce for new technologies. And of course most expansion of business activities necessitates an investment in working capital. When businesses undertake investment appraisal analysis they are encouraged to evaluate the cash flows associated with the project, but as we will see the tax treatment of the cash flows depends on the nature of the cash flow.

We will discuss the distortions that the tax system creates when a company is evaluating a project with a life of several years.

Investment in long-term projects and fiscal neutrality

There are a number of techniques used by companies to evaluate a capital project. We will confine ourselves to a consideration of discounted cash flow techniques using the net present value method. There are a large number of books which explain this method very well. The basic principle is that all cash flows are stated at their value today, termed their present value, by discounting them at the company's cost of capital. An example might help to explain the technique.

A company is considering investing £10,000 in a project which will generate a cash flow of £6,000 for two years starting one year after the initial investment. The company's after-tax cost of capital is 12%. A company's cost of capital might be the company's cost of debt. The after-tax rate is used because interest payments are tax deductible.

You need to undertake the following calculation in order to calculate the net present value.

Year value	Cash flow £	Discount factor 12%	Present £
0	(10,000)	1	(10,000)
1	6,000	0.8929	5,357
2	6,000	0.7972	4,783
		Net present value	140

Because the net present value is positive the investment should be undertaken. Projects which generate a negative net present value should be rejected.

Notes

- payments of cash are cash outflows and are shown as negative numbers
- the discount factor for each year is calculated by using the formula:

$$\frac{1}{(1+r)^t}$$

where r is the discount factor expressed as a decimal, that is 12% is written as 0.12, and t is the number of the year in which the cash flow arose
- the first cash flow, usually a cash outflow, is deemed to take place immediately and hence is recorded as occurring in year 0 and is already stated at its present value
- cash flows are deemed to arise at the end of the year in which they are recorded and so need to be discounted in full for that year.

From this example we can generate a test for fiscal neutrality. A tax is fiscally neutral if the decision about whether to undertake the investment is the same using the before-tax and after-tax cash flows. As you will see in Chapters 5 and 8 businesses in the UK pay tax on their profits approximately one year after the profits are earned. In addition capital allowances may be available when a business purchases fixed assets. Interestingly the capital allowances available are independent of the method of payment for the assets.

Activity

Which of the following are cash flows?

(a) payment of wages
(b) purchase of fixed assets
(c) allocation of fixed overheads
(d) rent paid
(e) depreciation
(f) tax paid on profits.

Feedback

Wages paid, rent paid and tax paid on profits are all cash flows as they have an immediate effect on the cash resources of the business. The allocation of fixed overheads and depreciation are accounting activities which do not have an effect on the cash resources of the business and so are not cash flows.

It is likely that the purchase of fixed assets will result in a cash flow; even an exchange of shares in return for assets would eventually have cash flow implications when dividends are paid. If assets are bought using credit the cash flows will be the payments required by the terms of the credit agreements. Of course if the assets are bought for cash the purchase price will be a cash flow.

When a business increases its level of activity it may also need to increase its investment in working capital. This increase is calculated by adding the increase in stock to the increase in debtors and deducting the increase in creditors to find the net increase. In general this increase is deemed to take place during the first year rather than immediately. There is often an assumption that the increase in working capital which takes place at the beginning of a project will be accompanied by a corresponding decrease in working capital during the final year of the project.

You now know all that you need to know about calculating a project's net present value and we can turn our attention to the impact of taxation on investment appraisal.

A little thought should persuade you that the only way for a tax system to be fiscally neutral is if tax is charged on positive cash flows at the same time as the cash flow arises, and tax relief should be available for cash outflows at the time the cash payment is made. If this situation exists and the rate of tax is 't' then if the before-tax net present value is £B then the after-tax cash flows will be £$B(1 - t)$. Provided the rate of tax is less than 100% if B is positive then $B(1 - t)$ will be positive. Equally if B is negative then $B(1 - t)$ will be negative. This means that so long as projects which give a positive net present value are accepted regardless of the numerical value of the net present value the before-tax decision will be the same as the after-tax decision and the system is fiscally neutral.

A government which taxes cash flows in this way is effectively going into partnership with its taxpayers. Profits and losses are shared between the business and the government in a predetermined ratio.

The impact of a time lag in the taxation of cash flows on investment appraisal

The UK corporation tax system does not tax cash flows. Instead profits are taxed and the tax is due nine months after the end of the accounting period. An activity may help you to determine the effect of such a delay.

Activity

Alrewas plc wishes to evaluate an investment opportunity. After an initial cash outflow of £10,000, which is fully deductible for tax purposes, there are cash inflows of £4,000 a year for each of the next five years. Tax is paid on the cash flows, at a rate of 20%, one year after the cash flow. Calculate the before-tax and after-tax net present value of the project. What would the after-tax net present value of the project have been if tax was paid in the year in which the cash flow arose? The company has a cost of capital of 10%.

Feedback

The before-tax net present value of the project is £5,163. The after-tax net present value of the project is £4,224. Both calculations support the decision to proceed with the project.

The after-tax net present value of the project if tax is paid and relief received without any time delay is £5,163 × $(1 - 0.2)$ = £4,130. This is lower than the after-tax net present value of the project with a time lag. Although the

Year	Cash flow £	Tax paid £	Discount factor 10%	Before-tax PV £	After-tax PV £
0	(10,000)		1	(10,000)	(10,000)
1	4,000	2,000	0.9091	3,636	5,455
2	4,000	(800)	0.8264	3,306	2,644
3	4,000	(800)	0.7513	3,005	2,404
4	4,000	(800)	0.6830	2,732	2,186
5	4,000	(800)	0.6209	2,484	1,987
6		(800)	0.5645		(452)
				5,163	4,224

company had to wait for a year to receive the benefit of the tax relief on the initial expenditure this was more than compensated for by the delay in payment of tax on the profits.

Hence it would be possible for a tax system which taxed cash flows with a time lag to lead to a positive after-tax net present value although the before-tax net present value was negative. It is not possible for the reverse situation to arise since for a project to be acceptable the positive cash flows must be greater than the cash outflows. Hence a delay in the payment of tax may lead companies to accept projects which otherwise would have been rejected.

The impact of the UK corporation tax system on investment appraisal

The UK corporation tax system does not tax cash flows, neither does it tax profits. The system is something of a hybrid with some accounting adjustments such as depreciation ignored for tax purposes and other expenses taxed on the accruals basis. In addition there is a nine-month gap between the end of the accounting period and the payment of tax.

Expenditure on a new project may be on any of the following items:

- land and buildings
- plant and machinery
- working capital
- advertising
- staff training.

You can probably think of some more examples but let us consider the tax treatment of each of these types of expenditure.

There is no tax relief on expenditure on land and buildings except for industrial buildings such as factories and warehouses which are eligible for industrial buildings allowances. We will consider the industrial buildings allowance in some detail in Chapter 5. Generally the allowance given is equal to 4% of the cost of the industrial building for the first 25 years of the building's life.

Expenditure on plant and machinery is likely to qualify for a writing down allowance of 25% of the reducing balance each year. Again we will consider the allowances available for expenditure on plant and machinery in detail in Chapter 5.

Expenditure on working capital, that is stock and debtors, is not eligible for any tax relief.

The costs of advertising and staff training is likely to be considered expenditure wholly and exclusively for the purpose of trade and so is fully deductible for Schedule D Case I purposes. Once again we will consider allowable expenses in Chapter 5.

As you can see there is a wide variety of tax treatments of expenditure incurred to set up a new project.

In the light of the tax treatment of different items of expenditure it seems unlikely that any move towards fiscal neutrality is feasible. However, the lower the rate of business tax the smaller the distortions caused by the tax system. The UK rate of company tax is the lowest in Europe which inevitably helps UK businesses to be competitive even if the UK tax system is distortive.

You may even consider that the present bias in the tax system is advantageous as it discriminates against projects which require investment in fixed and current assets in favour of labour intensive projects. With the current high levels of unemployment you may consider this to be a wise strategy.

Summary

In this chapter we have considered some of the distortions which exist in the current tax system. We have considered the distortions caused by both income and expenditure taxes for both individuals and companies. We have seen that lower marginal rates of tax are less likely to lead to distortions than high marginal rates of tax. In order to achieve low marginal rates of tax it will be necessary to levy the tax on as much income or expenditure as possible. For example, if VAT was extended to include food, children's clothing, books and newspapers it would be possible to reduce the rate of VAT and still generate the same amount of revenue for the government.

We can conclude that a broad tax base and low marginal rates of tax lead to fewer distortions than a narrow tax base with high marginal rates of tax.

Project areas

There are so many interesting projects contained within the material of this chapter it is hard to choose just one or two. A topical area is that of the disincentive to work shared by many single parents who simply cannot afford to work. A search for alternative systems of supporting these families which encourages parents to work would prove to be an interesting project.

Alternative bases of taxation

Introduction

The history of tax and the current tax environment was discussed in Chapter 1. In Chapter 2 the ways in which the UK system of taxation can distort the decision-making process of individuals and businesses were explored. In this chapter you will be able to develop the ideas introduced in Chapters 1 and 2. We will consider the impact of tax systems in general on the behaviour of individuals and businesses and then identify the desirable characteristics of a tax system. Once we have done this we will evaluate a number of bases of taxation.

At the end of this chapter you will be able to:

- discuss the concept of the incidence of taxation
- discuss the concept of the excess burden of taxation
- discuss the concept of economic rent
- identify the disincentive effects of taxation
- state and discuss the five desirable characteristics of a tax system
- state the range of tax bases which are available and discuss the merits and limitations of each tax base.

The incidence of taxation

The formal incidence of tax falls on those who must actually pay the tax while the effective incidence of tax falls on those whose wealth is reduced by the tax.

While it is not usually difficult to identify the formal incidence of tax it is, in practice, often impossible to identify the effective incidence of tax.

Consider the cost of a newspaper. Currently VAT is not levied on the sale of newspapers. If it were introduced the formal incidence of VAT would fall on the retailers who sell newspapers. The effective incidence is likely to fall not only on the retailers but also on the newspaper proprietors, their distributors and the individuals who buy newspapers. It is likely that the volume of sales of newspapers would fall leading to reduced profits for the newspapers, their distributors and the retailers. In addition, in order to reduce the impact of the tax on the volume of sales, the newspaper proprietors, their distributors and retailers may not pass on the full amount of the VAT to their readers but may reduce their profit margins instead.

Tax wedges

In the case of indirect taxes the tax wedge is the difference between the marginal cost of producing a good and the marginal benefit from consumption. In the UK then the tax wedge is equal to the VAT and/or customs duty levied on a sale. An item which is sold for £100 before VAT has a marginal benefit from consumption of £117.50 (£100 plus VAT at 17.5%), because this is what the purchaser is prepared to pay for it, and a marginal cost of producing the good of £100 since this is the price at which the seller is prepared to manufacture the good. Hence the tax wedge is £17.50, the amount of VAT which is due from the consumer.

In the case of an income tax system the tax wedge is the difference between the marginal value of leisure sacrificed by a worker and the marginal value to society of another hour of work.

In the case of taxes on unearned income the tax wedge is the difference between the gross and net after-tax rates of return.

Activity

Determine the variables which make up the tax wedge when a trader employs a new worker.

Feedback

The tax wedge will be equal to the difference between the total cost of the worker to the employer and the after-tax salary of the employee.

This difference will be made up of four elements: the income tax which is levied on the employee's salary, the employee's national insurance contributions, the employer's national insurance contribution, and finally the value of any business tax relief which will be available to the employer with respect to the cost of employing the extra member of staff.

The distorting effect of taxation is not dependent on the formal incidence of tax, rather it is dependent on the size of the tax wedge. For example, it is not important to draw a distinction between employer and employee national insurance but the total amount of national insurance which must be paid may lead to distortions.

The larger the tax wedge the greater the potential for distortions. A system of taxation will probably be less distortive if it contains many small distortions rather than one or two large distortions.

The ultimate payer of tax

The concept of the incidence of taxation is concerned with the question of who ultimately pays the tax. Look back to Chapter 2 to the activity where the gardener considers how much to charge for his labour. When determining his hourly rate the gardener decided how much money he wanted in exchange for his work and then added on the amount of tax which would be levied on him if he undertook the job, thus effectively passing the burden of his income tax liability on to his employer.

In theory the burden for indirect taxes, like VAT, falls on the final consumer. Yet there is evidence that manufacturers absorb some of the burden of VAT rather than passing it on in full to their customers. Most traders offered to fit double glazing free of VAT for some time after VAT was extended to double glazing thus absorbing the burden of taxation themselves.

Crowding out

The concept of the incidence of taxation is also concerned with the transfer of resources from the private sector to the public sector. Suppose, for example, that the government decides to stimulate the economy by increasing the number of employees in the public sector. It will achieve this in two ways: firstly taxes may increase, moving resources from the private sector and therefore reducing the level of activity in this sector. Secondly the government may borrow money to finance its expansion causing interest rates to rise and deterring the private sector from investing in new projects which now do not give an adequate return. This strategy then will cause a shrinking in the private sector which will reduce the size of the tax base and lead to an increase in the rates of tax needed to maintain the level of tax raised. This phenomenon is termed crowding out.

The excess burden of taxation

The substitution distortion

We have spent some time considering the distortive effect of taxation including the concept of substitution distortion whereby individuals consume one item rather than another because of the effect of taxation.

This substitution distortion is also called the excess burden of taxation. The burden of tax which is caused by a government transferring spending power from the taxpayer to the state is not, in itself, inefficient but if it is done in such a way as to affect the economic choices of the taxpayer the cost to the taxpayer is the excess burden of taxation. For example, as the Chancellor explained in his first budget of 1993, VAT was not then charged on domestic fuel but was levied on the costs of insulating a home. This distortion might have been influencing taxpayers to consume more energy to heat their homes rather than spending money on insulating their property. In an effort to remove this distortion, and to raise more revenue, the Chancellor announced his intention to extend the scope of VAT to domestic fuel, thus taxing both commodities on the same basis.

There are other examples of taxes which cause a distortion in the economic decisions made by a country's citizens. For some historical examples look again at Chapter 1. Look back to Chapter 2 and find out the effect that the marginal rate of income tax has on an employee's decision about working overtime. In addition look back to Chapter 2 for examples of the way in which taxes can distort the capital investment decisions of businesses. Investment projects which have a positive net present value before tax can have a negative net present value after tax if the tax system is not fiscally neutral. If this happens the company will have to use its money in some other way. Suppose that the company decides to distribute the funds to its shareholders. If this happens the shareholders suffer a loss equal to the before-tax net present value of the project. The community generally will have lost the benefit of the expenditure planned by the company. This may have been for goods or services, causing other businesses to lose orders. The total number of jobs may also fall. Finally the government has lost tax because the project was not undertaken.

The income distortion

The income distortion is the transfer of wealth from the taxpayer to the government. The income distortion then reduces the amount that the taxpayer can consume.

A lump-sum tax

The degree of income distortion will be dependent on the average rate of tax. The greater the average rate of tax the greater the income distortion. The degree of the substitution distortion will be dependent on the marginal rate of tax. It is argued by economists that a lump-sum tax where an individual pays a given amount of tax regardless of the amount of work which he undertakes would eliminate the substitution distortion when individuals decide whether to work harder or enjoy more leisure time.

If a lump-sum tax were to be introduced then a taxpayer's marginal rate of tax would be zero.

A lump-sum tax would be likely to affect the behaviour of individuals. The benefit of working for an extra hour will increase because there is no increase in taxation and so more work is likely to be undertaken. This does not mean that the lump-sum tax is not distortionary; it simply illustrates the distortions which exist in the tax system which prevails today.

The amount of a lump-sum tax paid by an individual must be independent of characteristics which the individual can influence. For example, a tax which increases with the educational and vocational qualifications of the individual is not a lump-sum tax because it may have a distortive effect on the decisions made by individuals about their education and training.

However, if only members of the workforce paid the lump-sum tax, there may be a distortionary effect as low paid individuals may be deterred from joining or remaining in the workforce.

Economic rent

Economic rent is the amount that a factor of production earns over and above what could be earned if it was put to its next best use. Some economists argue that economic rent should be subject to taxation.

The taxation of land

The first asset to be considered this way was land. Since there is only a finite amount of land it is a scare resource. Consider some farm land. The difference between the value of the crops and the cost of cultivating the land was the economic rent because there was no alternative use for the land.

However, today there are other uses for land, especially for building houses and other buildings. Land with planning permission is worth more than land without such consent. Under a system which taxes economic rent the increase in value brought about by planning permission should be taxable. Because planning permission is often difficult to obtain and local authorities only allow limited development in an area land with such permission can be very valuable. In theory it is feasible to tax such gains because landowners will still be better off by developing the land provided the tax is at a lower rate than 100%. A tax of this kind has been tried on several occasions, the last one being the Development Land Tax which was abolished in the early 1980s. In practice landowners, when faced with a tax of this type, often choose to 'wait and see' rather than realise the gain immediately in the hope that the tax will be abolished. To date this strategy has proved to be successful.

The economic rent of other assets

There are other assets whose value is enhanced because of the actions of governments. The most recent example of this has been the granting of the television franchises where companies were invited to bid for the right to broadcast in a region. Some companies lost their franchise and have had to find a new role for themselves as independent producers. Other companies bid so much for their franchise that it seems doubtful that they will earn even reasonable profits. These franchise payments can be considered to be a tax on economic rents.

An economic rent on housing

Now consider a homeowner. The economic rent of his or her home is the amount which the property could be let at on the open market.

In an income tax based system where income received is subject to taxation then a tax liability should arise on the value of this economic rent. This effectively treats a homeowner as both tenant and landlord. The payment of a notional rent has no tax consequences for the tenant in an income tax system but the notional rent received by the landlord would be taxable in the same way as any other income is taxable. In practice it may be difficult to persuade homeowners to pay tax on income which they have not, in fact, received. We will discuss income based tax systems later in this chapter.

If an expenditure tax system is in force (again this is discussed later in the chapter) the notional income received by the landlord has no tax consequences but the notional rent paid by the tenant would be subject to an expenditure tax. Once again it is unlikely that such a tax would be accepted by the electorate. Under an expenditure tax system it would also be theoretically possible for the homeowner to pay an expenditure tax when the property is acquired. In practice the barrier to home ownership that such a tax would create is likely to be unacceptable in the UK.

The desirable characteristics of a system of taxation

Stiglitz (1988) offers five desirable characteristics of a system of taxation. A system of tax should be:

- *Economically efficient*: it should not have an impact on the allocation of resources.
- *Administratively simple*: it should be easy and inexpensive to administer.
- *Flexible*: it should be easy for the system to respond to changing economic circumstances.
- *Politically accountable*: taxpayers should be able to determine what they are actually paying so that the political system can more accurately reflect the preferences of individuals.
- *Fair*: it should be seen to be fair in its impact on all individuals.

Other writers, including Adam Smith, have offered alternatives to Stiglitz but all the proposals are similar. One problem with all these lists is that their authors do not prioritise the desirable characteristics. Should we allocate each of the characteristics equal weight or are some more important than others? Are some of the characteristics so important that any successful system of tax must have them? Perhaps we should consider each of Stiglitz's characteristics before attempting to answer these questions.

Economic efficiency

A tax system is seen to be economically efficient if it does not distort the economic decisions which are made by individuals. We have already discussed the concept of economic efficiency in some detail in Chapters 1 and 2. In the early part of this chapter we have identified substitution distortions and income distortions and concluded that a lump-sum tax does not have a substitution distortion effect. In Chapter 2 we also considered both the income distortion effect and the substitution distortion effect of an expenditure tax, VAT.

Other examples of distortion include:

- *Planning for retirement.* An individual who invests funds in an approved pension fund obtains tax relief on contributions and the pension fund itself is exempt from both income and capital gains tax. This contrasts with an individual who proposes to finance retirement in some other way, perhaps by investing in a stamp collection, where the tax situation will be very different. No relief will be available for funds invested in the collection and capital gains tax will be levied when the collection is sold. However, the proceeds will be free of income tax.

- *Housing.* An individual who purchases his or her own home will obtain tax relief on some or all the interest paid on a loan to purchase the house. In contrast there is no tax relief on rent paid by an individual who chooses to rent his or her home rather than buy it.

Sometimes the distortions are intended in order to affect individuals' behaviour. Such taxes are termed corrective taxes. The examples above on pensions and housing may be considered corrective taxes. Another example is the subsidy which is sometimes paid to employers who provide jobs to individuals who have been unemployed for a long time.

We also have a number of examples of the impact that announcements have on people's behaviour. For example, if people believe that the duty on cigarettes will be increased in the budget they may purchase more cigarettes in the days before the budget in anticipation of an increase in tax.

Administrative simplicity

The costs of administering the tax system include not only the direct costs incurred by the government of the day but also the compliance costs of the taxpayer. Compliance costs are the costs which are imposed on a taxpayer when he or she complies with a given tax. Some commentators estimate that the compliance costs are five times as big as the direct costs. Currently there are proposals to reduce some of the compliance costs on sole traders and partnerships but the burden of accounting for PAYE, VAT and capital gains tax should not be underestimated.

Flexibility

A flexible tax is one which changes easily in response to changes in the economic cycle. Governments often aim to reduce the fluctuations in economic activities caused by the economic cycle. A flexible tax has a stabilising effect on the economy because it causes money to be taken out of a growing economy and reduces the amount of money that is taken out of the economy when it enters a recession.

Therefore, in times of recession a government might be content to see its receipts fall and increase its borrowing in order to give the economy a boost while during boom years a government might be happy to see its receipts increase thus moderating the boom.

An example of a flexible tax is income tax. When incomes rise the amount of tax raised increases without any action from the government and equally when income falls the amount of tax collected also falls. Because of the proportional nature of the UK income tax system the percentage change in the tax collected is greater than the percentage change in wages. If wages increase by, say, 10% in a year income taxes will increase by more than 10%

over the same period without a need for a change in the legislation and without a protest from taxpayers who accept that if their salaries increase their tax liability should also increase. Taxes will increase by a greater percentage than wages because marginal rates of tax are higher than average rates of tax. Another example of a tax which changes automatically is stamp duty on houses, which increases both as the number of houses sold increases and as the value of houses sold increases.

However, there is often a time lag between the decision to take some fiscal action, the implementation of the policy and the full impact of the tax on the economy. For example, during the 1980s there was great pressure from environ mentalists to reduce the lead emissions from petrol. In the late 1980s the duty on unleaded petrol was reduced to make it more attractive to use than leaded petrol. Demand for unleaded petrol increased as a result of the changes but there was a time delay while information about unleaded petrol was dissemi- nated throughout the population and car owners arranged to have their engines modified. The time lag for other changes may be shorter but the delay can cause instability. For example, if the government is faced with a severe recession it might expand the economy by borrowing in order to avoid high unemployment. This expansion might turn a recovery into a boom, leading to demands for cutbacks which might, once again, lead to recession. This cycle is termed the 'boom and bust' cycle for which successive UK governments have been criticised.

The rates of direct taxation are usually difficult to change, generating much political debate about the 'fairness' of each proposal. In addition the present government has made a number of commitments to refrain from increasing taxes. However, increasing employee national insurance contributions by 1% from 1994/95 did not seem to cause the political argument that increasing income tax by 1% would have done, despite the fact that both changes would have had the same effect on a taxpayer on average earnings of about £14,000.

Political accountability

For a tax system to be politically accountable it must legislate for all changes in taxation and the government must regularly offer itself to the electorate to gain a mandate for its policies.

For a tax system to be politically accountable the country's citizens need to be fully informed about the incidence of tax. Hence taxes where the incidence of tax is clear are to be preferred over taxes where there is disagreement and uncertainty about the ultimate payer of the tax. If this criterion is used then corporation tax is a bad tax because it is unclear whether the shareholders or consumers bear the ultimate burden of the tax. It is also argued by some economists that individuals are more aware of how much income tax they pay than how much VAT they pay, making income taxes more politically account- able than VAT.

In addition, the tax consequences of any financial transaction should be known in advance of the transaction being undertaken. In practice this is not always the case in the UK. In order to address this issue the government published a consultative document in November 1995 about pre-transaction rulings. By November 1996 ministers had concluded that while there was general support for such a scheme the potential difficulties were such that it was not feasible to introduce it immediately. In particular concerns were raised about the fee which would be levied on taxpayers using the service, the amount of information about the putative transaction which would be required by the Inland Revenue and the impact such a scheme would have on the existing informal arrangements between taxpayers and inspectors. At the time of writing the Inland Revenue are investigating the feasibility of introducing a product ruling scheme. Such a scheme would be restricted to retail products sold to taxpayers including financial instruments and savings plans.

As part of the new self-assessment regime a new system of free post-transaction rulings is to be introduced which will provide a ruling to a taxpayer after the transaction has been undertaken but before the taxpayer has submitted his or her tax return.

Fairness

A tax which is not seen to be fair is usually resented by the individuals called upon to pay it. The most recent example of a tax which failed, at least in part because it was seen to be unfair, was the community charge. The introduction of VAT on fuel is probably also seen to be unfair because the elderly, the infirm and families with young children spend a relatively high proportion of their income on heating which is generally considered to be a basic necessity of life.

There are two measures of the fairness of a tax system — horizontal equity and vertical equity:

- a tax system is horizontally equitable if taxpayers with equal taxable capacity bear the same tax
- a tax system has vertical equity if those whose need is greater suffer less tax.

Let us consider horizontal equity in more detail.

We have two problems of definition when considering horizontal equity. How will we identify taxpayers with equal taxable capacity? Two individuals doing the same job for the same money with the same personal circumstances are likely to have the same taxable capacity, but how do you compare the taxable capacity of an individual who has earned income with another who is unable to work but has substantial wealth? Equally an individual who prefers to spend his leisure time drinking incurs a greater tax liability than an individual who spends the same amount of money on trips to the theatre regardless of their relative taxable capacities. A married couple enjoys the benefit of the married couple's allowance which is not available to a couple who choose to live together even if they are identical in all other respects.

Now let us consider the matter of the tax to be paid by individuals with the same taxable capacity. Suppose we consider two individuals with the same lifetime income, one of whom earns the same amount for each year of his working life of 40 years while the other earns 20 times as much for only two years of his working life. Under a progressive tax system the first taxpayer will pay less tax than the second. Hence, for a tax to have horizontal equity it should be based on the lifetime income of the taxpayer. This approach is likely to prove difficult or impossible to operate in practice and in any case raises new difficulties. For example, how should individuals with different lifespans be taxed? Women, for example, have a significantly longer lifespan than men. If income is to be spread over a taxpayer's lifetime should women pay less tax than men on their taxable capacity because they will need to support themselves for more years? Many people would consider this to be unfair.

If we turn our attention to vertical equity we find new problems. To implement a tax system with vertical equity we must first decide who, in principle, should pay tax at the higher rate. Then we must decide how much higher that rate should be than the basic rate paid by other taxpayers, and finally we must devise a tax system which achieves our objectives.

An individual may be considered to have a greater ability to pay or to have a higher level of economic well-being or to receive more benefits from government spending. Any of these criteria might be used to identify individuals who should pay the higher rate of taxation. Even if the criteria to be used are agreed there will still be difficulties involved in measuring ability to pay, economic well-being or benefits received.

Suppose two individuals undertake the same job but the first chooses to work only the basic hours and spends his leisure time in his garden while the second chooses to work overtime each week. If income is used to determine economic well-being then the second individual will pay more tax than the first. But both employees had the same opportunity to earn extra money so is it fair that one of them should pay more tax than the other? If we consider the ability to earn an income then both will pay the same amount of tax.

So if we are to use the ability to pay as our criteria we must first decide whether we will use actual income or potential income. In practice of course it is actual income which is taxed. But even if we tax the actual income of taxpayers we may still have problems with equity. Suppose two individuals have the same income but the first saves money in order to provide for retirement while the second spends money as it is earned and depends on the state for support in old age. The first individual will pay tax on the return earned on the savings and so will pay more tax in total than the second individual, while the second receives more benefits from the state.

Some argue that tax paid should relate to the benefit received. That is, that those who benefit most from the services provided by the government should pay the most tax. This approach is occasionally used in the UK. For example, only those individuals who have a television in their living accommodation are required to contribute to the cost of the BBC by way of the licence fee. However, this is a crude measure of benefit. There is no way of evaluating how much benefit a taxpayer derives from watching BBC programmes. In addition the tax is difficult to collect and necessitates the use of a database of all addresses in the UK and detector vans to ensure compliance with the tax. There are relatively few services which can be taxed in this way. Defence is often quoted as a benefit which it is impossible for a citizen to choose whether to enjoy or not. It is often undesirable for other services to be withheld from citizens who do not contribute to their cost even if it were feasible. For example, there are instances in history when homeowners and businesses could subscribe to the fire service in rather the same way as a motorist can choose to join the AA or the RAC today. However, if a non-subscriber suffered a fire and the fire services did not provide their services it was possible that the fire would have spread to neighbours who had paid to have their property protected. In addition it is likely to be unacceptable to the community as a whole that some members of society are not helped by the fire services when they are in need.

Road tolls, for example on some bridges, are another way of taxing users rather than the whole population. However, road tolls are likely to lead to economic inefficiency because some road users will make an alternative choice rather than use the bridge and pay the toll giving a substitution distortion thus leading to an inefficient allocation of resources.

Thus it seems impossible that a significant amount of tax could be raised on this basis.

Utilitarians argue that a tax system will be fair if individuals make an equal sacrifice of utility. They undertake an analysis of individuals' utilities and then set tax rates so that the marginal utility of income, which is the loss in utility from taking a pound of income away from an individual, is the same for all individuals. It is then argued that taking a pound away from a rich individual causes him or her a lower loss of welfare than taking a pound away from a less well off individual. This leads to the conclusion that a tax system should be progressive although it does not help us to decide just how progressive the system should be. However, we have already discussed the problems created by high marginal rates of tax on work effort in Chapter 2 and this makes utilitarianism a less attractive argument.

You can see that this concept of fairness is extremely complex and we have done little more than introduce the subject.

Stiglitz revisited

Now that we have spent some time discussing each of Stiglitz's characteristics we can attempt to identify the most important of them.

In recent years two taxes proposed by the government have failed: the community charge and the increase in VAT on domestic fuel from 8% to 17.5%. The community charge replaced the rates in April 1990, and was itself replaced in April 1993 by the council tax. If we consider each of these taxes and try to identify the reasons for their failure we may be able to identify characteristics which a tax must have in order to be successful in the UK.

The community charge replaced the rates, a long-established but unpopular tax. Rather than levy tax on homeowners as the rates did, the community charge was levied on virtually all individuals over 18 years of age. The supporters of the community charge argued that it increased political accountability by making the individuals who were eligible to vote in local government elections responsible for paying for their elected council's expenditure proposals. Opponents of the community charge claimed that the tax was unfair because the majority of individuals were required to pay the same amount of tax regardless of their personal circumstances. Some individuals, including students and the unemployed, were able to pay a reduced amount but little relief was available for the majority of taxpayers. In practice the tax proved to be difficult to collect with many young adults simply disappearing from official records. Even now it is thought that it will take many years to collect the outstanding community charges owed. In addition to the administrative problems, protests about the unfairness of the community charge continued until it was replaced with the council tax.

The increase of VAT on domestic fuel was proposed in the spring budget of 1993. In April 1994 VAT was levied on domestic fuel at 8% and towards the end of 1994 the Chancellor attempted to introduce the legislation needed to increase the rate from 8% to 17.5%. In the event the House of Commons defeated the motion and the Chancellor was forced to abandon his proposal.

The defeat occurred despite measures announced in the budget to protect many of the less well off in society from the increase in VAT. These measures including substantial increases in the state pension as well as increases above inflation to a number of other state benefits.

The opponents of the tax argued that heating and lighting were essential for everybody, and not a luxury, and so should not be taxed at the full rate. They also argued that in general people on lower incomes spend proportionately more of their income on gas and electricity and so the increase would affect the poorest people in society disproportionately.

It would appear then that the community charge failed because it was difficult to collect and was considered to be unfair because it was regressive. The increase in VAT on domestic fuel was seen to be regressive and therefore unfair. Perhaps then the most important characteristic of a good tax system, in the UK at least, is that it should be, and be seen to be, fair.

Alternative tax bases

A considerable amount of debate has been generated by the question of the tax base which should be used to determine an individual's contribution to public funds. The five desirable characteristics of a good tax system should equip you to evaluate the following tax bases. We have already discussed two tax bases, the benefit theory of income tax and the ability to pay. In this section we will consider three further tax bases:

- wealth
- income
- expenditure.

Wealth

Look back to Chapter 1 and read about the history of wealth taxes. The first taxes were wealth taxes mostly because wealth is easier to tax than income. A wealth tax would replace taxes on unearned income and capital gains and is effectively a tax based on the ability to pay which was considered earlier in this chapter. A tax on wealth has the effect of redistributing wealth. However, there are a number of difficulties which arise when trying to value wealth.

Activity

List some of the things which may contribute to an individual's wealth.

Feedback

You have probably included some tangible assets in your list like land and buildings. Other assets include shares and securities and the market value of a business run by the individual. But for many people the present value of their future earnings and the present value of their pension fund are their most valuable assets. Look back to Chapter 2 for an explanation of the present value technique. The present value of an individual's future earnings is the estimated positive cash flows arising from his employment throughout his working life restated in present value terms. The courts already take account of potential earnings when awarding damages. However, we live in a rapidly changing world in which an individual may be faced with redundancy, retraining and second or even third careers during his or her working life. In practice it does not seem feasible to value the future earnings of every citizen. Since future pension rights are generally dependent on earned income it is also impossible to value the future pension of every citizen.

In practice then a wealth tax is a tax on assets. However, individuals who do not use a pension fund, for whatever reason, may accumulate assets in order to provide for old age and a wealth tax which is levied on assets but not pension rights will be inequitable.

In addition assets may provide additional benefits to their owner such as power and influence. For example, a wealthy individual is likely to be able to borrow money at a lower rate than is available to most citizens. It would be extremely difficult to ascribe a value to these economic benefits.

Finally, a wealth tax is likely to be expensive to administer, although property taxes, like the council tax, are relatively cheap to collect. The difficulties of a wealth tax are probably too great to enable it to be introduced in the industrialised world. However, a tax on expenditure may serve as a surrogate since it effectively taxes an individual's standard of living.

Although a full wealth tax may be impractical there are two taxes in the UK which could be considered to be, partly at least, wealth taxes, capital gains tax and inheritance tax. Together these taxes provided the Exchequer with less than 1% of its total revenue in 1996/97. This is about half of the average proportion of total revenue which is raised by wealth taxes in OECD countries.

One of the components of Conservative fiscal policy is the abolishment of both of these taxes and in recent years the threshold at which inheritance tax is levied has been increased substantially above that needed to compensate for inflation. The Conservative party argues that these two taxes, in common with other wealth taxes, discourage entrepreneurship and thus restrict economic growth. This view is not substantiated by a recent study of OECD countries which suggests that wealth taxes do not significantly affect the level of economic activity of a country.

One of the purposes of capital gains tax in the UK is to reduce tax avoidance. Taxpayers pay tax on their net chargeable gains in excess of the annual exemption limit, which is £6,500 for 1997/98, at their marginal rate of income tax. As a result there is relatively little incentive to realise capital gains rather than taxable income. If capital gains tax is abolished it is likely that many new measures will have to be introduced to restrict the scope for converting income into capital gains in order to limit the potential loss of income tax.

Inheritance tax serves no such purpose because it is almost entirely avoidable by taxpayers who undertake effective tax planning and are not unfortunate enough to die unexpectedly. However, there are a number of arguments in favour of an inheritance tax. Firstly, there is no evidence that a tax on inheritance affects individuals incentive to work. Secondly, it is argued that one role of tax is the transfer of wealth from the better off to the poorer in society. An inheritance tax is probably one of the best ways of achieving this redistribution of wealth. Of course there are many commentators who would not support such a role for taxation.

Income

Income is used as a tax base throughout the world. However, this does not mean that an income tax is without difficulties or that it is the best tax base to use. Our first problem arises when we try to define income.

Hicks defined income as the maximum value which a man can consume during a period and still expect to be as well off at the end of the period as he was at the beginning.

Hence if a tax system which taxes income is to be equitable it must allow for the erosion of the capital base caused by inflation. In times of inflation some of the income generated must be retained within the business in order to maintain the capital base. This sounds very reasonable but there are a number of difficulties which have deterred the Inland Revenue from implementing such a system. These problems include:

- determining how the value of the capital base should be measured
- the use of the word 'expect' in the definition. It does not tell how much an individual can consume with certainty, only what he can consume and expect to maintain his capital base. It does not help us to determine how to tax unpredicted profits, or losses.

Hicks himself claimed little usefulness for his definitions of income describing them as 'bad tools, which break in our hands'. In addition governments are reluctant to allow inflation to become an integral part of the tax system. At the moment some personal allowances and tax limits are increased in line with the increase in the retail price index unless the Chancellor elects to either freeze them or increase them by some other amount. Governments are reluctant to extend indexation for fear that it will fuel inflation once again.

In 1978 the Meade Committee reporting on *The Structure and Reform of Direct Taxation* considered a comprehensive income tax.

A comprehensive income tax is a tax which is levied on comprehensive income which is equal to the amount which an individual could consume without diminishing the value of his wealth. This can be restated in terms of actual events so that comprehensive income is equal to the amount which is consumed plus/(less) any increase/(decrease) in the value of the individual's wealth.

But this would result in all the difficulties described in the section on a wealth tax. Go back and re-read the section and you will find that it has already been rejected as being impractical.

Meade rejected the comprehensive income tax claiming that it was impracticable to introduce all the measures which would be necessary to adjust for inflation and supported the introduction of an expenditure tax.

Expenditure

Having rejected taxes on wealth and income let us finally consider expenditure taxes. An expenditure, or consumption, tax taxes what an individual takes out of the economy in a given period, unlike an income tax which taxes what is contributed to society. There is no need to value wealth which we have already concluded is impossible. The tax is only levied when the taxpayer spends money. All income is free of tax. Since an expenditure tax does not tax the return on an investment there is an encouragement to save provided that investors will save more if they can obtain a higher return.

An expenditure tax can incorporate personal allowances and varying rates of tax exactly as an income tax does. Hence it is possible for an expenditure tax to be progressive and to take account of a taxpayer's personal circumstances if it is considered desirable.

Activity

What percentage must an expenditure tax be levied at to replace an income tax of 23%?

Feedback

If we ignore the time value of money an expenditure tax of 29.87% is the equivalent of an income tax of 23%. However, because expenditure usually takes place after income is received the expenditure tax should be somewhat higher than this to compensate for the time lag between income and expenditure.

In addition, because savings are not taxed directly under an expenditure tax, the tax base will be somewhat narrower and so the expenditure tax will have to increase even more.

There are a number of ways of operating an expenditure tax system. The Meade Committee offered four alternatives.

- A *tax on value added*. This could operate in the same way as VAT. Note though that VAT is not strictly an expenditure tax, but an indirect tax. Look back to Chapter 1 for a discussion of indirect taxation. An expenditure tax will have to recognise an individual's personal circumstances which is something that a tax like VAT cannot do.
- A *tax on income with 100% capital allowances*. In Chapter 5 you will find out how a system of capital allowances would operate. Of course only a taxpayer could benefit from this system; a business with accumulated losses would not pay tax and so could not benefit immediately from an allowance for capital expenditure.
- A *tax on all income apart from investment income*. Go back and re-read the section on fairness for a discussion about the taxation of investment income.
- A *tax on consumption expenditure but not capital expenditure*. It was this system which was recommended by the Committee and we shall spend a little time considering how it would work in practice.

The Committee considered two forms of expenditure tax: a universal expenditure tax which is described below, and a two-tier expenditure tax which would collect a basic rate of tax through a system of VAT and higher rates of tax would be collected from taxpayers under a system such as the universal expenditure tax. This second system would be somewhat like our system of tax deducted at source where certain payments, such as interest, are paid after deduction of the basic rate of income tax, which is described in Chapter 1, and higher rate taxpayers are required to account for any additional tax payable on the receipt.

Under a universal expenditure tax a taxpayer's consumption expenditure would be calculated by adding the taxpayer's total realised income to any capital receipts, including the sale of capital assets and any amounts borrowed and deducting any expenditure which is not for the purposes of consumption including expenditure on capital assets and amounts repaid. Then tax could be levied on consumption expenditure at a number of rates if desired.

Expenditure taxes, particularly in the form of value added tax, have become popular with governments everywhere in recent years.

Income and expenditure compared

Income is used as a tax base almost everywhere but expenditure taxes are becoming more popular as a way of raising revenue. There are a number of reasons for preferring an expenditure tax to an income tax:

- It can be argued that it is fairer to tax consumption, that is the value of goods and services which an individual takes out of society, than to tax the contribution that he or she makes to a society in the form of either work effort or capital supplied. Remember that the difference between income and consumption is equal to savings. However, the individual who saves will eventually use savings for consumption and thus has merely deferred the expenditure tax rather than avoided it. Of course, it may be the beneficiaries of an individual's estate who use the savings for consumption but eventually the tax will be paid.
- An expenditure tax does not discriminate against individuals who defer their expenditure by saving. An income tax does discriminate against individuals who save in order to undertake consumption in the future by taxing the return on savings.
- The evidence is that savings are relatively inelastic. That is, the amount that is saved is not dependent on the return available. Hence an expenditure tax would not seriously distort the savings decision.

However, there are a number of potential disadvantages of an expenditure tax which make an income tax look more attractive:

- Because the return on savings is not subject to an expenditure tax it seems likely that the level of an expenditure tax will have to be higher than its equivalent income tax. This may prove to be a disincentive to work. Look back to Chapter 2 to find out how taxpayers behave when the rate of income tax is increased. People have become adept at valuing their work effort in terms of goods and services rather than money. This is important in times of inflation when people know that a certain increase in salary is necessary simply to maintain a given standard of living. Occasionally prices are given in terms of how many hours an individual on average wages must work in order to earn enough to buy the goods or services. If this is indeed how individuals think about the relationship between work and consumption then an increase in an expenditure tax will have a similar effect to an increase in an income tax. Hence an expenditure tax can still distort the decision to undertake extra work.

- Individuals who save in order to consume later are subject to uncertainty because they cannot be sure of the tax they must pay when they spend their savings. This uncertainty is not present in an income tax system.
- An expenditure tax still does not account for the privileges which accrue to those with wealth, such as being offered goods at reduced prices because of past patronage.
- Individuals usually have a changing pattern of income and expenditure over their lifetime. Many individuals spend more than they earn in the early years of their adult life and save in the middle years in order for expenditure to exceed income once again in retirement. This pattern may mean that individuals incur the greatest tax burden in years when their income is least able to provide for their needs.

Summary

In this chapter we have probably raised more questions than given answers. We began by attempting to identify the individual who actually suffers a loss in his or her wealth because of the requirement to pay tax. We found that the actual incidence of tax was often difficult to determine and that it was often different from the formal incidence. We then spent some time discussing some of the limitations of the existing tax system before identifying desirable characteristics of taxation. We then evaluated the feasibility of using wealth, income and expenditure as a tax base.

Project areas

There are many interesting questions which are inspired by the material dealt with in this chapter. However, it is important that any hypothesis which you wish to test is, in fact, testable. For example, the question of the funding of higher education is topical. A fascinating question is 'Should a graduate tax be used to fund higher eduction?' It would be possible to generate a discussion on the theoretical aspects of the question but it is difficult to see how you would undertake the necessary empirical work.

Discussion questions

Question 1. Is a lump-sum tax feasible?

Question 2. What corrective taxes, if any, would you like to introduce?

4 ▷ **Personal taxation**

Introduction

Individuals pay tax on their income for a fiscal year. Remember that the fiscal year 1997/98 runs from 6th April 1997 to 5th April 1998. The legislation uses a schedular system to determine the rules for taxing each source of income. For example, Schedule D Case I allows expenses which are wholly and exclusively incurred in the course of the business to be allowable deductions while Schedule E allows only expenses which are wholly, exclusively and necessarily incurred to be deducted. In recent years there have been some major changes in the way in which individuals are taxed. At the end of the 1980s independent taxation was introduced while self-assessment was introduced from 6th April 1996. We will consider both these changes later in this chapter.

In this chapter you will find out how to calculate the amount of income which is to be taxed and learn how to determine the amount of any reliefs and allowances which are available to a taxpayer. Once you have deducted the allowances and reliefs from the taxable income you will be able to compute a taxpayer's tax liability.

At the end of this chapter you will be able to:

- list income which is exempt from income tax
- describe the Schedules and Cases under which individuals pay income tax
- calculate the allowances and reliefs available to an individual
- describe the system of national insurance and calculate any national insurance contributions payable by both employers and employees
- prepare a simple personal tax computation for individuals and members of a family
- describe the system of self-assessment for individuals
- offer basic income tax planning advice to individuals and members of a family unit.

The schedular system of income tax

Remember that income is taxed using a schedular system. It is important to identify which Schedule and Case the income is taxed under because each Schedule and Case has its own rules which deal with the following:

- the income to be taxed
- allowable deductions, if any, from the income
- the basis of assessment
- the date on which tax should be paid.

With the exception of the basis of assessment the list is fairly self-explanatory. The basis of assessment is used to identify the income to be taxed in a fiscal year. We will consider the basis of assessment for each Schedule and Case in this chapter.

We will look at each of the Schedules and Cases in turn. In this chapter we will determine the income which is subject to tax, the expenses which can be set against the income for tax purposes and the date on which tax must be paid. In later chapters some of the Schedules and Cases will be considered in more detail. Specifically Schedule D Cases I and II will form the subject matter of Chapter 5 while Schedule A, Schedule D Cases III, IV, V and VI together with Schedule E will be dealt with in Chapter 6.

Direct assessment and income taxed at source

First we will discuss the differences between tax raised by direct assessment and tax deducted at source and consider a number of the bases of assessment which are used.

Income which is taxed by direct assessment is paid gross, while income taxed at source is paid after deduction of tax. The procedure by which income is paid net of tax was introduced at the beginning of the 19th century as an anti-avoidance measure. Look back to Chapter 1 for more details about the development of the income tax system. The following income is taxed at source:

- interest on most government stock
- interest paid by UK companies on debentures and loan stocks
- interest on bank deposit accounts paid to individuals
- interest paid on building society accounts
- dividends paid by UK companies
- income from deeds of covenant
- income from trusts, settlements and the estates of deceased persons
- patent royalties, but not copyright royalties
- annuities.

Income assessed under Schedule E is paid under PAYE (pay-as-you-earn), that is, the tax due on the income is deducted before the payment is made to the employee. This income is still technically taxed by direct assessment rather than taxed at source because the personal circumstances of the taxpayer are used to determine the amount of tax which should be deducted.

If individuals who are not liable to income tax, perhaps because their income is less than the personal allowances they are entitled to, receive income which has been taxed at source they can reclaim the tax which has been deducted.

This has not always been the case. Until 1991/92 tax was deducted at source from interest paid on building society accounts and could not be claimed back by non-taxpayers. When independent taxation was introduced married women with unused personal allowances were able to reclaim tax which had been deducted at source on all types of investment income apart from building society accounts. Building societies believed, the evidence suggests correctly, that 'housewives' would transfer their savings to accounts where they could reclaim the tax deducted at source. This led the building societies to success-fully lobby the government for a change in the law.

Basis of assessment

The basis of assessment is the way in which income is allocated to fiscal years for tax purposes. For example, Schedule E taxes income which is paid during the fiscal year. This is not the only basis of assessment which could be used. An alternative would be to tax income which is earned during the fiscal year. For most employees this would make no difference but for those who receive performance related bonuses which are paid in the fiscal year after the one in which they were earned the tax on the bonus would be payable before the bonus was actually received.

The legislation for the taxation under all of the Schedules and Cases is contained in the Income and Corporation Taxes Act 1988 (ICTA 1988).

Statutory total income

An individual's income from all sources during the tax year, as determined under the Schedules and Cases, is termed his or her statutory total income. The individuals taxable income is equal to his or her statutory total income less single person's allowance and reliefs.

Exempt income

The legislation specifically exempts certain income from income tax. You should be aware of the most significant exemptions which are:

- the first £70 interest from National Savings Bank ordinary accounts (ICTA 1988 s325)
- the increase in the value of national savings certificates
- premium bond prizes
- some social security benefits, including child benefit and housing benefit
- save-as-you-earn (SAYE) bonuses

- shares allotted to employees under approved profit sharing schemes (ICTA 1988 ss 135–137)
- educational grants and scholarships
- statutory redundancy pay, pay in lieu of notice and some payments up to a maximum of £30,000 made when an employment is terminated (ICTA 1988 ss90, 148, 188, 579 & 580).

Income which is not specifically exempt is subject to income tax under the schedular system which is dealt with in the next section.

Rates of tax

For the fiscal year 1997/98 the first £4,100 of taxable income is taxed at 20%. Taxable income between £4,100 and £26,100 is taxed at the basic rate of 23% and taxable income over £26,100 is taxed at the higher rate of 40%. The Conservative government in power since 1979 has often stated that its intention is to reduce the basic rate of income tax. For many years the target was a basic rate of 25% but once this was achieved a new target of 20% was set. It is expensive to reduce the rate for the whole basic rate band and so a new, lower rate band was introduced in April 1992. The government's long-term strategy is to extend this lower rate band and reduce the basic rate until the basic rate of tax is 20%.

The advantage of this tactic is that individuals with relatively low incomes benefit proportionately more than better off individuals. Look back to the example of Laura, Ashley and Ben in Chapter 1, to see why this is so. In the fiscal year 1997/98 it is estimated that more than seven million people will now pay tax only at a marginal rate of 20%. This is more than a quarter of all taxpayers.

Schedule A

All income from land and property is taxed under Schedule A. This includes income from furnished lettings and letting caravans and houseboats on permanent moorings. Taxable profits will be calculated by deducting total allowable expenses from total income from land and property. The basis of assessment will be the income for the fiscal year. This basis of assessment is usually termed the actual basis. The rules for determining allowable expenses are the same as for Schedule D Case I which is used to tax trading income. That is, the accruals basis will be used unless the income from property is very low, when the cash basis may be allowed.

Schedule D

In order to determine the profits or gains which are taxed under Schedule D it is necessary to determine whether or not the taxpayer is resident in the UK in the fiscal year. An individual is considered to be resident in the UK if he or she either spent over half of the fiscal year in the UK or has left the UK for permanent residence abroad and habitually spends more than three months of the year in the UK. For more information about residency look at the section on Schedule E in this chapter.

Individuals who are resident in the UK in the fiscal year are taxed on any annual profits or gains arising or accruing from any kind of property regardless of its location and from any trade, profession or vocation regardless of the location of the activity.

Individuals who are not resident in the UK in the fiscal year are taxed on the annual profits or gains arising or accruing from any property located in the UK and from any trade, profession or vocation carried on in the UK.

In addition tax is charged under Schedule D in respect of all interest of money, annuities and other annual profits or gains not charged under Schedule A or E, and not specifically exempted from tax (ICTA 1988 s18(1)).

Tax under Schedule D is charged under the Cases set out below. Schedule D Cases I and II are considered in detail in Chapter 5.

Case I

Profits from trades are taxed under Schedule D Case I (ICTA 1988 s18(3)). The normal basis of assessment for 1997/98 is the current year basis. Under the current year basis the basis period for a year of assessment is normally the 12 months to the accounting date ended in the fiscal year. However, there are a number of circumstances in which this simple rule cannot be applied, especially in the early years of trading, the final years of trading or years in which a business changes its accounting date. The rules which apply in most of these circumstances will be discussed in detail in Chapter 5. Expenses which are wholly and exclusively for the purpose of the trade are allowable deductions using the accruals basis.

Case II

Profits from professions or vocations are taxed under Schedule D Case II (ICTA 1988 s18(3)). The basis of assessment and calculation of allowable expenses are the same as for Schedule D Case I.

Case III

Interest received which has not had tax deducted from it is taxed under Schedule D Case III (ICTA 1988 s18(3)). Interest on the following is taxed under Schedule D Case III:

- National Savings Bank accounts other than the first £70 on National Savings Bank ordinary accounts which is exempt
- 3½% War Loan
- Government stocks held on the National Savings Stock Register
- loans between individuals.

The income assessable in a fiscal year is the interest arising within the year of assessment without any deductions (ICTA 1988 s64). Note therefore, that the accruals basis is not used. Some interest has tax at 20% deducted at source unless the recipient has elected to receive interest gross. An example of this is building society interest.

Case IV

Interest received from foreign securities is taxed under Schedule D Case IV (ICTA 1988 s18(3)). Foreign securities include debentures. The basis of assessment is the same as for Schedule D Case III (ICTA 1988 s65(1)).

Taxpayers who are resident but not ordinarily resident and/or not domiciled in the UK pay tax only on the amount remitted to the UK (ICTA 1988 s65(5)). Other taxpayers are liable to tax on the income arising from the securities.

Case V

Income from foreign possessions are taxed under Schedule D Case V. Such income includes dividends, rents, business profits and pensions but excludes income consisting of emoluments of any office or employment (ICTA 1988 s18(3)). The basis of assessment is the same as for Schedule D Case IV.

Case VI

Schedule D Case VI is used to tax annual profits or gains not falling under any other Case of Schedule D and not charged by virtue of Schedule A, C or E (ICTA 1988 s18(3)). In particular income from casual commissions, enterprise allowance payments, some capital sums from the sale of patent rights and post cessation receipts from a business are taxed under Schedule D Case VI. The basis of assessment is the profits or gains arising in the tax year.

Schedule E

Income from an office or employment is taxed under Schedule E (ICTA 1988 s19). It includes salaries, bonuses, benefits in kind and UK pensions. The basis of assessment is the actual income paid during the fiscal year. As we have seen tax is collected under the PAYE system; however, any additional tax is due 14 days after the issue of an assessment. There are in fact three cases for Schedule E depending on the residence of the taxpayer, the employer and the place of work.

It would be useful therefore to start by considering the concept of residence, ordinary residence and domicile.

The terms residence and ordinary residence are not defined in the legislation. The Inland Revenue has published a guidance booklet *Residents and Non-Residents – liability to tax in the UK* (IR20, 1986). In general a person cannot be resident for part of a tax year. He or she is either resident, or not resident, for the entire year of assessment. The only exception occurs when an individual either leaves the UK for permanent residence abroad or comes to the UK in order to take up permanent residence.

An individual is deemed to be resident in the UK if he or she:

- spends more than 183 days in the UK in the tax year (ICTA 1988 s336)
- has left the UK for permanent residence abroad but returns to the UK for periods which equal three months or more in the tax year. However, Statement of Practice 2/91 provides that 'any days spent in the UK because of exceptional circumstances beyond an individual's control (such as illness) are excluded from the calculation'.

A taxpayer is ordinarily resident if the UK is a regular choice of abode which forms part of the regular order of an individual's life.

A taxpayer may be resident, but not ordinarily resident, or ordinarily resident but not resident, or both resident and ordinarily resident in a tax year. A British citizen who has been ordinarily resident in the UK but who leaves for occasional residence abroad is deemed to be resident during his or her absence unless he can prove otherwise (ICTA 1988 s334).

An individual has a domicile of origin from the moment of birth. It is usually the domicile of the father but may be the domicile of the mother. An individual who is under 16 years old may acquire a domicile by dependence. An individual aged 16 or over may acquire a domicile of choice. To do this the individual must maintain a physical presence in the country concerned and must have evidence that he or she has a settled intention to remain there permanently or indefinitely.

Case I

Schedule E Case I assesses emoluments for any year of assessment in which the person holding the office or employment is both resident and ordinarily resident in the UK (ICTA 1988 s19(1)).

Foreign emoluments are defined as the emoluments of a person not domiciled in the UK from an office or employment under or with any person, body of persons or partnership resident outside, and not resident in, the UK. However, these shall be taken not to include the emoluments of a person resident in the UK from an office or employment under or with a person, body of persons or partnership resident in the Republic of Ireland (ICTA 1988 s192(1)).

Where the duties of an office or employment are performed wholly outside the UK and the emoluments from the office or employment are foreign emoluments, the emoluments shall be excepted from Schedule E Case I (ICTA 1988 s192(2)).

In addition, if the duties of an office or employment are performed wholly or partly outside the UK and any of those duties are performed in the course of a period which falls wholly or partly in that year and consists of at least 365 days, then in charging tax under Case I of Schedule E on the amount of the emoluments from that employment attributable to that period, or to so much of it as falls in that year of assessment, there shall be allowed a deduction equal to the whole of that amount (ICTA 1988 s193(1)).

Tax is collected under the PAYE system.

Case II

Income from an office or employment for duties performed in the UK when the employee is either not resident or is resident but not ordinarily resident in the UK is taxed under Case II (ICTA 1988 s19(1)). Foreign emoluments are dealt with as described under Schedule E Case I above. Where possible the PAYE system is used otherwise tax is collected directly, usually in four instalments.

Case III

The following income is taxed under Schedule E Case III:

- foreign emoluments earned wholly abroad by an employee who is either resident and ordinarily resident or resident but not ordinarily resident in the UK. The basis of assessment is the remittence basis, that is only income which is brought into the UK is assessed (ICTA 1988 s19(1)). Tax is collected after the end of the tax year
- every annuity, pension or stipend payable by the Crown or out of the public revenue of the UK other than annuities charged under Schedule C (ICTA 1988 s19(2))
- any pension which is paid otherwise than by, or on behalf of, a person outside the UK (ICTA 1988 s19(3))
- any pension or annuity which is payable in the UK by or through any public department, officer or agent of a government of a territory other than the UK, to a person who has been employed in relevant service outside the UK in respect of that service. A territory is any country which forms part of Her Majesty's dominions. Relevant service means in the service of the Crown or service under the government of a territory
- any pension or annuity which is payable to the widow, child, relative or dependant of any such person as is mentioned above. The person in receipt of the pension or annuity is chargeable to tax as a person resident in the UK (ICTA 1988 s19(4)).

If the emoluments from an office or employment, other than pensions, would fall in a year of assessment in which a person does not hold the office or employment, special rules apply. If the person has not yet held the office or employment the emoluments are treated as emoluments for the first year of assessment in which the office or employment is held. If the office or employment is no longer held by the person the emoluments are treated as emoluments for the last year of assessment in which the office or employment was held (ICTA 1988 s19(1)(4A)).

Schedule F

Dividends and other distributions from UK companies are taxed under Schedule F. Companies are taxed under Schedule F rather than individuals who receive the dividends together with a tax credit equal to 20/80ths of the dividend.

All distributions which are not specifically excluded are taxed as if they were a dividend. Income tax is levied on the aggregate of the distribution received and the related tax credit (ICTA 1988 s20). Non taxpayers are able to reclaim the tax credit. Lower rate and basic rate taxpayers are subject to tax at 20% on their dividends which means that the tax credit exactly equals the tax due on the dividend so that no further tax liability arises. Higher rate taxpayers are taxed at 40% on the aggregate of their dividends and the related tax credit. Like other taxpayers they are able to use the tax credit to reduce their tax liability.

Activity

Identify the Schedule and Case under which each of the following income is taxed:

(a) earnings from working part time in a pub
(b) earnings from appearing on television
(c) extra payments to an employee for undertaking a job which is more difficult than his normal job
(d) dividends paid to an individual who is the managing director of the company.

Feedback

Earnings received in the situations described in (a) and (c) are taxed under Schedule E since they are earnings from employment.

The situation in (b) is a little more complicated. If the taxpayer had a contract of service, as might be the case of a presenter who is required to appear in a programme on a fixed number of occasions during the period of the contract, then the income will be taxed under Schedule E. However, if the contract is for services, as might be the case of an expert who is asked to appear on a programme to give his expert opinion, the income will be taxed under Schedule D Case I. Look again at the way income is taxed under each of these schedules and think about the differences in the ways in which employees and self-employed individuals are taxed. We will consider these differences in detail in Chapter 6.

The dividends paid in (d) are taxed under Schedule F. The relationship of the shareholder to the company is not relevant.

Personal allowances and reliefs

Individuals are eligible to claim one or more allowances which are deducted from their total income to give their taxable income. The way in which allowances have changed in the latter half of this century offers a fascinating insight into our family life. As has already been said, until the Second World War a man on average income did not suffer income tax because his personal allowances were greater than his total income. At that time a family man would have been able to claim a married man's allowance which was substantially higher than the single personal allowance in order to reflect the costs of supporting a wife who did not work. In addition he received allowances if he had children.

A family was, until 1990, seen as a single tax unit and that unit was the husband. A married woman was not entitled to a personal allowance but her husband could claim the wife's earned income relief, which was of the same value as the single personal allowance. As its name suggests the relief was only available for earned income; a wife's investment income was taxed at her husband's marginal rate of tax even if she did not work.

Until the 1970s fathers also received tax allowances for any children in the family. However, these allowances were withdrawn and there was a compensatory increase in child benefit which was paid each week to mothers. This change was welcomed by almost everyone, especially groups concerned with child poverty. It was believed that the allowance was more likely to benefit the children if it was paid to the mother and it was paid regardless of the employment status of the husband thus providing some much needed income in times of unemployment. However, many people appear to have forgotten the transfer from allowances to benefit in the 1970s. Now the benefit is not always increased in line with inflation and there are pressure groups who campaign for the restriction of child benefit to families on relatively low incomes.

There are numerous examples of the Inland Revenue's attitude towards married women until the end of the 1980s. Until 1990 tax returns were completed by the husband and he was expected to make a return of both his own and his wife's earned and unearned income. Until recently if a married woman overpaid tax the Revenue sent any repayment due to her husband and all communications from the Revenue were addressed to the husband regardless of whether the husband or wife had initiated the correspondence. For many couples this arrangement was merely irritating but for others it was a source of great distress. Many women, for a variety of reasons, did not wish their husbands to know about either their earnings, or their savings, or both. However, for a small group of taxpayers there were some advantages to the system. If a husband had insufficient income to enable him to use his personal allowances he could apply the reliefs to his wife's income since, from the Revenue's point of view, her income was deemed to be his. In effect this meant that if a family consisted of a working wife and a husband with little or no income a personal allowance and a married man's allowance could be claimed whereas if the situation is reversed and the husband worked while the wife had no income, only the married man's allowance could be claimed.

However, at the end of the 1960s two schemes were introduced which were intended to reflect the changing role of women, especially professional women, in society. One of the schemes was intended to offer women some measure of privacy in their tax affairs. It enabled women to complete their own tax returns and enter into correspondence with the Revenue themselves. The personal allowances available to the couple were then split between the husband and wife in proportion to their income. Of course a curious taxpayer could easily deduce their spouse's total income from the amount of the allowances they received. The total tax paid by the couple was unchanged by this election (ICTA 1988 s283).

The second scheme was likely to be used by couples to reduce their total tax bill. The husband had to relinquish his married man's allowance and claim only the single person's allowance. In return his wife's liability to tax on her earned income was calculated without reference to his total income, enabling the couple to use the basic rate band twice, once in each tax computation. This election was only worth making if the couple were higher rate taxpayers and the wife had sufficient earned income to save more tax than was lost by her husband in forgoing the married man's allowance by using the basic rate of tax rather than her husband's marginal rate of tax (ICTA 1988 s287).

However, pressure grew during the 1980s for the reformation of the taxation of the family unit from two sources. Women demanded independence in tax matters, but perhaps even more importantly it became apparent that many couples were better off living together than getting married, especially if they had children and a mortgage. Consider a couple with two children with only the father working and a mortgage of £70,000. If the couple were married they could claim only the married couple's allowance together with tax relief on the interest paid on the first £30,000 of the mortgage. If the couple were not married they could each claim the single person's allowance and an additional personal allowance by claiming that each parent was responsible for one child. In addition both children were entitled to a single personal allowance. The mother could take the father to court and apply for maintenance payments for herself and their children which would provide them with sufficient income to utilise the personal allowances. Of course the mother and the children also had a basic rate tax band and if the father was a higher rate taxpayer more maintenance could be paid in order to save him tax at high rates. Finally the couple could each claim tax relief on the interest paid on £30,000 of the mortgage. You can see that it was possible for a couple who were not married to be several thousand pounds a year better off than a couple who were married. This was clearly nonsensical for a government which claimed to be the champion of the family. From 6th April 1990 a system of independent taxation was introduced which taxed individuals rather than family units.

Personal allowance (PA)

Every person who is UK resident is entitled to a personal allowance of £4,045 except for anyone in receipt of the age allowance. This includes children and married as well as single people (ICTA 1988 s257). There is provision in statute for the personal allowance to increase in line with inflation each year but this increase of £280 is three and a half times the rate of inflation (ICTA 1988 S257C).

Increases in personal allowances benefit less well off taxpayers proportionately more than better off taxpayers.

Married couple's allowance (MCA)

This allowance is currently available to a married man whose wife lives with him (ICTA 1988 s257A). The allowance equals £1,830 and is not subject to the indexation provision described above (FA 1992 s10(3)). Despite this the allowance was increased by £40 in the 1996 budget. In recent years the value of the allowance has been eroded by being restricted to lower rates of tax. In

1997/98 the relief is restricted to 15% and is therefore given as a credit against tax rather than as a deduction from statutory total income.

In any year of assessment in which her husband is entitled to the married couple's allowances under ICTA 1988 s257A, a woman may elect for half of the married couple's allowance to be transferred from her husband to herself (F(No 2)A 1992 s257BA(1)). A husband and wife may jointly elect for the entire married couple's allowance to be transferred to the wife (F(No 2)A 1992 s257BA(2)). Finally, if the joint election to transfer the allowance to the wife has been made, a husband may elect for one half of the allowance to be transferred back to him (F(No 2)A 1992 s257BA(3)). Once any of these three elections has been made it remains in force for subsequent years of assessment until it is either revoked or a further election is made (F(No 2)A 1992 s257BA(4)).

The married couple's allowance is reduced in the year of marriage by £1,830 × 1/12 for each complete tax month which passed before the wedding. A tax month runs from the 6th of one month to the 5th of the next month. The married couple's allowance is given in full in the year of divorce, separation or death of either spouse.

Widow's bereavement allowance (WBA)

This allowance is given to a widow, but not a widower, in the tax year in which her husband died and the following fiscal year provided that she has not remarried by the beginning of that year (ICTA 1988 s262). Like the married couple's allowance the widow's bereavement allowance is equal to £1,830 and the relief is restricted to 15% in 1997/98.

Age allowance (AA)

This allowance is available to a person aged 65 or over at any time during the tax year instead of the ordinary personal allowance (ICTA 1988 s257(2)). The age allowance is £5,220 for 1997/98. If either the husband or wife is 65 years or over during the tax year a married couple's allowance of £3,185 is available instead of the ordinary married couple's allowance (ICTA 1988 s257A(2)). This higher allowance is treated in exactly the same way as the ordinary married couple's allowance and is hence restricted to 15% for 1997/98. However, it is not possible for the allowance in excess of the basic allowance to be shared between the husband and wife.

If the person's statutory total income exceeds £15,600 the age allowance is reduced by £1 for each £2 of income over £15,600 until first the personal allowance has been reduced to the level of the normal personal allowance and then the married couple's allowance is reduced to the level of the normal married couple's allowance (ICTA 1988 s257(5)).

People aged 75 or over at any time during the tax year can claim a personal allowance of £5,400 and a married couple's allowance of £3,225 (ICTA 1988 ss257(3) & 257A(3)). Once again these allowances are reduced to a minimum of the ordinary personal allowance and married couple's allowance as before.

An individual who dies during the tax year in which they would have reached their 65th or 75th birthday is treated as if they had reached that age during the year (ICTA 1988 s257(4)).

> ### Activity
>
> Calculate the marginal rate of tax of a single person aged 70 with statutory total income of £16,000.

Feedback

The easiest way of tackling a question like this is to calculate the tax paid firstly for a taxpayer with statutory total income of £16,000 and then for a taxpayer with statutory total income of £16,008.

	£	£
Statutory total income	16,000	16,008
Less personal allowance		
£5,220 – (16,000 – 15,600)/2	5,020	
£5,220 – (16,008 – 15,600)/2		5,016
Taxable income	10,980	10,992

Hence an increase of £8 in statutory total income leads to an increase of £12 in taxable income. The marginal rate of tax in both situations is 23%. Hence the extra £8 of income results in an extra £2.76 (£12 × 23%) of tax which is an effective marginal rate of tax of 34.5% (£2.76/£8).

Additional personal allowance (APA)

This allowance of £1,830, restricted to 15% in 1997/98, is available when the claimant has a 'qualifying child' living with them for the whole or part of the tax year if the individual is either:

- a woman who is either single, or is not living with her husband but has the child living with her
- a man who is either single throughout the tax year, or whose wife is completely incapacitated for the whole of the tax year, or whose wife does not live with him at all during the tax year.

A qualifying child is:

- aged under 16 at the beginning of the tax year, or
- aged 16 or more at the beginning of the tax year but who is attending either a full-time course of education at an educational establishment or a full-time course of training of at least two years duration with an employer.

If the child is not legally the taxpayer's child he or she must also be under 18 at the beginning of the tax year and be maintained for the whole or part of the year at the expense of the taxpayer (ICTA 1988 s259).

A claimant may claim only one additional personal allowance for any tax year and a child can be a qualifying child only for one claimant in each tax year. If more than one taxpayer could claim the relief for a child the allowance will be apportioned between the claimants. The claimants may decide how to apportion the allowance. If they fail to agree the allowance will be apportioned by reference to the amount of time during which the child was resident with each claimant (ICTA 1988 s260).

If an unmarried couple live together as husband and wife only one additional personal allowance may be claimed by them regardless of the number of qualifying children. The claim is made for the youngest child. The additional personal allowance can be apportioned between the couple.

Blind person's allowance (BPA)

This allowance is given to taxpayers who are registered as blind with their local authority. The allowance is £1,280 for 1997/98. If the blind person has insufficient income to use the allowance in full the excess may be transferred to their spouse (ICTA 1988 s265).

Activity

Joanna married Simon on 16th August 1997. Joanna is 50 years old and has a 17-year-old son who is in the sixth form at school. Simon is 65 years old and registered blind. Calculate the allowances available to Joanna and Simon in the fiscal year 1997/98.

Feedback

Simon will be able to claim the age allowance of £5,220, subject to reduction if he has substantial income, and the blind person's allowance. In addition he will be able to claim the married couple's allowance of £3,185 reduced by a twelfth for each complete tax month in which he was not married. Joanna will be able to claim a personal allowance and an additional personal allowance because she has a qualifying child living with her. The additional personal allowance can be claimed only in the year in which the marriage took place.

The breakdown of marriage

You can now state which allowances are available to a married couple and explain the ways in which the allowances are restricted in the year of marriage. Finally we will consider the allowances which are available when a marriage ends, either by way of the death of one of the partners or by way of a legal separation.

We have already seen that the widow's bereavement allowance of £1,830 is given to a widow in the fiscal year in which her husband dies and the following year, unless she has remarried at the beginning of that year. In addition she receives a full additional personal allowance in the fiscal year in which her husband dies if she has a qualifying child living with her (ICTA 1988 s259). Her husband receives the full personal allowance and the full married couple's allowance for the fiscal year in which he dies.

If the wife dies her widower receives his personal allowance together with the married couple's allowance for the fiscal year in which she dies. The wife has a full personal allowance to set against her income up to the date on which she dies.

If the couple separate under a court order or separation deed, or in circumstances which are such that the separation is likely to be permanent, they are taxed as single people from the date of the separation. The husband will receive a personal allowance and the married couple's allowance in the year in which the separation took place. The wife will receive the additional personal allowance if she has a qualifying child living with her while the husband will only be able to claim the allowance if he has a qualifying child living with him from the year following the year of separation.

As you already know a couple can elect for the married couple's allowance to be shared between them in a variety of ways. If such an election is in force in the year of separation it remains in force. If one, or both, of the couple is eligible to receive part or all of the additional personal allowance in the year of separation there are restrictions on how much of the allowance they may receive in that year. For both the husband and the wife the aggregate of their share of the married couple's allowance and the proportion of the additional personal allowance received in the year of separation must not exceed the value of the married couple's allowance.

Charges on income

A charge on income is a recurring, legally enforceable, liability of the taxpayer of a type which income tax law allows as a deduction from the payer's total income to give statutory total income (TMA 1970 s8(8)).

The following payments are eligible to be treated as charges:

- payments of eligible interest
- covenanted payments to charity
- some one-off gifts to charities
- payments made for proper commercial reasons in connection with the individual's trade, profession or vocation
- payments of premiums under qualifying health insurance contracts for persons aged 60 and over
- some payments for vocational training.

Most charges are paid after deduction of basic rate tax, while copyright royalties and loan interest, paid other than under the MIRAS scheme or on loans to purchase annuities, are paid gross. In 1997/98 interest paid under the MIRAS scheme will be paid after deduction of tax at 15%.

Payments of eligible interest

Eligible interest is either mortgage interest paid under the MIRAS scheme or interest on loans to purchase annuities or other qualifying loan interest.

Interest paid on credit card balances and bank overdrafts does not qualify as a charge.

Interest paid on a mortgage, from a qualifying lender, which is used to buy the borrower's main residence falls within the MIRAS scheme (ICTA 1988 s369(1)). MIRAS stands for Mortgage Interest Relief At Source.

In order to claim relief on a loan to purchase a main residence the loan must be used to buy or develop land and buildings in the UK or Ireland for use as the taxpayer's only or main residence. Interest on a loan to purchase a large caravan or houseboat as a main residence is also eligible for the relief. The property must be occupied as the taxpayer's main residence within 12 months of acquisition for the loan to be a qualifying loan (ICTA 1988 s354). Only interest paid on the first £30,000 of any loan on a property is eligible for relief regardless of the number of people borrowing money to buy the property (ICTA 1988 s 357(1B)).

If a number of people borrow money to buy the same property the £30,000 limit is divided equally between all the borrowers (ICTA 1988 s356A(3)). However, if any of the borrowers does not fully utilise their limit the excess is transferable to the other borrowers (ICTA 1988 ss 356A(4), 356A(5), 356A(6), 356A(7) & 356A(8)).

If more than one loan is taken out the relief is allocated to loans in the order in which they were taken out (ICTA 1988 s371). Relief is not lost if the taxpayer ceases to use the house as a main residence for up to one year for any reason or up to four years because the borrower is moving elsewhere because of work (ICTA 1988 s356).

Tax relief on mortgage interest payments is restricted to 15% in 1997/98 (ICTA 1988 s369(1)).

An Inland Revenue concession allows a number of such absences due to work commitments provided that the borrower reoccupies the property for at least three months between each absence.

If the borrower moves house using a bridging loan then interest is allowed on the first loan for 12 months, or longer if the Inland Revenue agree after the second loan, which is also eligible for relief, has been taken out. Each loan has a £30,000 limit for relief giving a total of up to £60,000 (ICTA 1988 s355(1B)).

When a couple marry and one spouse leaves their own property to live with the other the relief is still available on the vacated property provided that it is sold within 12 months of being vacated. This relief extends to the situation where both spouses vacate the properties they owned before the date of the marriage and use bridging finance to purchase a third property as their main residence. Each loan has a £30,000 limit for relief giving a total of up to £90,000.

Other qualifying loans which are not covered by the MIRAS scheme are eligible for relief without limit. The relief is available at the taxpayer's marginal rate of tax. They include:

● *Loans to purchase plant and machinery*
  The loan must be used to purchase plant and machinery for which capital allowances are available. The relief is available to partners or Schedule E

employees. The relief is available for a maximum of three years from the end of the tax year in which the loan was taken out. If the asset is used partly for non-business purposes the relief is proportionately reduced (ICTA 1988 s359).

- *Loans to pay inheritance tax*
  The loan must be used by personal representatives to pay inheritance tax before a grant of representation. The relief is only available for 12 months (ICTA 1988 s364).

- *Loans to acquire an interest in a close company*
  The loan must be used to acquire ordinary share capital or to make a loan. The borrower must either, together with his associates, hold more than 5% of the ordinary share capital or hold some of the ordinary share capital and work for the greater part of the time in the management of the company. If any capital is repaid by the company the loan is deemed to have been reduced by this amount and the relief is accordingly reduced (ICTA 1988 ss360, 360A & 363).

- *Loans to invest in an employee-controlled company*
  The loan must be used to acquire ordinary shares either before, or within 12 months of, a company first becoming employee controlled. The company must be a UK unquoted trading company or the holding company of a trading group. A company is employee controlled if at least 50% of the issued ordinary share capital and voting power is owned by employees or their spouses. If one employee owns more than 10% of the shares he or she is deemed to own 10% when testing to see if the 50% rule is satisfied. Once again if any capital is repaid the relief will be reduced (ICTA 1988 ss361 & 363).

- *Loans to acquire an interest in a partnership*
  The loan must be used to either purchase a share in a partnership or introduce capital into a partnership or make a loan to a partnership to use wholly and exclusively for business purposes. The claimant must be a member of the partnership throughout the time during which interest is claimed. Limited partners are not eligible for this relief (ICTA 1988 ss362 & 363).

Donations to charity

To qualify as a charge a donation must either be by way of a deed of covenant or be a qualifying donation.

To qualify a deed of covenant must be made in favour of a charity, irrevocable by the payer and capable of exceeding three years. In addition it must not be made in exchange for any valuable consideration (ICTA 1988 s660(3)).

To be a qualifying donation under the Gift Aid scheme a gift must be to a charity and be worth at least £250 net of basic rate tax or £324.68 gross. The gift is deemed to be paid net of tax enabling the charity to reclaim the tax deducted. Relief is given for the gross sum paid at the taxpayers marginal rate of tax. The gift must not be subject to any condition which might lead to a repayment and total benefits which are received by the donor or any persons connected with him or her from the charity must not be worth more than the lower of 2.5% of the net gift and £250 in any one tax year (FA 1990 s25). In the year to 31st March 1996 a total of £330 million was donated under the Gift Aid scheme giving about £110 million in tax repayments to charity.

The payroll giving scheme was set up in the FA 1986. The scheme applies to employees who pay tax under the PAYE scheme and whose employer runs a scheme, which is approved by the Board of the Inland Revenue, which operates by withholding sums from them (ICTA 1988 s202(1) & (3)).

The employer pays the sums withheld to an agent, who is approved by the Board, and the agent pays them to a charity or charities. Alternatively the employer may pay the sums directly to the charity or charities (ICTA 1988 s202(4)). The sums must constitute gifts by the employee to the charity or charities concerned, must not be paid by the employee under a covenant, and must fulfil any conditions set out in the terms of the scheme concerned (ICTA 1988 s202(6). The maximum which can be donated under the payroll giving scheme by an employee in 1997/98 is £1,200 (ICTA 1988 s202(7)).

Provided that all the conditions of the scheme are met the sums withheld are treated as expenses of the employee incurred in the year in which they were paid (ICTA 1988 s202(2)). This effectively means that the employee is given tax relief for the donations made.

Medical insurance premiums for the over-60s

Premiums paid by an individual under an eligible private medical insurance contract for a UK resident aged 60 or over when the payment is made or for a UK resident couple at least one of whom is aged 60 or over when the payment is made are eligible for tax relief at a maximum rate of 24% (FA 1989 s54(1), (2) &(3)). The payments, which do not have to be paid by the individual insured by the contract, are made net of the basic rate of tax (FA 1989 s54(5)). If the payments are made under a contract for a married couple relief is still available even if one of the spouses is aged under 60 in the fiscal year. This relief will continue to be available even if the older spouse dies before the younger one attains the age of 60.

Copyright and patent royalties

Copyright royalties are paid gross unless the recipient is non-resident when they are paid net and the tax withheld is paid to the Inland Revenue (ICTA ss349(1) & 536).

Patent royalties are paid net of basic rate tax and the tax withheld is paid to the Inland Revenue (ICTA s349(1)).

National insurance contributions

As we have already seen in Chapter 1 national insurance was introduced in 1948 in order largely to provide for retirement pensions, unemployment and sickness benefit.

Initially national insurance was payable at a flat rate by both employees and employers. The intention was for the payment to represent an insurance payment rather than to tax people on the basis of an ability to pay. Thus the burden of the tax fell heaviest on the lowest paid, hence the tax was regressionary.

Over the next few years the amount which each contributor had to pay increased as social security expenditure grew. By 1961 the flat rate contribution was seen to be too great a burden on the lowest paid and earnings-related contributions were introduced. By 1975 the entire national insurance contribution was earnings related. Although national insurance is now assessed on a percentage basis there is an upper limit above which employees do not pay any extra national insurance. Hence the tax is still regressionary, that is that taxpayers on low incomes can pay a greater percentage of their income in tax than taxpayers on higher incomes, and leads to some rather strange marginal rates of tax as we saw in Chapter 2.

In addition neither employee nor employer national insurance contributions are payable on most benefits in kind making provisions of benefits in kind a tax efficient form of remuneration. Note that if an employee has a company car and/or fuel for private motoring the employer must pay Class 1A contributions, at 10% of the car and fuel scales, although the benefit is not subject to national insurance contributions by the employee.

National insurance contributions are collected by the Inland Revenue, using the PAYE system for Schedule E taxpayers, on behalf of the Department of Social Security.

A record is kept of an individual's national insurance contributions during their lifetime and gaps in contributions can lead to a loss of benefits and so NI still has some of the characteristics of an insurance scheme.

Unlike income tax which is charged on a taxpayer's income for the year, although it is collected monthly under PAYE, national insurance contributions are calculated according to the employee's income for the payment period. Hence, if a taxpayer works for a number of months during the year and then has no income for the rest of the year he or she may be able to reclaim some of the income tax already paid but no repayment of national insurance is possible. Income tax is termed a cumulative tax system because unused allowances cumulate, national insurance is a non-cumulative tax because unused allowances are lost.

There are four classes of national insurance contributions. Class 1 is paid by both employees, primary contributions, and employers, secondary contributions. Classes 2 and 4 are paid by the self-employed. Class 3 payments are made on a voluntary basis in order to maintain rights to some state benefits.

Employees over pensionable age, 65 for a man and 60 for a woman, are not required to make national insurance contributions. However, the employer's contribution, at the non-contracted out rate, is still payable.

National insurance contributions for 1997/98 are:

Class 1

Pay per week £	Employee first £62/week %	excess up to £465/week %	Employer on all earnings %
Below 62.00	0	0	0.0
62.00 – 109.99	2	10	3.0
110.00 – 154.99	2	10	5.0
155.00 – 209.99	2	10	7.0
210.00 – 465.00	2	10	10.0
Over 465.00	2	10	10.0

If the employee is a member of a contracted out occupational pension scheme employee contributions remain at 2% on the first £62 income per week but contributions on the excess up to £465 per week reduce to 8.4%. The employer's contribution is reduced by 3% on earnings between £62 and £465 a week. Outside of these limits his contribution is unchanged from the non-contracted out contribution.

Class 1 contributions are based on the employee's gross pay without deducting pension contributions.

Class 2
The self-employed pay national insurance contributions of £6.15 per week for 1997/98 provided annual profits are at least £3,480.

Class 3
Anyone can pay voluntary contributions of £6.05 per week to maintain rights to some state benefits.

Class 4
The self-employed pay 6.0%, for 1997/98, of their profits between lower and upper limits, which are £7,010 and £24,180 for 1997/98. Profits above the upper limit are not subject to national insurance contributions. For Class 4 national insurance contribution purposes profits are the taxable profits under Schedule D Case I and II less capital allowances, trading loss and trade charges on income. Class 4 contributions are paid together with the associated income tax liability, in two instalments on 1st January in the tax year and on 1st July following it. Under the new rules payment will be on 31st January in the tax year and on 31st July following it.

Taxpayers making Class 1 national insurance contributions at the higher rate are eligible to receive unemployment benefit and earnings related state pension which Class 2 and Class 4 contributors are ineligible to receive.

A full basic pension is paid to individuals who, for at least nine out of every ten years of their deemed working life, have paid at least the equivalent of the lower earnings limit contribution for the whole year. The deemed working life is from 16 to 65 for a man and from 16 to 60 for a woman although the retirement age for men and women will be equalised in due course.

As we have seen national insurance contributions are levied on earned income. This provides a distortion in the tax system between earned income and investment income. A taxpayer with taxable income of less than £24,180 will have a marginal rate of tax of 33% on earned income but only 23% on unearned income. This anomaly may encourage shareholder/directors of family businesses to draw relatively low salaries and pay dividends in order to reduce national insurance contributions.

Example

Rosemary owns all the share capital of the company in which she works full time. Rosemary wishes to extract all of the after tax profits of the company. The profits adjusted for tax, before her director's salary, was £40,000 in the accounting year ended 31st March 1998.

Calculate Rosemary's total tax and national insurance liability if she draws the maximum salary possible. How would Rosemary's position change if she did not draw a salary and instead all of the profits were paid out as dividends?

Solution

We will begin by assuming that Rosemary does not receive any benefits in kind from the company and that she has no other income and suffers no charges on income.

The before tax cost to the company of paying a salary to Rosemary is the amount of her gross salary together with the employer's national insurance contributions. We know from the question that the cost to the company of paying the salary will be £40,000. We can find the amount of Rosemary's salary by solving the following equation:

$$\text{Salary} + 10\% \times \text{Salary} = £40,000$$

Solving it we find that Salary = £36,364.

Now we can find Rosemary's tax liability by determining her income tax liability and Class I employee national insurance contributions.

Rosemary's income tax computation for 1997/98

	£
Salary	36,364
Less personal allowance	4,045
Taxable income	32,319
Tax	
£4,100 @ 20%	820
£22,000 @ 23%	5,060
£6,219 @ 40%	2,488
Tax liability	8,368

Class 1 national insurance contributions are £2,160 ((£62 × 2% + (£465 − 62) × 10%) × 52).

Hence Rosemary's salary suffers total deductions of £10,528 (£8,368 + £2,160). The company has suffered total deductions of £3,636 (£40,000 − £36,364). Hence the total tax payable by the company and Rosemary is £14,164 (£10,528 + £3,636).

If Rosemary does not draw a salary but receives the profits of the company by way of dividends, the tax position will be rather different. The payment of dividends does not have national insurance implications for either the company or Rosemary. However, now that the company has made a profit a liability to corporation tax equal to 23% of the taxable profit will arise. In addition when a company pays a dividend it must pay advance corporate tax at a rate of 20/80ths of the dividend paid. The advance corporate tax can be used in two ways. Firstly, the company can deduct the advance corporate tax from its corporation tax liability. Secondly, the shareholders can use the advance corporation tax as a tax credit. Non-taxpayers can even receive a repayment of the tax credit. All of this is explained in more detail in Chapter 8.

The corporation tax payable is £9,200 (23% × £40,000). Hence the maximum net dividend which can be paid is £30,800. The advance corporation tax on a dividend of £30,800 is £7,700 (£30,800 × 20/80).

Rosemary will receive a dividend of £30,800 together with the related tax credit of £7,700.

Rosemary's income tax computation for 1997/98

	£
Gross dividend	38,500
Less personal allowance	4,045
Taxable income	34,455
Tax	
£26,100 × 20%	5,220
£8,355 × 40%	3,342
Tax liability	8,562
less tax credit	7,700
Tax payable	862

Remember that dividends are deemed to be the top slice of income and are taxed at 20% unless the taxpayer's marginal rate of tax is 40% when they are taxed at 40%. Since the first £26,100 of income is taxed at 20% or 23% it is only the dividends in excess of this amount that are taxed at 40%.

Hence the total tax payable by the company and Rosemary is:

	£
Income tax payable	862
Advance corporation tax payable	7,700
Mainstream corporation tax payable	
(£9,200–£7,700)	1,500
Tax payable	10,062

As you can see the way in which profits are extracted from a company can have a dramatic effect on the tax liability. However, it is important that before such decisions are made non-tax considerations are taken into account. A decision based solely on tax consequences may not be in the best interests of the company, or the directors, in the long term.

In practice there are benefits to taking some salary from a company. For example, if Class 1 national insurance contributions are paid a range of benefits including pensions, sickness benefit and maternity pay become available. In addition pension contributions can only be made out of earned income not investment income.

Personal tax computations

First we will look at a pro forma of a personal tax computation.

To make the pro forma easier to follow illustrative numbers have been included in the computation.

The following notes may help you to follow the example:

- *Earned income*

  The earned income is taxed under Schedule D Case I and so must be the income from a trade. From the Schedule D Case I profits the taxpayer can deduct personal pension contributions. Capital allowances are deducted from trading profits in order to calculate the Schedule D Case I profits. Capital allowances are granted to taxpayers who purchase fixed assets. They are sometimes described as tax depreciation. As you have probably guessed capital allowances are given instead of depreciation. In some other countries the amount of tax relief is closely linked to the amount of depreciation charged in the profit and loss account but in the UK there is no link between the two. Capital allowances are dealt with in detail in Chapter 5. Pension contributions, up to certain limits, are also allowable deductions from earned income. You will be able to read about personal pensions in Chapter 6.

- *Investment income*

  Most investment income is paid after deduction of tax at source. Look back to Chapter 1 for an explanation of why this is done. The bank deposit interest and the building society interest have had tax deducted at 20%. So if the gross interest is £100 the net interest received is £80. The gross income received is included in a tax computation and then the taxpayer is given a tax credit which is equal to the tax deducted at source.

  Remember that investment income is taxed at either 20% or 40%. The higher rate applies if the taxpayer's taxable income before investment income exceeds £26,100. Investment income is deemed to be the highest part of the taxpayer's income. In Chapter 8 you will learn about the imputation system of corporation tax and the tax treatment of dividends.

- *Charges*

  Most charges are paid net of basic rate tax. The taxpayer paid £385 to the charity under the deed of covenant and is deemed to have withheld £115 (£385 × 100/77) at source. The amount paid, together with the tax withheld, is deducted from investment income in the tax computation.

- *Allowances*

  Raj is married and since no election has been made to apportion the married couple's allowance between them he is entitled to the full married couple's allowance as well as a personal allowance.

Raj: Income tax computation 1997/98

	£	£	Tax suffered £
Earned income			
Schedule D Case I		37,000	
Less capital allowances		1,000	
		36,000	
Less personal pension contributions		3,000	
		33,000	
Investment income			
Dividends £1,000 × 100/80	1,250		250
Bank deposit interest £3,200 × 100/80	4,000		800
Building Society interest			
£800 × 100/80	1,000		200
	6,250		
Less charges on income paid			
Covenanted payment to charity £385 × 100/77	500		
Net investment income		5,750	
Statutory total income (STI)		38,750	
Less allowances			
Personal allowance		4,045	
Taxable income		34,705	1,250
Income tax			
Lower rate £4,100 × 20%		820	
Basic rate £22,000 × 23%		5,060	
Higher rate £8,605 × 40%		3,442	
£34,705		9,322	
Less tax reductions: married couple's allowance			
£1,830 × 15%		275	
Tax borne		9,047	
Add tax retained on charges paid net (£115)		115	
Tax liability		9,162	
Less tax deducted at source		1,250	
Tax payable		7,912	

- *Income tax rates*

  Remember that dividends and interest are taxed at 20% unless the taxpayer is a higher rate taxpayer in which case they are taxed at 40%. Because Raj's income taxed at 40% exceeds the gross value of the dividends and interest received it is not necessary to deal with the dividends and interest separately. In other examples in the book you will learn how to account for the dividends and interest which are received by basic rate taxpayers.

- *Income tax reductions*

  Income tax reductions are amounts deducted in the tax computations in order to compute the tax borne. The concept of income tax reducers has recently been introduced by the Inland Revenue. Income tax reducers are not eligible for tax relief at the taxpayer's marginal rate of tax. In 1997/98 relief is available on tax reducers at only 15%.

- *Tax borne*

  Tax borne is the amount of tax which the taxpayer is liable for because of his own personal circumstances.

- *Tax liability*

  The tax liability is equal to the tax borne together with the tax retained on the charges paid. This is the total amount of tax which the taxpayer is responsible for accounting for to the Inland Revenue.

- *Tax payable*

  The tax payable is equal to the tax liability less the tax which has been deducted at source from income received by the taxpayer. The tax payable must be remitted to the Inland Revenue. There are a number of complicated rules which are used to determine when the tax must be paid. These arrangements are beyond the scope of this book.

Self-assessment

In Chapter 1 we reported that self-assessment will be introduced for the first time in the UK for the fiscal year 1996/97. Self-assessment is already used in a number of other countries, including the USA, Australia and Germany. Despite the government's opportunity to draw on the experience of other countries many commentators fear that there will be many difficulties in the first year in which self-assessment operates. In this section we will consider the way in which the new system is intended to operate and then briefly attempt to identify the areas which are most likely to cause difficulties to taxpayers, their agents and the Inland Revenue.

The new tax return

The self-assessment tax return will be sent to taxpayers on 6th April 1997. The return comprises a form on which taxpayers must fill in details of their income and capital gains for the fiscal year 1996/97 and a number of supporting schedules. Taxpayers will be sent only those supporting schedules which the Inland Revenue deems necessary and will have to request additional schedules if needed. The onus will be on taxpayers to ensure that they complete all the necessary schedules. It is anticipated that relatively few taxpayers will require all the supporting schedules. Taxpayers who would rather use a computer will be provided with the necessary software by the Inland Revenue. The software will provide a taxpayer with an electronic tax return and guidance on completing the return.

The major benefits of self-assessment are thought to include:

- each taxpayer needing to deal with only one tax office. Under the old system taxpayers might deal with several tax offices if they received income from a number of sources
- reduction to only two dates on which tax will be due to be paid. Under the old system each Schedule and Case had its own dates for payment. As a consequence some taxpayers were required to pay tax on several different dates
- a reduction in costs to the Inland Revenue because it will no longer need to issue estimated assessments and then agree final assessments with large numbers of taxpayers.

There may be some disadvantages associated with the system of self-assessment:

- the Inland Revenue have announced that the system of penalties and interest on overdue tax will be enforced more rigorously in the future
- it will no longer be acceptable to submit an incomplete tax return by the due date and provide the missing information later as was often done under the old system. Instead taxpayers will be required to provide reasonable estimates of income where exact figures are not known and pay tax based on those estimates. If the correct figures lead to a subsequent increase in the tax due a liability to interest may arise
- taxpayers whose affairs are not in order by April 1997 may find themselves in a certain amount of difficulty when attempting to comply with the requirements of self-assessment.

Income tax planning points for couples

Under the system of independent taxation married women are able to include their investment income as well as their earned income in their tax computation. If a wife's marginal rate of tax is lower than her husband's it is tax efficient to shift income from the husband to the wife. There are broadly two ways of doing this. Firstly, investments held in the husband's name could be transferred to his wife. There is no capital gains tax liability arising from a transfer between spouses. These investments might include shares in a family business, in which case dividends paid on the shares would be taxed at the lower rate.

The second opportunity for shifting income from the high taxpayer to the low taxpayer is where a business is being run by one or both of the spouses. For example, it is possible to pay a wage to a wife who deals with telephone calls and paperwork for the business. The alternative is to set up in business as a partnership in which case a wife can be allocated a share of the profits. A similar strategy can be adopted with adult children with low marginal rates of tax. If a partnership is established then it is the responsibility of the partners to agree the profit-sharing ratio and the Inland Revenue will not challenge such an agreement. However, if a relative is employed by a sole trader, partnership or company the Inland Revenue may wish to be satisfied that the payment is wholly and exclusively for the purpose of trade. In the case of *Copeman v Flood* (1941) a farmer employed his son and daughter as directors of the company and they each received a salary of £2,600. The son was aged 24 and had some business experience but the daughter was only 17 and unable to carry out the duties of a director. Both did undertake some duties for the company. It was held that the entire salary was not an expense incurred wholly and exclusively for business purposes. The Commissioners were asked to decide how much of the payments should be allowable based on the actual work carried out by the son and daughter.

Summary

This chapter has provided you with the framework which will enable you to apply the legislation discussed in later chapters.

In order to calculate an individual's tax liability it is necessary to undertake a number of steps:

- Identify each source of income for a taxpayer.
- Determine the Schedule and Case which is used to calculate the taxable income for each source of income.
- Use the rules of the Schedule and Case to determine the basis of assessment for each source of income.
- Calculate the income which is assessable and determine any deductions from that income which are allowed for tax purposes. This will enable you to calculate the taxable income from each source of income.
- Determine all the allowances and reliefs which the taxpayer can claim. To do this you must know whether or not the taxpayer is married, their age and details of any charges on income paid.
- Now you can calculate the tax liability of a taxpayer.

The possibilities for tax planning for families were also discussed in this chapter. You should be able to suggest ways in which a married couple can legitimately minimise the amount of tax they pay. Strategies you should be aware of include:

- transferring income-earning assets to the spouse with the lowest marginal rate of tax
- employing members of the family in a family business or admitting them to a partnership in order to take advantage of their low marginal rates of tax.

The legislation which relates to national insurance contributions was also discussed in this chapter enabling you to calculate the national insurance liability of any individual or employer.

Finally we discussed the new system of self-assessment. We considered the operation of the new system and briefly discussed its likely advantages and disadvantages.

In conclusion you are now able to read the next three chapters which build on the foundations which have been laid in this chapter.

Questions

Question 1 (based on ACCA December 1990).

Independent taxation of husband and wife includes the following features:

(a) A personal allowance is given to everyone.

(b) The married couple's allowance is given initially to the husband but can be transferred to the wife if the husband has insufficient income to use it.

(c) A separate income tax computation is made for each spouse and each spouse is entitled to a basic rate band (currently £22,000).

(d) A separate exemption for capital gains is available for each spouse (currently £6,500).

These rules present opportunities to reduce the direct tax burden on married couples.

Required

(a) Set out in general terms the strategy to be followed to maximise the benefits of the system.

(b) Describe the basic steps to be taken to achieve those benefits.

Question 2.

Janet and Dave have lived together for two years. Janet has a son Mark aged 15 who lives with them. Janet earned £26,000 during 1997/98. She also received an annual bonus in August in respect of the year ended on the previous 31st March of £3,000. She contributed £2,002 net to her pension fund during the year. Janet owns a cottage in North Yorkshire which she let from 1st October 1997 at an annual rent of £8,000 payable quarterly in advance. Her allowable expenses for the year amounted to £1,000.

Dave earned a salary of £16,000 in the tax year 1997/98. He also had some investment income of £3,000 net from a bank deposit account. Dave has taken out a covenant with Save the Children for four years from 1st January 1997 under which he agreed to pay £308 each year net of income tax to the charity.

Required
Compute Janet and Dave's tax payable for 1997/98.

Question 3 (based on ACCA Tax Framework June 1994).

(a) With effect from 1993/94 the basic married couple's allowances may be allocated by one of four methods.
    For each method, state how the allowance is allocated and by whom and by when the necessary action must be taken.

(b) Abel and Zoë were married on 17th May 1995 when they were both 20. On 21st March 1996 Zoë gave birth to twins, Brendan and Yvonne. On 7th June 1996 Abel and Zoë separated in circumstances likely to be permanent, Brendan staying with his father and Yvonne staying with her mother. On 7th December 1996 Abel and Zoë were divorced. From 6th July 1996 Abel was required by a court order to pay maintenance of £30 per week to Zoë. These amounts were to be increased on 1st January 1998 to £50 per week by court order.

Neither Abel nor Zoë plans to re-marry nor live with a new partner. Abel was in full-time employment. Zoë did not work and had no income from state benefits after 7th June 1996.

Required
State the amount of the allowances to which Abel and Zoë are entitled for the tax years 1995/96, 1996/97 and 1997/98. (You may assume that allowances in 1995/96 were the same as in 1996/97.)

Hint
In each of the years Abel can claim tax relief on the maintenance payments up to a limit equal to the married couple's allowance. In 1994/95 relief was limited to 20%. From 1995/96 onwards relief was limited to 15%. Zoë will not be liable for tax on the maintenance payments received from Abel.

5 ▷ Business taxation

Introduction

In this chapter we will study the taxation of unincorporated businesses. In fact unincorporated businesses are not treated as separate entities for tax purposes. Rather the schedular rules are used to calculate the taxable income under Schedule D Case I and II. In the case of a sole trader the taxable income is then included in the taxpayer's tax computation.

At the end of this chapter you will be able to:

- state the badges of trade and use them to identify trading activities
- adjust business profits for tax purposes
- apply the opening year rules to new businesses
- apply the closing year rules on the cessation of a business
- undertake capital allowance computations
- calculate the tax payable, or repayable, when an unincorporated business incurs trading losses
- offer simple tax planning advice to sole traders.

Introduction to Schedule D Cases I and II

Look back to Chapter 4 to find out how income which is taxed by direct assessment is assessed for tax purposes. Such income is taxed under a Schedule. The basis of assessment depends on which Schedule the income is assessed under. Income from a trade is assessed under Schedule D Case I and income from a vocation or profession is taxed under Schedule D Case II. There are some small differences in the way that the tax due is calculated under these two Cases, but for our purposes we can treat them as being the same.

There are nearly three and a half million people, or 13% of the workforce, who are taxed under Schedule D Case I or II. While some Schedule D Case I and II taxpayers run large businesses many are running relatively small undertakings. In general, sole traders and partners are assessed on the profits which are derived from the accounting period which ends in the fiscal year.

Before any assessment under Schedule D Case I is made it is first necessary to demonstrate that trading is taking place. Once the existence of trading has been established you will need to undertake a number of steps in order to determine the Schedule D Case I assessment for a fiscal year. These are:

1. determine which accounts will form the basis period for the fiscal year
2. adjust the accounting profits in order to derive the taxable profits, that is the Schedule D Case I or II assessments.

Once the Schedule D Case I assessment has been determined you will need to establish the tax implications of any investment in fixed assets. Finally, you will need to be able to deal with any Schedule D Case I losses which arise.

Identification of trading activities

Until recently it was very important to determine whether a receipt was trading income or not. Before 1965, if a receipt was not deemed to be trading income then it was likely to be a capital gain and so was not taxable. Since 1965 capital gains have been taxable but until 1988 capital gains were taxed at 30%. This rate was usually lower than the taxpayer's marginal rate of tax.

Today the distinction is less important because capital gains are taxed at the taxpayer's marginal rate of tax. In fact a taxpayer would probably prefer to be taxed under Schedule D Case I today. However, it is still necessary to differentiate between a trade and a hobby. For most of us hobbies cost money; the Inland Revenue will not give us tax relief on these losses although relief is often available for losses incurred during the course of trading.

The statutory law does not define trading although the TA 1988 s832(1) states that it 'includes every trade, manufacture, adventure, or concern in the nature of a trade'. We must therefore look to case law for guidance in determining whether trading is, in fact, taking place.

The Royal Commission on the Taxation of Profits and Income (1955: Cmd 9474) suggested that there were six 'badges' which can help to determine whether or not a transaction is, in fact, trading. None of the badges offer a conclusive test of trading although some are stronger than others. If trading is taking place it is likely that there will be evidence of the existence of more than one 'badge'.

Badges of trade

The six badges of trade are:

● *The subject matter of the transaction*
If the property which forms the subject matter of the transaction does not provide either income or enjoyment to the owner, it is likely that the transaction will be deemed to be trading. It seems unlikely that commodities or manufactured articles which are normally the subject of trading will form the subject of an investment rather than a trade.

In *Rutledge* v *IRC* (1929) the taxpayer bought one million rolls of toilet paper from a bankrupt German firm for £1,000 while in Berlin on business. The rolls were sent to the UK and the taxpayer endeavoured to sell them.

Eventually he found a buyer who bought the whole quantity for £12,000, affording him a considerable profit. The transaction was held to be 'in the nature of a trade' largely because of the quantity of the goods involved.

Hence even a single transaction can be seen to be trading.

In contrast in *IRC v Reinhold* (1953) the taxpayer was not held to be trading. He had bought four houses within two years intending to sell them. The Court of Session stated that 'heritable property is not an uncommon subject of investment' and hence the taxpayer was not trading. In the recent case of *Marson v Morton* (1986) the taxpayer bought land intending to develop it but in fact sold it. The taxpayer was held not to be trading, confirming that land can be held for investment purposes even though it does not yield an income.

- *The frequency of similar transactions*

Although a single transaction can be considered to be trading the repeated undertaking of transactions in the same subject matter may be seen to indicate that trading is being conducted.

In *Pickford v Quirke* (1927) the taxpayers formed a syndicate to buy and resell cotton mills. There were four such transactions. The membership of the syndicate was not identical for each transaction. It was held that any one transaction would not have constituted trading but the four taken together did.

Hence subsequent transactions can cause an income tax liability to arise on the earlier transactions.

- *The circumstances responsible for the realisation*

There is a presumption that trading is not occurring if the property is disposed of to raise money for an emergency. Other circumstances which indicate that trading is not taking place include sales by executors of the deceased's property and sales by liquidators and receivers of the assets of an insolvent company. In the case of *The Hudson's Bay Company v Stevens* (1909) the taxpayer company had sold off a large quantity of land over a number of years which it had acquired in return for the surrender of its charter. The company was held not to be trading, the court offering the following explanation: 'The company are doing no more than an ordinary landowner does who is minded to sell from time to time as purchasers offer, portions suitable for building of an estate which has devolved upon him from his ancestors.'

- *Supplementary work on or in connection with the property realised*

Trading is more likely to be taking place if either work is done on the property to make it more marketable, or an organisation is set up to sell it. The courts decided that if there is an organised effort to obtain profit there is a source of taxable income but in the absence of such effort the presumption will be that trading is not taking place.

In *Cape Brandy Syndicate v IRC* (1927) a group of accountants bought 3,000 casks of Cape brandy, blended it with French brandy, recasked it and sold it in lots over the next 18 months. They were held to be trading because they did not simply buy an article which they thought was cheap and then resell it. The syndicate bought the brandy intending to transport it, modify its character and recask it so as to enable it to be sold in smaller quantities.

- *The motive of the transaction*

  There is some evidence of trading taking place if the objective of undertaking the transaction is to make a profit. However, even in the absence of a motive to make a profit it may still be concluded that trading is taking place. The subject matter of the transaction may be crucial.

  In *Wisdom v Chamberlain* (1968) the taxpayer, a well-known comedian, bought silver bullion as a hedge against the anticipated devaluation of the pound. It was held that the taxpayer had undertaken an adventure in the nature of a trade when he realised a profit three months later because the transaction was entered into on a short-term basis with the sole intention of making a profit from the purchase and sale of a commodity.

- *The length of ownership*

  The presumption is that the shorter the period of ownership the more likely it is that trading is taking place. However, this is a weak badge of trade because the short period of ownership can often be discounted by the taxpayer, perhaps by demonstrating a need for cash at the time of the sale. Hence there are many exceptions from this as a universal rule.

In conclusion we will consider the case of *Edwards v Bairstow and Harrison* (1956) who were selling secondhand plant but claimed that they were not trading. In deciding that the appellants were trading Lord Radcliffe said:

> It is said that there was no organisation for the purposes of the transaction. But in fact there was organisation, as much of it as the transaction required. It is true that the plant was not advertised for sale, though advertisements asking for plant were answered by the respondents. But why should they incur the cost of advertising if they judged that they could achieve the sale of plant without it? It is said that no work had been done on the maturing of the asset to be sold. But such replacement and renovation as were needed were in fact carried out, and I can see no reason why a dealer should do more work in making his plant saleable than the purposes of sale require. It is said that neither of the respondents had any special skill from his normal activities which placed him in an advantageous position for the purposes of this transaction. It may be so, though one of them was the employee of a spinning firm. In any case the members of a commercial community do not need much instruction in the principles and possibility of dealing, and I think that, given the opportunity, the existence or non-existence of special skill is of no significance whatever. It is said finally, that the purchase and sale of plant lent itself to capital, rather than commercial, transactions. I am not sure that I understand what this is intended to mean. If it means that at the relevant period there was no market for secondhand plant in which deals could take place, there is no finding to that effect and all the facts that are recited seem to be against the contention. If it means anything else, it is merely an attempt to describe the conclusion which the respondents would wish to see arrived at on the whole case.

There remains the fact which was avowedly the original ground of the Commissioners' decision — 'this was an isolated case'. But, as we know, that circumstance does not prevent a transaction which bears the badges of trade from being in truth an adventure in the nature of trade. The true question in such cases is whether the operations constitute an adventure of that kind, not whether they by themselves or they in conjunction with other operations, constitute the operator a person who carries on a trade. Dealing is, I think, essentially a trading adventure, and the respondents' operations were nothing but a deal or deals in plant and machinery.

Adjustment of profits

Now that you are able to identify trading activities you need to be able to calculate the taxable profits. Taxable profits are made up of the difference between trading receipts and allowable expenses during a period of assessment.

In order to calculate the taxable profits you will need to:

- determine which accounting period will form the basis of assessment for the fiscal year
- identify taxable income and allowable expenditure which relates to the basis period.

In this section we will discuss the identification of the basis of assessment in general terms. Then we will determine what are trading receipts and finally we will consider allowable expenses.

Recognition of income and expenditure

Clearly it is important to determine in which period income and expenditure will be recognised. Unfortunately there is no legislation to help us and in practice the taxpayer must agree a basis with the Inland Revenue.

There are three acceptable ways of recognising income and expenditure:

- The earnings basis, where the normal accounting principles are used, for example the accruals and realisation concepts apply. Stock must be valued at the lower of cost (using FIFO) and market value. Work in progress is usually valued using absorption costing although marginal costing can be used. Most taxpayers use the earnings basis.
- The cash basis, where income and expenditure are only recognised when the related cash flow occurs. The Inland Revenue is usually reluctant to allow the cash basis to be used because of the potential to manipulate the profit figure. However, barristers, who cannot sue for their fees, and authors, who only earn their royalties when they are received, are usually allowed to use the cash basis.
- The conventional or bills delivered basis, where only bills received or issued are used. Solicitors are usually allowed to use the bills receivable basis after they have been self-employed for three years provided that they agree to invoice clients regularly.

Once a basis is agreed it will continue to be used unless the taxpayer elects to use an alternative basis. Of course, if he wishes to change he must first obtain Inland Revenue approval.

We will now look in detail at the calculation of the Schedule D Case I income.

Trading receipts

A receipt is a trading receipt if it is a payment for services or goods. Payments made on a voluntary basis for some personal quality of the taxpayer are not deemed to be trading receipts. In *Murray v Goodhews* (1976), Watneys paid ex gratia lump sum payments to landlords of public houses when they terminated tied tenancies, partly as an acknowledgement of the good relationship they had with their tenant and partly to preserve their good name. These sums were held not to be trading receipts in the hands of the landlords since the amounts of the payments had no connection with the profits earned or barrelage taken by any house nor was it linked with future trading relations between Watneys and the taxpayer.

However, in *McGowan v Brown and Cousins* (1977), the taxpayer, an estate agent, received a low fee for acquiring property for a company in the expectation that he would be retained to deal with letting the property. The company paid the taxpayer £2,500 as compensation when they retained another agent to deal with the lettings. The payment was held to be a trading receipt despite the lack of a legal obligation to pay it.

The receipt must be income not capital. This distinction has proved difficult to draw and a number of tests have been developed by lawyers over a long period of time. Perhaps the most obvious test is to determine if the asset is part of the fixed capital or is part of working capital of the business. The difficulty is that whether an asset is an item from stock in trade or a capital asset depends on the type of business being carried on.

Another test which can be applied is the 'trees and fruit' test, where the tree is considered to be the capital which produces the fruit which is income.

This test may result in a payment being divided into capital and revenue parts as in the case of *London and Thames Havens Oil Wharves Ltd v Attwooll* (1967) where £100,000 compensation was paid after a tanker crashed into a jetty, causing serious damage. The sum was split into a capital sum which was intended to be used to rebuild the jetty and a revenue receipt which was compensation for loss of income due to the accident.

A number of other receipts may also be considered to be trading receipts because they are seen to be compensation for loss of revenue earnings. These include receipts which relate to:

- restrictions on commercial activities
- restrictions on the short-term use of commercial assets, although a receipt relating to a permanent restriction is deemed to be capital
- cancellations of commercial contracts or connections which are relatively small compared to the size of the business. Receipts which are compensation for contracts which are large compared to the size of the business are deemed to be capital
- appropriations of unclaimed deposits and advances
- the sale of information. This receipt is covered by statute (TA 1988 ss530 and 531) unlike the four above which have been decided by means of case law. Provided that the vendor continues to trade after the sale the receipt will be treated as a trading receipt

- a trade debt which has been deducted as a trading expense and is subsequently cancelled is treated as a trade receipt (TA 1988 s94).

Goods disposed of other than in the ordinary course of business must be accounted for, at market value, as a trading receipt. In *Sharkey v Wernher* (1956) the taxpayer who ran a stud farm as a business also raced horses as a hobby. She transferred five horses from her stud farm to her racing stables and recorded the cost of breeding the horses as a receipt of the stud farm. The Revenue argued that the market value of the horses should be entered in the accounts. It was held that horses which were transferred from the stud farm to her racing stable must be entered in the accounts as a receipt at their market value rather than their cost.

The rule derived from this case applies to goods taken by owners for their own use as well as goods they give to others. The rule is also applied if goods are sold at less than their market value. However, provided that the disposal can be shown to have been made for genuine commercial reasons the rule in *Sharkey v Wernher* does not apply and a trader may make a disposal at whatever value he chooses. Additionally the rule applies to traders only. It does not apply to professional persons. In *Mason v Innes* (1967) the novelist Hammond Innes gave the manuscript of *The Doomed Oasis* to his father. The writer had deducted allowable travelling expenses from his income which had been incurred while researching the book. The Inland Revenue wanted to assess the writer on the market value of the script. Lord Denning, the Master of the Rolls, said:

> Suppose an artist paints a picture of his mother and gives it to her. He does not receive a penny for it. Is he to pay tax on the value of it? It is unthinkable. Suppose he paints a picture which he does not like when he has finished it and destroys it. Is he liable to pay tax on the value of it? Clearly not. These instances . . . show that . . . *Sharkey v Wernher* does not apply to professional men.

Deductible expenses

For expenditure to be an allowable deduction from income it must satisfy three criteria. It must be a revenue item. It must be incurred wholly and exclusively for the purposes of the trade, profession or vocation. Finally it must not be specifically disallowed as a deductible expense by statute.

The following sums are specifically disallowed as deductions when calculating the Schedule D Case I or Case II profits:

- any expenses which are not wholly and exclusively incurred for the purposes of the trade, profession or vocation
- any payment for the maintenance of the trader, his or her family or accommodation and any payments made for any domestic or private purposes distinct from the purposes of the trade, profession or vocation
- the rent of the whole or any part of any dwelling-house or domestic offices. However, if some part of the accommodation is used for the purposes of the trade, profession or vocation then any rent which is *bona fide* paid for that part of the accommodation up to a maximum of two-thirds of the total rent will be allowable

- any amount spent on repairs of premises or for the supply, repairs or alterations of any assets employed for the purposes of the trade, profession or vocation in excess of the amount actually expended for those purposes
- any loss which is not connected with or arising out of the trade, profession or vocation
- any capital employed in improvement of premises occupied for the purposes of the trade, profession or vocation
- any debts, except bad debts, proved to be such, and doubtful debts to the extent that they are respectively estimated to be bad
- any sum recoverable under an insurance or contract of indemnity
- expenditure incurred for private rather than business purposes
- any annuity or other annual payment (other than interest) payable out of the profits or gains
- any interest paid to a person not resident in the UK if and so far as it is interest at more than a reasonable commercial rate
- any royalty or other sum paid in respect of the user of a patent
- most expenditure on hospitality is disallowed but any entertainment of *bona fide* employees is allowed without limit
- gifts are generally disallowed but gifts to customers costing less than £10 which carry a conspicuous advertisement for the business are allowed provided they are not food, alcohol or tobacco (ICTA 1988 s74).

However, some of the expenses which are included in the above list may be allowed if it is in the normal course of the taxpayer's business to make such provision.

There are a number of areas of difficulty with this legislation. Some of it has been dealt with through further legislation – for instance, renting business property by means of a lease is dealt with by TA 1988 s87. Other problems have been addressed by the development of case law, for instance the distinction between capital and revenue expenditure.

By extra-statutory concession small gifts to local charities made for trading purposes are deductible. Also by extra-statutory concession relief is available for trade receipts and trade debts, the proceeds of which cannot be remitted to the UK.

In a press release the Inland Revenue announced that living expenses incurred during business visits abroad, excluding expenses attributable to holidays taken abroad, are deductible in computing profits of the trade.

The costs incurred by companies in valuing their land for the purposes of complying with the Companies Act 1985 are deductible for tax purposes.

Expenditure on a training course for the proprietor of a business which is intended to provide new expertise, knowledge or skills brings into existence an intangible asset of enduring benefit to the business and is capital expenditure. However, if attendance is to update expertise, knowledge or skills already possessed the expenditure is normally regarded as revenue expenditure.

The incidental costs of obtaining finance by means of a qualifying loan or the issue of qualifying loan stock or a qualifying security and the incidental costs of obtaining finance by those means shall be treated as expenses of management and are deductible (ICTA 1988 s77(1)). That is if the interest paid on a loan is tax deductible then the incidental costs of obtaining finance are also deductible.

A qualifying loan and qualifying loan stock is defined as a loan or loan stock the interest on which is deductible in computing, for tax purposes, the profits or gains of the person by whom the incidental costs in question are incurred. A qualifying security is any deep discount security in respect of which the income elements are deductible in computing the total profits of the company by which the incidental costs in question are incurred (ICTA 1988 s77(2)).

The incidental costs of obtaining finance means expenditure on fees, commissions, advertising, printing and other incidental matters but not including stamp duty being expenditure wholly and exclusively incurred for the purpose of obtaining the finance (whether or not it is in fact obtained), or of providing security for it or of repaying it (ICTA 1988 s77(6)).

Note that sums paid in consequence of, or for obtaining protection against, losses resulting from changes in the rate of exchange between different currencies or for the cost of repaying a loan or loan stock or a qualifying security so far as attributable to its being repayable at a premium or to its having been obtained or issued at a discount are not deductible expenses for tax purposes (ICTA 1988 s77(7)).

Look back to Chapter 4 to see how charges are dealt with. Charges paid are disallowed in the Schedule D Case I computation because they are relieved in the personal tax computation. Hence interest paid on long-term loans which are charges are disallowed. Interest paid on other types of loans including overdrafts, credit cards and hire purchase agreements will be allowable provided they satisfy the wholly and exclusively rule. However, interest paid on overdue tax is not an allowable expense.

Any payments made which are held to be contrary to public policy such as fines and penalties are disallowable. However, in practice deductions for parking fines incurred by employees parking the employer's cars during the course of their employer's business are usually allowed although fines incurred by directors and proprietors are never allowed.

Similarly if a business suffers from a theft by a member of staff the loss will be an allowable expense but a misappropriation by a director or proprietor will not be deductible (*Curtis v J & G Oldfield* (1933)).

The law is consistent in its treatment of revenue income and expenditure. The tests that were used to determine whether a receipt was capital or revenue are also used to test whether expenditure is capital or revenue. However, in the case of *Lawson v Johnson Matthey plc* (1992) a payment of £50 million was made as part of a deal with the Bank of England in order to save the banking subsidiary from a threat of insolvency. Despite the size and one-off nature of the payment it was allowed as revenue expenditure.

This distinction between capital and revenue expenditure has become more important in recent years with the phasing out of 100% first-year allowances on capital expenditure. Now, if expenditure is deemed to be capital, the taxpayer can only claim a maximum 25% writing down allowance in the year in which the expenditure is incurred.

When considering whether legal and professional charges are allowable we need to look first at the status of the item to which they relate. For example, fees and charges incurred in respect of capital assets and non-trading items are not deductible.

Activity

For each of the following legal and professional charges decide whether they are allowable deductions for the purposes of Schedule D Case I:

1. Charges incurred in issuing shares.
2. Charges incurred when obtaining a long (more than 50 years) lease.
3. Charges for trade debt collection.
4. Charges incurred with respect to an action for breach of contract.

Feedback

The first two charges would be disallowable because they relate to non-revenue items while the third charges would be allowable and the fourth charges would be allowable provided that the contract has the quality of revenue and not capital.

However, it is not possible to classify all legal and professional charges using this rule. For example, the normal fees for preparing accounts and agreeing tax liabilities are allowable while legal fees incurred during tax appeals are not deductible regardless of the outcome of the appeal. However, accountancy expenses incurred due to an Inland Revenue investigation will be allowable provided that taxable profits for earlier years are not increased and if an increase is made to the taxable profits of the year under review this does not lead to interest charges or penalties.

Amounts spent on repairs to an asset will generally be allowable for tax purposes but amounts spent on improvements will be disallowed, although they may be eligible for capital allowances. In general the normal accounting principles are used as guidance when differentiating between revenue and capital expenditure but case law has been used to decide marginal cases.

You need to know some of the details of the main cases in order to be able to identify revenue and capital expenditure. We will begin by contrasting the decisions made in the cases of *Law Shipping Co Ltd* v *IRC* (1924) and *Odeon Associated Theatres Ltd* v *Jones* (1972) which both concern the cost of making good dilapidations which existed at the time of acquisition. We will then contrast the cases of *Samuel Jones & Co (Devondale) Ltd* v *CIR* (1951) and *Brown* v *Burnley Football and Athletic Co Ltd* (1980) to differentiate between repairing and replacing assets.

The first area of difficulty involves expenditure which is incurred to renovate assets soon after they were acquired. In *Law Shipping Co Ltd* v *IRC* (1924) a ship, which was built in 1906, was bought in December 1919 for £97,000. The ship was ready to sail with freight booked at the time of purchase. The periodical survey of the ship was then considerably overdue and exemption from survey had had to be obtained. The ship was granted a Lloyd's Certificate for a single voyage to enable it to be taken into dock to undergo its survey. The purchaser had to spend £51,558 on repairs. It was agreed that the expense of keeping a ship, which is employed in trade, in proper repair is an expense necessary for the purpose of trade, even if that expense is deferred. In fact had the purchaser's predecessors undertaken the repairs they would have been able to set the costs against their income for tax purposes. However, the accumulation of repairs represented by the expenditure was an accumulation which extended partly over a period during which the ship was employed, not in the purchaser's trade, but in that of the purchaser's predecessors.

A ship which is dilapidated is worth less than a ship which has been well maintained and is in good condition. The condition of the ship at the time of the sale was reflected in the price paid. The value of the ship was presumably increased by the repairs undertaken and hence some of the cost of the repairs should be treated as capital expenditure since they increased the value of a capital asset.

It was held that most of the expenditure was incurred because of the poor state of repair of the vessel when it was bought and this amount was disallowed but £12,000 of the expenditure was allowed for post-acquisition repairs.

In the contrasting case of *Odeon Associated Theatres Ltd v Jones* (1972) a cinema had been bought which was in a fairly dilapidated condition after the Second World War. The cinema was used for a number of years by its new owners before it was refurbished. All of the refurbishment expenditure was allowed despite the poor condition of the cinema when it was bought.

There are some essential differences between the two cases which led to the differing conclusions. When the cinema was bought the purchase price was not reduced to reflect the condition of the property which was both usable and used immediately after purchase. In the *Law Shipping* case the purchase price did reflect the condition of the ship which was not seaworthy immediately after purchase. Finally the Court of Appeal decided that the costs of refurbishment were deductible expenses in accordance with accounting principles.

The second area which has depended on case law for clarification concerns the question of repair or replacement. That is, has an asset been repaired or replaced? In the case of *Samuel Jones & Co (Devondale) Ltd v CIR* (1951) expenditure on a new chimney to replace the existing one was allowable because the chimney was held to be a subsidiary part of the factory.

In the case of *Brown v Burnley Football and Athletic Co Ltd* (1980) the football club replaced a wooden spectators' stand with a concrete structure which also provided additional accommodation. The expenditure was disallowed because the entire stand, which was held not to be part of a larger asset, but a distinct and separate part of the club, was replaced.

Payments to employees will usually be allowable deductions provided that they are in the interest of the business.

For example, travelling expenses incurred when travelling to work are disallowable but travelling expenses incurred in the course of business are deductible. This seemingly simple ruling is still open to dispute. For example, it may not be easy to decide exactly where an individual's work commences. Recently there was a report in *The Guardian* about a taxpayer who is the only employee, and major shareholder, of a company which designs oil platforms who was in dispute with the Inland Revenue over travel and accommodation expenses. The company paid for its employee to travel, often hundreds of miles, in order to work. Now, as we will see in Chapter 6, an employee's expenses are taxable benefits unless they are wholly, exclusively and necessarily incurred in the performance of employment duties (TA 1988 s198). The Inland Revenue argued that the taxpayer's costs in getting to the area and arranging a place to stay merely enabled him to be available for work each day. This means that the costs of travel and accommodation are private expenses, paid by the company, which are therefore taxable benefits. However, if the taxpayer had been taxed under Schedule D Case I the expenses would have been an allowable deduction because the expense was incurred wholly and exclusively for the purpose of the business. Indeed employees of large companies who receive similar payments are not taxed on them because there is a presumption that they are based at the company's offices so that the expenses are incurred in the course of their duties because they are travelling between sites.

The following week the same writer, David Brodie, reported that an accountant in Wiltshire had a client in similar circumstances. The accountant successfully claimed the payments as allowable deductions by quoting from a Revenue Statement of 13th February 1981 which exempts construction workers from tax on their expenses and then went on to argue that it would contravene the Taxpayers' Charter to limit the concession to one particular industry. The accountant concluded his statement by saying that individual tax inspectors are prepared to operate this concession.

As you will remember only expenditure which is wholly and exclusively for the purposes of business will be deductible. There are two situations in which businesses risk falling foul of this requirement. The first is when a payment is held to be too remote from the business for it to be considered to be wholly and exclusively for the purposes of business. The second is when expenditure has two purposes, one business and the other private, the expenditure is likely to fail the 'wholly and exclusively' test and be disallowable because of a duality of purpose.

When deciding whether subscriptions and donations are allowed we can use the 'wholly and exclusively' rule. For example, trade subscriptions are likely to be allowable while donations to a charity will probably only be allowable if they are relatively small and to local charities. Subscriptions and donations to political parties are usually disallowable but in the case of *Morgan v Tate and Lyle Ltd* (1954) a political donation to the Conservative Party was allowed because it was made in order to resist the nationalisation of the sugar industry proposed by the Labour Party which would have led to the cessation of the business.

Any appropriations from the business, including a salary or interest on capital paid to the owner, are disallowable. In *Caillebotte v Quinn* (1975) the taxpayer, a self-employed carpenter, claimed the difference between the cost of eating at home, 10p, and the cost of eating in a cafe, 40p, for those days when he was working away from home. It was held that the expenditure was disallowable because he ate to live as well as to work and so the expenditure was tainted by the private purpose. There have been a number of other cases testing this legislation, one of the most recent being in *Mackinlay v Arthur Young McClelland Moores & Co* (1990) where the House of Lords ruled that removal costs paid to two partners to move house were disallowable. It was accepted that the partnership benefitted from the move because the partners were able to work at different offices but that there was duality of purpose. The House of Lords also confirmed that the rules for sole traders also apply to unincorporated partnerships.

Although it is not possible to split a purpose into a business and a personal purpose, it may be possible to split a payment and allow the business portion as a deductible expense. The most widespread example of this is the treatment of expenses relating to a car which is used for both business and pleasure. The proportion of business miles compared to total miles determines the proportion of the expenses such as servicing, insurance and petrol which is an allowable deduction. As you have already seen section 74 of ICTA 1988 enables taxpayers who undertake all, or part, of their business from their own home to deduct part of the costs of running the house from their Schedule D Case I profits.

If a taxpayer leases premises he or she is likely to pay a premium when the lease is granted as well as a rent. A part of the premium paid will be allowed as a deductible expense for tax purposes. The lessee can claim the amount on which the landlord is assessed spread over the life of the lease. Hence in order to determine the relief available you need to determine the Schedule A assessment on the lease premium which is dealt with in Chapter 6. Look at the Activity 'Amanda' in Chapter 6 to see how the Schedule A assessment is determined.

Expenditure can only be a deductible expense from trading income if it was incurred on or after the date on which the business commences to trade. However, expenses incurred in the seven years prior to this date will be treated as a loss which arises in the year of commencement (TA 1988 s401). This may seem rather strange to you. However, as you will see in the next section, trading profits in the first period of accounts are likely to be taxed more than once. Conversely then an expense incurred in the same period is likely to be eligible for tax relief more than once. By allowing the expenditure as a loss rather than a trading expense this multiple relief is avoided.

Pro forma for the adjustment of trading profits

You can now identify taxable revenues and allowable deductions for Schedule D Case I purposes and you are able to allocate these revenues and expenses to periods of account. Finally you will find it helpful to use this pro forma to undertake the adjustment of profits to the Schedule D Case I assessment.

Computation of the Schedule D Case I assessment

		£	£
Net profit per accounts			20,000
Add	expenditure in the accounts which is not deductible under Schedule D Case I	3,000	
	income taxable under Schedule D Case I not directly credited to the P & L account	1,000	4,000
			24,000
Less	income in the accounts which is not taxable under Schedule D Case I	2,000	
	expenditure not in the accounts which is deductible under Schedule D Case I	3,000	5,000
Schedule D Case I income			19,000

Basis of assessment

In this section we will discuss the current year basis which was introduced in 1997/98 for all unincorporated businesses as part of the self-assessment regime.

Current year basis

The normal basis of assessment for 1997/98 onwards is the current year basis. Under the current year regime the general rule is that the profits arising in the tax year will be assessed in the tax year (ICTA 1988 s60(1)). This is sometimes termed the actual basis because the actual profits arising in the tax year for the basis of assessment in the tax year. In particular the profits in the tax year in which the business commenced will be taxed on the actual basis (ICTA 1988 s61(1)). However, if a sole trader or partnership uses an annual accounting date which is not 5th April the basis of assessment of a fiscal year will be the 12 months to the accounting date which falls in the fiscal year (ICTA 1988 s60(2)). Since few businesses will use 5th April as an accounting date the accounting period ended in the fiscal year will normally form the basis period for the fiscal year.

There are some circumstances in which the normal basis of assessment cannot be applied and we will consider these now.

Assessments in the early years of trading

As we have already said, the basis of assessment for the commencement year, that is the fiscal year in which the taxpayer begins to trade, is the profits which arose in the fiscal year (ICTA 1988 s61 (1)).

If, in the second fiscal year, the accounting date falling in that year is less than 12 months from the commencement date, the basis of assessment is the profits arising in the first 12 months of trading (ICTA 1988 s61 (2)). If the accounting date falling in that year is at least 12 months from the commencement date the basis of assessment is the profits arising in the 12 months to the accounting date (ICTA 1988 s62 (2). If the first period of account is so long that there is no accounting date in the second year of assessment the basis of assessment is the profits arising in the fiscal year (ICTA 1988 s61 (2)).

The basis of assessment in the third fiscal year will be the period of account ending in the year provided that the second fiscal year contains an accounting date. If this is not the case the basis of assessment is the profits arising in the 12 months to the accounting date in the third year.

All subsequent years, apart from the year of cessation, will be taxed on the current year basis (ICTA s60 (3)).

It is likely that some profits will be taxed more than once in the early years of trading. Overlap profits are the amount of profits or gains which are included in the computations for two successive years of assessment (ICTA 1988 s63A (5)). The overlap period is the number of days in the period in which overlap profits arose (ICTA 1988 s63A (5)).

Activity

Daniel, Peter, Laura and Rachel graduated in June 1997 from Leeds Business School and they each decided to become self-employed as sole traders. From the following details identify the basis periods for each of them for their first four years of assessment.

- Daniel began to trade on 1st July 1997 and drew up accounts to 5th April 1998 and 5th April thereafter.
- Peter also began to trade on 1st July 1997 but drew up accounts to 30th June 1998 and 30th June thereafter.
- Laura also began to trade on 1st July 1997 but elected to draw up accounts to 31st May 1998 and 31st May thereafter.
- Rachel didn't begin to trade until 1st January 1998 and then produced accounts to 30th April 1999 and 30th April thereafter.

Feedback

Daniel

Fiscal year	Basis period	Explanation
1997/98	9 months to 5/4/98	Actual basis for year of commencement
1998/99	year to 5/4/99	12 months to the accounting date
1999/00	year to 5/4/00	12 months following previous basis period
2000/01	year to 5/4/01	12 months following previous basis period

Peter

Fiscal year	Basis period	Explanation
1997/98	9 months to 5/4/98	Actual basis for year of commencement
1998/99	year to 30/6/98	12 months to the accounting date
1999/00	year to 30/6/99	12 months following previous basis period
2000/01	year to 30/6/00	12 months following previous basis period

Laura

Fiscal year	Basis period	Explanation
1997/98	9 months to 5/4/98	Actual basis for year of commencement
1998/99	year to 30/6/98	First 12 months
1999/00	12 months to 31/5/99	12 months to the accounting date
2000/01	12 months to 31/5/00	12 months following previous basis period

Rachel

Fiscal year	Basis period	Explanation
1997/98	3 months to 5/4/98	Actual basis for year of commencement
1998/99	year to 5/4/99	Actual basis
1999/00	year to 30/4/99	12 months to the accounting date
2000/01	year to 30/4/00	12 months following previous basis period

These four examples illustrate most of the possibilities in the early years of trading.

Activity

For each of Daniel, Peter, Laura and Rachel calculate the overlap periods, if any.

Feedback

Daniel
No period forms part of the basis period of more than one year of assessment and hence Daniel does not have an overlap period.

Peter
The nine-month period from 1st July 1997 to 5th April 1998 is part of the basis period for 1997/98 and 1998/99 and hence is an overlap period. To calculate the overlap profits find 9/12 of the profits for the year to 30th June 1998.

Laura
Like Peter the nine-month period from 1st July 1997 to 5th April 1998 is part of the basis period for 1997/98 and 1998/99 and hence is an overlap period. In addition the month of June 1998 is part of the basis period for 1998/99 and 1999/00 hence is also an overlap period.

Rachel
The 11-month period from 1st May 1998 to 5th April 1999 is part of the basis period for 1998/99 and 1999/00 and hence is an overlap period.

Assessments in the closing years of trading

Where a sole trader or partnership ceases to trade in a year of assessment other than the commencement year the basis period for the year of cessation will begin immediately after the end of the basis period for the preceding year of assessment and end on the date on which the business is permanently discontinued (ICTA 1988 s63).

This rule applies even if the final accounting period is less than 12 months long. If a business does not trade for many years and a year of assessment might fall under the early year rules or the year of cessation rules section 63 takes precedence.

Before you can determine the basis periods in the year of cessation you need to know one more thing. If a business has more than one accounting date in the fiscal year the legislation treats the latest of the accounting dates at the accounting date for tax purposes (ICTA 1988 s60(5)).

Activity

Kathy had been in business for many years, making up accounts to 30th April, when she ceased to trade on 31st March 2000. Her adjusted profits for the final three accounting periods were:

	£
Year ended 30.4.98	42,000
Year ended 30.4.99	44,000
Period ended 31.3.00	40,000

Calculate the Schedule D Case I assessments for the final two years of assessment.

Feedback

The final year of assessment is 1999/00 and hence the penultimate year of assessment is 1998/99.

Fiscal year	Basis period	Schedule D Case I assessment
1998/99	year to 30.4.98	£42,000
1999/00	23 months from 1.5.98 to 31.3.00	£84,000 (£44,000 + £40,000)

Relief for overlap profits

Remember that under the current year rules the basis of assessment in which the business ceases to trade is the final accounting period. Because some profits are taxed more than once in the opening years the Inland Revenue gives some relief by way of overlap relief. There are two situations in which overlap relief can be claimed. Relief can be claimed in the fiscal year in which the business changes its accounting date provided that this results in the assessment of a period which is more than 12 months long. The details of this relief are beyond the scope of this text. The second occasion on which relief can be claimed is the fiscal year in which the business ceases to trade. If the business does change its accounting date and claims overlap relief, any unused relief can be carried forward to be used when the business ceases to trade (ICTA 1988 s63A(3)). When overlap relief is given in the year of cessation the maximum relief is equal to the overlap profits.

Jim commenced trading on 1st January 1996 and made up accounts to 31st December each year. He ceased to trade on 31st December 2001. His tax adjusted profits are:

Period	Assessment £
y/e 31.12.96	48,000
y/e 31.12.97	24,000
y/e 31.12.98	36,000
y/e 31.12.99	40,000
y/e 31.12.00	36,000
y/e 31.12.01	48,000

Determine the Schedule D Case I profits for each of the relevant fiscal years.

Feedback

Fiscal year	Basis period	Assessment £	Note
95/96	1.1.95–5.4.96	12,000	(i)
96/97	y/e 31.12.96	48,000	(ii)
97/98	y/e 31.12.97	24,000	
98/99	y/e 31.12.98	36,000	
99/00	y/e 31.12.99	40,000	
00/01	y/e 31.12.00	36,000	
01/02	y/e 31.12.01	36,000	(iii)

The assessments are:

Notes
- (i)   The profits are time apportioned £48,000 × 3/12.
- (ii) The overlap profits are £12,000 (3/12 × £48,000).
- (iii) The taxable profits of £48,000 are reduced by the overlap profits of £12,000.

You can now determine the Schedule D Case I assessment for a fiscal year. Now you need to be able to calculate the capital allowances available for a fiscal year.

Capital allowances

You will remember that depreciation is not an allowable expense for tax purposes. Relief for capital expenditure is given by means of capital allowances.

The legislation relating to capital allowances is contained in the Capital Allowances Act 1990 (CAA 1990). Capital allowances are available to businesses on certain capital expenditure. Under the old rules capital allowances were deducted from the Schedule D Case I income of individuals. Under the new, current year basis rules, capital allowances are an allowable expense for tax purposes (FA 1994 s211 (1)). This measure will bring the rules for income tax in line with corporation tax. Capital allowances continue to be an allowable deduction when calculating the Schedule D Case I income of a company.

Capital allowances are given for years of assessment. The basis period for a year of assessment is used to determine the fiscal year in which additions and disposals will be incorporated into the capital allowances computation.

Writing down allowances are not available in the year in which a business ceases to trade. However, balancing allowances or charges are calculated instead.

For expenditure on capital assets to be eligible for capital allowances it must fall into one of these categories:

- plant and machinery
- industrial buildings
- patents
- know-how, and
- agricultural buildings and works.

The first two categories are the most important and so we will concentrate on these.

Plant and machinery

The CAA 1990 does not contain a definition of plant and machinery and so it is necessary to look to case law for guidance.

There has been a considerable amount of case law on the subject. One of the most important is *Yarmouth* v *France* (1887) in which the status of a horse was questioned. Lindley LJ concluded:

> There is no definition of plant in the Act: but in its original sense, it includes whatever apparatus is used by a businessman for carrying on his business, not his stock-in-trade which he buys or makes for sale; but all goods and chattels, fixed or moveable, live or dead, which he keeps for permanent employment in his business.

A number of subsequent cases refined the definition. In *Wimpy International Ltd* v *Warland* (1988) three types of asset were excluded from the definition of plant and machinery:

- assets which are not used for carrying on the business
- assets with a useful life of less than two years
- assets which form part of the setting in which the business was carried on, as opposed to assets actively used in the business.

This judgment is the result of a number of earlier cases. In would be useful for us to review some of the more interesting ones.

The last requirement is referred to the 'function v setting' test and has generated a considerable number of cases. In *CIR* v *Barclay Curle & Co* (1969) the costs of building a dry dock was held to be expenditure on plant and machinery because the dock played an active part in the operation of the company's trade. In *Cooke* v *Beach Station Caravans Ltd* (1974) the costs of excavating and installing a swimming pool were held to be expenditure on plant and machinery because the swimming pool performed a function, that of giving buoyancy and enjoyment to the swimmers.

In *Benson v Yard Arm Club* (1978) a ship which was being used as a floating restaurant was held to be ineligible for capital allowances because it failed the functional test. However, in *CIR v Scottish and Newcastle Breweries Ltd* (1982) it was held that light fittings, decor and murals performed the function of creating an atmosphere and so were plant. In contrast in *Wimpy International Ltd v Warland* (1988) a floor was held not to be plant despite making the restaurant attractive to customers.

In a more recent case, *Carr v Sayer* (1992), quarantine kennels were held not to be plant despite being purpose built.

In the case of *Brown v Burnley Football and Athletic Co Ltd* (1980) expenditure on a new stand was held not to be plant because it did not perform a function. You will remember that Burnley Football and Athletic Co Ltd had also failed to claim the expenditure as a repair because the entire stand was replaced. Today such expenditure would be allowed under the special provisions stated below.

The following expenditure is deemed to be plant and machinery:

- expenditure on equipment in order to comply with fire regulations for a building occupied by the trader (CAA 1990 s69)
- expenditure on thermal insulation in an industrial building (CAA 1990 s67)
- expenditure in order to comply with statutory safety requirements for sports grounds (CAA 1990 s70)
- expenditure on computer software (CAA 1990 s67A).

In order to claim capital allowances a person carrying on a trade must incur capital expenditure on the provision of machinery or plant wholly and exclusively for the purposes of the trade and the machinery or plant belongs to him (CAA 1990 s24(1)). The extent to which assets can be described as plant and machinery is highlighted in *Munby v Furlong* (1977) when a barrister successfully argued that his law library was plant because it was the apparatus used for carrying on his business.

For each chargeable period, apart from a period which ends with the cessation of trade, for which the qualifying expenditure exceeds any disposal value, a writing down allowance is available equal to 25% of the excess, reduced proportionately for short basis periods (CAA 1990 s24(2)). The 1996 budget contained proposals to reduce the writing down allowances from 25% to 6% for expenditure on plant and machinery with a working life of more than 25 years. This reduced percentage will apply to expenditure incurred on or after 26th November 1996. However, if a contract is entered into before 26th November 1996 and the expenditure is incurred before 1st January 2000 the new rules will not apply. The Chancellor argued that the new rules will bring the tax treatment of such assets more in line with their accounting treatment. Certainly such an intention is in line with the tax treatment of depreciation in many other countries. In practice it seems likely that relatively few businesses will be affected by these changes as few items of plant and machinery are normally considered to have a useful life of 25 years or more. The Exchequer expects to increase tax receipts by £325 million in 1998/99 and £675 million in 1999/00.

In general, the rules will only apply to businesses spending more than £100,000 per annum on such long-life assets and the full 25% writing down allowance will continue to be available for expenditure on:

- machinery or plant in a building used wholly or mainly as, or for purposes ancillary to, a dwelling-house, retail shop, showroom, hotel or office
- sea-going ships and railway assets bought before the end of 2010. The tax treatment of expenditure in this category incurred after this date will be reviewed in due course.

In addition expenditure on long-life assets which is below a *de minimis* limit will not be subject to the new rules. The *de minimis* limit for a company will equal £100,000 divided by one plus the number of companies associated with it. We will deal with associated companies in Chapter 8. The *de minimis* limit will also apply to sole traders and partnerships provided that the sole trader or, in the case of a partnership, at least half the partners, devotes substantially the whole of their time to carrying on the business. However, the *de minimis* limit does not apply to expenditure on plant and machinery on which the previous owner received allowances at the reduced rate.

With the exception of cars, leased assets, long-life assets and assets with a private use element, all qualifying expenditure is aggregated into a pool from which the disposal value is deducted and the writing down allowance is then calculated. The taxpayer may also be able to elect for some assets to be de-pooled and we will study this later.

Capital allowances pro forma

Once again if you know the way to lay out a computation you will be able to calculate the capital allowances for a business.

Capital allowances on the general pool for plant and machinery

	Pool £	Allowances £
1997/98		
Written down value b/f	50,000	
Additions	20,000	
	70,000	
Disposals	10,000	
	60,000	
Writing down allowance	(15,000)	15,000
Written down value c/f	45,000	
Allowances for 1997/98		15,000
1998/99		
Additions	27,000	
	72,000	
Disposals	32,000	
	40,000	
Writing down allowance	(10,000)	10,000
Written down value c/f	30,000	
Allowances for 1998/99		10,000

The qualifying expenditure for a chargeable period is the excess of the qualifying expenditure for a chargeable period immediately preceding the chargeable period in question (CAA 1990 s25).

The disposal value is equal to the lower of the net proceeds of disposal, including any insurance money received, and the capital expenditure incurred on the acquisition of the machinery or plant.

Leased assets and cars costing less than £12,000 are aggregated in a separate pool to the general pool (CAA 1990 s39). The calculation of the writing down allowances is exactly as for the general pool.

All or part of the writing down allowance can be waived by the taxpayer. Any amount waived simply has the effect of increasing the balance of qualifying expenditure which is eligible for capital allowances in future years. Clearly it is usually in the interest of the business to claim tax relief as quickly as possible.

Activity

List reasons which might lead a business to waive or reduce the writing down allowance.

Feedback

A business might waive the writing down allowance on the following occasions:

- if taxable profits would be reduced to such an extent that it would not be possible for the taxpayer to use all of his or her personal allowances
- if the taxpayer believed that his or her marginal rate of tax would increase significantly in future years.

In the year in which there is a cessation of trade a balancing allowance or charge may arise. If the balance of qualifying expenditure exceeds any disposal value a balancing allowance equal to the whole of the excess is given (CAA 1990 s24(2)). If the disposal value exceeds the balance of qualifying expenditure a balancing charge equal to the excess will be levied on the taxpayer (CAA 1990 s24(5)).

Activity

Catherine retired on 31st December 1997 after trading for many years. On 6th April 1997 the tax written down value of the pool was £10,000 and of the car, which was used totally for the purposes of the business, was £4,500. The car had originally cost £6,000.

Catherine sold the plant and machinery for £12,000 and the car for £3,000 when she retired. Calculate the capital allowances and charges for 1997/98.

Feedback

The capital allowances computation is:

	Pool £	Car £	Allowances £
1997/98			
WDV b/f	10,000	4,500	
Disposal proceeds	(12,000)	(3,000)	
	(2,000)	1,500	
Balancing allowance		(1,500)	1,500
Balancing charge	2,000		(2,000)
Net capital allowances			(500)

If the machinery is only partly used for the purpose of trade the capital allowances and charges described above are reduced by the fraction A/B where A is the proportion of the time during which the asset was used for the purpose of trade while B is the total period of ownership (CAA 1990 s27). A separate capital allowances computation must be carried out for each asset with an element of private use rather than their inclusion in the pool.

Cars which cost more than £12,000 are termed expensive motor cars. Such cars are not pooled but are the subject of separate computations (CAA 1990 s34(1)). The writing down allowance is limited to a maximum of:

- £3,000 or, if the period is part only of a year, a proportionate part of £3,000, and
- if the person carrying on the trade is regarded as having incurred a part only of the expenditure actually incurred on the provision of the motor car, a proportionate part of £3,000 or, if the period is part only of a year, that proportionate part proportionately reduced (CAA 1990 s34(3)).

For cars purchased before 11th March 1992 the definition of an expensive car applied to cars costing more than £8,000 and the writing down allowance is limited to £2,000 per annum.

When the car is disposed of the balancing allowance or charge is calculated in the normal way and is reduced if there is a private use element as described above.

Activity

Roger has traded for many years making up accounts to 31st December each year. On 31st August 1997 he bought a car for £20,000 and agreed with the Inland Revenue that it was used 75% of the time for business purposes. He sold the car on 28th February 1999 for £12,000. Determine the capital allowances which can be claimed on the car.

Feedback

The capital allowances computation is:

	Expensive car £	Allowances £
1997/98		
Acquisition	20,000	
WDA	3,000 × 75%	2,250
WDV c/f	17,000	
1998/99		
Proceeds	(12,000)	
	5,000	
Balancing allowance	(5,000) × 75%	3,750

There are also restrictions on the tax relief available if an expensive car is hired rather than bought. If a car, which cost more than £12,000 when new, is hired the expenditure allowed for tax purposes equals the cost when new reduced in the proportion which £12,000 together with one half of the excess bears to the cost when new (CAA 1990 s35(2)). Hence the maximum allowable deduction from profits when leasing an expensive car is:

$$\frac{£12,000 + 1/2\ (P - £12,000)}{P} \times R$$

where P is the cost of the car when new and R is the annual rental cost. For contracts which commenced before 11th March 1992 the limit is £8,000 rather than £12,000 and is substituted in the formula.

The taxpayer may elect for certain machinery and plant to be treated as a short-life asset and de-pooled in order for the balancing allowance to be claimed when the asset is disposed of (CAA 1990 s37(1)). The election must be made not more than two years after the end of the chargeable period, or its basis period, in which the capital expenditure was incurred and is irrevocable (CAA 1990 s37(2)). However, if the asset is not disposed of in a chargeable period ending on or before the fourth anniversary of the end of the chargeable period in which the cost of the asset was recorded then the tax written down value of the asset is transferred to the pool at the beginning of the next chargeable period (CAA 1990 s37(5)).

The Act identifies assets which cannot be treated as short-life assets, these are:

- ships
- motor cars, and
- machinery or plant provided for leasing (CAA 1990 s38).

Industrial buildings

An industrial building is a building or structure in use for the purposes of:

- a trade carried on in a mill, factory or other similar premises, or
- a transport, dock, inland navigation, water, sewerage, electricity or hydraulic power undertaking, or
- a tunnel, bridge or toll road undertaking, or
- a trade which involves the manufacture or storage of goods or materials, or

- a trade involving working of any mine, oil well or other source of mineral deposits, or
- ploughing or cultivating land (other than land occupied by the person carrying on the trade) and other agricultural operations on such land, or threshing the crops of another person, or
- catching or taking fish or shellfish.

A building provided by a person carrying on any such trade or undertaking for the welfare of workers employed by that person is deemed to be an industrial building (CAA 1990 s18(1)).

The legislation specifically excludes any building or structure in use as, or as part of, a dwelling-house, retail shop, showroom, hotel or office from the definition of an industrial building (CAA 1990 s18(4)).

In his Autumn Statement of 1992 the then Chancellor Norman Lamont introduced an initial allowance of 20% for expenditure on industrial buildings, hotels and agricultural buildings and works provided that the contract to construct the building was entered into between 1st November 1992 and 31st October 1993 and the building was brought into use on or before 31st December 1994.

A writing down allowance of 4% straight line is also available when the building is brought into use. The initial allowance and the writing down allowance can be claimed in the same year. In order to be eligible for a writing down allowance a person must have an interest in the building, which must qualify as an industrial building, at the end of the basis period for the chargeable period (CAA 1990 s3). When a building is the subject of a long lease the lessee is deemed to be the person having an interest in the building provided that both the lessor and the lessee make an election (CAA 1990 s11).

Expenditure incurred on preparing, cutting, tunnelling or levelling land in order to prepare the land as a site for the installation of machinery or plant is treated as expenditure on an industrial building for capital allowance purposes (CAA 1990 s13).

The writing down allowance is reduced for short basis periods for both income tax and corporation tax purposes.

Activity

Bob has traded for many years and makes up accounts to 30th June each year. On 1st January 1993 he bought a new factory for £100,000 which was brought into use on 1st May 1993. Determine the industrial buildings allowance available for 1994/95, 1995/96, 1996/97 and 1997/98.

The capital allowances available are:
Industrial buildings and structures, including qualifying hotels and commercial buildings, occupied for the purpose of trade in enterprise zones are eligible for an initial allowance of 100% of the cost, including VAT, provided the site was included in the zone not more than ten years before the expenditure (CAA 1990 s1). There is no requirement that buildings in an enterprise zone be in use in order to claim the allowance but only the last buyer before the building is brought into use may claim the allowance (CAA 1990 s10A(8)).

Feedback

	Building £	Allowances £
1994/95		
Cost	100,000	
Initial allowance	(20,000)	20,000
	80,000	
WDA 4% × Cost	(4,000)	4,000
WDV c/f	76,000	
Allowances available		24,000
1995/96		
WDA 4% × Cost	(4,000)	4,000
WDV c/f	72,000	
Allowances available		4,000
1996/97		
WDA 4% × Cost	(4,000)	4,000
WDV c/f	68,000	
Allowances available		4,000
1997/98		
WDA 4% × Cost	(4,000)	4,000
WDV c/f	64,000	
Allowances available		4,000

The initial allowance is not available for any part of the cost which has been met by a grant. The taxpayer may waive any part of the initial allowance. Any allowance so waived will be written off on a straight line basis over the four years from the date on which the building is brought into use.

If the building was not in use as an industrial building on the last day of the basis period and was not used for any other purpose the writing down allowance is still available provided that the period of disuse is temporary (CAA 1990 s15). In practice so long as the building is used as an industrial building at some time in the future the period of disuse will be considered to be temporary. However, if the building is used for a non-industrial purpose a notional writing down allowance continues to be deducted as before but no capital allowance may be claimed by the taxpayer (CAA 1990 s8(7)).

If the asset is disposed of within 25 years of the date on which the building was first used a balancing allowance or charge may arise (CAA 1990 s4(1) & (2)). If there are no proceeds of disposal or the proceeds do not exceed the residue of the expenditure immediately prior to disposal a balancing allowance equal to the excess of the residue of the expenditure over the proceeds will be given (CAA 1990 s4(2A)). If the proceeds do exceed the residue of expenditure a balancing charge equal to the amount by which proceeds exceed the residue of expenditure will be made (CAA 1990 s4(4)).

Activity

Ian has traded for many years and prepares accounts to 31st December each year. On 30th September 1991 he bought an industrial building for £500,000 and brought it into use immediately. He sold it on 31st March 1997 for £600,000 to Diane who makes up accounts to 30th September. Diane brought the building into use immediately. Determine the industrial building allowances available to Ian and Diane.

Feedback

Industrial building allowances are available as follows:

	Building £	Allowances £
Ian		
1992/93		
Cost	500,000	
WDA 4% × Cost	(20,000)	20,000
WDV c/f	480,000	
1993/94		
WDA 4% × Cost	(20,000)	20,000
WDV c/f	460,000	
1994/95		
WDA 4% × Cost	(20,000)	20,000
WDV c/f	440,000	
1995/96		
WDA 4% × Cost	(20,000)	20,000
WDV c/f	420,000	
1996/97		
WDA 4% × Cost	(20,000)	20,000
WDV c/f	400,000	
1997/98		
Residue before sale	400,000	
Proceeds (limited to cost)	500,000	
	(100,000)	
Balancing charge	100,000	(100,000)
Diane		
1997/98		
Residue before sale	400,000	
Balancing charge	100,000	
Residue after sale	500,000	

The building has a total tax life of 25 years. Ian owned the building for 4 years six months leaving a remaining tax life of 20 years six months when Diane bought the building.

The writing down allowance which Diane can claim for each of the next 20 years is £24,390 (£500,000/20.5). In the following year she can claim the final writing down allowance of £12,200 (£500,000 – £24,390 × 20).

Activity

Suppose that in the above activity from 30th September 1992 to 31st May 1994 Ian used the building to run an indoor market rather than using it for industrial purposes. All the other information is unchanged. Determine the industrial building allowances available to Ian and Diane.

Feedback

Industrial building allowances are available as follows:

	Building £	Allowances £
Ian		
1992/93		
Cost	500,000	
WDA 4% × Cost	(20,000)	20,000
WDV c/f	480,000	
1993/94		
Notional WDA 4% × Cost	(20,000)	
WDV c/f	460,000	
1994/95		
Notional WDA 4% × Cost	(20,000)	
WDV c/f	440,000	
1995/96		
WDA 4% × Cost	(20,000)	20,000
WDV c/f	420,000	
1996/97		
WDA 4% × Cost	(20,000)	20,000
WDV c/f	400,000	
1997/98		
Residue before sale	400,000	
Proceeds (limited to cost)	500,000	
	(100,000)	
Balancing charge	100,000	

The balancing charge is limited to the total allowances given.

Balancing charge		(60,000)
Diane		
1997/98		
Residue before sale	400,000	
Balancing charge	60,000	
Residue after sale	460,000	

The writing down allowance which Diane can claim for each of the next 20 years is £22,439 (£460,000/20.5). In the following year she can claim the final writing down allowance of £11,220 (£460,000 − £22,439 × 20).

Patents

If patent rights are purchased a pool is formed, on which a writing down allowance of 25% per annum, on a reducing balance basis, is available provided that the patent rights are used for trading purposes. The rules for balancing allowances and charges are as for the general pool for plant and machinery. If sale proceeds exceed the original cost the deduction from the pool is limited to the original cost, as for plant and machinery, but the excess of proceeds over the original cost is taxed under Schedule D Case VI.

Scientific research

Scientific research expenditure which is not capital is an allowable deduction from trading profits for tax purposes (CAA 1990 s136(1)). Scientific research expenditure which is of a capital nature is eligible for a 100% capital allowance in the year in which the expenditure was incurred (CAA 1990 s137). Any disposal proceeds will be deemed to be trading receipts.

Agricultural buildings and works

Capital expenditure on farmhouses, farm buildings, cottages, fences, drainage and similar works is eligible for capital allowances (CAA 1990 s124(1) & (2)). In addition to a writing down allowance of 4% per annum using the straight line basis which is available from the year in which the expenditure was incurred, an initial allowance of 20% was available for expenditure between 1st November 1992 and 31st October 1993 provided that the building was brought into use by 31st December 1994. This gives agricultural buildings, like industrial buildings, a 25-year tax life.

When an agricultural building is disposed of the writing down allowances in the year of sale is time apportioned for both the seller and the purchaser. For example, if the sale takes place half way through the seller's accounting period he or she will receive half of the annual allowance. If the purchaser has a different year end and so the date of the sale falls only a third of the way through their accounting period they will be entitled to two-thirds of the annual allowances. However, if the seller and buyer make a joint election a balancing allowance/charge is calculated for the seller in the same way as it is for industrial buildings.

Losses

You can now calculate the Schedule D Case I assessment and the capital allowances for any fiscal year. Finally you need to be able to deal with losses. Calculating a loss is simple. You only need to undertake the adjustments of profits which you practised earlier in this chapter. A loss can only be relieved once. However, there are a number of ways of relieving a loss and it is this that we will concentrate on in this section.

Trading losses

A taxpayer who incurs a trading loss has a number of alternative ways of relieving the loss. Some losses are only available in particular circumstances. For example only losses incurred in the first four years of trading can be relieved under s381. Each relief has advantages and drawbacks. The taxpayer will often have to choose between receiving a rebate quickly and maximising the amount of relief which can be claimed. If tax relief is received there is a risk that the taxpayer will be left with too little income to fully utilise his or her personal allowances. If a personal allowance is not claimed during a tax year it is lost forever and so the relief has been wasted.

As already stated a loss is calculated using the normal Schedule D Case I adjustments of profit computation. If the adjustment results in a loss rather than a profit the assessment is taken to be nil and the loss is eligible for loss relief.

The loss can be relieved by:

- carrying forward and setting against future trading profits under s385 ICTA 1988
- setting against total income of the fiscal year in which the loss arose and/or the preceding year under s380 ICTA 1988
- carrying back and setting against total income arising in the three fiscal years before the loss arose provided the loss arose in the first four years of trading under s381 ICTA 1988
- carrying forward and setting against income received from a limited company when the loss making business is incorporated under s386 ICTA 1988
- carrying back and setting against trading income of the previous three fiscal years when the business ceases to trade under s388 ICTA 1988.

We will deal with each of these losses in turn.

Section 385 ICTA 1988: carry forward of trading losses

Losses are carried forward and set against the first available profits. The losses can be carried forward without time limit but have to be relieved against profits from the same trade.

Activity

Pat has been trading for many years and makes up accounts for calendar years. Her results for recent years are as follows:

Year ended	£
31.12.97	(7,600)
31.12.98	2,500
31.12.99	10,300

Determine Pat's assessments if she claims loss relief under s385.

Feedback

	1997/98 £	1998/99 £	1999/00 £
Schedule D Case I	0	2,500	10,300
Less s385 relief	0	2,500	5,100
Taxable profit	0	0	5,200

To keep track of the loss relief it is often helpful to maintain a loss memorandum as a working paper.

Loss memorandum	£
Trading loss	7,600
Less: claim in 1998/99	(2,500)
	5,100
Claim in 1999/00 (balance)	(5,100)
	0

Once an s385 election has been made there is no flexibility: the first available profits have to be used to relieve the loss. If the taxpayer has little income from other sources this may lead to a loss of personal allowances. There is also a delay in receiving the relief, until the year of assessment following the year in which profits are made. As well as having potentially serious cash flow implications the relief is worth less because it is received in the future rather than now. This is particularly so if tax rates are falling because the tax rate applied to the relief is the one in force when the relief is received. In addition the law is strict about what exactly constitutes the same trade. In *Gordon and Blair Ltd v IRC* (1962) losses incurred from the trade of brewing could not be carried forward and relieved against profits earned from bottling. Whether the same trade is being carried on is a question of degree and so the facts of each case must be considered carefully. Hence there is an element of risk in choosing to receive relief under s385.

Section 387 ICTA 1988: relieving excess trade charges

Remember that charges, regardless of the purpose for which they were incurred, are deducted from the taxpayer's income from all sources although for historical reasons they are often first set against investment income.

For the purpose of section 387 charges are subdivided into trade charges and non-trade charges. A trade charge is a charge which has been incurred wholly and exclusively for the purpose of the trade. Examples of trade charges are patent royalties and some interest payments. The most common example of a non-trade charge is a charitable deed of covenant.

When an individual has insufficient taxable income to fully relieve their charges relief may be available under section 387. First all the non-trading charges should be relieved against whatever income there is. Any non-trading charges which are not relieved in this way cannot be relieved in any other way. Next trade charges should be set against any remaining income. Any trade charges which are not relieved in this way can be carried forward and relieved against future trading profits in the same way as losses are relieved under section 385.

Section 380 ICTA 1988: relieving trading losses against total income

Under section 380 a trading loss can be relieved against a taxpayer's statutory total income. The loss in a basis period is the loss, for s380 purposes, of the fiscal year. If there is an overlapping period the loss is deemed to arise in the earlier of the fiscal years for which it forms the basis of assessment.

Section 380 does offer some flexibility to the taxpayer. The taxpayer can elect to use the loss in the year in which it was incurred and/or in the preceding fiscal year. However, the taxpayer cannot choose how much relief is claimed in each year; the loss must be fully relieved if there is sufficient statutory total income. Remember that statutory total income is made up of income from all sources during the tax year, as determined under the Schedules and Cases.

The loss can also, at the taxpayer's election, be set against net chargeable gains for the year. The exemption limit and capital losses brought forward from previous years are ignored for this purpose. The loss must first be relieved against statutory total income for the year. The claim can only be made provided the taxpayer is still undertaking the same trade at the beginning of the tax year in which the claim is made.

We will deal with capital gains tax in detail in Chapter 7 but it might help you to attempt the activity below if you know a little about the tax now. The basis of assessment for capital gains is fiscal years. Hence in the tax year 1997/98 taxpayers will pay tax on their chargeable gains realised between 6th April 1997 and 5th April 1998. Individuals, but not companies, are entitled to an annual exemption limit of £6,500 in 1997/98, that is the first £6,500 of chargeable gains are not subject to taxation. Individuals pay tax on their chargeable gains at their marginal rate of income tax. Hence higher rate taxpayers pay tax at 40% on their chargeable gains.

Activity

Graham has been trading for many years and has the following results:

Year end	£
31 December 1997	7,000
31 December 1998	(500)
31 December 1999	(12,000)
31 December 2000	1,500

His capital gains are as follows

	£
1997/98	1,000
1998/99	9,000
1999/00	2,000
2000/01	500

Graham receives £4,000 (gross) each year from a building society investment account. Calculate the maximum loss relief claims which can be made under s380. You may assume that the annual exemption limit for capital gains was £6,500 for all of the years.

Feedback

Assessments	1997/98 £	1998/99 £	1999/00 £	2000/01 £
Schedule D Case I	7,000	Nil	Nil	1,500
Taxed interest	4,000	4,000	4,000	4,000
Statutory total income	11,000	4,000	4,000	5,500
Less s380 relief	(500) (i)	4,000 (ii)	4,000 (iii)	Nil
	10,500	Nil	Nil	6,500
Chargeable gain	1,000	9,000	2,000	500
s380 relief		(4,000) (iv)		
		5,000		
Less annual exemption	6,500	6,500	6,500	6,500

Loss memorandum

	£	£
Trading loss	500	12,000
s380 (i)	(500)	
(ii)		(4,000)
(iii)		(4,000)
(iv)		(4,000)
		12,000

Notes on example:

(i)   The loss arising in the year ended 31st December 1998 is relieved under s380 in 1997/98.

(ii) The loss arising in the year ended 31st December 1999 is carried back and relieved under s380 in 1998/99.

(iii) The remaining loss arising in the year ended 31st December 1999 is set against statutory total income of the fiscal year 1999/00.

(iv) Graham has elected to set the balance of the unrelieved loss against his net chargeable gains of the fiscal year prior to the year in which the loss arose. By doing this he has lost £2,500 of the annual exemption limit for chargeable gains.

Once again the taxpayer risks losing personal allowances when making a claim under s380. In addition, if he makes the election to relieve the loss against net capital gains he risks losing the annual exemption limit.

However, there is more flexibility than under s385 because the taxpayer can choose which years to relieve the loss against. In addition the taxpayer can receive a cash refund immediately which might be very welcome. The loss is set off against earned income first and then investment income. Although the amount of tax paid is not affected there may be an adverse effect on the amount of pension premiums which can be eligible for tax relief.

Activity

Helen commenced trading on 1st June 1996 with 31st December as her year end. In the period to 31st December 1996 Helen incurred a loss of £12,000. In the year to 31st December 1997 the loss incurred rose to £18,000.
  Calculate the loss which can be relieved under s380.

Feedback

Fiscal year	Basis period	Loss £	Notes
1996/97	1.6.96–5.4.97	16,500	(i)
1997/98	1.1.97–31.12.97	13,500	(ii)

Notes

(i)   The loss is made up of the aggregate of the loss to 31st December 1996 of £12,000 and the loss in the period 1st January 1997 and 5th April 1997 £4,500 (£18,000 × 3/12).

(ii) The loss is made up of the loss for the basis period of £18,000 less the portion of the loss which had been dealt with in 1996/97 £4,500.

Section 381 ICTA 1988: relief for losses in the early years of a trade

Under section 381 the loss is calculated by reference to basis periods. Like s380 relief, the loss cannot be double counted and so any loss in an overlap period is deemed to be a loss in the earlier fiscal year only. The loss can be carried back and set against the total income assessable in each of the three previous years starting with the earliest year first. The taxpayer cannot restrict the claim. If the loss is sufficiently large it must be set against all three years.

Activity

John worked for a company retailing menswear until 31st December 1994. On 1st January 1995 he set up his own business distributing menswear to businesses across the north of England. His Schedule E income was as follows:

Fiscal year	Income £
1992/93	7,000
1993/94	8,000
1994/95	9,000
1995/96	4,000

His trading profits/(losses) were as follows:

Accounting period	Profit/(loss) £
6 months to 30.6.96	(5,000)
y/e 30.6.97	(4,000)
y/e 30.6.98	(2,000)
y/e 30.6.99	1,000

Calculate the net income tax assessment for each of the years involved assuming that claims are made under s381. To do this you need first to calculate the allowable loss for each of the fiscal years in which a loss is incurred. Then the allowable loss can be carried back and set against the Schedule E income using s381.

Feedback

The first fiscal year in which the allowable losses arise is 1995/96. Allowable losses are:

Fiscal year	Basis period	Allowable loss	Note
1995/96	1.1.96–5.4.96	(2,500)	(i)
1996/97	1.1.96–31.12.96	(4,500)	(ii)
1997/98	1.7.96–30.6.97	(2,000)	(iii)
1998/99	1.7.97–30.6.98	(2,000)	(iv)

Notes

(i)   Three months loss is allowable in 1995/96. Hence allowable loss is £2,500 (£5,000 × 3/6).

(ii)   The loss of the first period plus six months loss from the second period less the overlap loss is allowable in 1996/97. Hence the allowable loss is £4,500 (£5,000 + (£4,000 × 6/12) – £2,500).

(iii)   The loss for the year to 30th June 1997 less the overlap loss is allowable in 1997/98. Hence the allowable loss is £2,000 (£4,000 – £2,000).

(iv)   The loss for the year to 30th June 1998 is the allowable loss in 1998/99.

Now we can relieve the allowable losses. Losses are relieved in chronological order.

	1992/93 £	1993/94 £	1994/95 £	1995/96 £
Schedule E	7,000	8,000	9,000	4,000
s381 relief				
1995/96	(2,500)			
1996/97		(4,500)		
1997/98			(2,000)	
1998/99				(2,000)
Assessable income	5,500	3,500	7,000	2,000

The assessable income for 1996/97, 1997/98 and 1998/99 is zero.

Section 386 ICTA 1988: relief for losses when a business is transferred to a company

Where a business is converted into a company and the same trade is carried on after the conversion, relief can be claimed under s386 provided that the consideration is wholly or mainly made up of shares. The relief is available for the unrelieved trading losses of the unincorporated business. Under the old rules the loss cannot be increased by capital allowances. Because capital allowances are treated as an allowable expense under the new rules all businesses will be able to get relief for them in the future.

The loss must be set against the first available income from the company with earned income taking priority over interest received and dividends from the company.

Section 388 ICTA 1988: terminal loss relief

When a business ceases terminal loss relief may be claimed. First, losses must be relieved using all the other reliefs. Any losses still unrelieved can be carried back and set against total income of the three fiscal years preceding the year in which the business ceased to trade.

As before you need to calculate the amount of loss relief before you can set it against taxable income.

The terminal loss is made up of:

- the trading loss from 6th April to the date of cessation
- the trading loss from 12 months before the date of cessation to the following 5th April
- any trading charges unrelieved in the final fiscal year;
- a proportion of the unrelieved trading charges from the penultimate fiscal year to make up 12 months' trading charges.

If the trading result is a profit in either the year of cessation or the penultimate year of trading it is taken to be zero for the purpose of the above computation.

Activity

After making a loss Helen decided to cease to trade on 30th September 2001. Helen's trading results in recent years have been:

Accounting period	Profit/(loss) £
y/e 31.12.97	15,000
y/e 31.12.98	12,000
y/e 31.12.99	6,000
y/e 31.12.00	1,000
p/e 30.9.01	(9,000)

Feedback

The terminal loss is made up of:

Narrative	Loss £	Notes
Trading loss:		
in year of cessation	(6,000)	(i)
proportion of penultimate fiscal year	(2,750)	(ii)
Terminal loss	£8,750	

Notes

(i)   Basis period for year of cessation is 6.4.02–30.9.02, a six-month period. Allowable loss is £9,000 × 6/9.

(ii) Basis period for penultimate year is 1.10.01–5.4.02, a six-month period. Allowable loss is 3/9 × £9,000 – 3/12 × 1,000.

Now that we know how much terminal loss can be claimed you need to be able to relieve the loss. Remember that the loss can be carried back and set against total income of the three fiscal years preceding the year in which the business ceased to trade taking the later years first.

Activity

Using the information in the previous activity relieve Helen's terminal loss and determine the revised assessments for the fiscal years 1997/98 to 2000/01.

Feedback

	1997/98 £	1998/99 £	1999/00 £	2000/01 £
Sch D Case I	15,000	12,000	6,000	1,000
s388 relief		(2,000)	(6,000)	(1,000)
Revised assessment	15,000	10,000	0	0

Summary

The main theme of the chapter has been the determination of the tax liabilities of sole traders by calculating the Schedule D Case I assessment less any capital allowances and losses. In order to do this you need to be able to undertake the following:

- identify trading by differentiating between hobbies, trading and capital transactions. You can also use the badges of trade to determine whether a single transaction is a trading activity
- determine which profits fall to be taxed in a fiscal year
- calculate any capital allowances which are available by using the legislation and case law to determine which allowance can be claimed and then calculate the relief which can be claimed
- determine the extent of any loss, identify which loss reliefs are available and explain the advantages and disadvantages of each of the reliefs.

Project areas

This chapter provides a rich source of material for projects including the:

- effectiveness of capital allowances
- impact of taxation on reported profit.

A successful project will be stated in terms of a question to be answered or a hypothesis to be tested. The areas identified above yield the following questions which would make interesting dissertation titles:

- Does increasing capital allowances lead to increased investment in plant and machinery?
- Do businesses reclassify expenditure in order to minimise the tax they pay?

Discussion questions

Question 1. Roger has a large garage and has always enjoyed tinkering with cars. In recent years he has found that he has actually made a small amount of money by buying cars, doing them up and after using them for a while selling them for more than he paid for them.

How would you decide whether Roger has a hobby or is trading?

What additional information would you require before you could make a decision?

Question 2. What tax advice would you give to two brothers planning to start a business selling and installing computer systems to dentists?

Computational questions

Although the first question relates to a company rather than a sole trader or partnership you will be able to answer it using the information contained in this chapter because the rules governing the taxation of trading profits of companies are similar to the rules which apply to individuals and partnerships. The biggest difference between the taxation of companies and the taxation of unincorporated businesses is that companies are taxed on the profits which arise in an accounting period rather than using the fiscal years which are used for Schedule D Case I taxpayers.

Question 1 (based on CIMA May 1992).

The following events occurred and were reflected in the profit and loss account of Q plc for its year ended 31st March 1998.

Debits

(a) Expenditure of £8,500 was incurred on the reconstruction of a roof on a secondhand warehouse which was recently purchased. This had been damaged in a fire some months before Q plc acquired it.

(b) During the year the sales director was convicted of an embezzlement and the amount of the loss, as established in court, was £18,000.

(c) Due to a contraction of the trade, a works manager was made redundant. His statutory redundancy entitlement was £12,000 and the total gratuitous lump sum paid to him (including the £12,000) was £38,000.

(d) For the whole of the year, one of the senior managers was seconded to work full-time for a national charity. Her annual salary, included in the salaries charged in the profit and loss account, was £24,000. Also included in the salaries figure was the salary of a manager, amounting to £18,000, who was, throughout the above period, wholly engaged in working for a subsidiary of Q plc.

(e) Costs of £24,000 were incurred in constructing a creche to be used for employees' children. Administration costs include £8,000 in respect of the running costs of the creche incurred during the year.

Credits

(f) £24,000 was received from an insurance company in respect of damage caused to processing plant as a result of a fork-lift truck colliding with it. The cost of repairing the plant was £18,000 and this was credited against the repairs account. The additional £6,000 was an agreed sum paid for loss of profits while the plant was unusable and this was credited to the profit and loss account.

(g) A gain of £30,000 arose on the sale of investments. No details of the original cost of disposal price are given at this stage.

(h) Q plc has included in its sales figure for the year, sales amounting to £50,000 to X Ltd, a company in which a director of Q plc has an interest. These sales have been heavily discounted and, if they had been made at the normal retail price, would have been sold for £80,000.

Required

Indicate, giving full reasons and quoting case law where appropriate, how each of the above items would be dealt with in arriving at the adjusted Schedule D Case I profit figure for the year.

You must state in your answer whether each item would be added to or subtracted from the profit shown by the profit and loss account (which is not given) or left unadjusted.

Question 2 (based on ACCA Paper 7 June 1994, part b only).

Bill, who starts to trade on 1st April 1996 and makes up accounts to 31st March, erects a poultry house on 31st December 1998 at a cost of £30,000.

On 31st December 2000 he sells the poultry house and the land on which it stands to Ben, whose accounting date is 30th June and who started to trade on 1st July 1996. The poultry house is sold for £20,000.

Required

Show the allowances which Bill and Ben can claim for all relevant years:

(i) assuming Bill and Ben make an election on the sale; and

(ii) assuming no election is made.   (5 marks)

Question 3 (based on ACCA Paper 7 December 1994, part a only).

Joseph Kent commenced in business on 1st October 1995 as a joiner making conservatories. His tax-adjusted profits before capital allowances were as follows:

	£
Period to 31.12.96	35,000
Year ended 31.12.97	24,000
Year ended 31.12.98	42,000

Capital additions and disposals were as follows:

Additions	£
1.10.95 car(1) (at valuation)	12,200
1.10.95 trailer	2,000
1.10.95 plant and machinery	8,000
1.12.97 car(2)	13,000

Disposals	£
1.12.97 car(1)	7,000
1.1.97 plant and machinery (at less than cost)	2,000

Private use of cars (1) and (2) has been agreed with the Revenue at 20%. No claim is made to treat any of the assets as short-life assets.

Joseph manufactured the conservatories in rented premises until 1st January 1998 when he purchased a new factory unit for £20,000 on an industrial estate (not an enterprise zone). All assets were brought into use immediately on acquisition.

Required
Calculate the taxable profits for the years 1995/96 to 1998/99 inclusive, and the overlap profits carried forward. (18 marks)

Question 4 (based on ACCA Paper 7 December 1994).

Jacqueline retired from her do-it-yourself shop on 28th February 1998 after a 20-year trading period. Overlap profits on commencement were £2,000.

Her adjusted profits/loss had been agreed with the Inland Revenue as follows:

	£
Year ended 31.3.95	6,000 profit
Year ended 31.3.96	13,000 profit
Year ended 31.3.97	8,000 profit
Period to 28.2.98	14,500 loss

Jacqueline has investment income of £6,000 for 1997/98 only. You should assume that the current basis period rules have applied throughout the life of the business.

Required
   (a) Show the final taxable profits for 1994/95, 1995/96, 1996/97 and 1997/98 after claiming terminal loss relief. (7 marks)
   (b) Identify an alternative loss relief claim, and state whether it would be better than terminal loss relief. (4 marks)

Income from other sources

Introduction

In Chapters 1 and 4 you read about the Schedular system which has been used to tax income for nearly 200 years. You learnt that to calculate the tax liability from the receipt of income it is necessary to identify the Schedule and Case under which the receipt is taxed. In Chapter 5 you studied Schedule D Cases I and II, which are used to tax income from trades, vocations and professions.

In this chapter you will learn about the detail of most of the remaining Schedules and Cases. Only then will you be able to prepare an individual's tax computation. We will not consider Schedule D Cases III, IV and V in any more detail than is given in Chapter 4.

At the end of this chapter you will be able to:

- calculate an individual's taxable income under Schedule A
- state the tax treatment of income which is taxed under Schedule D Case VI and calculate an individual's taxable income under Schedule D Case VI
- state the tax treatment of emoluments from an office or employment, including benefits in kind, and calculate an individual's taxable income under Schedule E
- state the legislation which relates to pension contributions
- determine the maximum pension contribution which may be made by an individual in a fiscal year
- prepare a tax computation for an individual.

We will use the framework of the schedular system to provide a structure for this chapter starting with Schedule A.

Schedule A

All income from property in the UK is taxed under Schedule A. Taxable income from property is calculated in the same way as trading profits are computed under Schedule D Case I.

The basis of assessment will be the income for the fiscal year. Income will be computed using the accruals basis. However, for very small simple businesses, for example income from one property, it is likely that the cash basis will be acceptable. The accounts will include the total income from property in the UK regardless of the source less total allowable expenses. Allowable expenses include:

- expenses incurred wholly and exclusively for the purpose of trade
- capital allowances for plant and machinery which enable taxpayers to carry on their business
- an allowance equal to 10% of the relevant receipts from furnished lettings to give relief for the wear and tear of furniture and equipment provided. Relevant receipts are gross receipts less any sums for services which would normally be borne by the tenant (Statement of Practice A19). Payment of the council tax by the landlord would be an example of such a payment. Alternatively a taxpayer may elect to use the renewals basis. The renewals basis entitles the taxpayer to deduct the cost of replacing furniture. Note however that the initial costs of acquiring furniture are not allowable expenses
- interest paid.

Income assessed under Schedule A is to be treated as investment income for tax purposes. This means that, among other things, no national insurance liability will arise on Schedule A income.

Loss relief

In general losses arising under Schedule A are carried forward and set against the first available Schedule A profits (ICTA 1988 s379A(1)). Some losses attributable to capital allowances or agricultural expenses may be set against the taxpayer's total income in the fiscal year in which the loss arose and/or the following fiscal year. If the loss is claimed for both years it is deemed to be claimed for the earlier year first (ICTA 1988 s379A). The maximum relief available with respect to capital allowances is equal to the lower of the excess of capital allowances over balancing charges and the Schedule A loss for the fiscal year. The maximum relief available with respect to agricultural expenses is equal to the lower of all expenses related to land used for animal husbandry excluding loan interest and the Schedule A loss for the fiscal year (ICTA 1988 s379A(4)).

When the loss is claimed under section 379A(3) the taxpayer cannot elect to restrict the losses claimed even if this means that some personal allowances are lost. Any loss still unrelieved after a section 379A(3) claim can be carried forward and set against future Schedule A profits.

Furnished holiday lettings

Holiday lettings are assessed under Schedule A. However, the regulations which apply to Schedule D Case I are used to determine the taxable income. Capital allowances can be claimed, relief for the disposal of business assets is available and loss relief can be claimed under the regulations which apply to losses incurred by traders. Because the profits are treated as earned income the taxpayer can provide for retirement by making contributions to a pension fund. Relief from capital gains tax including rollover relief, retirement relief, relief for gifts of business assets and relief for loans to traders are also available. Note that the basis period rules for Schedule A apply to income from furnished holiday lettings.

To be eligible for this advantageous treatment the accommodation must be let commercially with a view to realising profit. The property must be available for letting to the public for at least 140 days in the fiscal year and must have actually been let for 70 of the 140 days. For at least seven months of the fiscal year, including the 70 days, the property must not normally be occupied by the same tenant for more than 31 days.

The 'rent a room' scheme

If an individual lets one or more furnished rooms in his or her main residence rents received up to a limit of £4,250 in 1997/98 are exempt from tax under Schedule A. If another individual is also receiving rent from letting accommodation in the same property the limit of £4,250 will be halved. If the gross rents exceed the limit the total amount received will be taxable unless the taxpayer has elected to be taxed on the alternative basis when the gross receipts less £4,250 or £2,125 if the limit is halved, without any deductions for either expenses or capital allowances will be taxed.

Premiums on leases

When a lease is granted the lessee often has to pay a premium to the lessor. In fact sometimes the lessor receives very little rent for the duration of the lease but has to depend on the lease premium for income from the property.

Tax is paid on the value of the premium less 2% of the premium for each complete year of the lease after the first year.

Written as a formula then tax due equals

$$P - (P \times (L - 1) \times 2\%)$$

where P is the premium on the lease and L is the length of the lease.

Activity

Amanda granted a 21-year lease on a property on 1st January 1997 for an initial premium of £30,000 and an annual rent of £6,000 payable monthly in advance. Determine Amanda's Schedule A assessment for 1996/97 and 1997/98.

Feedback

In 1996/97 the assessment on the premium of the lease is £18,000 (£30,000 − (2% × (21 − 1) × £30,000)). The rent due in 1997/98 is £2,000 (£6,000 × 4/12). Hence the total Schedule A assessment for 1996/97 is £20,000 (£18,000 + £2,000).

In 1997/98 the Schedule A assessment will be £6,000.

The lessor can deduct the annual equivalent of the amount on which the landlord is liable to pay tax in each year of the lease. In the activity above Amanda's tenant would be able to claim a deduction of £18,000/21 = £857 in each year of the life of the lease.

Schedule D Case VI

Schedule D Case VI is used to tax annual profits or gains not falling under any other Case of Schedule D and not charged by virtue of Schedule A, C or E (ICTA 1988 s18(3)). The main types of income which are taxed under Schedule D Case VI are:

- income from the sale of patent rights
- commissions earned on a casual basis
- the sale of future earnings.

Emoluments from an office or employment

The rest of this chapter will be taken up with the legislation which relates to employees. Since employees form a majority of the working population the regulations which apply to the taxation of employees is clearly very important. Emoluments, pensions and unemployment benefit are taxed under Schedule E. Emoluments are defined as all salaries, fees, wages, perquisites and profits whatsoever. In general income is taxed in the year of receipt. In recent years the Inland Revenue has extended the range of occupations which are taxed under Schedule E. For example, many individuals who work in television are no longer deemed to be self-employed but are now considered to be employees. While you are reading this chapter and undertaking the activities you might like to identify the reasons for the Revenue's tactics.

Basis of assessment

Pensions and unemployment benefit are taxed on the accruals basis and benefits in kind are taxed when they are provided. However, in general emoluments are taxed on the receipts basis, that is, they are taxed in the fiscal year in which the date of the receipt falls.

For all employees, other than directors, the date of receipt is deemed to be the earlier of the date on which payment is made and the date on which there is an entitlement to payment. This legislation is intended to prevent employees from transferring emoluments, such as bonuses, to a fiscal year in which their marginal rate of tax is lower.

Activity

When might a taxpayer's marginal rate of tax be likely to fall?

Feedback

There are two reasons for a fall in a taxpayer's marginal rate of tax. Firstly, he or she might suffer a drop of income, or an increase in allowable deductions, which reduces his or her highest rate of tax. This might occur if a taxpayer plans to retire and so transfers a bonus from the final fiscal year which was worked to the next fiscal year in which was retirement.

Secondly, there might be, as there has been since 1979, a trend towards lower tax rates so that the tax payable falls from one year to the next even though income remains constant.

There are additional restrictions on the date of a receipt if the employee is a director who is likely to be in a position to influence the treatment of an emolument. Directors' earnings are taxed in the fiscal year which contains the earliest of the following dates:

- the date of receipt as determined by the above legislation
- the date when the emolument is charged in the company's accounting records
- the end of the company's period of account in which the amount arose provided that it had been determined by then
- the date on which the amount is determined if it is after the end of the company's period of account.

Allowable expenses

As we saw in Chapter 4 the basic rule is that only expenses which are wholly, exclusively and necessarily incurred in the performance of their duties will be allowable deductions from an employee's Schedule E income. In practice it is difficult to claim expenses as a deduction from Schedule E emoluments. However, trade unions and associations sometimes negotiate special allowances, particularly for safety equipment.

As you might expect there is a substantial amount of case law which is used to identify expenditure which is an allowable deduction for the purposes of Schedule E.

In *Brown* v *Bullock* (1961) the employee, a bank manager, was required by his employers to join a London club. His subscription was held not to be an allowable deduction because it was not necessary for the performance of his duties.

In *Lupton* v *Potts* (1969) a solicitor's articled clerk was not able to claim the costs of his examination fees because the expenditure was held not to be incurred wholly and exclusively in the performance of his duties.

Some expenditure is specifically allowed as a deduction from Schedule E emoluments. This includes:

- contributions to an approved occupational pension scheme
- premiums paid to approved personal pension plans
- subscriptions to professional bodies listed by the Inland Revenue, provided it is relevant to the duties of the employment.

In addition travelling expenses incurred necessarily in the performance of the duties of the employment and capital allowances on plant and machinery necessarily provided for use in the performance of those duties are allowable deductions. Note then that the expenditure need not be wholly and exclusively for the performance of an employee's duties. However, to be allowable such expenditure must be incurred in the performance of the duties. Expenditure which is incurred in order to put an employee in a position which enables him to perform his duties, for example travel expenses from home to work, are not allowable deductions. Recently the House of Lords disallowed the cost of newspapers bought by journalists arguing that buying and reading the newspapers was preparation for work rather than part of the performance of their duties.

In *Pook* v *Owen* (1970) a doctor was telephoned at home by the hospital where he worked as a part-time consultant. He sometimes gave instructions to staff at the hospital before travelling to work. It was held that he was travelling between sites since his work started when he answered the phone at home and so his travelling costs between his home and the hospital were allowable expenses. However, a taxpayer will not be able to claim travelling expenses from his home to work because he chooses to undertake some of his duties at home.

The Inland Revenue published a consultative paper in early 1996 on potential changes to the current Schedule E rules on employees' travel and subsistence expenses. The proposals dealt with 'site-based' employees and employees travelling to a temporary place of work. A 'site-based' employee is one who has no fixed place of work but who is required to perform duties at several sites by their employer. From 6th April 1998 the Inland Revenue intends to allow such 'site-based' employees to set the costs of travelling to and from the sites against their Schedule E income and to obtain relief for subsistence expenses when staying at a site. It also proposes to clarify the basis on which relief is given for travel and subsistence expenses to employees working at a temporary place of work. In addition the paper contained proposals to simplify the Schedule E legislation and reduce the employer's compliance and administration expenses.

Benefits in kind assessable on all employees

In addition to receiving a wage or salary many employees receive other benefits because of their employment. These benefits may include subsidised lunches, non-contributory pensions, private health care and company cars.

The tax treatment of some benefits in kind is dependent on the status of the taxpayer while the tax treatment of other benefits in kind is independent of the status of the taxpayer. We will start with the general rule for benefits in kind and consider those benefits which are assessable in the same way on all employees. Then we will turn our attention to the tax treatment of benefits given to higher paid employees and directors.

By concession, some benefits received by employees by reason of their employment are not assessed to tax under Schedule E. For example, the free coal received by miners is not chargeable to tax (Extra-statutory Concession A6).

Apart from items which are specifically dealt with in the legislation the general rule is that all employees are assessed on the cash equivalent of the benefit. The cash equivalent is taken to be the amount that the benefit could be sold for. This rule tends to operate in favour of the employee because benefits in kind may have either no resale value, for example a season ticket for rail travel or a company car, or a low resale value, such as the secondhand value of a suit.

However, there are some special rules which relate to specific benefits in kind. All employees are assessed on the provision of living accommodation and vouchers.

Employees who receive cash vouchers, credit tokens or exchangeable vouchers will be assessable on the cost to the employer of providing the benefit. However, luncheon vouchers with a value of up to 15p per day are not subject to tax in the hands of the employee.

If an employee is provided with accommodation by an employer, which is not job related, the employee will be assessed to tax on the annual value of the property less any contributions made. The annual value is taken to be the rateable value, if available, or a value estimated by the Inland Revenue if the property does not have a rateable value (Press Release 19.4.90). However, if the property is rented by the employer the employee will be assessed on the higher of the annual value and the actual rent paid.

If the accommodation either cost over £75,000 or, if acquired more than six years before it was first provided to the employee, its market value on the date it was first provided to the employee was over £75,000, a further assessment is made on the employee. The additional benefit is equal to the excess of the cost of providing the accommodation over £75,000 multiplied by the official rate. The official rate is the interest rate given by the Treasury. The cost of providing the accommodation includes the costs of any improvements undertaken before the start of the tax year as well as the purchase price of the property.

As an extra-statutory concession if the same accommodation is provided to several employees or directors during a fiscal year the maximum total assessable benefit relating to that accommodation will be limited to the assessable benefit that would have arisen if only one employee had been provided with the accommodation. The extra-statutory concession also waives the further assessment on accommodation which cost over £75,000 where the basic accommodation charge is based on the open market rental value.

If the accommodation provided is job related then no assessment to tax under Schedule E arises on employees other than directors, who may still incur a tax liability. Accommodation is job related if either:

- the employee is required to live in the accommodation for the proper performance of his or her duties; or

- the employment is of the kind where it is customary to provide accommodation or the accommodation is provided to enable the better performance of the employee's duties; or
- the accommodation is provided for reasons of security.

If living accommodation is provided by reason of a person's employment then alterations and additions to the accommodation which are of a structural nature, or repairs, which would be required if the property were leased under the Landlord and Tenant Act 1985, are not assessable benefits under ICTA 1988 s154 (ICTA 1988 s155(3)).

All employees are also assessed on the amount of any loan which is written off by reason of their employment.

Some benefits in kind are specifically excluded from assessment to tax in the hands of all employees. In-house sports facilities for employees are not liable to tax.

Employees are not assessed on the benefit of any entertainment which is provided by third parties provided that the following conditions are fulfilled:

- the entertainment was not provided, or procured, by the employer or persons connected to the employer, and
- the entertainment was not provided in recognition of services which have been or are to be performed (ICTA 1988 s155(7)).

A list of connected persons can be found in Chapter 7.

Employees, by way of an extra-statutory concession, are not assessable on long service awards provided that they have worked for the organisation for at least 20 years, have not received a similar award within the past ten years and the cost to the employer of the award is no more than £20 per year of service. Rewards for suggestions are taxable but again there is an extra-statutory concession that exempts awards provided there is a formal suggestions scheme which is open to all employees and all of the following conditions are met:

- the suggestion relates to activities which are outside the scope of the employee's normal duties
- if the award is more than £25 it is only made after a decision has been taken to implement the suggestion
- awards over £25 either do not exceed 50% of the expected net financial gain during the first year after implementation or do not exceed 10% of the expected net financial gain during the first five years after implementation
- awards over £25 are shared equitably between any employees making the suggestion.

If the award exceeds £5,000 the excess is always taxable.

The costs of relocation if an employee has to move for work reasons up to a maximum of £8,000 are not taxed as a benefit in kind. If expenses of more than £8,000 are paid the employee will be assessed on the excess over £8,000 as a benefit in kind. Note that it is not necessary for a taxpayer to sell his house in order to qualify for the relief to be paid free of taxation.

A nursery place at a workplace nursery is not a taxable benefit. All other forms of childcare provision, including cash or vouchers, provided by the employer are taxable.

Benefits in kind assessable on higher paid employees and directors

In the first part of this section you will learn how to identify employees who are affected by the legislation which is applied to higher paid employees and directors. The rest of the section will deal with the detail of the legislation.

A higher paid employee is one whose emoluments are £8,500 a year or more. Emoluments include not only salaries, commissions and fees but also reimbursed expenses and benefits in kind, valued as if the taxpayer were a higher paid employee, other than the benefit of receiving a loan to purchase a home which would qualify for tax relief at the lower rate.

A director is any person who either acts as a director or on whose instructions the directors are accustomed to act, other than a professional advisor.

If a director owns 5% or less of the company's share capital and is either a full-time working director or the company is either non-profit-making or is established for charitable purposes he or she is not subject to these rules unless he or she is also a higher paid employee.

The general rule on benefits in kind is that if an employee or members of the employee's family or household, by reason of employment, receive any benefits, they are to be treated as emoluments of the employment and are chargeable to income tax under Schedule E at an amount which is equal to the cash equivalent of the benefit (ICTA 1988 s154(1)). The cash equivalent of any benefit chargeable to tax under section 154 is an amount equal to the cost of the benefit, less so much of it as is made good by the employee to those providing the benefit (ICTA 1988 s156(1)). In *Pepper* v *Hart* (1992) the House of Lords decreed that cost meant the marginal cost to the provider rather than the average cost. This will often have the effect of substantially lowering the value of the benefit to be taxed. Of course if it is not possible to directly attribute any costs to the provision of the benefit to the taxpayer then there will be no assessable benefit. Notice that for a benefit in kind to be taxable it is not necessary for the employer to provide it, it is simply necessary that the benefit is provided to the taxpayer or family by reason of the taxpayer's employment.

If an asset is provided for the use of a higher paid employee or a director then the assessable benefit is the annual value which is the greater of 20% of the market value of the asset when first provided as a benefit to an employee, and the rent paid by the employer if the asset was rented. If ownership of the asset is subsequently transferred to the employee the assessable benefit is the greater of the excess of the current market value of the asset over the price paid by the employee and the excess of the market value of the asset when it was first provided to the employee over the total of the annual benefits assessed on the employee for that asset.

There are a number of exceptions to these general rules. A taxpayer is not assessable on the benefit of a car parking space at or near his or her place of work (ICTA 1988 s155(1A)). Pensions, annuities, lump sums or gratuities provided by an employer, when an employee dies or retires, for the employee, his or her spouse, children or dependants are not subject to ICTA 1988 s154 (ICTA 1988 s155(4)).

Meals which are provided in the employer's canteen for the staff generally are not an assessable benefit (ICTA 1988 s155(5)).

If the employee is provided with medical treatment outside the UK when the need for the treatment arises while the employee is outside the UK for the purpose of performing duties of employment there is no assessable benefit under ICTA 1988 s154 (ICTA 1988 s155(6)). Similarly no assessable benefit arises if the employer provides insurance for the employee against the cost of such treatment (ICTA 1988 s155(6)).

One of the most important benefits in kind, in terms of the number of employees receiving it, is the company car. All higher paid employees and directors are assessed on a benefit if they are provided with a company car. Company cars became widespread during the 1970s for a number of reasons. The most important was the wages legislation in force at the time which attempted to limit increases in wages. Providing cars to some employees was a way of rewarding employees despite the legislation. It then became apparent that providing company cars to employees was extremely tax efficient. The employer could deduct the full cost of providing the car and the employee suffered relatively little tax on the benefit. Finally the provision of a company car did not lead to an increase in the national insurance contributions of either employees or employers. During the 1980s Nigel Lawson turned his attention to the taxation of company cars and over a number of years the tax on the benefit has increased very substantially. While there may still be some tax advantages which encourage the use of company cars the benefits are lower than in the past. Employers are required to pay national insurance contributions on company cars but employees are still not required to pay national insurance contributions on the benefit. Look at the table at the back of the book to find the tables which give the assessable benefit of company cars which is called the scale charge. From 1994/95 all cars are assessed on their list price. This may have the effect of stopping car manufacturers from quoting a high list price and then offering discounts.

If the employee or director makes a contribution for any private use of the car the amount of the contribution is deducted from the scale charge. If the business travel is more than 2,500 miles per year the scale charge is reduced by a third. If the business travel is more than 18,000 miles per year the scale charge is reduced by two-thirds. Both of these limits are proportionately reduced if the car is available for only part of the year, but only continuous periods of at least 30 days are taken into account for tax purposes.

No tax liability arises on a pool car provided that the following conditions are met:

- the car was made available to, and actually used by, more than one employee and, in the case of each of them, it was made available to him by reason of his employment, but it was not ordinarily used by one of them to the exclusion of the others
- in the case of each employee any private use was merely incidental to the business use
- the car was not normally kept overnight on or in the vicinity of any residential premises where any of the employees was residing (ICTA 1988 s159(2)).

In addition to the scale charge for the benefit of the car if the employee receives the benefit of fuel for his private use he or she is assessed on the benefit of the fuel. A table is used to determine the amount of the taxable benefit when an employee is provided with private fuel. Look at the back of the book for the fuel charges for 1997/98. If the employee makes a contribution to the cost of the fuel which he has used, but does not reimburse the entire cost, the assessable benefit is not reduced. Hence, if the employee is going to make a contribution it is more tax efficient if he or she contributes to the cost of the car rather than to the cost of the fuel.

If an employee is provided with a mobile telephone and it is available for his, or his family's, private use then the cash equivalent of the phone is an assessable benefit (ICTA 1988 s159A(1)). The cash equivalent of the benefit is £200 for each mobile telephone made available in the year (ICTA 1988 s159A(2)). However, if for any year there is no private use of the mobile telephone or the employee is required to, and does, make good the full cost of any private use of the mobile telephone then the cash equivalent of the benefit for that year is nil (ICTA 1988 s159A(3)). If the phone is unavailable for any part of a year the cash equivalent of the benefit for that year shall be reduced proportionately (ICTA 1988 s159(4)).

A director can only claim to be living in job-related accommodation if as well as meeting the conditions given above he or she has an interest in less than 5% of the company and he or she is either a full-time working director or the company is non-profit-making or is a charity unless the accommodation is provided as part of special security arrangements.

Higher paid employees who are provided with living accommodation are assessed on the benefit of the accommodation, as described above. They are also taxed on any other expenses which are paid by the employer which relate to the accommodation, for example the cost of heating and lighting, repairs and 20% a year of the cost of any furniture provided. If the accommodation is job related the maximum assessment of ancillary services is 10% of the employee's net emoluments. Net emoluments is the Schedule E assessment after any allowable expenses and pension contributions but excluding the cost of any ancillary services. If the accommodation is not job related the taxpayer will be assessed on the full cost to the employer of providing any ancillary services.

Activity

Alexandra has a house in Yeovil and normally lives there but she has been transferred to London for two years to establish a new branch of the company she works for. Her gross salary in 1997/98 is £30,000. She has been provided with a flat in Mayfair which has an annual value of £1,000. In 1997/98 the company paid £5,000 in ancillary services. Alexandra made a contribution of £1,000 to these services. She also pays £3,000 a year into a pension fund.
Determine Alexandra's Schedule E assessment for 1997/98.

Feedback

Schedule E assessment: Alexandra

	£	£
Salary		30,000
Less pension contributions		3,000
		27,000
Accommodation benefits		
Annual value (exempt)		
Ancillary services	5,000	
Restricted to 10% of £27,000	2,700	
Less employee's contribution	1,000	1,700
Schedule E assessment		28,700

If a higher paid employee or director, or a member of her family, had a loan which was obtained by reason of her employment and either no interest was paid on the loan for the year or the amount of interest paid on the loan in the year is less than interest at the official rate she will be assessed, at her marginal rate of tax, on the cash equivalent of the benefit of the loan. The cash equivalent is equal to the difference between the interest paid, if any, and the interest calculated at the official rate (ICTA 1988 s160(1)). However, if the total amount of any loans do not exceed £5,000 no tax liability will arise.

The amount of the loan is normally taken to be the average of the balance at the beginning of the year and the balance at the end of the year if the loan had been in existence throughout the year. Otherwise the balance on the dates on which the loan was taken out and/or repaid are used instead and only complete tax months in which the loan existed are taken into account. A tax month runs from the 6th of the month to the 5th of the following month. However, the taxpayer can make an election for interest at the official rate on the outstanding balance to be calculated on a daily basis, which is obviously more accurate. If an employer makes loans to employees on the same terms and conditions as are available to the public and a substantial number of such loans are made to the public no liability to tax will arise.

Activity

List the main differences between the taxation of a Schedule D Case I taxpayer and a Schedule E taxpayer. Who do you think enjoys the more advantageous treatment?

Feedback

You might have written your answer using different headings but you should have noted most of the following points.

Basis of assessment
Employees are taxed on the basis of the income received in the current year while self-employed taxpayers are taxed on the taxable profits for the accounting period

which ended in the fiscal year. This provides a small advantage for taxpayers with accounting dates which are early in the fiscal year, the end of April for instance, particularly in times of inflation or growth because of the relatively long delay between earning the profits and paying tax on them.

Allowable deductions
The self-employed can claim relief for expenses which are incurred wholly and exclusively for the purpose of trade while the employed can only gain relief for expenses which are wholly, exclusively and necessarily incurred in the performance of their duties. It is likely therefore that the self-employed will be able to claim a far larger total deduction from income than employees. For example, if an academic purchases a computer to enable him to produce teaching materials at home no deductions for the costs of the computer will be allowable. However, a freelance lecturer who takes the same action will be able to claim a capital allowance for the cost of the computer.

National insurance
The self-employed must pay both Class 2 and Class 4 national insurance contributions and yet receive few benefits in return for their contributions. Employees also pay national insurance contributions but in return become entitled to sickness benefit, maternity benefit and unemployment benefit.

Administration
Most self-employed individuals use the services of an accountant and certainly find themselves spending some time maintaining records which are required by the tax authorities. Employees usually incur few expenses when dealing with tax matters. This difference is likely to remain despite the introduction of self-assessment.

The taxation of investments available to employees

If employees are given, or sold, the right to buy shares at a price which is lower than the quoted share price a taxable benefit arises. The employee is taxed on the difference between the market price of the shares and the aggregate of the cost, if any, of acquiring the rights and the cost of buying the shares.

If there is a change in the rights or restrictions on some of the company's shares, called a chargeable event, which causes the value of the employee's shares to rise the increase will be assessable under Schedule E. Ex-employees will also be liable to tax under Schedule E if a chargeable event occurs within seven years of their employment with the company ending. If there is a change in the rights or restrictions which affects all of the shares of the same class it is not treated as a chargeable event and no tax liability arises.

However, there are a number of special schemes which, if approved by the Inland Revenue, offer tax breaks to employees who obtain shares in the company or participate in the profits of the company.

We will start by identifying the general conditions which must be satisfied in order for an employee to subscribe to shares in the company which employs them and then consider each of the following schemes:

- approved share option schemes
- profit-sharing schemes
- employee share-ownership plans.

Approved share option schemes

Where there is a genuine offer to the public of shares in a company at a fixed price or by tender and a director or employee is entitled, by reason of his or her office or employment, to an allocation of the shares, in priority to members of the public and the following conditions are satisfied:

- the total number of shares offered to employees and directors of the company is not more than 10% of the shares subject to the offer
- all persons entitled to such an allocation are entitled to it on similar terms
- persons entitled are not restricted wholly or mainly to persons who are directors or whose remuneration exceeds a particular level
- the directors and employees must pay at least the fixed price or the lowest price successfully tendered or the notional price for the shares.

Any benefit derived by the director or employee from his entitlement shall not be treated as an emolument of his office or employment (FA 1988 s68(1), (1A), (2) & (2A)).

If employees are given, or sold, an option to acquire shares there is a liability to tax under Schedule E when the option is exercised. Tax is levied on the difference between the market value of the shares on the date on which the option was exercised and the amount paid for the option together with the amount paid for the shares.

However, if the shares are acquired through an approved share option scheme and the option is exercised between three and ten years after the granting of the option there is no income tax liability when either the option is granted or the option is exercised (ICTA 1988 s185).

When the shares acquired through an approved share option scheme are disposed of any capital gain will be subject to capital gains tax in the normal way. You will learn how to calculate the capital gains tax liability when a taxpayer disposes of shares in Chapter 7.

If the market value of the shares when the option was received exceeds the amount paid to obtain the right together with the price at which the shares are acquired by exercising the right there may be a charge to income tax under Schedule E (ICTA 1988 s185(6)).

In order for a scheme to be approved a number of conditions must be satisfied. Some of the most important conditions are:

- The shares must be fully paid up, irredeemable and not subject to any restrictions which do not apply to all of the shares of the same class (ICTA 1988 Sch 9 s12(1)).
- Only full-time directors and employees who work for the company for at least 20 hours a week may join the scheme. However, a person may exercise rights under the scheme after he has ceased to work for the grantor (ICTA

1988 Sch 9 s27(1) & (4)). The scheme does not have to be open to all employees.

- At any time the maximum value of shares which any individual can hold the rights to under share option schemes set up by the same company cannot exceed the greatest of the following:
  - £100,000
  - four times the amount assessed under PAYE during the current year
  - four times the amount assessed under PAYE during the preceding year
  - four times the amount assessed under PAYE during the period of 12 months beginning with the first day during the current year of assessment in which an assessment under PAYE arises provided there was no assessment under PAYE during the preceding year (ICTA 1988 Sch 9 s28(2)).

  The value of the shares is taken to be the market value of the shares on the date on which the rights were obtained (ICTA 1988 Sch 9 s28(3)).
- The exercise price of the option must not be significantly less than the market value of shares at the date that the option was granted (ICTA 1988 Sch 9 s29(1).

Profit-sharing schemes

A profit-sharing scheme will be approved by the Board if it is administered by trustees and the Board is satisfied that every participant in the scheme is bound in contract with the grantor:

- to permit his shares to remain in the hands of the trustees throughout the period of retention, and
- not to assign, charge or otherwise dispose of his beneficial interest in his shares during that period, and
- if he directs the trustees to transfer the ownership of his shares to him at any time before the release date, to pay to the trustees before the transfer takes place a sum equal to income tax at the basic rate on the appropriate percentage of the locked-in value of the shares at the time of the direction, and
- not to direct the trustees to dispose of his shares at any time before the release date in any other way except by sale for the best consideration in money that can reasonably be obtained at the time of the sale or, in the case of redeemable shares in a workers' co-operative, by redemption (ICTA 1988 Sch 9 s2(2)).

The period of retention is the period beginning on the date on which they are appropriated to the participant and ending two years later or, if it is earlier:

- the date on which the participant ceases to be a director or employee of the company because of injury, disability or redundancy, or
- the date on which the participant reaches the age specified in the scheme, or
- the date of the participant's death, or

- in a case where the participant's shares are redeemable shares in a workers' co-operative, the date on which the participant ceases to be employed by either the co-operative or its subsidiary (ICTA 1988 Sch 10 s2).

Provided that the above conditions are fulfilled there will not be an income tax liability when the beneficial ownership of the shares passes to the participant (ICTA 1988 s186(1) & (2)).

However, the participant will be subject to tax on any dividends received in respect of the shares. In addition a charge to income tax under Schedule E will arise if the trustees become, or the participator becomes, entitled to receive a capital receipt in respect of the shares before the release date.

If the trustees dispose of any of a participant's shares at any time before the release date or, if it is earlier, the date of the participant's death, then the participant shall be chargeable to income tax under Schedule E for the year of assessment in which the disposal takes place (ICTA 1988 s186(4)).

For the purposes of capital gains tax a person who is a participant in relation to an approved profit-sharing scheme shall be treated as absolutely entitled to his shares as against the trustees of the scheme (TCGA 1992 s238(1)). Hence when the shares are transferred to the participator from the trustees no capital gains tax arises but if the shares are disposed of by the participant a capital gains tax will be levied on any chargeable gain. The allowable cost is the market value of the shares when they were transferred to the employee. There is no allowable deduction for any charge to income tax (TCGA 1992 s238(2)).

Employee share-ownership plans

Tax relief under Schedule D Case I is available if a UK resident company transfers funds to the trustees of a qualifying employee share-ownership trust for the benefit of some or all of its employees. In order to obtain tax relief the trustees must apply the sum for one or more qualifying purposes within nine months of the end of the period of account in which the funds were transferred (FA 1989 s67(1), (2) & (5)).

As well as payments to beneficiaries under the terms of the trust deed the acquisition of shares, repayments of loans and interest on loans and the meeting of expenses are all qualifying purposes (FA 1989 s67(4)).

When a chargeable event occurs the trustees will be taxed at a rate equal to the basic rate of tax plus an additional 10% under Schedule D Case VI on the chargeable amount (FA 1989 s68s(2)).

A chargeable event occurs whenever the trustees make a transfer of securities which is not a qualifying transfer. In addition a chargeable event occurs if trustees retain securities on the expiry date, which is seven years after they were acquired, or expend a sum for a purpose other than a qualifying purpose (FA 1989 s69(1)).

The FIFO basis, that is earlier acquisitions are deemed to be disposed of before later acquisitions, is used for matching purposes (FA 1989 s69(7)).

When the shares are transferred to employees a charge to income tax will arise on the difference between the market price of the shares and the consideration provided by the employee. However if the shares are transferred to an approved profit-sharing scheme the income tax liability can be avoided.

Pensions

A working individual can derive a pension from three sources: the state pension scheme, occupational pension schemes and personal pension schemes. The state pension scheme is funded from national insurance contributions. Contributions to the state pension scheme have no income tax consequences although state pensions, like occupational pensions and personal pensions, are taxable in the hands of the recipient. Both occupational pension schemes and personal pensions schemes have income tax implications and it is these we will study in this section.

Occupational pension schemes

Occupational pension schemes are available for employees who elect to join a pension scheme set up by their employers. An employee cannot be required to join a pension scheme by his employer.

An employer has considerable scope for flexibility in setting a scheme up but for contributions by employees to be deductible for income tax purposes a scheme must be Inland Revenue approved.

In order to obtain Inland Revenue approval a scheme must meet all of the following conditions:

- the scheme is intended to provide benefits to employees or their dependents
- the employer is a contributor to the scheme
- no repayment of an employee's contribution can be made under the scheme (ICTA 1988 s590(2)).

In addition the following conditions must be satisfied:

- any benefit for an employee is a pension on retirement at age between 60 and 75 which does not exceed one-sixtieth of the employee's final remuneration for each year of service up to a maximum of 40 years
- any benefit for an employee's widow or widower takes the form of a pension payable on the death of the employee after retirement which does not exceed two-thirds of any pension or pensions payable to the employee
- no other benefits are payable under this scheme
- a scheme may allow for an employee, on retirement, to obtain, by commutation of his pension, a lump sum not exceeding a total of three-eightieths of his final remuneration for each year of service up to a maximum of 40 years (ICTA s590(3)).

Note that the maximum lump sum which can be taken is one and a half times final remuneration as this is three-eightieths up to a maximum of 40 years for each year of service.

In practice the Inland Revenue may approve schemes which do not meet all of the conditions set out above. In particular some approved schemes offer:

- a pension of two-thirds of final salary after less than 40 years' service

- a pension for the widows of employees on death in service, or for the children or dependants of employees
- a lump sum of up to four times the employee's final remunerations plus a refund of contributions on the death in service of the employee
- benefits to be payable on retirement within ten years of the specified age, or on earlier incapacity
- benefits additional to those provided by a scheme to which the employer is a contributor (ICTA 1988 s591).

Clearly contributing to a pension fund is an extremely tax efficient way of saving for one's retirement. In the FA 1989 the Chancellor limited the tax advantages of saving via a pension fund. This was done by placing an upper limit on the earnings on which an approved pension scheme can be based. In the fiscal year 1997/98 the maximum earnings are £84,000 (Statutory Instrument 1992/624). This earning cap has the effect of restricting the maximum pension to £56,000 (2/3 × £84,000) and the maximum tax-free lump sum to £126,000 (1.5 × £84,000).

If a scheme is Inland Revenue approved:

- income from investments or deposits held for the purposes of the scheme are exempt from income tax (ICTA 1988 s592(2))
- sums paid by an employer by way of contribution under the scheme shall be allowable deductions from Schedule D Case I or II in the chargeable period in which the sum is paid (ICTA 1988 s592(4))
- a lump sum, not paid by way of ordinary annual contribution, paid by the employer may be deemed to be an allowable deduction in either the year in which it was paid or a number of years at the Board of Inland Revenue's discretion (ICTA 1988 s592(6)
- any contribution paid under the scheme by an employee shall, up to a maximum of 15% of either the gross emoluments or the earning cap, be deductible from his Schedule E income (ICTA 1988 ss 592(7) & 592(8))
- contributions by an employer are not regarded as benefits in kind in the hands of the employee.

An employee is free to make additional voluntary contributions to increase his or her retirement benefits provided that his total benefits do not exceed the limits set out above and that his total contributions do not exceed 15% of gross emoluments, limited to the earnings cap of £84,000 (ICTA 1988 s592(8A)). Additional voluntary contributions are paid net of basic rate tax. If an employee makes additional voluntary contributions no lump sum, in commutation of a pension, shall be allowed (ICTA 1988 Sch 23 s7(2)).

Personal pension schemes

Employees can use a personal pension scheme if either their employer does not operate a pension scheme or they choose not to join their employer's occupational pension scheme. They are also used by the self-employed. Like occupational pension funds the investments bought with the premiums are free of both income tax and capital gains tax. Pensions drawn are treated as earned income in the hands of the beneficiary. Personal pensions are taxed under Schedule E.

A personal pension scheme must only provide some or all of the following benefits (ICTA 1988 s633):

- An annuity which commences when the member of the scheme is aged between 50 and 75 years. However, if the member becomes incapable through infirmity of body or mind of carrying on his own occupation or any occupation of a similar nature for which he is trained or fitted the annuity may commence before the age of 50. The annuity may also commence before the age of 50 if the Board of the Inland Revenue are satisfied that the member's occupation is one in which persons customarily retire before that age (ICTA 1988 s634(3)). Any annuity paid must be payable for life and may continue to be paid for up to ten years after the member's death (ICTA 1988 s634(4) & (5)). The annuity must not be capable of assignment or surrender, except that an annuity for a term which is certain may be assigned by will or by the annuitant's personal representatives in the distribution of his estate (ICTA 1988 s634(6)). The maximum sum which can by used to provide a lump sum or an annuity for the taxpayer's dependants is 5% of net relevant earnings (ICTA 1988 s640(3)). We will define net relevant earnings later on in this section.
- A lump sum, provided that the member makes an election to receive a lump sum on or before the date on which an annuity, as described above, is first payable to him or her (ICTA 1988 s635(1)). The right to payment of the lump sum must not be capable of assignment or surrender (ICTA 1988 s635(5)).
- The payment, after the death of a member, of an annuity to the surviving spouse of the member or to the member's dependants at the time of his or her death (ICTA 1988 s636 (1) & (2)).
  The annuity must be payable for the life of the annuitant (ICTA 1988 s636(4)). If the annuity is payable to the surviving spouse of the member who is under the age of 60 at the time of the member's death the annuity may be deferred. If the annuity is deferred, the date to which it is deferred must not be later than:
  – the date on which the surviving spouse is aged 60, or
  – where the member's annuity is payable to the surviving spouse for a term of not more than ten years and the spouse reaches the age of 60 before the time when the member's annuity terminates, that time (ICTA 1988 s636(5)).
- The payment of a lump sum on the death of the member before he or she attains the age of 75 (ICTA 1988 s637(1)).

There are a number of other restrictions which must apply for a scheme to be approved:

- The permitted maximum for a year of assessment is the aggregate of the relevant percentage, which is generally 17.5%, of the member's net relevant earnings for the year and any unused relief from the six years of assessment preceding the current one (ICTA 1988 s638(4) & (5)). The maximum of 17.5% includes any amount used to provide a lump sum or annuity for the taxpayer's dependants.

Net relevant earnings equals the aggregate of earnings under Schedule D Cases I, II and income from furnished holiday lettings taxed under Case VI and Schedule E for the year less capital allowances, loss relief, Schedule E deductions and the excess of trade charges over other income (ICTA 1988 s623(6)). Like occupational pensions net relevant earnings are limited to a maximum of £84,000 for 1997/98 (ICTA 1988 s640A).

In the case of individuals whose age at the beginning of the year of assessment is over 35 the relevant percentage is as follows:

Age	Relevant percentage
36–45	20
46–50	25
51–55	30
56–60	35
61 and over	40 (ICTA 1988 s640(1))

Where personal pension arrangements are made by an employee whose employer makes contributions under the arrangements, the maximum amount that may be deducted or set off in any year of assessment shall be reduced by the amount of the employer's contributions in the year (ICTA 1988 s640(4)).

A contribution paid by an individual under approved personal pension arrangements made by him or her shall be deducted from or set off against any relevant earnings of his or her for the year of assessment in which the payment is made (ICTA 1988 s639(1)).

A Schedule E taxpayer may deduct an amount equal to income tax at the basic rate from the contribution when it is paid (ICTA 1988 s639(3)). The scheme administrator shall accept the amount paid after the deduction in discharge of the individual's liability to the same extent as if the deduction had not been made and may recover an amount equal to the deduction from the Board (ICTA 1988 s639(4)). Schedule D Case I and II taxpayers must make the contribution without deduction of tax.

An individual who pays a contribution to an approved personal pension scheme may elect for all or part of the contribution to be treated as paid in either:

- the fiscal year preceding the year it was paid in, or
- if the individual had no net relevant earnings in that preceding year of assessment, in the year of assessment before that (ICTA 1988 s641(1)).

Unused relief is the difference between the premiums paid to a personal pension scheme and the appropriate percentage of net relevant earnings. If an individual has unused relief in a year of assessment, the unused relief can be carried forward for six years in order to increase the maximum allowable premium. The relief for a year of assessment is used before any unused relief brought forward. Relief brought forward is used on a FIFO basis (ICTA 1988 s642(1)).

In the November 1994 budget the Chancellor proposed to allow members of approved personal pension schemes to defer purchasing an annuity up until the age of 75 while withdrawing amounts during the deferral period. The amounts withdrawn should be approximately the same as an annuity which the fund could have provided. This measure was proposed in order to help individuals who retire at a time when annuity rates are very low. The ability to make withdrawals from the accumulated fund will enable taxpayers to retire and receive an income from their pension fund while waiting for annuity rates to increase.

At the moment this facility will only be available to members of personal pension schemes. However, there is pressure on the government to extend the option to individuals paying into either retirement annuity schemes, the forerunner of personal pension schemes, or occupational pensions which use a money purchase formula rather than the final salary.

Summary

In this chapter we have focused on the taxation of income from land and buildings and income from employment. Since the majority of the workforce are employees it is an important area of study. Broadly every benefit received by reason of an employment is taxable but very few deductions are allowable. The tax treatment of individuals with gross emoluments of less than £8,500 a year is more generous than that of other employees. However, this limit has not increased for more than a decade and so more and more employees are subject to the more stringent tax regime which applies to those earning at least £8,500 a year without a commensurate increase in real incomes. There are some tax planning opportunities for employers and employees. These include the provision of benefits in kind and planning for retirement. There are also a number of special schemes such as approved share option schemes which are dealt with in Chapter 2.

Project areas

The taxation of rental income and income from employment provide a number of interesting areas to research. Probably the most straightforward is to undertake a comparison of the taxation of employment throughout the EU. An interesting area of research is the question of extending the existing tax relief for workplace nurseries to all kinds of child-care costs. However, the collection of data should be carefully thought out.

Discussion questions

Question 1. Income from employment, described as a contract of service, is taxed under Schedule E while income from self-employment, described as a contract for services, is taxed under Schedule D Case I. How might you decide whether an individual is employed or self-employed?

Question 2. What are the advantages of income from holiday lettings being considered to be trading income?

Computational questions

Question 1 (based on ACCA June 1991).

Arthur owned a furnished house in a holiday resort which was available for commercial letting when not occupied by Arthur and his family.

In the tax year 1997/98 it was let for the following periods, no letting to the same person exceeding 30 days.

Month	Days	
April	7	
May	14	
June	7	
July	31	
August	30	— occupied by Arthur
September	14	

Apart from the above periods and two weeks in April when it was being decorated the house was available for letting throughout the tax year. The total rent received was £1,900 and the following expenditure was incurred.

	£
Insurance	550
Repairs and decorating	616
Water rates	160
Accountancy	160
Cleaning	60
Advertising	480
Replacement furniture	140

The annual allowance of 10% of rent (less water rates) has been agreed for wear and tear of furniture.

Arthur has also purchased two shops in the resort:

Shop 1. The annual rent was £3,000 on a tenant's repairing lease which expired on 24th June 1997. Arthur took advantage of the shop being empty to carry out repairs and decorating. The shop was let to another tenant on a five-year tenant's repairing lease at £4,000 per annum from 29th September 1997.

Shop 2. The shop was purchased on 10th April 1997 and required treatment for dry rot. Arthur also undertook some normal redecorating work before the shop was let on 29th September 1997 on a seven-year tenant's repairing lease at an annual rent of £6,000. A premium of £2,000 was received from the incoming tenant upon signing the lease on 29th September 1997.

The rent for both shops was due in advance on the usual quarter days which are 25th March, 24th June, 29th September and 25th December.

The following expenditure was incurred:

	Shop 1 £	Shop 2 £
Insurance	190	300
Ground rent	10	40
Repairs and decorating	3,900*	5,000†
Accountancy	50	50
Advertising for tenant	100	100

Notes

*Includes £2,500 for re-roofing the shop following gale damage in February 1997. Because the roof had been badly maintained the insurance company refused to pay for the repair work.

†Includes £3,000 for dry rot remedial treatment. The dry rot was present when the shop was bought in April 1997.

Required

Calculate the income assessable on Arthur for 1997/98 from the house and both shops and show how any losses would be dealt with.

Question 2 (based on ACCA December 1990).

Maurice Thistlethwaite, aged 53, is a research chemist with Pulsating Paints Ltd. His wife Marjorie, aged 52, is a teacher with North Shires County Council. Details of their income and outgoings for the year ended 5th April 1998 are as follows.

(a) Gross salaries

Maurice   £24,407
Marjorie   £17,000

Maurice paid 5% of his salary to an approved pension scheme and Marjorie paid 6% of her salary to the teachers' pension scheme.

(b) Pulsating Paints Ltd paid a private health insurance benefit for Maurice of £275 and also provided him with a new 1,500cc petrol-engined car costing £14,500 on 6th November 1997. His total mileage from that date to 5th April 1998 was 8,000 miles of which 1,000 was on business. The company paid all running costs of the car, £1,200, including Maurice's private petrol.

(c) Maurice paid £100 to a professional body of which he was a member and Marjorie paid £60 to her teaching union. Marjorie also purchased an academic gown during the year at the request of her employer. This cost £75.

(d) Marjorie made free-standing additional voluntary contributions to a UK life assurance company of £900 (after relief for basic rate income tax). It had been agreed with the Inland Revenue that the contributions would be eligible for relief from both basic and higher rate tax.

(e) On 1st January 1996 Maurice began performing as a magician at local charities and social clubs. It had been agreed with the Inland Revenue to treat the income as trading income and adjusted profits have been agreed as follows.

Year ended 31st December 1996   £2,000

Year ended 31st December 1997   £3,000

Out of this income Maurice paid the maximum amount (based on the 1997/98 assessment only) to a personal pension scheme in February 1998.

(f) Maurice and Marjorie had joint accounts with the Barland Bank plc on which interest of £600 was paid and with the Barchester and Bognor Building Society on which interest of £4,000 was paid.

(g) Investments in UK companies were held in joint names and dividends of £3,500 were received.

(h) Mortgage interest of £800 (gross) was paid in respect of a loan on the family home. The mortgage was a joint one with each spouse paying one half of the interest. The interest payments were made under the MIRAS arrangements.

(i) Following the sale of investments during the year, profits of £17,100 had been agreed with the Inland Revenue for capital gains tax purposes. The investments had been held in joint names.

(j) Maurice had entered into deeds of covenant as follows:

(i) with his daughter Antonia on 25th August 1995 for £2,000 per annum (gross). Antonia is a full-time student at London University

(ii) with the local parish church on 25th April 1995 for £250 per annum (net after income tax).

Required

Calculate the income tax and capital gains tax liabilities for 1997/98 of Mr and Mrs Thistlethwaite.

Question 3 (based on ACCA Taxation December 1993).

Martin was appointed sales director of Multiple Mechanics Ltd on 1st July 1997. His employment package was as follows:

1. Annual salary of £30,000 payable in equal instalments in arrears on the last day of each month.

2. A commission related to sales and payable annually shortly after the company's year end, 31st March. The commission to 31st March 1998, £2,700, was paid on 30th April 1998.

3. Company car, a Mercedes diesel 3000cc. The car was first registered on 1st August 1993 and cost £30,000 when new. All running expenses, including private fuel, were to be paid for by the company but Martin was to pay the company £50 per month for private use of the car and £20 per month for private fuel, whatever the amount used. His total mileage from appointment to 5th April 1998 was 16,000, of which 1,000 were private. These mileage figures were evenly spread over the period. The fuel consumption of the car averaged 30 miles per gallon, a gallon costing an average £2.30.

4. A clothing allowance of £600 per annum payable monthly on the first day of each month.

5. Medical health insurance which cost the company £600 per annum payable monthly on the first day of each month. The premium had been reduced because of group membership. If Martin had paid the premium himself it would have cost him £800 per annum.

6. A furnished flat, annual value £1,200, which was provided rent free until such time as Martin could find a suitable house in the locality, which was not until the summer of 1998. The flat had cost £120,000 in 1996 and the furniture had cost £10,000 at the same time.

Required
Show the amounts assessable under Schedule E on Martin for the tax year 1997/98.

7 ▷ Capital gains tax

Introduction

Until capital gains tax was introduced in 1965 capital receipts were largely free of tax. Much of the incentive to classify a receipt as capital rather than revenue has now been removed by the introduction of capital gains tax although there are still differences between the operation of income tax and capital gains tax as you will see. During its relatively brief life capital gains tax has undergone many changes as successive chancellors attempted to improve the tax. Chancellor Clarke was no exception: in the Finance Act 1994 he restricted the amount of loss relief that could be claimed.

After reading this chapter you will be able to:

● describe the introduction and development of capital gains tax
● calculate the capital gains tax liability which arises as a result of a range of transactions
● describe the reliefs available to taxpayers
● discuss the use of tax planning to reduce the liability to capital gains tax.

Background

The first attempt to tax capital gains was in 1962. The tax was replaced in 1965 by James Callaghan, the Labour Chancellor, by capital gains tax which was intended to tax profits which were not subject to income tax. You will remember that taxes are sometimes introduced because they are seen to be fair. Capital gains tax is certainly an example of this. The proportion of direct taxation raised by capital gains tax has reduced in recent years due to the introduction of the indexation allowance. During the 1970s increases in an asset's value caused by inflation were taxed along with increases in the real value of the asset. Since 1982 only real gains have been subject to capital gains tax. Today capital gains tax accounts for only 1% of the revenue raised by direct taxation but as James Callaghan said at the time, the tax was not primarily introduced to raise income but to 'provide a background of equity and fair play'. By taxing capital gains it is also possible to reduce the incentive to manipulate the tax affairs of an individual to create capital gains rather than income.

There is no intention to subject a receipt to both income tax and capital gains tax. The general rule is that if a receipt is subject to income tax no capital gains tax liability will arise although there is no legislation which prevents a receipt being taxed twice.

Look again at some of the cases in Chapter 5 which are used to determine whether trading has occurred. Some of these cases would not be brought today because if the receipt is not seen to be a trading receipt it will be dealt with as a capital receipt. Of course there are differences between the treatment of capital gains and income. For example, capital gains cannot be included in the calculation of net relevant income for pension purposes. The tax was not intended to be retrospective so only gains which arose after 6th April 1965 are liable to tax. There were two ways of achieving this. Firstly the 'budget day value' at 6th April 1965 could be substituted for the original cost of assets acquired before that date. This would enable the tax to be levied only on gains which arose after 6th April 1965. The second solution was to 'time-apportion' the gain. That is the total gain which arose throughout the period of ownership was calculated and then apportioned, on a time basis, to the periods of ownership prior to and subsequent to 6th April 1965. Only the gain which was attributable to the later period of ownership was subject to capital gains tax. In practice the rules were sometimes more complicated than is described here but the broad principles are accurate.

Since it was introduced there have been substantial changes to the legislation. In 1971 the liability to capital gains tax on death was abolished and in 1982 the Chancellor, Geoffrey Howe, introduced measures which gave taxpayers some relief for inflation.

When capital gains tax was first introduced no relief was given for the effects of inflation. Broadly speaking tax was paid on the difference between the allowable costs of acquiring the asset and the disposal proceeds. This led to increases in value which were due to inflation, rather than to a real appreciation in the value of an asset, being taxed. In 1985 the law was amended to give full relief, for capital gains tax purposes, for increases in the retail price index (RPI).

In 1988 the tax was rebased so that gains before 1982 were not liable to taxation. This was achieved by undertaking two computations when an asset held on 31st March 1982 is disposed of, one using the allowable cost of the asset and the second using the market value on 31st March 1982. If both computations yield an indexed gain the smaller of the gains becomes chargeable. If both computations yield a loss the smaller of the two losses becomes allowable, although for disposals on or after 30th November 1993 the indexation allowance cannot be used to create or increase a loss. If one computation results in a gain and the other gives a loss then there is neither a chargeable gain nor an allowable loss. Taxpayers can also make an irrevocable election for the market value on 31st March 1982 to be used instead of the actual costs for all of their assets, except quoted securities, which were held on 31st March 1982.

In 1992 there was a Consolidation Act and legislation relating to capital gains tax is now contained in the Taxation of Chargeable Gains Act 1992 (TCGA 1992).

Capital gains tax is a complicated tax and each year interested parties lobby the Chancellor to simplify or even abolish the tax. Indeed it is one of Prime Minister John Major's stated aims to abolish capital gains tax.

The charge to capital gains tax

A liability to capital gains tax arises when a chargeable person makes a chargeable disposal of chargeable assets. You need to be able to define each of these terms and list exemptions to capital gains tax.

Chargeable person

A chargeable person may be:

- *An individual who is either resident or ordinarily resident in the UK during the tax year in which the chargeable disposal occurs* (TCGA 1992 s2(1))
  If the individual is resident and domiciled in the UK disposals anywhere in the world may give rise to a capital gains tax liability. If he or she is resident but non-domiciled only gains from the disposal of assets held in the UK or remitted to the UK will be within the scope of capital gains tax. If an individual is neither resident nor ordinarily resident in the UK but undertakes a trade, profession or vocation via a branch or agency based in the UK, disposals of assets used in the course of the business will be within the scope of capital gains tax. If either the trade ceases or the assets are exported there is a deemed disposal, at the market value, for capital gains tax purposes (TCGA 1992 s10(1)).

- *A trustee*
  The residence of a trust is dependent on the residency status of the majority of the trustees. If the majority of the trustees are resident or ordinarily resident in the UK and the administration of the trust is undertaken in the UK the trust will be deemed to be UK resident.
  If the trust becomes non-resident capital gains tax will be charged on unrealised gains at the date when the trust becomes non-resident as well as on subsequent gains which are realised by the trustees.
  A capital gains tax liability may arise when a trustee makes a chargeable disposal. This may occur when he sells trust assets or when a beneficiary becomes absolutely entitled to trust assets. No charge arises if an individual becomes absolutely entitled due to a death. Trustees may be able to claim hold-over relief. The loss relief provisions for individuals also apply to trusts. The rate of capital gains tax in respect of gains accruing to trustees of an accumulation or discretionary settlement in a year of assessment is equal to the sum of the basic and additional rates of income tax for the year (TCGA 1992 s5(1)).

- *A personal representative*
  Personal representatives are deemed to acquire the assets at the market value at the date of death of the testator. When the personal representatives make disposals a liability to capital gains tax may arise. The annual exemption limit is available to the personal representatives for the three years commencing with the year of death of the testator to set against any chargeable gains which arise when assets from the estate are disposed of (TCGA 1992 s3(7)). For these three years the treatment of chargeable gains and allowable losses will be exactly as they would have been if the testator were alive.

- *A partner in a business*
  A partnership does not have a separate legal identity. When a partnership makes a chargeable disposal of partnership assets the individual partners are individually liable to tax in proportion to their share of the capital gain.

The legislation contains a list of exempt persons. These are:

- charities using gains for charitable purposes
- approved superannuation funds
- local authorities
- registered friendly societies
- approved scientific research associations
- authorised unit and investment trusts.

Companies are not chargeable persons for capital gains tax purposes. However, corporation tax is charged on their profits which includes their chargeable gains. Corporate chargeable gains are calculated in exactly the same way as for chargeable persons although there are some special rules, for example when a disposal is made to another member of a group of companies. We will discuss these situations in Chapters 8 and 9.

Chargeable disposal

The term chargeable disposal includes the sale or giving of all or part of an asset. It also includes the loss or destruction of an asset (TCGA 1992 s24) and the receipt of a capital sum in return for the surrender of rights to assets (TCGA 1992 s22). Examples of this are the sale of rights which attach to shares when a company makes a rights issue. The chargeable disposal is deemed to take place when the title to the asset passes to its new owner.

A number of disposals are exempt disposals and do not give rise to a capital gains tax liability. These are:

- transfers of assets on death. The assets are deemed to be acquired by their new owners at their value at the date of death
- transfers of assets to provide security for a loan or mortgage
- gifts to charities and national heritage bodies.

The taxpayer may elect for a capital sum, received by way of compensation for any kind of damage to an asset, not to be treated as a disposal provided that:

- the capital sum is wholly applied in restoring the asset, or
- the capital sum is used to restore the asset except for a part which is not reasonably required for the purpose and which is small in comparison with the whole capital sum, or
- the amount of the capital sum is small, as compared with the value of the asset (TCGA 1992 s23(1)).

In practice a capital sum is deemed to be small if it is less than 5% of the value of the asset. To obtain the relief at least 95% of the capital sum must be used to restore the asset.

If this election is made the capital sum is deducted from the allowable cost incurred prior to receiving the capital sum. It is not possible for this calculation to reduce the allowable costs to below zero (TCGA 1992 s23).

Chargeable assets

All assets are chargeable assets unless they are specifically exempted from capital gains tax. Here is a list of some of the exempt assets:

- motor vehicles (TCGA 1992 s263)
- national savings certificates, premium bonds and SAYE deposits (TCGA 1992 s121)
- foreign currency provided it was for private use (TCGA 1992 s269)
- decorations for valour unless the chargeable person purchased them (TCGA 1992 s126)
- damages for personal or professional injury (TCGA 1992 s51)
- life assurance policies when disposed of by the original beneficial owner (TCGA 1992 s210(2))
- works of art or scientific collections given for national purposes are treated as being disposed of on a no gain/no loss basis (TCGA 1992 s258(1))
- gilt-edged securities, for example Treasury loans, Treasury stocks, Exchequer loans and War loans (TCGA 1992 s115)
- qualifying corporate bonds (TCGA 1992 s115)
- the disposal of debts, other than debts on a security, by the original creditor (TCGA 1992 s251)
- pension and annuity rights (TCGA 1992 s237)
- betting winnings (TCGA 1992 s51).

In addition in certain circumstances tangible moveable property, also called chattels, are exempt from capital gains tax and we will consider these later.

If a taxpayer disposes of exempt assets no chargeable gain, or allowable loss, arises.

The basic computation

First we will study the computation of the chargeable gain or allowable loss. Then we will take a number of transactions together with the taxpayer's income liable to tax in order to calculate the amount of capital gains tax which must be paid.

Broadly the chargeable gain is calculated by deducting allowable expenditure and any indexation allowance from the net proceeds received.

The pro forma for calculating the chargeable gain or allowable loss is:

	£
Gross proceeds on disposal (or market value)	12,000
Less incidental costs of disposal	(2,000)
Net proceeds	10,000
Less allowable costs	2,500
Unindexed gain/(loss)	7,500
Less indexation allowance	1,000
Indexed gain/(Unindexed loss)	6,500

The numbers have been used to make the pro forma easier for you to understand.

We will now consider each of these elements of the capital gains tax computation in turn.

Gross proceeds on disposal

In general the proceeds received from an 'arm's length' transaction are used. An arm's length transaction occurs when vendor and purchaser are not connected in any way that could affect the price agreed between them. That is the price is one which two strangers might mutually agree. However, if the disposal is not a bargain at arm's length the consideration is deemed to be the market value of the asset regardless of the value of any consideration actually given.

Disposals to connected persons and gifts are always taken to be not at arm's length. The market value is also used if the consideration for the disposal cannot be valued.

Connected persons are defined in the TCGA 1992 as follows:

- an individual is connected to his or her spouse, siblings, direct ancestors, lineal descendants and their spouses. He or she is not connected to lateral relatives like uncles, aunts, nephews and nieces
- companies are connected to each other if they are under common control. A company is connected to a person if, either alone or with individuals connected to him or her, that person controls it
- an individual is connected to his or her partners and their spouses and relatives except for acquisitions and disposals of partnership assets under *bona fide* commercial arrangement
- a trustee is connected with the settlor of the trust, any person connected with the settlor and any close company in which either the trustee or any beneficiary of the trust is a participator. A trustee is not connected with the beneficiaries of the trust.

Sometimes a taxpayer may try to reduce tax liability by disposing of assets piecemeal to connected persons. For example, a majority shareholder may pass shares on to the next generation in a series of small gifts. If it were not for the anti-avoidance legislation this would give a lower market value than if the shares were transferred by way of one transaction.

However, if a taxpayer disposes of related assets in a series of linked transactions to connected persons the disposal proceeds for each disposal are a proportion of the value of the aggregate of the assets transferred. Transactions are deemed to be linked if they occur within six years of each other.

There are strict rules for calculating the market value of some assets. When calculating the market value no reduction is made if several assets are sold at the same time. So if a large number of shares are disposed of to a connected person no account is taken of any reduction in the share price due to the size of the disposal. For example, the market value of quoted securities is taken to be the lower of the:

- 'quarter-up': the lower of the two prices quoted in the Daily Official List plus a quarter of the difference between the two prices
- 'mid price': half way between the highest and lowest prices at which bargains were recorded on the date of disposal excluding bargains at special prices.

Incidental costs of disposal

The incidental costs of disposal include all commissions and fees which relate to the sale such as legal costs, valuation fees and the cost of advertising.

Allowable costs

Allowable costs include the following:

- The base cost of acquiring the asset. This will usually be the purchase price. However, there are a number of situations in which some other value will be used. For example, if the asset is inherited rather than bought, the market value at the date of death will be an allowable cost. There are other examples which we will consider later on.
- Any incidental costs of acquisition such as legal fees.
- Any capital expenditure incurred in enhancing the asset or establishing, preserving or defending title to, or a right over, an asset. For enhancement expenditure to be allowed the benefits of the expenditure must be reflected in the state or nature of the asset at the time of disposal. There are a number of specific exclusions from this category of allowable expenses. These are the costs of repairs, maintenance and insurance and any expenditure which is either an allowable deduction for income tax purposes or was met by public grants, such as home improvement loans.

The indexation allowance

The indexation allowance is applied to all items of allowable costs but not any incidental costs of disposal. The allowance is designed to compensate for the percentage increase in the retail price index from the later of March 1982 and the month in which the asset was acquired to the month in which the disposal took place.

Hence the indexation factor is:

$$\frac{\text{RPI for month of disposal} - \text{RPI for month of acquisition disposal (or March 1982)}}{\text{RPI for month of acquisition (or March 1982)}}$$

The indexation factor should be stated as a decimal correct to three decimal places.

The indexation allowance is equal to the indexation factor multiplied by the allowable cost. If there is enhancement expenditure this also is indexed but from the date of the expenditure not from the date of acquisition of the asset.

Remember that it is not allowable for the indexation allowance to turn an unindexed gain into an indexed loss or to increase an unindexed loss.

If the allowable costs exceed the net proceeds a loss is deemed to have been made for capital gains tax purposes.

Calculation of the capital gains tax liability

Basis of assessment

The basis of assessment depends on whether the gain was made by a company or an individual.

Companies are not liable to capital gains tax but pay corporation tax on the net chargeable gains arising in the accounting period less unrelieved losses brought forward (TCGA 1992 s8(1)). Hence the basis of assessment for companies is the accounting period. The calculation of the chargeable gain or allowable loss is as for individuals. In Chapter 8 you will find out how to determine the capital gains to be included in a company's corporation tax computation.

For individuals capital gains tax is charged on the chargeable gains accruing during the year of assessment after the deduction of:

- allowable losses accruing during the year, and
- any allowable losses accruing from a previous year of assessment which have not already been allowed as a deduction from chargeable gains (TCGA 1992 s2(2)).

Allowable losses cannot be carried back except on the occasion of the taxpayer's death.

A year of assessment runs from 6th April to the following 5th April (TCGA 1992 s288(1)). Capital gains tax is charged on a current year basis. The tax is payable on the later of the first of January following the year of assessment and 30 days of the issue of a notice of assessment (TCGA 1992 s7). Hence for disposals made in the fiscal year 1997/98 the tax is payable on 31st January 1999. In order to maximise the gap between making the disposal and paying the tax, disposals should be made as early as possible during the fiscal year.

Rate of tax

For individuals, but not companies, there is an annual exemption for each tax year. It is increased in line with the increase in the RPI and rounded up to the next multiple of £100 each year (TCGA 1992 s3(3)). The annual exemption limit operates something like personal allowances for the purposes of income tax. For 1997/98 the annual exemption limit is £6,500.

The rate of tax applied to net chargeable gains in excess of this limit is the rate of income tax which would apply if they were the top slice of income (TCGA 1992 s4).

Activity

In 1997/98 James, a single person, has Schedule E income of £24,000 and net chargeable gains of £15,000. Calculate James' capital gains tax liability.

Feedback

James' capital gains tax liability is calculated as follows:

	£
Income	
Schedule E	24,000
Less personal allowance	4,045
Taxable income	19,955
Capital gains tax	
Chargeable gains	15,000
Less annual exemption	6,500
	8,500
Capital gains tax payable	
(26,100 − 19,955) = 6,145	
6,145 × 23%	1,413
2,355 × 40%	942
	2,355

In our example the taxpayer does not pay interest on a mortgage. If he had, the computation would have remained unchanged. Interest paid which is eligible for lower rate tax relief cannot be deducted from income when computing the capital gains tax liability.

The use of losses

As already discussed the capital gains tax liability is calculated by reference to the net gains for the fiscal year. That is the total amount of the gains less the total amount of the losses. However, if the chargeable gains less allowable losses for the year do not exceed the exempt amount for the year no deduction will be made, for that year, from any allowable losses carried forward from a previous year or carried back from the year in which the individual dies. If the net chargeable gains for the year do exceed the exempt amount the deduction from that amount from allowable losses carried forward from a previous year shall not be greater than the excess (TCGA 1992 s3(5)).

Activity

Brian has the following chargeable gains and allowable losses:

	Chargeable gain £	Allowable loss £
1997/98	1,000	10,000
1998/99	6,000	3,000
1999/00	8,000	1,000

You may assume that the annual exemption limit is £6,500 for all the years involved.
How will the losses be relieved?

Feedback

1997/98

£1,000 of the loss will be set against the chargeable gain leaving £9,000 of the loss unrelieved and thus available to carry forward.

1998/99

The entire loss of £3,000 will be set off against the chargeable gains. None of the loss brought forward will be used because the net gain £3,000 (£6,000 − £3,000) is less than the annual exemption amount.

So the loss carried forward is still £9,000.

1999/00

The entire loss of £1,000 will be set off against the chargeable gain leaving a net gain of £7,000 (£8,000 − £1,000). This exceeds the annual exemption amount by £500 (£7,000 − £6,500). Hence £500 of the £9,000 loss brought forward will be relieved in 1998/99 giving net chargeable gains of £6,500 which will be fully relieved by the exemption limit and the losses carried forward to 2000/2001 are £8,500.

This legislation offers considerable tax planning opportunities. For example, if an allowable loss has been made in a year the use of the loss can be maximised by either ensuring the chargeable gains made in the year exceed the allowable losses by at least the exempt amount or by ensuring that no chargeable gains are realised in the same year.

When a taxpayer dies capital losses arising in the tax year in which he or she dies can be carried back to the previous three fiscal years, later years first. The loss can be used to reduce the net gains to an amount which is just covered by the annual exemption amount each year.

Husband and wife

Capital gains tax is somewhat complicated in its treatment of spouses. For most purposes a husband and wife are treated as two separate people. They each have the full annual exemption limit and each pays tax on their capital gains at their marginal rate of tax. It is not possible for losses to be transferred from one spouse to the other.

If an asset is jointly owned any chargeable gain, or allowable loss, will be apportioned between the husband and wife by reference to the beneficial interest of each in the asset.

Disposals between a husband and wife living together are treated on a no gain or loss basis. This is done by taking the net proceeds to be such that the chargeable gain is nil regardless of any consideration actually given.

It is not possible to use the indexation allowance to create or increase a loss. As a result there is some complexity in the treatment of transfers between spouses.

If the spouse making the chargeable disposal acquired the asset on a no gain/no loss basis before 1st April 1982 a computation based on the March 1982 market value, as well as one using the original cost, will be made (TCGA 1992 s55 (1)). If the asset was acquired on a no gain/no loss basis after 1st April 1982 but before 30th November 1993 and the transferring spouse originally acquired the asset before 1st April 1982 the spouse making the chargeable disposal will be deemed to have held the asset at 31st March 1982 (TCGA 1992 s55 (5)). This means that a computation using the March 1982 market value should be made.

Special rules apply if the asset was also transferred between the spouses before 30th November 1993. If the chargeable disposal leads to an allowable loss under the new rules the allowable loss will be increased by the rolled-up indexation. If the unindexed gain or loss is nil the allowable loss will be equal to the rolled-up indexation. If there is an unindexed gain and the indexation allowance would normally be sufficient to reduce the chargeable gain to nil the allowable loss will be equal to the difference between the unindexed gain and the rolled-up indexation (TCGA 1992 s55 (8)). The rolled-up indexation allowance is equal to the allowance which would have been available to a transferring spouse had they made a chargeable disposal on the date on which the no gain/no loss transfer was made (TCGA 1992 ss55 (7b), 55(9), 55(10) and 55 (11)).

As you would expect, the chargeable gain on assets which were acquired by the transferring spouse after 31st March 1982 will be calculated using the original cost rather than the March 1982 market value. If the asset is also transferred on a no gain/no loss basis before 30th November 1993 the spouse making the chargeable disposal will be deemed to have acquired the asset on the date on which the transfer was made. The allowable cost for the chargeable disposal will be the transferring spouse's allowable cost plus the indexation allowance to the date of the transfer. The indexation allowance on the chargeable disposal is calculated from the date of the transfer and is subject to the normal restrictions. If the asset is transferred on a no gain/no loss basis on or after 30th November 1993 the transfer value is the aggregate of the cost to the transferring spouse and the indexation allowance from the date the asset was first acquired to the date of the transfer. If the chargeable transfer leads to an unindexed loss the loss should be reduced by the amount of the indexation allowance included in the no gain/no loss transfer. However, this reduction cannot create an unindexed gain.

These rules obviously give great scope for tax planning. Assets can be transferred between spouses before their final disposal to make the best use of annual exemption limits and low marginal rates of tax. The legislation also offers opportunities to maximise the benefit to be obtained from capital losses.

The disposal of chattels, assets held at 31st March 1982, the part disposal of assets and negligible value claims

Now that you are able to calculate the chargeable gain on a disposal there are some special situations which you need to be able to deal with. Broadly speaking there are two potential difficulties when calculating a chargeable gain. Firstly, it may not be possible to use the proceeds actually received when a disposal is made and secondly allocating allowable costs may not be straightforward. For example, suppose an individual buys a large plot of land and then sells a small part of it. It is likely that the large plot is worth more per acre than the part sold. If the taxpayer is allowed to apportion costs by reference to the areas sold a lower chargeable gain will arise than if the cost is apportioned according to the market value of the part disposed of and the part retained. Perhaps understandably then the legislation lays down that the allowable costs are allocated according to market values when part disposals are made.

Chattels

We have already defined chattels as tangible movable property. Assets such as cars, paintings and horses are chattels. Securities and land are not chattels. Wasting chattels are chattels with an estimated remaining useful life of 50 years or less. Hence a horse is a wasting chattel.

Broadly, wasting chattels are exempt from capital gains tax. However, there are two special rules we must consider. First you will remember that cars are exempt from capital gains tax. Secondly, assets which are used during the course of a trade, profession or vocation and are eligible for capital allowances are subject to capital gains tax even if they are wasting chattels.

The capital gains tax computation for such assets depends on whether an unindexed loss arises or not. If an unindexed loss arises the allowable cost is reduced by the lower of the unindexed loss and the capital allowances including any balancing allowance or charge given for the asset. If a gain is made the rules set out next, relating to the relief available for chattels, apply.

A relief is available for chattels subject to capital gains tax which have a relatively low value. If the proceeds of sale are £6,000 or less, no capital gains tax liability will arise. This is true even if the asset was eligible for capital allowances. If the sale proceeds exceed £6,000 the chargeable gain is equal to the lower of $(5/3) \times$ (gross proceeds − £6,000) and the indexed gain. It is not possible to give a benchmark of when it is no longer worth making both calculations, and so for relatively low value chattels both calculations will have to be made.

Activity

Jack sold a bible in June 1997 for £6,600. He had bought the book for £100 in November 1984 in an antique shop.
  Calculate the chargeable gain.

Feedback

	£
Proceeds	6,600
Less cost	100
Unindexed gain	6,500
Indexation allowance	
$\dfrac{155.8 - 91.0}{91.0} = 0.712$	
0.712×100	71
	6,429
$\dfrac{5}{3} \times (\pounds 6,600 - 6,000) = \pounds 1,000$	

The chargeable gain is the lower of £6,429 and £1,000.
Hence the chargeable gain is £1,000.

If a chattel is sold for less than £6,000 any allowable loss is calculated as if the chattel had been sold for £6,000. This will have the effect of reducing or extinguishing the loss but cannot create a gain.

Not all wasting assets are chattels. Examples include registered designs and copyrights with less than 50 years to run. In such cases the allowable cost is the full original cost of the asset written down over its useful life on a straight line basis. The indexation allowance is also given on this reduced cost.

Activity

Stephen sold a registered design with a remaining life of 15 years for £12,000 in March 1998, which had cost £10,000 in March 1987.
Calculate the chargeable gain.

Feedback

	£
Proceeds	12,000
Allowable cost	
$10,000 \times \dfrac{15}{26}$	5,769
Unindexed gain	6,231
Indexation allowance	
$\dfrac{158.5 - 100.6}{100.6} = 0.576$	
$0.576 \times 5,769$	3,323
Indexed gain	2,908

Chattels for which capital allowances are available and which are used throughout their period of ownership in a trade, profession or vocation do not have their allowable cost written off.

Assets held on 31st March 1982

Remember that in 1985 capital gains tax was rebased to 31st March 1982. This means that gains which arose due to ownership of an asset before this date are not subject to tax.

In order to find out how much of the gain is subject to tax two computations are carried out. One computation uses the actual cost of the asset while the other uses the market value on 31st March 1982. In both cases the indexation allowance is based on the higher of the actual cost and the 31st March 1982 market value. When the 31st March 1982 market value is used, enhancement expenditure before 31st March 1982 is excluded from the computation. This is reasonable because the March 1982 market value should already reflect the value of any such expenditure.

If both calculations produce gains the chargeable gain is the lower of the two.

If both calculations produce losses the allowable loss is the smaller of the two.

If one calculation results in a loss and the other in a gain there is deemed to be neither a gain or a loss.

Activity

Rex bought a holiday cottage in 1975 for £25,000. The legal and survey fees relating to the acquisition were £500. He built a garage in 1978 for £1,500. In September 1985 central heating was installed at a cost of £3,000. The house was valued at only £20,000 in March 1982 because of plans to build an industrial estate nearby but in 1983 planning permission was refused and the industrial estate was built ten miles away. In January 1998 the house was sold for £60,000. Rex had to pay estate agency fees of £1,000, £600 related to the sale and £400 related to maintenance of the property during the time it was for sale, and £300 in legal fees.
  Compute the chargeable gain or allowable loss.

Feedback

	Cost £	31.3.82 Value £
Gross proceeds	60,000	60,000
Less incidental costs of disposal:		
estate agency fees	600	600
legal fees	300	300
Net proceeds	59,100	59,100
Less cost 1975	(25,000)	
costs relating to the acquisition	(500)	
enhancement cost 1978	(1,500)	
31.3.82 market value		(20,000)
enhancement cost 1985	(3,000)	(3,000)
Unindexed gain	29,100	36,100
Less indexation allowance		
On original cost:		

$$\frac{158.0 - 79.4}{79.4} = 0.990$$

0.990 × £25,500	(25,245)	(25,245)

On enhancement cost 1978

$$\frac{158.0 - 79.4}{79.4} = 0.990$$

0.990 × £1,500	(1,485)	(1,485)

On enhancement cost 1985

$$\frac{158.0 - 95.4}{95.4} = 0.656$$

0.656 × £3,000	(1,968)	(1,968)
Indexed gain	402	7,402

Because both computations give a gain the smaller gain of £402 based on the original cost is used.

Part disposals

A taxpayer may dispose of all or part of an asset. For example, she may dispose of one chair from a set of four. Alternatively she may dispose of a part share in an asset, for example selling a third interest in a painting. A part disposal may still be a chargeable disposal.

Only part of the allowable cost is included in the capital gains tax computation. To calculate this multiply the allowable cost which relates to the entire asset by

$$\frac{A}{A + B}$$

where A is the value of the part disposed of and B is the market value of the remainder. The amount which is eligible for the indexation allowance is similarly reduced (TCGA 1992 s42).

To some extent this legislation acts as an anti-avoidance measure. If we take the example of the chairs a set of four valuable chairs will be worth more than the aggregate values of a single chair and a set of three and equally a set of three chairs will be worth less than three-quarters of the value of the four chairs. This leads to a lower allowable cost and indexation allowance and so a higher chargeable gain.

Activity

Susan gave a third interest in a painting of her father, which had been commissioned at a cost of £30,000 in April 1982, to her daughter on the occasion of her 21st birthday in June 1997. The market value of the third disposed of was estimated to be £20,000. The market value of the remaining two-thirds of the painting was estimated to be £55,000.
  Calculate Susan's chargeable gain.

Feedback

The allowable cost using market value at 31st March 1982 is:

$$\frac{20,000}{20,000 + 55,000} \times £30,000 = £8,000$$

	£
Proceeds (deemed to be market value)	20,000
Less allowable cost	8,000
Unindexed gain	12,000
Less indexation allowance	
$\dfrac{155.8 - 81.0}{81.0} = 0.923$	
0.923 × £8,000	7,384
Indexed gain	4,616

The legislation which deals with the part disposal of small areas of land is a little different.

  Provided the total amount or value of the consideration for all disposals of land made by the transferrer in the year does not exceed £20,000 if there is a transfer of land which forms part of a holding of land and the amount or value of the consideration for the transfer does not exceed one-fifth of the market value of the holding immediately before the transfer the transfer shall not be treated as a disposal (TCGA 1992 s242(1) & (3)). The consideration is then deducted from any allowable expenditure when computing a gain on any subsequent disposal of the holding (TCGA 1992 s242(2)).

  A taxpayer can claim for a transfer of land, forming part of a holding of land, to an authority exercising or having compulsory powers to purchase the land not to be treated as a disposal. The consideration for the transfer must be small, in practice less than 5% of the market value of the holding immediately before the transfer. The transferrer must not have taken any steps by advertising, or otherwise, to dispose of any part of the holding or to make his or her willingness to dispose of it known to the authority or others (TCGA 1992 s243(1) & (2)). Once again the consideration is then deducted from any allowable expenditure when computing a gain on any subsequent disposal of the holding (TCGA 1992 s243(2)).

When a subsequent disposal takes place the indexation allowance is calculated on the original cost, rather than the cost reduced by the consideration. Then a negative indexation allowance is calculated on the value of the consideration, based on the date on which the part disposal took place.

Negligible value claims

If an asset becomes effectively worthless the taxpayer can make a negligible value claim in which the asset is deemed to be sold at its then market value and immediately reacquired at the same value. This enables the taxpayer to create a capital loss which can be relieved in the normal way. Of course the allowable cost on any subsequent disposal is the market value at the date of the negligible value claim.

We have now considered most of the special situations which you need to be aware of. However, there are two more which you need to know something about. The first is the treatment of quoted securities and the second is the treatment of dwelling-houses which either have some element of private use as well as being used for other purposes or are not considered the taxpayer's principle private residence throughout the period of ownership.

Quoted securities

Matching

Special rules are needed for quoted securities because a taxpayer may undertake many transactions in quoted securities and in these cases a 'matching problem' may arise. Suppose a taxpayer acquires some ordinary shares in a company on several different dates. When he makes a disposal it will be necessary to calculate the allowable cost of the shares. This is much the same problem as arises in the valuation of stock and many of the same techniques offer solutions, for example FIFO, LIFO and average cost. In addition there are circumstances when it may be difficult to identify the appropriate allowable costs, for example when rights and bonus issues are made. Since 1985 an indexed weighted average cost has been used as we will see.

During the relatively brief life of capital gains tax a number of strategies have been adopted to deal with this matching problem. At the same time efforts were made to reduce tax avoidance. Remember that tax avoidance is legal.

For example, a taxpayer may wish to realise a gain or loss without relinquishing the shares. Perhaps he will want to realise a gain to use the annual exemption limit to the full, or he may wish to realise a loss in order to set it against gains on other disposals. Without anti-avoidance legislation this could be done by selling the shares and immediately buying them back. If this is done in the same period of account for the stock exchange, normally two weeks long, the transaction costs are relatively low. However, as you will see anti-avoidance legislation makes this transaction unrewarding if the objective is to reduce any capital gains tax liability.

The legislation has not been changed to any major extent since 1985 and so we now seem to be in a period of stability. However, in order to calculate a capital gains tax liability today, you will still need to know something of the legislation which was in force prior to 1985.

First, however, you must understand the matching rules which are in force today.

Shares which are disposed of are matched in the following order:

- shares acquired on the same day
- shares acquired in the previous nine days on a FIFO basis
- shares in the FA 1985 pool
- shares in the FA 1982 holding
- shares bought before 6th April on a LIFO basis.

Of course securities must be matched to identical securities. If a taxpayer holds 'A' shares and 'B' shares in the same company a disposal of 'A' shares can only be matched against acquisitions of 'A' shares.

The composition of the FA 1985 pool

Each 1985 pool is made up of shares of the same class in the same company so a person may have to maintain a number of FA 1985 pools.

The FA 1985 pool includes the following securities:

- shares acquired on or after 6th April 1982 and held on the 6th April 1985
- shares acquired on or after 6th April 1985.

The FA 1985 pool for companies is the same as for individuals but the relevant date is 1st April rather than 6th April.

Shares acquired between 6th April 1982 and 5th April 1985 are included in the FA 1985 pool at the cost of acquisition plus the indexation allowance for the period from the date of acquisition to April 1985 (March 1985 for companies).

The legislation describes disposals and further acquisitions of shares which change the indexed value of the pool as 'operative events'. Before each operative event is dealt with in the pool the indexed value of the pool is changed to reflect the change in the RPI from the date of the last operative event to the date of the new operative event. This increase is termed the indexed rise rather than an indexation allowance.

The indexed rise is calculated in the same way as the indexation allowance but this time the indexation factor applied to the indexed cost of the pool is not rounded to three decimal places. Note that the rounding rule does apply to the indexation factor used to establish the pool on 6th April 1985.

When an acquisition occurs the shares acquired are added to the pool at their allowable cost, which will be either their purchase price, or their market value on the date of acquisition. When a disposal takes place the proportion of shares disposed of is used to find the proportion of the indexed cost which should be deducted from the net proceeds. No further indexation allowance is available.

Activity

Nancy undertakes the following transactions in ordinary shares of XYZ plc:

	Number of shares	Value £
2 January 1983 bought	1,000	2,200
6 January 1985 bought	1,500	4,000
6 January 1988 bought	500	1,800
15 May 1997 sold	1,000	7,000

Calculate the chargeable gain.

Feedback

First we must set up the FA 1985 pool.

	Number of shares	Cost £	Indexed pool
2nd January 1983	1,000	2,200	2,200
4th January 1985	1,500	4,000	4,000
	2,500		6,200
Indexation allowance			
$\dfrac{94.8 - 82.6}{82.6} = 0.148$			
$0.148 \times 2,200$			326
$\dfrac{94.8 - 91.2}{91.2} = 0.039$			
0.039×4000			156
		6,200	6,682
Indexed rise			
$\dfrac{103.3 - 94.8}{94.8} \times £6,682$			599
Acquisition	500	1,800	1,800
	3,000	8,000	9,081
Indexed rise			
$\dfrac{155.5 - 103.3}{103.3} \times 9,081$			4,589
			13,670
Disposal	1,000		
Proportion applicable to sale			
1,000/3,000		2,667	4,557
	2,000	5,333	9,113

	£	£
Proceeds		7,000
Less cost		2,667
Unindexed gain		4,333
Less indexation allowance		
(4,557 – 2,667)		1,890
Chargeable gain		2,443

The composition of the 1982 holding

All shares of the same class and same company acquired between 6th April 1965 and 5th April 1982 (31st March for companies) are pooled at their allowable cost in the 1982 holding. Any subsequent disposal has an allowable cost which is taken to be a proportion of the cost of the pool. An indexation allowance calculated from April 1982 until the date of the disposal is also available.

Activity

Robert undertakes the following transactions in shares of ABC plc:

	Number of shares	Value £
5th June 1975 bought	1,000	2,000
10th November 1979 bought	1,000	3,000
4th July 1981 bought	1,000	4,000
10th July 1997 sold	2,000	18,000

The market value per share on 31st March 1982 was £4.50.
Calculate the chargeable gain.

Feedback

First find the value of the 1982 holding.

	Number of shares	Cost £
5th June 1975	1,000	2,000
10th November 1979	1,000	3,000
4th July 1981	1,000	4,000
	3,000	9,000

	Pool cost	31st March 1982 market value
	£	£
Proceeds	18,000	18,000
Less pool cost		
$\frac{2,000}{3,000} \times £9,000$	6,000	
31st March 1982 value		
$2,000 \times 4.5$		9,000
Unindexed gain	12,000	9,000
Indexation allowance		
$\frac{156.0 - 79.4}{79.4} = 0.965$		
$0.965 \times 9,000$	8,685	8,685
Indexed gain	3,315	315

Robert's chargeable gain is £315, the lower of the two gains.

An investor's share holdings can change for a variety of reasons other than simply buying and selling shares. The simplest reason is probably a bonus issue whereby some of a company's reserves are capitalised and shareholders receive extra shares in proportion to their existing holding.

Another simple situation, for capital gains tax purposes at least, occurs when there is a stock split so that one old share is replaced by, for example, two new shares.

More complex situations include rights issues, takeovers and mergers and capital distributions. We will consider each of these in turn.

Bonus issues and share splits

In these situations no change to the value of the holding has occurred. The change is to the number of shares held. All that is needed is to increase the number purchased at each time purchases, prior to the bonus issue or share split, were made.

Ruth has had the following transactions in shares in LMN plc.

	Number of shares	Value £
4th June 1972 purchased	1,000	900
10th June 1982 purchased	600	1,000
14th June 1989 purchased	400	1,000
2nd January 1990 bonus issue of one for two		
10th September 1997 sale of	2,000	6,000

The market value on 31st March 1982 was £1.20 per share.
Calculate the chargeable gain.

Feedback

The first step is to set up the FA 1985 pool and then the 1982 holding. Then the disposal can be dealt with.

FA 1985 pool

	Number of shares	Cost £	Indexed pool
10th June 1982	600	1,000	1,000
Indexation allowance			
$\dfrac{94.8 - 81.9}{81.9} \times 0.158$			
0.158×1000			158
Value at 6 April 1985			1,158
Indexed rise			
$\dfrac{115.4 - 94.8}{94.8} \times £1,158$			252
			1,410
Addition June 1989	$\dfrac{400}{1,000}$	$\dfrac{1,000}{2,000}$	$\dfrac{1,000}{2,410}$
Bonus issue January 1990	$\dfrac{500}{1,500}$		
$\dfrac{156.5 - 115.4}{115.4} \times £2,410$			858
			3,268
Disposal September 1997	1,500	2,000	3,268

The 1982 holding

	Number of shares	Cost £	31.3.82 Value £
Acquisition 4th June 1972	1,000	900	1,200
Bonus issue 2nd January 1990	$\dfrac{500}{1,500}$	$\underline{}$ 900	$\underline{}$ 1,200

To calculate the chargeable gain it is necessary to undertake two computations, one dealing with the disposal from the FA 1985 pool and the second dealing with the disposal from the 1982 holding.

FA 1985 pool

	£
Proceeds £6,000 × $\dfrac{1,500}{2,000}$	4,500
Less cost	2,000
Unindexed gain	2,500
Less indexation allowance (3,268–2,000)	1,268
Indexed gain	1,232

1982 holding

	Cost £	31.3.82 Value £
Proceeds £6,000 × $\dfrac{500}{2,000}$	1,500	1,500
Less cost £900 × $\dfrac{500}{1,500}$	300	
31.3.82 value £1,200 × $\dfrac{500}{1,500}$		400
Unindexed gain	1,200	1,100
Less indexation allowance		
$\dfrac{156.5 - 79.4}{79.4} = 0.971$		
0.971 × 400	388	388
Indexed gain	812	712

The chargeable gain is £712. The total chargeable gain is £1,944 (£1,232 + £712).

Rights issues

When a rights issue is made existing shareholders are given the right to subscribe to new shares at what is supposed to be an attractive price. For the purposes of capital gains tax rights issues are aggregated with the shares which conveyed the rights. This is illustrated in the next activity. When the indexation allowance is calculated expenditure on a rights issue is deemed to be made on the date of the rights issue. If the rights are sold rather than exercised the proceeds are treated as a capital distribution and the rules relating to capital distributions are used to calculate any chargeable gain.

Activity

Suppose that in the above example Ruth had taken up a one for two rights issue at a cost of £1 per share on January 1990 rather than receiving a bonus issue. Calculate the chargeable gain on the subsequent disposal.

Feedback

Ruth's transactions now are:

	Number of shares	Value £
4th June 1972 purchased	1,000	800
10th June 1982 purchased	600	1,000
14th June 1989 purchased	400	1,000
2nd January 1990 rights issue of one for two	1,000	1,000
10th September 1997 sale of	2,000	6,000

The market value on 31st March 1982 was £1.20 per share.

As before we will first set up the FA 1985 pool and the 1982 holding before dealing with the disposal.

FA 1985 pool 10th June 1982 £	Number of shares	Cost £	Indexed pool
	600	1,000	1,000
Indexation allowance $\dfrac{94.8 - 81.9}{81.9} \times 0.158$			
0.158×1000			158
Value at 6 April 1985			1,158
Indexed rise $\dfrac{115.4 - 94.8}{94.8} \times £1,158$			252
			1,410
Addition June 1989	$\underline{400}$	$\underline{1,000}$	$\underline{1,000}$
	1,000	2,000	2,410
Indexed rise $\dfrac{119.5 - 115.4}{115.4} \times £2,410$			86
			2,496
Rights issue January 1990	$\underline{500}$	$\underline{500}$	$\underline{500}$
	1,500	2,500	2,996
$\dfrac{156.5 - 119.5}{119.5} \times £2,996$			928
			3,924
Disposal September 1997	$\underline{1,500}$	$\underline{2,500}$	$\underline{3,924}$

The 1982 holding

	Number of shares	Cost £	31.3.82 value £
Acquisition 4th June 1972	1,000	900	1,200
Rights issue 2nd January 1990	500	500	500
	1,500	1,400	1,700

Once again to calculate the chargeable gain it is necessary to undertake two computations, one dealing with the disposal from the FA 1985 pool and the second dealing with the disposal from the 1982 holding.

FA 1985 pool

	£
Proceeds $£6,000 \times \dfrac{1,500}{2,000}$	4,500
Less cost	2,500
Unindexed gain	2,000
Less index allowance $(3,924 - 2500)$	1,424
Indexed gain	576

1982 holding

	Cost £	31.3.82 value £
Proceeds $£6,000 \times \dfrac{500}{2,000}$	1,500	1,500
Less cost $£900 \times \dfrac{500}{1,500}$	300	
31.3.82 $£1.2 \times 1,000 \times \dfrac{500}{1,500}$		400
Less cost of rights $£500 \times \dfrac{500}{1,500}$	167	167
Unindexed gain	1,033	933
Less indexation allowance		
$\dfrac{156.5 - 79.4}{79.4} = 0.971$		
$0.971 \times £400$	388	388
$\dfrac{156.5 - 119.5}{119.5} = 0.310$		
$0.310 \times £167$	52	52
Indexed gain	593	493

The chargeable gain on the disposal from the 1982 holding is £493. The total chargeable gain is £1,069 (£576 + £493).

Capital distributions

A capital distribution is a repayment of share capital rather than a dividend which is paid from income.

A capital distribution is a part disposal and provided it has a value of more than 5% of the value of the shares the normal part disposal rules apply.

However, if the capital distribution is 5% or less than the value of shares the distribution can be deducted from the allowable cost of the shares. This has the effect of deferring the gain until a future disposal occurs. The Inland Revenue are able to exercise their discretion when applying this rule although the taxpayer may appeal if the deduction is disallowed.

If a deduction is made from the allowable cost, when a subsequent disposal is made, the indexation allowance is calculated in two parts. First the full indexation allowance based on the original allowable cost is calculated. Secondly, an allowance based on the deduction indexed from the date of the small disposal to the date of the subsequent disposal is calculated. The indexation allowance used for the subsequent disposal is the first allowance less the second allowance.

Reorganisations

During a reorganisation new shares and possibly debentures are exchanged for the original shareholding. If the exchange is for only one class of securities, for example ordinary shares, there is no difficulty, the allowable cost of the original holding becomes the allowable cost of the new holding.

If shares are exchanged for more than one class of securities, such as ordinary shares and debentures, it is necessary to apportion the allowable cost of the original securities to the new holdings. If all the new securities are quoted the allowable cost is split in proportion to their market values on the first day on which they are quoted after the reorganisation.

Takeovers and mergers

The way in which share exchanges which occur during a takeover or merger are valued is exactly as you might expect from reading the sections on reorganisations and capital distributions.

New shares and securities received in exchange for existing holdings do not lead to a capital gains tax liability. Their allowable cost is derived from the allowable cost of the original holding as described in the section on reorganisations. If new capital is introduced it is an allowable cost. If part of the consideration is in the form of cash a capital distribution is deemed to have taken place and the procedure described in the section on capital distributions is followed.

Principal private residence

An individual's principal private residence, including grounds of up to half a hectare, is exempted from capital gains tax provided that he or she has occupied the whole of the residence throughout the period of ownership.

This exemption has helped to contribute to the attitude of homeowners to any increase in the value of their property. Homeowners are in a unique position to become highly geared with loans of up to 100% of the value of the house available at times during the boom in house prices in the 1980s. This meant that even a small increase in the value of houses could generate a spectacular and tax-free increase in the value of the owner's equity. This has led to a sense of economic well-being when the price of houses goes up among the 65% of households who own their own homes. Few people see increases in house prices in the same light as increases in other commodities such as cars or furniture. Imagine, for a moment, the impact of applying capital gains tax to principal private residences. Increases in value would no longer be seen as beneficial because of the large amount of tax which may be payable each time an individual moves. There is some pressure on the government to levy tax on the gains made by homeowners but it is hard to imagine a government accepting the level of unpopularity which would surely be the result.

A husband and wife can claim only one principal private residence between them unless they are legally separated. If the taxpayer has not occupied the residence throughout his period of ownership a capital gains tax liability may arise. To calculate the proportion of the gain which is exempt from capital gains tax multiply the total gain by:

$$\frac{\text{Period of deemed occupation since 31st March 1982}}{\text{Total period of ownership since 31st March 1982}}$$

Remember that capital gains which arose prior to 31 March 1982 are not taxable.

Provided that the residence was the taxpayer's principal private residence at some time during his period of ownership the last 36 months of ownership are deemed to be a period of occupation even if the taxpayer nominates another property to be his principal private residence during this period. This measure is designed to help taxpayers who have moved house and are trying to sell their old house in today's economic climate.

There are a number of other occasions on which a period of absence can be treated as a period of deemed occupation provided that the property both before and after the period of absence, although not necessarily immediately before or immediately after, was occupied as the taxpayer's principal private residence. The periods of deemed absence are not affected if the property is let during them.

The periods of deemed occupation are:

- any periods totalling three years
- any periods during which the taxpayer was required to live abroad in order to fulfil employment duties
- any periods totalling four years during which the taxpayer was required to work elsewhere in the UK in order to fulfil employment duties.

Strictly each period of absence should be followed by a period of occupation. However, as an extra-statutory concession, if a taxpayer's employment requires him to work in the UK immediately followed by a period of working abroad or vice versa the periods will still be allowed as periods of deemed occupation.

Example

John bought a house on 10th January 1978 for £30,000. He lived in the house until 30th June 1980 when he obtained work in another part of the country. The house was let until he returned on 1st April 1983. On 1st May 1988 he went to work abroad until 1st May 1993 when he returned to UK and moved in with his fiancée. The house was sold on 1st January 1998 for £120,000. John incurred fees and costs of £5,000 relating to the sale. The house was estimated to be worth £45,000 on 31st March 1982.

Solution

It is first necessary to calculate the proportions of exempt and chargeable months to the period of ownership since 31st March 1982.

Period	Exempt months	Chargeable months
10.1.78 – 31.3.82 ignored	0	0
1.4.82 – 31.3.83 (working away)	12	0
1.4.83 – 30.4.88 (occupied)	61	0
1.5.88 – 31.12.94 (see below)	0	80
1.1.95 – 1.1.98 (last 36 months)	36	0
	109	80

The period from 1st May 1988 to 31st December 1994 is not exempt because the absence was not followed by a period of owner occupation.

Now the chargeable gain can be calculated:

	£	£
Gross proceeds		120,000
Incidental costs of disposal		5,000
Net proceeds		115,000
Less 31.3.82 value		45,000
Unindexed gain		70,000
Less indexation allowance		
$\dfrac{158.0 - 79.4}{79.4} = 0.990$		
£45,000 × 0.990		44,550
Private residence exemption		25,450
	109	14,678
Chargeable gain	189	10,772

No computation based on cost needs to be done because it would clearly produce a higher gain.

Taxpayers who own more than one residence may nominate which is to be deemed their main residence. This is done by giving notice to the Inspector of Taxes within two years of acquiring the second residence. It is possible to vary the nomination at a later date. In order to elect for a residence to be a main residence the taxpayer must, at times, reside in the property. If no written election is made the question of residence will be decided by the Inspector of Taxes by reference to the facts.

Taxpayers living in job-related accommodation will be able to claim any residence which they own as a principal private residence provided that they intend to occupy it as their main residence in due course. Look back to Chapter 6 for a definition of job-related accommodation.

Lettings

If a lodger lives with a family sharing living accommodation and eating with them there is no liability to capital gains tax. However, if part or all of a property is let for residential purposes, the principal private residence exemption may extend to gains which relate to the period of letting.

This relief is available if:

- the owner is absent and lets the property during a period which is not considered a deemed period of occupation
- only part of the property is let.

The relief available is the lowest of:

- the gain accruing during the letting period
- £40,000
- the total gain which is exempt under the principal private residence provisions.

However, this relief cannot turn a gain into an allowable loss for capital gains tax purposes.

If part of the residence is used wholly for business purposes the gain which is attributable to the use of that part is taxable. This is an important point to bear in mind when deciding whether to claim that part of a residence is used exclusively for business purposes, perhaps an office or a workshop. In the short term it may be possible to set some expenses against income for income tax purposes but it may give rise to a substantial liability for capital gains tax purposes in the future.

Reliefs from capital gains tax

As you have already seen capital gains tax is largely intended to create a fair and equitable system of tax and to limit the incentives to create a capital receipt rather than a revenue receipt. However, there are a number of situations when relief is available to mitigate the impact of capital gains tax. For example, the profit on the sale of a taxpayer's principal private residence is exempt from capital gains tax. This measure may not surprise you, maintaining the favoured tax treatment of home ownership which we are already familiar with from the rules for income tax.

There are also special reliefs available on retirement from a business. These recognise the fact that taxpayers often provide for retirement by investing in the growth of the business rather than contributing to a pension fund.

Businesses often sell an asset intending to replace it with another. For example, a business may move to new premises and thus sell existing land and buildings in order to purchase new property. Rollover relief may be available if the proceeds from a sale of assets are invested in new assets. You may consider this to be entirely reasonable since, although a liability to capital gains tax has arisen, the business is clearly no better off. In reality the taxpayer has simply exchanged one asset for another.

If the new asset is a depreciating asset then the taxpayer may claim holdover relief rather than rollover relief.

If a taxpayer makes a chargeable disposal for less than the market value of the asset then, providing both the donor and the beneficiary make an election, some or all of the chargeable gain can be deferred and transferred to the beneficiary by means of gift relief. This enables assets to be passed from one generation to the next without a capital gains tax liability arising.

We will consider each of these reliefs in turn.

Retirement relief

Relief from capital gains tax is given in any case where a material disposal of business assets is made by an individual who, at the time of the disposal, has attained the age of 50 or has retired on the grounds of ill-health below the age of 50 (TCGA 1992 s163(1)). Note that if the individual is 50 or over he can claim retirement relief regardless of whether he actually retires. A person shall be treated as having retired on the grounds of ill-health if the Board are satisfied that he has ceased to be engaged in and, by reason of ill-health, is incapable of engaging in work of the kind which he previously undertook and is likely to remain permanently so incapable (TCGA 1992 Sch 6 s3(1)).

A disposal of business assets is:

- a disposal of the whole or part of a business, or
- a disposal of one or more assets used in the business until it ceased to be carried on, or
- a disposal of shares or securities of a company (TCGA 1992 s163(2)).

In order to claim the relief the business must be owned, throughout the 12 months prior to the disposal, by:

- the individual making the disposal, or
- a trading company which is the individual's personal company, in which he works full time in a managerial or technical capacity, or
- a trading company which is a member of a trading group of which the holding company is the individual's personal company, and that individual works full time, in a managerial or technical capacity, in one of the companies in the group (TCGA 1992 s163(3) & (4) & (5) & Sch 6 1(2)).

A company is an individual's personal company if he exercises at least 5% of the voting rights in the company (TCGA 1992 Sch 6 1(2)).

Additionally, in order to claim retirement relief, when the disposal is of one or more assets, the disposal must take place within one year after the date on which the business ceased to trade (TCGA 1992 Sch 6 s1(2)).

A group of companies for capital gains tax purposes is a 51% group. Look in Chapter 8 for a definition of groups.

The chargeable gain is equal to excess of the appropriate proportion of the gains of the disposal over the maximum relief available (TCGA 1992 Sch 6 s7(1)).

The appropriate proportion is found by dividing the company's chargeable business assets by the company's chargeable assets. Both valuations should take place immediately before the disposal takes place (TCGA 1992 Sch 6 s7(2)).

Every asset is a chargeable asset apart from assets which would not have given rise to a chargeable gain if they had been disposed of immediately before the date of disposal (TCGA 1992 Sch 6 s7(3)). In practice stock, debtors, cash, motor cars and items of plant and machinery which cost less than £6,000 are the main examples of assets which are not chargeable assets.

Similarly if there is a qualifying disposal of the shares or securities of a holding company the chargeable gain is equal to the excess of the appropriate proportion of the gains of the disposal over the maximum relief available (TCGA 1992 Sch 6 s8(1)).

If a 51% subsidiary is not a wholly owned subsidiary the value of its chargeable assets and chargeable business assets of the subsidiary are reduced by the fraction A/B where A is the amount of that share capital owned, directly or indirectly, by the holding company and B is the whole of the ordinary share capital of the subsidiary (TCGA 1992 Sch 6 s8(4)).

A chargeable business asset is an asset, including goodwill but not including shares or securities or other assets held as investments, which is used for the purposes of the trade (TCGA 1992 Sch 6 s12(2)). In practice shares and securities and assets which are held for investment purposes are not chargeable business assets.

If the conditions outlined above are met throughout the ten-year period prior to the date of disposal the maximum retirement relief that can be claimed is the first £250,000 of the gain and one half of any gain between £250,000 and £1,000,000. If the conditions are met for only a proportion of the ten-year period the limits are reduced proportionately. Since in order to claim the relief the conditions must have been met for at least one year the smallest possible proportion is 10% (TCGA 1992 Sch 6 s13(1)).

If the individual has met the conditions for retirement relief in two businesses one after the other within the ten-year period prior to the disposal the two periods of involvement can be added together for the purposes of determining the maximum relief available provided the time between the involvement in the two businesses is not more than two years (TCGA 1992 Sch 6 s14(2)).

Strictly relief can only be claimed for two or more businesses if the final qualifying business had been undertaken for at least a year. In April 1994 the Inland Revenue announced an extra statutory concession. From 14th April 1994 taxpayers will not have to satisfy this requirement in order to add together several periods of business activity provided that all of the other conditions have been met (Statement of Practice U5).

Rupert, a company director, owns 50% of the ordinary share capital of Eco Ltd. He retired on his 60th birthday, 12th June 1997. Rupert had bought the shares in 1980 for £100,000 and sold them on 12th June 1997 for £800,000. The March 1982 value of the shares was £250,000. On the date the shares were sold the company had the following assets:

	£
Goodwill	100,000
Plant (cost £600,000)	300,000
Premises (cost £400,000)	600,000
Investments	100,000
Net current assets	500,000
	1,600,000

Calculate Rupert's chargeable gain.

Feedback

The chargeable business assets are goodwill, plant and premises with an aggregate value of £1,000,000. The chargeable assets are equal to the chargeable business assets plus the investments giving a total value of £1,100,000.

Because the March 1982 valuation is higher than the original cost it is only necessary to undertake one calculation using the March 1982 value in order to give the smallest gain.

	£	£
Proceeds		800,000
Less March 1982 valuation		250,000
Unindexed gain		550,000
Less indexation allowance		
$\dfrac{155.8 - 79.4}{79.4} = 0.962$		
$0.962 \times £250,000$		240,500
		309,500
Less retirement relief		
Exempt amount	250,000	
$50\% \times £(309,500 \times \dfrac{1,000,000}{1,100,000} - 250,000)$	15,682	
		265,682
Chargeable gain		43,818

Reinvestment relief

Remember that rollover relief is intended to provide relief when all of the proceeds from the sale of a business asset are reinvested in another business asset. In contrast reinvestment relief is available when some or all of the proceeds from the disposal of an asset or a material disposal of shares in a qualifying company are reinvested in a qualifying investment (FA 1993 Sch 7 s164A(1)). The relief is only available to individuals or a body of trusteees, not companies.

A disposal of shares is a material disposal of shares in a qualifying company if throughout the 12 months before the disposal the company is the reinvestor's unquoted personal company which is a trading company or the holding company of a trading group and the reinvestor has worked full time for the company (FA 1993 Sch 7 s164A(4)).

In order to obtain the relief the acquisition must be made within one year before and three years after the date of the disposal (FA 1993 Sch 7 s164A(9)).

In common with retirement relief, reinvestment relief is only available on the proportion of the gain which relates to chargeable business assets (FA 1993 Sch 7 s164C(1) &(2)).

An individual is deemed to have acquired a qualifying investment when he acquires at least 5% of the eligible shares of a qualifying company (FA 1993 s164A(8)). A company is a qualifying company if it is an unquoted trading company undertaking a qualifying trade or an unquoted holding company which only holds shares in qualifying subsidiaries (FA 1993 s164G).

From 29th November 1994 a company is eligible to be a qualifying company regardless of the proportion of land or buildings that it holds. From the same date the Chancellor also relaxed the definition of a qualifying trade to include property development and farming.

Activities which are not qualifying trades are:

- dealing in land, in commodities or futures or in shares, securities or other financial instruments
- dealing in goods otherwise than in the course of an ordinary trade of wholesale or retail distribution
- banking, insurance, money-lending, debt-factoring, hire purchase financing or other financial activities
- leasing, hiring or receiving royalties or licence fees
- providing legal or accountancy services
- providing services of facilities for a trade carried on by another person which is not a qualifying trade (TCGA 1992 s164I (2)).

The relief available is equal to the lower of the:

- gain on the original disposal
- cost of the qualifying investment
- market value of the qualifying investment at the date on which it was acquired if it was not acquired in a transaction at arm's length
- relief claimed by the taxpayer (TCGA 1992 s164A (2)). When the relief is claimed the qualifying investment's base cost is reduced by the amount of the reinvestment relief (FA 1993 Sch 7 s164A(2)).

When the relief is claimed the qualifying investment's base cost is reduced by the amount of the reinvestment relief (FA 1993 Sch 7 s164A(2)).

Interaction with retirement relief

Reinvestment relief should be claimed before retirement relief is dealt with (TCGA 1992 s164BA (1)). However, any reduction under reinvestment relief should be first given against the amount which would otherwise be chargeable after retirement relief (TCGA 1992 s164BA (3)). Were this not to be the case every £2 of reinvestment relief claimed would reduce retirement relief by £1 when the 50% rate was applicable.

Work through the following example to see how the two reliefs inter-react in practice.

Example

Laura sold shares in a qualifying company for the purposes of retirement relief, in which she has been a full time working director for 10 years, in May 1997 for £500,000. She had acquired the shares in 1980 for £30,000. The shares had a market value of £60,000 on 31st March 1982. Laura was 68 in April 1997 and is considering reinvesting in a qualifying investment in August 1997. Laura has made other chargeable disposals in the year which have fully utilised her annual exemption limit. Laura has sought your advice about how much to reinvest in order to obtain the maximum deferral.

Solution

First calculate the chargeable gain, assuming that Laura does not reinvest any of the proceeds.

	£	£
Proceeds		500,000
Less allowable cost (March 82 value as this is higher than the original cost)		(60,000)
Unindexed gain		440,000
Less indexation allowance		
$\frac{155.5 - 79.4}{79.4} = 0.958$		
$0.958 \times £60,000$		(57,480)
Gain before retirement relief		382,520
Less retirement relief		
£250,000 × 100%	250,000	
50% × (£382,520 − £250,000)	66,260	(316,260)
Chargeable gain		66,260

Now we can say that to defer all the capital gains tax Laura should reinvest £66,260.

Suppose Laura chose to reinvest only £60,000. In this case the chargeable gain will be:

	£
Proceeds	500,000
Less rolled over gain	(60,000)
	440,000
Less allowable expenditure	(60,000)
Unindexed gain	380,000
Less indexation allowance	(57,480)
	322,520
Less retirement relief (as above)	(316,260)
Chargeable gain	6,260

Note that provided Laura has no other chargeable gains in the year this disposal will not give rise to a capital gains tax liability.

Rollover relief

If the consideration which a taxpayer obtains for the disposal of assets used for the purposes of the trade is used, by him, to acquire other assets which are also used only for the purpose of the trade rollover relief may be available (TCGA 1992 s152(1)). Both the old and the new assets must fall into one, but not necessarily the same one, of the following classes:

- Class 1:
  - any land or building or part of a building used only for the purpose of trade
  - fixed plant or machinery which does not form part of a building
- Class 2:
  - ships, aircraft and hovercraft
- Class 3:
  - satellites, space stations and spacecraft
- Class 4:
  goodwill
- Class 5:
  - milk quotas and potato quotas.
- Class 6:
  - ewe and suckler cow premium quotas (TCGA 1992 s155).

In order to claim the relief the new assets must be acquired between 12 months before and three years after the disposal of the old assets (TCGA 1992 s152(4)). It is not necessary for the old and new assets to be used in the same business.

If rollover relief is claimed the chargeable gain is deducted from the allowable cost of the new asset. If the total proceeds from the sale of the old asset are reinvested in the new asset full relief will be given. However, if some of the proceeds are not reinvested then a chargeable gain equal to the lower of the chargeable gain before rollover relief and the amount which has not been reinvested will be subject to capital gains tax immediately.

Mike bought a factory in March 1987 for £500,000 and sold it for £950,000 in September 1997. He bought a ship in November 1997 for £800,000. Determine any chargeable gain that arises on the sale of the factory assuming that rollover relief is claimed and compute the base cost of the ship bought in November 1997.

Feedback

Disposal of factory

	£
Proceeds	950,000
Less allowable cost	500,000
Unindexed gain	450,000
Indexation allowance	

$$\frac{156.5 - 100.6}{100.6} = 0.556$$

$0.556 \times £500,000$	278,000
Indexed gain	172,000
Less amount not reinvested	
£950,000 – £800,000	150,000
Gain eligible to be rolled over	22,000

The chargeable gain is £150,000

Base cost of the ship

Cost	800,000
Less rolled over gain	22,000
Base cost of the ship	778,000

Holdover relief

Rollover relief cannot be claimed if the replacement asset is depreciable. That is if it is, or within the next ten years will become, a wasting asset. Remember that a wasting asset has a life of 50 years or less and so holdover relief is going to apply to any replacement asset with a life of 60 years or less. Plant and machinery is always treated as a depreciating asset while land and buildings are never treated as depreciating assets.

Holdover relief is available if the proceeds are reinvested in a depreciable asset. The relief is given by reducing the amount of the chargeable gain and making a reduction of the same amount in the expenditure allowable in respect of the replacement asset (TCGA 1992 s154(1)).

The held-over gain gives rise to a chargeable gain on the earlier of:

- the date on which the taxpayer disposes of the replacement asset
- the date on which the replacement asset ceases to be used for the purposes of a trade carried on by the taxpayer
- ten years after the date of the acquisition of the replacement asset (TCGA 1992 s154(2)).

If, before the held-over gain crystallised, the replacement asset is itself replaced by an asset which is not a depreciating asset then some or all of the held-over gain can be transferred to the new asset (TCGA 1992 s154(4) & (5)).

Activity

May bought a workshop in February 1972 for £25,000 and ran a business making and selling soft furnishings. In July 1981 she sold the premises for £40,000 and in August 1981 she bought plant for £50,000 to use in the new premises she was renting. In January 1984 May bought a new workshop for £35,000 and in October 1997 she sold the machinery for £80,000. The March 1982 value of the plant was £55,000.

Determine May's chargeable gains on each of the transactions.

Feedback

July 1981 disposal	£
Proceeds	40,000
Less allowable costs	25,000
Gain	15,000

The entire proceeds of £40,000 were reinvested in plant and so the £15,000 gain can be held over.

January 1984 purchase
When the workshop, not a depreciating asset, was bought part of the held-over gain could be rolled over to the new workshop.
The £5,000 not eligible to be rolled over will continue to be held over until the charge crystallises ten years after acquisition in August 1991.

	£
Total gain held over	15,000
Less proceeds not reinvested £40,000 – £35,000	5,000
Gain eligible to be rolled over	10,000

August 1991
The held-over gain of £5,000 crystallised and was chargeable to capital gains tax in 1991/92.

October 1997 disposal	Cost £	1982 market value £
Proceeds	80,000	80,000
Less cost	50,000	
1982 market value		55,000
Unindexed gain	30,000	25,000
Less indexation allowance		
$\dfrac{156.9 - 79.4}{79.4} = 0.976$		
$0.976 \times £55,000$	53,680	53,680
Loss	Nil	Nil

Since it is not possible to create a loss using the indexation allowance the chargeable gain is nil.

Gift relief

Gift relief is available if an individual makes a disposal, otherwise than as a bargain at arm's length, of a qualifying asset and both the transferrer and the transferee elect for the transferrer's gain to be reduced to nil. If the election is made the transferee is deemed to acquire the asset at its market value less the gain which would otherwise have arisen. If the transferee provides some consideration the deferred gain is equal to the gain less any excess of the consideration over the allowable costs, excluding the indexation allowance. This deferred gain is termed the held-over gain (TCGA 1992 s165(1) & (4)).

For the purposes of gift relief an asset is a qualifying asset if:

- it is, or is an interest in, an asset used for the purposes of a trade, profession or vocation carried on by:
  - the transferrer, or
  - his or her personal company, or
  - a member of a trading group of which the holding company is his or her personal company or
- it is shares or securities of a trading company, or of the holding company of a trading group, and either:
  - the shares are neither quoted on a recognised stock exchange nor dealt with in the Unlisted Securities Market: or
  - it is the transferrer's personal company (TCGA 1992 s165(2)).

If the taxpayer makes a disposal by way of a gift to a charity or for national purposes, or for a consideration which would give rise to an allowable loss, then the disposal and acquisition shall be treated as being made for such consideration as to secure that neither a gain nor a loss accrues on the disposal. The recipient of the asset is deemed to have acquired the asset at the same time and for the same consideration as the donor of the gift (TCGA 1992 s257(2)).

A gift is deemed to be for national purposes if it is made to the National Gallery, the British Museum, the National Trust or universities, among others (IHTA 1984 Sch 3).

Alan sold a small paper recycling plant to his daughter Sarah on 30th April 1997. The plant had a market value of £300,000 but Alan sold it to Sarah for £100,000 and claimed gift relief. Alan had bought the business in May 1982 for £50,000. Sarah intends to sell the business in March 1998 and believes that she will be able to obtain a price of £400,000. Determine Alan's chargeable gain and advise Sarah on the amount of any chargeable gain she will be assessed on when she sells the business.

Feedback

	£
Alan	
Deemed proceeds	300,000
Less allowable cost	50,000
Unindexed gain	250,000
Less indexation allowance	
$\dfrac{155.2 - 81.6}{81.6} = 0.902$	
$0.902 \times £50,000$	45,100
Indexed gain	204,900
Less gain held over	
£204,900 − (£100,000 − £50,000)	154,900
Chargeable gain	50,000
Sarah	
Proceeds	400,000
Less allowable cost £300,000 − £154,900	145,100
Unindexed gain	254,900
Less indexation allowance	
$\dfrac{158.5 - 155.2}{155.2} = 0.021$	
$0.021 \times £145,100$	3,047
Chargeable gain	251,853

Alan's chargeable gain is £50,000 while Sarah's chargeable gain will be £251,853 if she sells the business as planned.

If both retirement relief and gift relief are available retirement relief must be deducted first. Any gain remaining can be held over.

Tax planning

Capital gains tax is a tax which is amenable to tax planning because the timing of events is often within the control of the taxpayer. Tax planning is also an important issue because it is possible to incur a significant capital gains tax liability if good advice is not taken.

Consider the disposal of a company on retirement. The taxpayer can sell either the shares of the company or the business's assets and wind the company up.

If the assets are sold a capital gains tax liability will accrue to the company. When the company is then liquidated the taxpayer will incur a second capital gains tax liability on the gain received on the shares. He may be able to use retirement relief to mitigate the second charge but the total amount of tax paid is obviously likely to be relatively high.

If the shares are sold then only the gain on the shares will be taxable and once again the retirement relief can be used to mitigate the charge.

However, for a number of reasons the purchaser may rather buy the assets than the shares. If the company is sold the purchaser also acquires the liabilities and obligations of the company whereas acquiring the assets is more straightforward.

These factors, together with many more, will become part of the negotiations which are entered into before the business is sold.

Regardless of whether the assets or the shares are disposed of there are a number of points to be borne in mind when disposing of a business. If possible defer the disposal until the taxpayer is eligible for the maximum retirement relief. If the taxpayer is married ensure that both the spouses have an interest in the business so that each can claim retirement relief.

In general, capital disposals should be made as early as possible in the fiscal year in order to delay the payment of tax as much as possible. An individual or married couple should try to fully utilise their annual exemption limit each year since if it is not used it cannot be carried forward.

If at all possible losses should not be wasted by being set against current gains which would otherwise have benefited from the annual exemption limit.

It is important to obtain good tax advice before making a large disposal so that any exemptions and reliefs available can be claimed.

Summary

Capital gains tax was introduced in 1965. In the early years there were many changes in the legislation which were needed to correct fundamental flaws in the original legislation. One of the most important developments was the introduction of the indexation allowance. Of course this also significantly reduced the amount of tax which was collected but it might be argued that it made the tax 'fairer' which seems to be one of the most important characteristics of capital gains tax. The rate of change in the legislation has slowed somewhat in recent years suggesting that the tax is now largely working as originally intended.

Taxpayers, both individuals and companies, pay tax on their chargeable gains. However, there is considerable scope for tax planning as the taxpayer can often choose the date on which to make the disposal. There are a number of reliefs which are available to taxpayers including relief on a principal private residence and retirement relief, rollover relief, holdover relief and gift relief. Remember also that gains on assets held in pension funds and personal equity plans are not subject to income tax or capital gains tax. These reliefs, together with the annual exemption limit, enable most individuals to avoid any liability to capital gains tax.

Project areas

Once again capital gains tax offers a number of worthwhile projects. One particularly interesting question is: 'Is capital gains tax fair?' It is a difficult area but could yield a successful project for a good student. A comparative study could also form the basis of an interesting project.

Discussion topic

It is sometimes possible for individuals to arrange their affairs in order to have receipts taxed as income rather than a capital gain and vice versa. For example, directors planning to sell a family company could either pay themselves high salaries taxable under Schedule E or take relatively low salaries thus increasing the funds retained in the business leading to a higher value for their shares when the company is sold. List the taxation consequences of making this decision and discuss the circumstances in which income may be preferable to capital gains.

Computational questions

Question 1 (based on ACCA June 1990).

(a) Adrienne sold 2,000 ordinary shares in The Paramount Printing Company plc, a quoted company, on 4th August 1997 for £18,000. She had bought ordinary shares in the company on the following dates.

	Number of shares	Cost £
12th April 1970	1,500	4,000
1st May 1988	1,500	5,000

The value of each of the shares on 31st March 1982 was £4.
No election has been made or is to be made to have all pre-March 1982 acquisitions rebased to March 1982.

Required
Calculate, before annual exemption, the capital gain assessable on Adrienne for 1997/98.

(b) James purchased a house in Oxford, 'Millhouse' on 1st July 1983 and took up immediate residence. The house cost £50,000. On 1st January

1984 he went to work and live in the United States where he stayed until 30th June 1986. On 1st July 1986 James returned to the UK to work for his United States employers in Scotland where it was necessary for him to occupy rented accommodation. On 1st July 1987 his mother became seriously ill and James resigned from his job to go and live with her. His mother died on 30th September 1988 leaving her house to James. James decided to continue to live in his mother's house and finally sold 'Millhouse' on 30th June 1997 for £200,000. The value of the house on 31st March 1982 was £75,000.

Required
Calculate, before annual exemption, the capital gain assessable on James for 1997/98. No election has been, or will be, made to have all pre-31st March 1982 acquisitions rebased to 31st March 1982.

Question 2 (based on ACCA December 1988).

(a) Arthur bought 300 hectares of land for £120,000 on 1st February 1988. On 1st July 1997 he sold 50 hectares of the land for £40,000. On 1st July 1997 the value of the remaining 250 hectares was £187,500.

Required
Calculate Arthur's capital gain for 1997/98 (before annual exemption).

(b) Margaret sold her holiday home, which had never been her main residence, on 6th April 1997 for £65,000. She had purchased the home on 6th April 1971 for £3,000. The following amounts of enhancement expenditure were incurred:

6th October 1975	Central heating system	£1,000
6th May 1985	Extension to rear of house	£4,000

The value of the house on 31st March 1982 has been agreed with the Inland Revenue as £25,000.

Required
Calculate Margaret's capital gain for 1997/98 (before annual exemption).

(c) On 3rd August 1997, her 55th birthday, Anne retired from running her nursing home and gave the business to her daughter, Jocelyn. Both Anne and Jocelyn are resident and ordinarily resident in the UK. Anne had owned the business for the previous 15 years.

Her accountant had agreed the chargeable gain with the Inland Revenue at £200,000, before any reliefs.

Required
State the reliefs (other than annual exemption) which can be claimed and outline the effect of claiming them.

Question 3 (based on ACCA June 1989).

(a) On 6th April 1968 Edward acquired for £5,000 a small workshop where he carried on his trade as a furniture maker. On 6th April 1997 he sold the workshop for £120,000 and moved on 10th April 1997 to smaller premises which cost £114,000. Edward was born in 1943. The market value of the workshop on 31st March 1982 was £60,000.

Required
Calculate Edward's capital gain for 1997/98 (before annual exemption), assuming that Edward makes any necessary claim to reduce his capital gain. Edward has not elected to have all pre-31st March 1982 acquisitions rebased to 31st March 1982.

(b) On 31st August 1997, his 56th birthday, Robert retired from his newsagent's business which he had owned since 1st September 1986. The sale proceeds were £425,750 and the allocation of this amount was agreed with the purchaser of the business.
The relevant details are as follows.

	Cost £	Sale proceeds £
Goodwill (September 1986)	10,000	180,000
Shop premises (September 1986)	80,000	240,000
Movable fittings (April 1991)	2,000	1,500
Trading stock (July 1994)	1,500	1,750
Motor van (October 1993)	3,000	2,500
		425,750

Required
Calculate Robert's capital gain for 1997/98 (before annual exemption), arising from the disposal of the business assets. Robert has not elected to have all pre-31st March 1982 acquisitions rebased to 31st March 1982.

(c) Michelle bought an antique vase in January 1980 for £2,000 and sold it in November 1997 for £8,000. £800 sales commission was deducted from the sale price. The vase was valued at £4,000 on 31st March 1982.

Required
Calculate Michelle's gain for 1997/98 (before annual exemption). Michelle has not elected to have all pre-31st March 1982 acquisitions rebased to 31st March 1982.

(d) Explain the rules governing rollover relief on the replacement of business assets and state how the relief is granted.

Question 4 (based on ACCA Tax Framework June 1994).

(a) On 31st July 1997, his 56th birthday, Oskar Barnack retired as sales manager of European Traders Limited and sold his 10% ordinary shareholding in the company. He had been a full-time employee of the company for 12 years. The sale of the shares on 31st July 1997 realised £550,000. Oskar inherited the shares on 1st August 1989 at a valuation of £125,000.
The market values of the assets of the company at 31st July 1997 were:

	£
Land and buildings	700,000
Goodwill	300,000
Shares held as an investment	200,000
Stock	160,000
Bank and cash balances	25,000
Government securities	220,000

Required
Calculate Oskar's chargeable gain for 1997/98, before annual exemption.

(b) Walter purchased his business premises in October 1976 for £10,000. In May 1986 he gave them to his son Darren when the value was £50,000. The appropriate joint election for gift relief was made. The value of the premises on 31st March 1982 was £40,000. In April 1997 Darren sold the premises for £200,000.

Required
Calculate the capital gain assessable on Darren for 1997/98, before annual exemption.

(c) *Required*
Calculate the capital gains assessable for 1997/98 and any losses carried forward in each of the following situations:
   (i)   Marlene had capital gains for the year 1997/98 of £12,000 and capital losses for the year 1997/98 of £8,000.
   (ii)   Moira had capital gains for the year 1997/98 of £12,000 and capital losses brought forward of £8,000.
   (iii) Marina had capital gains for the year 1997/98 of £3,000 and capital losses brought forward of £8,000.
   (iv)   Melissa had capital gains for the year 1997/98 of £12,000, capital losses for the year 1997/98 of £8,000 and capital losses brought forward of £4,000.

8 Corporation tax

Introduction

Corporation tax is charged on the profits of companies, and the Corporation Tax Acts apply, for any financial year for which Parliament so determines (ICTA 1988 s6(1)). Until 1965 companies, were taxed under the income tax legislation. In 1965 a reform of the tax system led to the introduction of corporation tax. As you will learn in this chapter there are both similarities and differences in the way in which companies are taxed compared to sole traders and partnerships which are subject to income tax. At the end of this chapter you will be able to:

● describe the imputation system of taxation
● state the basis of assessment of tax for companies
● determine the profits chargeable to corporation tax
● calculate any tax payable or repayable when the quarterly returns for dividends and charges paid or received are completed
● calculate a company's mainstream corporation tax
● state the date on which the mainstream corporation tax is due
● compute the loss relief available to a company.

The liability to corporation tax

For corporation tax purposes a company is defined in the Companies Act 1985 as being either a corporate body or an unincorporated association. Hence the definition of a company extends to organisations such as clubs and political associations which are therefore subject to corporation tax. Remember that the definition excludes partnerships which are taxed under Schedule D Case I.

UK resident companies are liable to corporation tax on their total world-wide profits arising in an accounting period regardless of whether the profits are remitted to the UK or not (ICTA 1988 s12(1)). However, dividends received from other UK resident companies are not liable to corporation tax (ICTA 1988 s208). The capital gains of a company are not subject to capital gains tax. However, its capital gains are subject to corporation tax (ICTA 1988 s6(3)).

A company is deemed to be UK resident if it is either incorporated in the UK or if its central management and control are exercised in the UK (FA 1988 s66(1)). A company is still deemed to be resident in the UK, even if it is no longer carrying on any business or it is being wound up outside the UK, if it was resident in the UK immediately prior to it ceasing to trade or being wound up (FA 1988 s66(2)).

Non-resident companies are liable to UK corporation tax if a trade is carried on in the UK through a branch or agency. The trading profits arising, directly or indirectly, from the branch or agency are liable to UK tax whether or not they arise in the UK. Income from property or rights either used by, or held by or for the branch or agency is chargeable to corporation tax, as are any chargeable gains arising from the disposal of assets which were situated in the UK (ICTA 1988 s11(1) & (2)).

The imputation system of taxation

Background

In Chapter 3 we considered whether companies should be liable to tax and reviewed the principal methods of taxing companies. When corporation tax was first introduced the classical system was used. Under the classical system the relationship between a company and its shareholders is ignored. A company pays tax on its profits without reference to its dividend policy and its shareholders pay tax on their dividends received without receiving any relief for the tax already paid by the company. This is a simple system but does lead to distributed profits being taxed twice, once in the hands of the company and then again in the hands of the shareholders.

In 1973 this problem of double taxation of distributed profits led to a switch to the imputation system under which shareholders are given a tax credit for the corporation tax which has been paid by the company. The tax credit can be used to offset any liability to income tax. Look again at the way in which dividends are included in a tax computation under Schedule F in Chapter 4.

For 1997/98 the tax credit is set at a rate of 20%. Taxpayers receive a tax credit equal to 20/80th of any dividend received from a UK company. Gross dividends, that is the dividend together with the related tax credit received by basic rate taxpayers, are subject to income tax at a rate of 20%. This means that lower rate and basic rate taxpayers are able to use their tax credit to satisfy their tax liability. Higher rate taxpayers are taxed at a rate of 40% on their gross dividends received although of course they are able to use the tax credit to reduce the tax liability. Non-taxpayers are able to reclaim the tax credit.

In order to compare the imputation system with the classical system we will use an example.

Example

Aberdeen plc earned a taxable profit of £2 million in the accounting period ended on 31st March 1998. The company paid a dividend of £800,000 on 18th

February 1998. Corporation tax was at 33% for the whole of the year. Gross dividends are taxed at a basic rate of 20%, although higher rate taxpayers are taxed at a rate of 40% on their gross dividends.

Aberdeen plc's position

	Classical system £'000	Imputation system £'000
Schedule DI	2,000	2,000
Corporation tax liability	660	660
Distributable income	1,340	1,340
Dividends paid (gross)	1,000	
Dividends paid (net)		800
Retained earnings	340	540

Note that under the classical system a net dividend payment of £800 (£1,000 × 80%) is made to the shareholders and an additional £200 (£1,000 × 20%), which is the income tax deducted at source, is paid to the Inland Revenue. Hence the cost of paying a dividend to Aberdeen's shareholders under the classical system is £1,000 (£800 + £200).

Under the imputation system once again a net dividend of £800 is paid and £200 advance corporation tax is paid to the Inland Revenue. However, the advance corporation tax is, within limits, deductible from Aberdeen plc's corporation tax liability and so paying the dividend has a net cost of only £800 under the imputation system. If the advance corporation tax is not deductible from the corporation tax liability the dividend will have a net cost of £1,000. We will consider the set off of advance corporation tax later in this chapter.

Shareholder's position

	£'000	£'000
Dividend received	800	800
Income tax deducted at source	200	0
Tax credit	0	200
Gross dividend	1,000	1,000
Income tax liability at 20%	200	200
Less: tax deducted at source	200	0
tax credit	0	200
Tax due	0	0

The shareholder considered in this example was a basic rate taxpayer. As you can see the shareholder's tax position was the same whichever system was used. A little thought should convince you that all shareholders enjoyed the same tax treatment under both systems. A non-taxpayer was able to reclaim either the tax deducted at source or the tax credit while a higher rate taxpayer was required to pay the same amount of additional tax under either system.

The imputation system in detail

When a UK company pays a qualifying distribution to its shareholders it must also pay advance corporation tax (ACT) to the Inland Revenue (ICTA 1988 s14(1)).

A distribution is a qualifying distribution unless it is an issue of redeemable share capital or any other security which is not issued wholly in exchange for new consideration (ICTA 1988 ss 14(2) & 209(2c)).

The advance corporation tax payable is the amount or value of the distribution multiplied by the fraction

$$\frac{I}{100 - I}$$

where I is set by the Finance Act each year (ICTA 1988 s14(3)). For 1997/98 I is 20%.

The ACT paid is treated as a tax credit in the hands of the shareholder as well as a deduction from the company's corporation tax liability.

Activity

Using the rate of ACT for 1997/98 calculate the ACT payable if a dividend of £400 is paid. Add the ACT to the dividend – this is called the franked payment.

Feedback

The ACT payable is equal to $£400 \times \dfrac{20}{100 - 20} = £100.$

The franked payment is £500 (£400 + £100).

Calculation of the corporation tax payable

Income is computed under Schedule D Cases I to VI on the full amount of the profits or gains or income arising in the accounting period (whether or not received in or transmitted to the UK), without any other deduction than is authorised by the Corporation Tax Acts (ICTA 1988 s70(1)).

For corporation tax purposes income received which is taxable under Schedule D Case V is dealt with under the rules for Schedule D Case I income (ICTA 1988 s70(2)).

In order to calculate the corporation tax payable you will need to undertake a number of steps. These are:

1. Determine the accounting period(s) which are to be assessed.
2. Adjust profits for tax purposes and allocate income and allowable expenditure to the correct period.
3. Calculate the profits chargeable to corporation tax.
4. Ascertain the rate(s) at which corporation tax will be charged.

1. Determining the accounting period to be assessed

Look for the similarities and differences between the basis of assessment for companies and unincorporated traders when reading this section.

Corporation tax is assessed and charged for any accounting period of a company on the full amount of the profits arising in the period, whether or not received in or transmitted to the UK, without any other deduction than is authorised by Acts of Parliament (ICTA 1988 s12(1)).

An accounting period of a company shall begin, for corporation tax purposes, whenever:

● the company comes within the charge to corporation tax, usually on commencement to trade
● an earlier accounting period of the company ends without the company then ceasing to be within the charge to corporation tax (ICTA 1988 s12(2)).

An accounting period of a company shall end, for the purposes of corporation tax, on the earliest of the following:

● 12 months after the beginning of the accounting period
● an accounting date of the company or, if there is a period for which the company does not make up accounts, the end of that period
● the commencement of a winding up
● the date on which the company ceases to be UK resident
● the date on which the company ceases to be liable to corporation tax (ICTA 1988 s12(3)).

Activity

Apply the above rules to determine the periods of account when a company changes its year end from 31st December to 31st March by having a 15-month accounting period starting on 1st January 1997.

Feedback

The 1st January 1997 is the start of an accounting period because it is immediately after the end of the previous accounting period. Since it ends 12 months after it starts the first accounting period must run from 1st January 1997 to 31st December 1997.

The second accounting period must commence as soon as the first one finishes and so it begins on 1st January 1998. It ends at the end of the period of account which is 31st March 1998.

2. Allocating adjusted profits to accounting periods

In the activity above you found that the 15-month period of account was split into two accounting periods for tax purposes, the first one 12 months long and the second one three months long. We must now split the profits between the two periods in the following way:

- Schedule D Case I, II and VI income before capital allowances is apportioned on a time basis (ICTA 1988 s72). In our example 12/15ths would be included in the first accounting period while the remaining 3/15ths would be included in the second accounting period.
- Capital allowances, including balancing allowances and charges, are calculated for each accounting period. Writing down allowances are reduced for short accounting periods.
- Other income is allocated on an actual basis to the period to which it relates. For example, bank interest is allocated to the period in which it is received while rent is allocated to the period in which it is due.
- Charges are allocated to the period in which they are paid.
- Chargeable gains are allocated to the period in which they are realised.

Now you need to be able to adjust the company's trading profits for tax purposes. As for income tax the easiest way of calculating the Schedule D Case I profits is to follow the pro forma given here. Numbers are used in the pro forma to make it easier to follow.

Schedule D Case I adjustment of profits
Adjustment of profits for the accounting period ended on 31st December 1997

	£'000	£'000
Net profits per accounts		3,270
Add expenditure disallowed under Sch DI		530
		3,800
Less: Income not assessable under Sch DI	120	
Expenditure not included in the accounts which is an allowable deduction	180	
Capital allowances	500	
		800
Schedule D Case I income		3,000

Notice that the computation is very similar to the one prepared under the rules for income tax.

Charges are treated in the same way as they are for income tax purposes being disallowed in the Schedule D Case I computation and relief given by way of a deduction from total profits.

In Chapter 5 you saw that the incidental costs of obtaining a qualifying loan or qualifying loan stock are allowable deductions from the Schedule D Case I profit.

A loan or loan stock is not a qualifying loan or qualifying loan stock if it carries the right to conversion within three years into either shares or the acquisition of shares or other securities which are not themselves a qualifying loan or qualifying loan stock.

If the right is not, or is not wholly, exercised before the expiry of the three-year period the loan shall be regarded as a qualifying loan or qualifying loan stock (ICTA 1988 s77(3) & (4)). However, if the right is partly exercised within the three-year period only a proportion of the expenses will be allowed. The proportion allowed will be the same as the proportion of the right which has not been exercised. To the extent that some of the incidental costs of obtaining finance are incurred before the expiry of the three-year period they shall be treated as being incurred immediately after the three-year period expires (ICTA 1988 s77(5)).

3. Profits chargeable to corporation tax

Now that the Schedule D Case I income has been computed we can calculate the profits chargeable to corporation tax. Once again we will use a pro forma with numbers in it to demonstrate how to do this.

Profits chargeable to corporation tax for the accounting period ended on 30th September 1997	£'000
Schedule D Case I	3,000
Schedule D Case III	1,000
Schedule D Case IV	110
Schedule D Case V	390
Schedule D Case VI	300
Schedule A	200
Taxed income (gross)	300
Chargeable gains	700
Total profits	6,000
Less charges on income (gross)	(1,000)
Profits chargeable to corporation tax (PCTCT)	5,000

You need to know a little more about some of these items before you are ready to calculate the profits chargeable to corporation tax. We will consider the relevant points in the order in which they appear in the pro forma.

Schedule D Case III

Interest is included in the accounts on the accruals basis while the basis of assessment is the interest received. This may lead to the figure included in the profit and loss account to be different from the figure which needs to be included in the tax computation. The basis for Schedule D Case III for companies is the current year basis, that is the interest received during the accounting period.

Schedule A

Until 5th April 1995 individuals and companies were taxed in the same way under Schedule A. From 6th April 1995 the way in which rent and other income from land and buildings is taxed has changed for individuals while the Schedule A legislation is unchanged for companies. In this chapter we will deal with the old Schedule A rules which apply to companies. The new rules for individuals have been dealt with in Chapters 4 and 6.

Rents due, premiums on leases, ground rents and payments for sporting rights are all taxed under Schedule A provided that the land is located in the UK. Profits or gains arising from a company's occupation of any woodlands which are managed on a commercial basis are not subject to tax under Schedule A.

In order to calculate the taxable income under Schedule A you must be able to do the following:

1. determine the basis of assessment
2. identify the receipts which are taxed under Schedule A
3. calculate the allowable deductions
4. relieve any losses which have arisen under Schedule A.

Basis of assessment

The basis of assessment is the rent 'due and payable' in a chargeable accounting period. That is rent is taxed, not on the accruals basis, or on a cash basis, but on the basis of when it is due to be received.

The accounts must include full details about properties let at full rent, properties let on a tenant's repairing lease and properties let at other than full rents together with any other chargeable items. The taxable profit or loss on each lease must be calculated.

A lease is taken to be at a full rent if the rent paid under the lease is sufficient, taking one year with another, to defray the cost to the lessor of any expenses of maintenance, repairs, insurance and management of the premises subject to the lease which fall to be borne by him (ICTA 1988 s24(7)). A lease at full rent is often referred to as a landlord repairing lease.

A tenant's repairing lease is a lease where the tenant is obliged to maintain and repair the whole, or substantially the whole, of the premises which are the subject of the lease (ICTA 1988 s24(6)).

Taxable receipts

The assessment for the year is made on the assumption that all sources of income and all amounts relevant in computing profits are the same as the previous year (ICTA 1988 s22(2a)).

Rent includes a payment by the tenant to cover the cost of maintenance and repairs to the property which are not required, by the lease, to be carried out by the tenant (ICTA 1988 s24(6)b).

If rent receivable is not paid then provided that the company proves that it did not receive the payment and that either this was because of the default of the payee and it has taken any reasonable steps available to it to enforce payment, or that the company waived payment of the amount in order to avoid hardship to his tenant, then the company is treated as if it had not been entitled to that amount and a repayment of tax will be made if appropriate (ICTA 1988 s41(1)).

Income from holiday lettings is not taxed under Schedule A. It is deemed to be trading income and is taxed under Schedule D Case VI as is income from furnished lettings.

Allowable deductions

The following deductions from income are specifically allowed when computing the Schedule A taxable income:

(a) maintenance, repairs, insurance and management charges
(b) any other services provided by the taxpayer, which he was obliged to provide, but in respect of which he received no separate consideration
(c) any rates such as the council tax and the business tax which the taxpayer rather than the tenant is liable to pay
(d) any rent, ground rent or other periodical payment which relate to the land (ICTA 1988 s25(2)).

The Inland Revenue uses considerable discretion when interpreting this section and in practice most types of expenditure which are of a revenue nature are allowable. For example, the costs of employing staff to decorate, clean, garden and collect rents are allowable deductions. In addition insurance costs and legal and accountancy costs are allowable. However, insurance premiums for policies which provide compensation for loss of rents are not deductible.

Expenditure for maintenance or repairs which was required to remedy dilapidations arising in the period before the property was owned by the company will not be allowable for deduction against tax; rather it will be an allowable cost for capital gains tax purposes (ICTA 1988 s25(4)).

Expenses incurred during a period in which the property is occupied by the owner will not be deductible for Schedule A purposes although they may be eligible for relief under Schedule D Case I.

Interest payable is not an allowable deduction for the purposes of Schedule A. However, provided that in any period of 52 weeks during which interest is payable the property is let at a commercial rent for more than 26 weeks and when not let is either available for letting at such a rent or is only prevented from being occupied at a commercial rent because of repair or construction work being carried out, the interest paid can be deducted as a charge (ICTA 1988 s355(1)). Only interest on the first £30,000 of a loan is eligible for relief if the property is the only or main residence of an individual. However, interest payable can only be set off against Schedule A income. Unrelieved interest can be carried forward and set against income from property without limit.

A void period is a period in which there is no tenant leasing the property (ICTA 1988 s25(2)). Generally expenses incurred during a void period are not allowable deductions. However, expenditure during a void period may be allowable if it began either with the termination of an earlier lease at a full rent or when the company acquired the property and ends with a lease at a full rent (ICTA 1988 s25(5)).

If there is a void period between the date of acquisition of the property and the date when the property was first let expenditure in the void period is allowable provided that it relates to dilapidations which occurred after the property was acquired. If there is a void period between two tenancies expenditure which was incurred during the void period will only be allowed if both the leases were at full rent. In both cases allowable expenses incurred in the void period are relieved by being set against the income from the lease following the void period even if this creates or increases a loss for tax purposes.

As you might expect any capital expenditure which improves the property will not be an allowable deduction for Schedule A purposes although it may be an allowable cost for capital gains tax purposes. This will then exclude expenditure on improvements such as central heating, extensions and double glazing from being allowable deductions from Schedule A income.

Capital allowances are available for machinery and plant provided for use, or used by a person entitled to rents or receipts falling within Schedule A for the maintenance, repair or management of premises in respect of which those rents or receipts arise as they apply in relation to machinery or plant provided for use or used for the purposes of a trade (ICTA 1988 s32(1)).

Allowances and balancing charges are added to the amount of any expenditure on maintenance, repair or management of the premises which is deductible when computing the profits or gains for the purposes of Schedule A and deducting the amount on which any such charge is to be made from that expenditure (ICTA 1988 s32(3)).

Loss relief

If a company owns several properties it may be able to set expenses relating to some properties against income received from others. The income and expenditure for all leases at full rent are pooled for tax purposes enabling losses on some properties to be set against profits on others (ICTA 1988 s25(7)).

If a loss is made on the pool of full rent leases it can be carried forward to be set against the first available profits from full rent leases of the same property or other landlord repairing leases (ICTA 1988 s31(3)).

Excess expenditure on a property let under a tenant's repairing lease can be carried forward to be set against future profits from the same or other full rent leases of the same property (ICTA 1988 s31(3)). Alternatively, by concession, the loss may be set against the income from the pool of leases at full rent (IR leaflet IR27). Note that losses can only be carried forward in this way if the loss creating property is either let continuously on full rent leases or any void period is both preceded by and followed by full rent leases.

We have defined a full rent lease and a tenant's repairing lease. A third type of lease is a lease which is not at full rent, sometimes called a lease at a nominal rent, that is the lease is not expected to generate a profit over a number of years. If a loss is incurred on such a lease, which is likely, it can only be relieved by carrying forward to set against future profits on the same lease, that is the same tenant, in the same property, under the same lease. In practice then it is likely that the loss will remain unrelieved.

Activity

Myston Ltd has the following income. Determine Myston's Schedule A assessment for the accounting period for the year ended 31st March 1998.

Property A
This property was let under a tenant's repairing lease. The rent, which was £2,600 a year until December 1997, is payable quarterly in advance on the usual quarter days. The rent increased to £3,000 a year beginning with the December 1997 payment. The allowable expenses for the year were £4,000.

Property B
This property was let under a landlord repairing lease. The annual rent of £7,200 was payable quarterly in advance on the usual quarter days. The allowable expenses for the year were £1,500.

Property C
This property was let under a landlord repairing lease. The annual rent of £7,800 was payable quarterly in advance on the usual quarter days. The rent due on 25th March 1998 was not received until 10th April. The allowable expenses for the year were £1,000.

Property D
This property was let under a tenant repairing lease. The property was let for the first time in the fiscal year on 29th September 1997 at a rent of £7,800 a year payable quarterly in arrears on the usual quarter days. The allowable expenses for the year were £800.

Property E
This property was let under a lease at a nominal rent of £600 a year payable in advance on the first of each month. Allowable expenses in the year to 31st March 1998 were £1,000.

Feedback

Myston's Schedule A assessment for year ended 31st March 1998					
	A	B	C	D	E
	£	£	£	£	£
Income	2,800	7,200	7,800	3,900	600
Expenditure	4,000	1,500	1,000	800	1,000
Profit/(loss)	(1,200)	5,700	6,800	3,100	(400)

Properties B and C are landlord repairing leases and so can be pooled. Profits on landlord repairing leases £5,700 + £6,800 = £12,500.

Any loss on a tenant's repairing lease can be set against the profits of the landlord repairing leases. The loss on property A can be relieved this way £12,500 − £1,200 = £11,300. Finally, the profit from other tenant's repairing leases can be added to determine the Schedule A assessment. The Schedule A assessment is £11,300 + £3,100 = £14,400.

Notes
Property A: The income receivable is made up of two payments at the old rate of £650 a quarter and two payments at the new rate of £750 a quarter.
Property C: The rent received on 10th April is still assessable in the year to 31st March 1998 because the basis of assessment is the rent receivable during the accounting period.
Property E: Because the property is let at a nominal rent any loss incurred can be relieved only against future profits from the same tenancy. Hence the loss of £400 cannot be relieved in the current period and must be carried forward.

Schedule D Case VI

Remember that Schedule D Case VI is used to tax annual profits or gains not falling under any other Case of Schedule D and not charged by virtue of Schedule A, C or E (ICTA 1988 s18(3)). In particular corporate income from furnished lettings is taxed under Schedule D Case VI. The basis of assessment under Schedule D Case VI is the income received during the fiscal year. Allowable deductions include all the deductions which would have been allowed under Schedule A together with the cost of repairing and insuring the contents of the property and an allowance for wear and tear of the furniture which is equal to 10% of the rent. If the premises are occupied by the company for part of the year the allowance is reduced proportionately.

Losses suffered on furnished lettings assessed under Schedule D Case VI can be set against any Schedule D Case VI profits in the year in which the loss arose. The loss can also be carried forward to be set against future Schedule D Case VI profits.

The legislation allows a taxpayer to elect for the part of the rent which relates to the premises to be taxed under Schedule A rather than Schedule D Case VI for a year of assessment. This creates Schedule A income which can be used to relieve Schedule A losses which arose on either tenant's repairing leases or leases at full rent.

Furnished holiday lettings are also assessed under Schedule D Case VI. The regulations which apply to Schedule D Case I are used to determine the taxable income.

Taxed income

Taxed income includes all income received net of basic and lower rate tax. Examples include interest received from a UK company, patent royalties and bank interest but not copyright payments or building society interest.

Taxed income is included in the tax computation at its gross value, that is the amount received together with the tax credit. This may be different from the amount included in the profit and loss account.

Dividends received from UK companies are excluded from the tax computation because they are not subject to corporation tax.

Chargeable gains

Companies are not liable to capital gains tax but their chargeable gains and allowable losses, which are calculated in exactly the same way as for individuals, are subject to corporation tax (ICTA 1988 s6(3)). However, unlike individuals, companies do not have an annual exemption to set against their chargeable gains.

Charges paid

Just like income tax, charges are usually payments made net of basic rate tax. Patent royalties, covenanted payments and some one-off donations to charities are all charges.

If donations to charity are to be treated as a charge they must be paid net of basic rate tax. However, donations to charities which are made wholly and

Activity

Bournemouth Ltd had the following results for the year ended 31st March 1998.

	£'000	£'000
Gross profit on trading		1,200
Investment income		300
Profit on sale of investments		200
		1,700
Less: Depreciation	100	
Directors' emoluments	150	
Patent royalties payable	30	
Audit and accountancy fees	45	
Legal costs	20	
Salaries	100	
Premium on lease written off	25	
Miscellaneous expenses	30	
		500
Net profit for year		1,200

	£'000
(a) Investment income	
Investment income comprised the following:	
Dividends from UK companies (gross)	200
Loan interest from UK company (gross)	100
(b) Profit on sale of investment	
The profit on the sale of investment relates to a sale of quoted ordinary shares during the year. The chargeable gain is £150,000.	
(c) Legal costs	
Legal costs comprised the following:	
expenditure:	
Costs re issue of debentures	5
Costs re issue of shares	12
Costs re renegotiations of directors'	
service agreements	3
(d) Lease premium	
The lease premium written off relates to a lease taken out at the beginning of the accounting period for a warehouse for a period of 17 years. The premium paid was £25,000.	
(e) Capital allowances	
Capital allowances have been agreed at £50,000	

Calculate the profits chargeable to corporation tax

exclusively for the purpose of the trade will be allowable deductions from the Schedule D Case I profits. Of course no payment can be both an allowable deduction from the Schedule D Case I profits and a charge. An example of such a donation might be a gift to an employees' welfare organisation.

The charges which are added back in the adjustments of profits computation are equal to the amount which is included in the profit and loss account. This figure will usually be determined using the accruals basis rather than the cash paid basis. The amount allowed as a charge in the calculation of profits chargeable to corporation tax is the cash paid plus any tax withheld if the charge was paid net. Hence the two figures may not be the same.

Before you attempt an activity there is a final word to say about capital allowances. The capital allowances computation is exactly the same as for a sole trader or partnership. However, companies do not own any assets with a private use element. If the directors, or other employees, have the private use of an asset the capital allowances are not reduced. Under the rules for income tax the directors, or other employees, are assessed on the value of the benefit under the Schedule E rules.

The preceding activity is intended to give you an opportunity to determine the profits chargeable to corporation tax from a profit and loss account. You can find out how to deal with the premium on a lease in the section on Schedule A in Chapter 6. It is a complicated question and so you might find it difficult to get everything right on your first attempt.

Feedback

First you needed to calculate the Schedule D Case I income.

Schedule D Case I

	£'000	£'000
Net profit per accounts		1,200
Add: Depreciation	100	
Patent royalties	30	
Legal costs	12	
Lease premium written off	25	
		167
		1,367
Less: Investment income	300	
Profit on sale of investments	200	
Capital allowances	50	
Lease premium (Working 1)	1	
		551
Schedule D Case I income		916

Working 1
The amount of the lease assessable on the landlord under Schedule A is £25,000 − £25,000 × (17 − 1) × 2% = £17,000. The amount which is allowable in the accounting period ended 31st March 1998 is £17,000/17 = £1,000.

Now you can calculate the profits chargeable to corporation tax.

	£
Schedule D Case I	916,000
Taxed income	100,000
Chargeable gains	150,000
	1,166,000
Less charges paid: patent royalties	30,000
Profits chargeable to corporation tax	1,136,000

4. The rate of corporation tax payable

The rate of corporation tax is set for financial years, rather than the fiscal years of the income tax legislation. A financial year (FY) runs from 1st April to the following 31st March: the financial year 1997 runs from 1st April 1997 to 31st March 1998. The rate of corporation tax for a financial year is set in arrears in the Finance Act (ICTA 1988 s8(5)). Hence the rate for the financial year 1997 will be set in the Finance Act 1998. In practice in recent years Chancellors have offered companies advance notice of the rates. During the mid-1980s the rate of corporation tax was reduced in stages from 52% to 35% at the same time as the first year allowances for plant and machinery were phased out. The changes were legislated for in advance. More recently in the Finance Act 1991 the Chancellor set the rate for the financial year 1990 to 34% and the rate for the financial year 1991 to 33%.

Look back to Chapters 1 and 3 for a full discussion of the impact of these changes. Briefly the changes led to a broadening of the tax base, by reducing the rate of capital allowances on plant and machinery from 100% to 25%, and enabled the Chancellor to reduce the tax rates while maintaining the level of taxation raised from companies. Many manufacturing companies found themselves paying corporation tax for the first time for many years. The generous capital allowances given previously had shielded them from corporation tax entirely. Companies which did not invest heavily in plant and machinery benefited greatly from the reduction in the rate of corporation tax. Hence the move tended to benefit service industries with high labour costs and low capital investment at the expense of manufacturing industries.

In the 1996 budget the Chancellor introduced measures to reduce the capital allowances for plant and machinery with an expected useful life of at least 25 years to 6%. Look back to Chapter Five for a full discussion of these proposals. The new rules will only apply to companies who spend more than £100,000 a year on such long-life assets. This limit of £100,000 must be shared equally between associated companies. For example, a company which has three associated companies will have an annual limit of £25,000 (£100,000/4).

Companies are associated with each other if either one controls the other or if both are controlled by the same person or persons, who may be individuals, partnerships or companies (ICTA 1988 s13(4)). Associated companies do not have to be UK resident.

Control for these purposes is defined as holding over 50% of the share capital or 50% of the voting power or being entitled to over 50% of the distributable income or of the net assets in a winding up (ICTA 1988 s416).

You should have realised that companies with year ends other than 31st March will straddle two financial years which may have differing rates for corporation tax.

If the rate for the two years is the same, as it often is, there is no difficulty. The profits chargeable to corporation tax are taxed at the rate prevailing for the two years.

If the rate does change between the two years the profits chargeable to corporation tax are apportioned to the two financial years on a time basis (ICTA 1988 s8(4)).

Cardiff Ltd has 30th June as a permanent accounting date. In the year to 30th June 1991 Cardiff generated profits chargeable to corporation tax of £4 million. In the financial year 1990 the full rate for corporation tax was 34% while in the financial year 1991 the rate was reduced to 33%. Calculate Cardiff Ltd's tax liability for the year to 30 June 1991.

Feedback

Profits	Tax rate %	Tax liability £
£4m × 9/12	34	1,020,000
£4m × 3/12	33	330,000
	Tax payable	1,350,000

The first nine months of the accounting period fall in the financial year 1990 and so the profits attributable to this period are taxed at 34%. The remaining three months of the accounting period fall in the financial year 1991 and so the profits attributable to this period should be taxed at only 33%.

Franked investment income is made up of dividends received from another UK resident company and the related tax credit (ICTA 1988 s238(1)). You have already seen that such dividends are not subject to corporation tax.

Companies whose profits chargeable to corporation tax plus franked investment income are not more than £300,000 are taxed at the small companies rate which is equal to the basic rate of income tax which for financial year 1997 is 23% (ICTA 1988 s13). Over 85% of companies are either taxed at the small companies rate or benefit from tapering relief.

If a company's profits chargeable to corporation tax plus franked investment income exceeds this lower limit it is taxed at a rate of 33%. However, if a company's profits chargeable to corporation tax plus franked investment income exceeds £300,000 but is not more than £1,500,000 tapering relief, or small companies relief, is available (ICTA 1988 s13(2)).

The tapering relief is equal to:

$$\text{Fraction} \times (M - P) \times \frac{I}{P}$$

where M is the upper limit of £1,500,000, P is the profits chargeable to corporation tax plus franked investment income and I is the profit chargeable to corporation tax (ICTA 1988 s13(2)).

The fraction for FY 1997 is 1/40. In the financial year 1996 the small companies rate was 24% and the fraction was 9/400.

If a company's accounting period straddles two financial years in which the upper and lower limits for the small companies relief change the accounting period is split into two, the first one ending on 31st March, and the second one beginning on the 1st April and ending on the date of the accounting period. The tax is calculated for each period separately. All income and expenditure is apportioned on a time basis regardless of when any payments or receipts occurred. The upper and lower limits are proportionately reduced on a time basis.

Activity

Doncaster Ltd reported profits chargeable to corporation tax of £500,000 for the accounting period ended 30th June 1994. The lower limit for the financial year 1993 was £250,000 and the upper limit was £1,250,000. The lower limit for the financial year 1994 was £300,000 and the upper limit was £1,500,000. The marginal relief fraction for both years was 1/50. Calculate the profits which will be allocated to each period and find the limits which are used to determine the rate at which the company will pay tax.

Feedback

	Financial year 1993 £	Financial year 1994 £
Lower limits	$250,000 \times 9/12$ = 187,500	$300,000 \times 3/12$ = 75,000
Upper limits	$1,250,000 \times 9/12$ = 937,500	$1,500,000 \times 3/12$ = 375,000
PCTCT	$500,000 \times 9/12$	$500,000 \times 3/12$

Nine months of the accounting period fall in the financial year 1993 while the remaining three months fall in the financial year 1994. The profits and limits for the financial years are shown above.

Now that you can calculate the profits chargeable to corporation tax and determine the rate of tax at which a company will pay tax you are able to calculate a company's corporation tax liability.

Activity

Ealing plc has profits chargeable to corporation tax of £290,000 and franked investment income of £40,000 for the year ended 31st March 1998. Calculate Ealing's corporation tax liability.

Feedback

	£
PCTCT	290,000
FII	40,000
Profits	330,000

The profits lie between £300,000 and £1,500,000 so tapering relief applies.

	£
Corporation tax on PCTCT £290,000 × 33%	95,700
Less tapering relief	
1/40 × £(1,500,000 – 330,000) × 290,000/330,000	25,705
Corporation tax liability	69,995

If a company has a short accounting period the upper and lower limits are reduced proportionately (ICTA 1988 s13(6)). If a company has one or more associated companies the upper and lower limits are divided by the total number of companies associated with each other (ICTA 1988 s13(3)).

Activity

Felixstow plc prepared accounts for nine months to 31st December 1997. Felixstow has profits chargeable to corporation tax of £160,000 and franked investment income of £40,000. Felixstow has one associated company. Determine the corporation tax payable.

Feedback

	£
PCTCT	160,000
FII	40,000
Profits	200,000

The limits for tapering relief are reduced by a quarter because the accounting period was only nine months long. The limits are then divided by the total number of associated companies, in this case there are two associated companies.

Hence the lower limit is £300,000 × 9/12 × 1/2 = £112,500 and the upper limit is £1,500,000 × 9/12 × 1/2 = £562,500.

	£
Corporation tax payable on PCTCT 160,000 × 33%	52,800
Less tapering relief	
1/40 × £(562,500 – 200,000) × 160,000/200,000	7,250
Corporation tax liability	45,550

Calculation of the mainstream corporation tax payable

Now that you can determine the corporation tax liability of a company you must undertake a number of adjustments in order to ascertain the mainstream corporation tax.

The mainstream corporation tax is the amount of tax which the company must pay to the Inland Revenue after the end of the tax year to settle the company's corporation tax liability for the accounting period.

Basically a company can set any ACT paid, and not repaid, and any income tax suffered against its corporation tax liability.

The steps you will need to undertake are:

1. Calculate the net ACT balance and the net income tax paid and check that the ACT balance is less than the maximum ACT set-off.
2. Determine the mainstream corporation tax payable.

Finally you will need to be able determine the date on which the mainstream corporation tax must be paid.

Calculation of the net act and income tax paid

Quarterly accounting for ACT

At the beginning of this chapter you learnt how to calculate the ACT which is payable whenever a company pays a dividend.

Now we will study a more complex situation when a company not only pays dividends but also receives them from other UK companies. Look at the sections on Schedules and Cases in Chapter 4 to find out how dividends from foreign companies are dealt with for tax purposes.

As you have already seen if a company receives a dividend from a UK company it also receives a tax credit equal to 20/80 of the dividend received. The dividend together with the tax credit is termed franked investment income (ICTA 1988 s238(1)). Because the dividend received has been paid out of income which has already been subjected to UK corporation tax the franked investment income received is not taxable in the hands of another UK company.

When paying a dividend a company need only pay ACT on the excess of dividends paid over dividends received thus enabling it to use the tax credit it has received.

Activity

Gisburn plc received a dividend of £400 from another UK company and paid a dividend of £1,000. Calculate the ACT payable.

Feedback

The franked investment income received is £400 × 100/80 = £500. The franked payment made is £1,000 × 100/80 = £1,250.

The ACT payable is equal to:

(Franked payment – Franked investment income) × 20%.

Hence Gisburn plc must pay ACT of £(1,250 – 500) × 20% = £150.

The financial year is divided into quarters ending on 31st March, 30th June, 30th September and 31st December. In addition, if the company's year end is not one of these quarter dates, the quarter in which the year end falls is divided into two periods with the first one ending on the company's accounting date.

The company must submit form CT61, together with any ACT payable, within 14 days of the end of each quarter in which either a franked payment is made or franked investment income is received.

Activity

Halifax plc has paid and received the following dividends during the year ended 31st March 1998.

Date	Dividends received £	Dividends paid £
10th April 1997	1,280	
10th June 1997		2,240
1st July 1997	640	
15th October 1997	3,520	
15th November 1997		1,920
9th January 1998	1,280	
20th March 1998		640

Return period	Franked payment £	Franked investment income £

Complete the table allocating franked payments and franked investment income to return periods.

Feedback

Your table should be completed as follows:

Return period	Franked payment £	Franked investment income £
Quarter to 30.6.97		
10.4.97		(1,600)
10.6.97	2,800	
Quarter to 30.9.97		
1.7.97		(800)
Quarter to 31.12.97		
15.10.97		(4,400)
15.11.97	2,400	
Quarter to 31.3.98		
9.1.98		(1,600)
20.3.98	800	

Now you have calculated the franked payments and the franked investment income for each return period we can determine the ACT to be paid or the ACT which can be reclaimed. As you might expect the revenue will not allow a company to claim a repayment of ACT unless it has actually paid it. Unless a loss relief claim is made it is not possible for a company to reclaim the tax credit which is attributed to its franked investment income.

Quarterly returns

Now we can complete the quarterly return.

Return period	FP £	FII £	Cumulative £	ACT paid (repaid) £
Quarter to 30.6.97				
10.4.97		(1,600)		
10.6.97	2,800			
			1,200	240
Quarter to 30.9.97				
1.7.97		(800)		
			(800)	(160)
			400	80
Quarter to 31.12.97				
15.10.97		(4,400)		
15.11.97	2,400			
			(2,000)	(80)
			(1,600)	Nil
Quarter to 31.3.98				
9.1.98		(1,600)		
20.3.98	800			
			(800)	
Surplus franked investment income c/f			(2,400)	

Note that in the quarter to 31.12.97 only the ACT which had been paid and not reclaimed in a previous quarter in the current accounting period could be reclaimed. The balance is surplus franked investment income which can be carried forward to be set against ACT due in the future.

If an accounting period straddles 6th April in a year in which the rate of ACT changes the period is divided into two notional accounting periods for ACT purposes. The first period ends on 5th April. ACT paid in the first of these periods cannot be repaid if franked investment income exceeds franked payments in the second of these periods. The surplus franked investment income must be carried forward to the next accounting period. Any ACT not repaid in either of these periods can be set against the company's corporation tax liability in the normal way.

The set-off of ACT against a corporation tax liability

ACT which has not been repaid can be set against a company's corporation tax liability for the accounting period subject to a maximum set-off which is equal to the rate of the tax credit for dividends (20%) times the profits chargeable to corporation tax. If the rate of tax changed during the accounting period leading to the creation of two nominal accounting periods the profits chargeable to corporation tax are apportioned to each period on a time basis in order to calculate the maximum set-off.

Activity

Calculate the maximum ACT set-off for Ipstones Ltd who had profits chargeable to corporation tax of £200,000 for the year to 30th June 1997.

Feedback

The maximum ACT set-off is 20% × £200,000 = £40,000.

Any ACT paid in excess of the maximum ACT set-off is termed surplus ACT and can be relieved by carrying it forward to future accounting periods or carrying it back to accounting periods which began in the six years preceding the year in which the ACT was paid.

ACT which is carried back is subject to the maximum set-off, which is calculated as described above. The ACT must be relieved in the later years first. This is sometimes termed the LIFO basis, last in first out.

ACT can also be carried forward indefinitely but must be used as soon as possible. Once again the amount which can be set off is limited to the maximum set-off.

Calculation of the mainstream corporation tax

The corporation tax liability reduced by the ACT set-off is termed the mainstream corporation tax liability.

Activity

Jarrow Ltd began trading on 1st April 1995 and has the following results:

	Accounting period to		
	31.3.96	31.3.97	31.3.98
	£'000	£'000	£'000
Schedule D Case I	143	200	170
Schedule D Case III	20	20	20
	163	220	190
Chargeable gains	2	10	40
	165	230	230
Charges	(30)	(30)	(30)
PCTCT	135	200	200
FII	8	40	20
'Profits'	143	240	220
Franked payments	53	200	300

Jarrow Ltd has no associated companies.

Calculate Jarrow Ltd's mainstream corporation tax liabilities for each of the above years.

Feedback

	Accounting period to		
	31.3.96	31.3.97	31.3.98
	£'000	£'000	£'000
ACT paid			
£(53 – 8) × 20%	9		
£(200 – 40) × 20%		32	
£(300 – 20) × 20%			56
Maximum set-off 20% × PCTCT	(27)	(40)	(40)
Surplus ACT	0	0	16
Surplus ACT carried back	8	8	(16)
Corporation tax			
on PCTCT at 25%/24%/23%	30	48	46
ACT set-off	17	40	40
MCT due	13	8	6

Income tax paid and withheld

The treatment of taxed income, also called unfranked investment income, and charges is very similar to the treatment of franked investment income and franked payments. In fact they are both dealt with on the same form CT61, albeit in different sections. Of course income tax is withheld at a rate of 23%, equivalent to the basic rate of income tax, rather than the lower rate which applies to franked investment income and franked payments. Until 6th April 1997 tax was withheld at a rate of 24%. You will remember that when dealing with dividends paid and received, form CT61 includes franked investment income and franked payments. Similarly charges and taxed income are recorded gross in form CT61. However, when dealing with taxed income and charges the form includes only the tax suffered and the tax deducted. In addition there are other differences between the treatment of unfranked income and charges and franked investment income and franked payments. The two main differences are that taxed income is subject to corporation tax whilst, as we have seen, franked investment income is not and there is a maximum set-off for ACT while there is no limitation on the amount of income tax which can be set off.

However, it is important that franked payments and income are dealt with separately to unfranked income and charges. You might like to think of them as being like oil and water. They are both liquids but they do not mix.

You will remember that in the corporation tax computation charges are deducted from income at their gross amount rather than the amount actually paid. However, as you have already seen, companies deduct basic rate tax at source from charges and pay only the net amount. Effectively the company acts as an agent for the Inland Revenue and must pay the tax deducted to the Revenue.

In the same way as a company must pay any ACT due to the Revenue within 14 days of the end of a quarter period in which the dividend was paid the tax deducted from charges must be paid to the Revenue within 14 days of the end of the quarter period in which the charge was paid.

However, the company may deduct any tax which has been withheld on unfranked investment income received, from the tax it has withheld from its charges paid, from its payment to the Revenue. That is it only pays income tax on the excess of charges paid over its taxed income received. You will have realised that this is exactly the same as for franked payments and franked investment income. Of course since taxed income and charges are usually stated gross it is not necessary to gross them up whereas we do need to gross up dividends paid and received.

Any income tax suffered which is not eligible for repayment through the quarterly accounting system can be set against the corporation tax liability without limit provided that the company makes a separate repayment claim at the end of the year.

If there is a change in the basic rate of income tax during an accounting period there is no need to split the accounting period into two notional periods. The cumulative total simply includes the tax deducted and the tax suffered regardless of the rate at which it is deducted or suffered.

Activity

Kelsoe plc has the following taxed income and charges for the year to 30th September 1997.

		£
18.11.96	Charge paid	12,000 (gross)
20.2.97	Income received	16,000 (gross)
30.3.97	Charge paid	12,000 (gross)
20.8.97	Income received	16,000 (gross)

Complete the following table.

Return period	Income tax deducted £	Income tax suffered on income £	Cumulative £	Income tax paid/ (repaid) £

Feedback

Return period	Income tax deducted £	Income tax suffered on income £	Cumulative £	Income tax paid/ (repaid) £
1.10.96–31.12.96	2,880		2,880	2,880
1.1.97–31.3.97	2,880	(3,840)	(960) 1,920	(960)
1.7.97–30.9.97		(3,680)	(3,680) (1,760)	(1,920)

Notes

The payment of income tax of £2,880 which relates to the charge paid on 18th November 1996 is due on 14th January 1997, 14 days after the end of the return period.

No return is made for the third quarter in the accounting period because no payments were made or received during the quarter.

In the final quarter only £1,920 of the income tax suffered at source is repayable because the repayment is limited to the income tax which has already been paid during the accounting period.

The final balance of £1,760 will be set against the company's corporation tax liability after deducting any ACT. If the corporation tax less deductible ACT is less than £1,760 a repayment of the income tax suffered will be made.

Payment of corporation tax

The mainstream corporation tax is payable nine months after the end of the accounting period. Companies will have to pay the estimated corporation tax on the due date, that is, nine months after the end of the accounting period, even if the exact amount is not known by that date. The company must file complete accounts, computations, the return form and any corporation tax still outstanding on the filing date, which is 12 months after the end of the accounting period. This system is called pay and file.

The Inspector of Taxes will only raise an assessment if he or she believes that the filed computation understates the amount of tax which is payable. If the amount of tax paid is either late or too little a company may be liable for interest payments or penalties or both.

Self-assessment for companies will be introduced in 1999 at the earliest. Under the proposed self-assessment regime there will not be any major changes in the way in which companies file their returns or pay taxes. The companies tax return will also act as the assessment of the companies tax liability.

Losses

Now that you are able to calculate a company's mainstream corporation tax liability you are ready to deal with the situation which arises when companies make losses.

There are a number of ways in which a loss can be relieved. Although there are some similarities between the taxation of individuals and companies when losses are made it is probably easier to treat them completely separately. Unlike the adjustment of profits for Schedule D Case I where a little common sense might help you to find the right answer it is necessary to learn the rules for loss relief. One of the easiest ways of learning the rules is to use a pro forma.

There are a number of different ways of incurring a loss and a number of different reliefs which are available. Briefly these are:

- *Trading losses*
  Trading losses can be: set against other income of the same accounting period, carried back and set against trading income of earlier accounting periods, carried forward and set against future trading income or set-off against franked investment income.
- *Capital losses*
  Capital losses can be set against current or future capital gains.
- *Schedule A losses:*
  Corporate Schedule A losses were dealt with earlier in this chapter.

We will start by studying each of the reliefs available for trading losses. In each case you will be given a pro forma which will help you tackle the problems at the end of the chapter.

Loss relief by setting against future trading income (ICTA 1988 S393(1))

If a company carrying on a trade incurs a loss in the trade in an accounting period the company can claim for the loss to be set off, for the purposes of corporation tax, against trading income from the trade in future accounting periods.

If, within three years, there is both a change in the ownership of a company and a major change in the nature or conduct of a trade carried on by the company losses incurred in an accounting period beginning prior to the change in ownership cannot be carried forward and set against trading profits earned in an accounting period ending after the change in ownership under section 393 (ICTA 1988 s768(1)). Note that for the purposes of section 768 an accounting period is deemed to end on the date of the change of ownership (ICTA 1988 s768(2)).

A major change in the nature or conduct of a trade includes a major change in the type of property dealt in or services or facilities provided, in the trade or a major change in customers, outlets or markets of the trade. The Revenue may consider that such a major change has taken place even if the change is the result of a gradual process which began outside the three-year period identified above (ICTA 1988 s768(4)).

In a Statement of Practice published in 1994 the Inland Revenue offered guidance as to what would be considered to be a major change in the nature or conduct of a trade. In addition to the factors mentioned in the legislation the Revenue would consider changes in other factors such as location of business premises, suppliers, management, staff, methods of manufacture and pricing or purchasing policies to indicate that a major change may have occurred.

When considering whether a change is a major change the Inland Revenue would compare conditions applying before and after the change during any period of three years which include the date of the change of ownership. All of the relevant factors will be considered although it may be that a change in only one factor may be sufficient to constitute a major change. Changes which are solely intended to increase efficiency or keep pace with developing technology or management techniques will not be considered to be major. Similarly a rationalisation in the product range or a replacement of unprofitable items with new items of a kind related to those already being produced will not constitute a major change. To further clarify the matter the Statement of Practice includes seven examples. The following changes would not be considered to be major changes:

- a company manufacturing kitchen fitments in three obsolescent factories moves production to one new factory. This would be allowed on the grounds of increased efficiency

- a company manufacturing kitchen utensils replaces enamel by plastic, or a company manufacturing timepieces replaces mechanical by electronic components. This would be allowed on the grounds of keeping pace with developing technology
- a company operating a dealership in one make of car switches to operating a dealership in another make of car satisfying the same market. This would be allowed on the grounds that it is not a major change in the type of property dealt in
- a company manufacturing both filament and fluorescent lamps, of which filament lamps form the greater part of the output, concentrates solely on filament lamps. This would be allowed on the grounds that it is a rationalisation of the product range without a major change in the type of property dealt in.

The following changes would be considered to be major changes:

- a company operating a dealership in saloon cars switches to operating a dealership in tractors. Such a change would be considered a major change in the type of property dealt in
- a company owning a public house switches to operating a discothèque in the same, but converted, premises. Such a change would be considered a major change in the services of facilities provided
- a company fattening pigs for their owners switches to buying pigs for fattening and resale. Such a change would be considered a major change from providing a service to being a primary producer (Statement of Practice 10/91 issued in July 1994).

Provided that the company is deemed to have carried on the same trade the trading income from the trade in succeeding accounting periods shall be treated as reduced by the amount of the loss. Only losses which have not been relieved by carrying back to an earlier accounting period can be relieved in this way. The loss must be set against the first available trading profits (ICTA 1988 s393(1)).

If the charges paid in an accounting period exceed the amount of the profits against which they are deducted and include payments made wholly and exclusively for the purposes of a trade carried on by the company the excess of those payments can be treated as a trading expense for the purpose of section 393(1) (ICTA 1988 s393(9)). This means that unrelieved trading charges can be added to any trading losses being carried forward under s393(1). Unrelieved charges which are not wholly and exclusively for the purposes of trade, for example deeds of covenant to charities, cannot be relieved under s393(1). However, a claim for group relief of both trade and non-trade charges can be made by members of a group. We will consider group relief in the next chapter. In addition non-trade charges can be set against any trading income for the year in which they are paid before trading charges, which can be carried forward, and relieved.

An example should help to explain this section and will also serve as a pro forma for you to use when you attempt questions yourself.

Example

London Ltd has the following results for the three years to 31st March 1998

	31.3.96 £	Year ended 31.3.97 £	31.3.98 £
Trading profit (loss)	(10,000)	6,500	6,000
Non-trade charges	500	500	500
Trade charges	800	800	800

Calculate the profits chargeable to corporation tax for each of the years concerned.

Solution

	31.3.96 £	Year ended 31.3.97 £	31.3.98 £
Schedule D Case I	Nil	6,500	6,000
Less s393(1) loss relief		(6,500)	(5,100)
non-trading charges	0	0	(500)
trading charges	0	0	(400)
PCTCT	0	0	0

Loss memorandum

Trading loss for y/e 31.3.96	10,000
Add: unrelieved trading charges for y/e 31.3.96	800
Loss carried forward @ 1.4.96	10,800
Less s393(1) relief in y/e 31.3.97	(6,500)
	4,300
Add: unrelieved trading charges for y/e 31.3.97	800
Loss carried forward @ 1.4.97	5,100
Less s393(1) relief in y/e 31.3.98	(5,100)
	0
Add: unrelieved trading charges for y/e 31.3.98	400
Loss carried forward @ 1.4.98	400

Note the way in which a loss memorandum has been used. It is a good way of keeping track of the way in which the loss has been relieved.

Loss relief against total profits (ICTA 1988 s393A(1))

If a company, carrying on a trade, incurs a loss in the trade the company may claim for the loss to be set-off for the purposes of corporation tax against profits, before charges, from any source of the accounting period in which the loss arose and against the profits before non-trade charges of preceding accounting periods which fall wholly or partly within a period of three years immediately preceding the accounting period in which the loss is incurred provided the company was then carrying on the trade giving rise to the loss. In each period in which the loss is relieved sufficient profits are left unrelieved to enable trade charges to be relieved except for the year in which the loss arose. The amount of the reduction which may be made to the profits of an accounting period falling partly before the beginning of the three-year period shall not exceed a part of those profits which are proportionate to the part of the accounting period falling within the three years (ICTA 1988 s393A(1) & (2)).

In order to claim the relief it is necessary to show that the trade was being carried on on a commercial basis and with a view to the realisation of gain in the trade in the accounting period in which the loss was incurred (ICTA 1988 s393A(3)).

Note that when within any period of three years there is both a change in the ownership of a company and a major change in the nature or conduct of a trade carried on by the company, it will not be possible to set a loss incurred by the company in an accounting period ending after the change in ownership against any profits of an accounting period beginning before the change in ownership under section 393A(1) (ICTA 1988 s768A(1)).

Relief must be claimed for the current period before any loss can be carried back to earlier periods. The carry back is on a LIFO basis, that is the loss is carried back to more recent periods before earlier periods.

Once again an example will help you to see how the relief is calculated in practice and provide you with a pro forma to use for your own work.

Example

Maidstone Ltd has reported the following results for the period from 1.4.93 to 30.9.97.

| | Period ended | | | | |
	31.3.94 £	30.9.94 £	30.9.95 £	30.9.96 £	30.9.97 £
Trading profit/ (loss)	3,000	(4,000)	15,000	12,000	(29,000)
Schedule A	800	800	800	800	800
Chargeable gains	900	0	200	0	2,000
Non-trading charges	300	0	300	300	300
Trade charges	1,200	600	1,200	1,200	1,200

Maidstone did not make a claim for the loss incurred in the six months to 30th September 1994 to be relieved under s393A(1).

Calculate the profits chargeable to corporation tax for each of the periods affected assuming that loss relief under s393A(1) is claimed for the loss in the year ended 30th September 1997.

Solution

	Period ended				
	31.3.94 £	30.9.94 £	30.9.95 £	30.9.96 £	30.9.97 £
Schedule D I	3,000	0	15,000	12,000	0
Less s393(1)	0	0	4,000	0	0
	3,000	0	11,000	12,000	0
Schedule A	800	800	800	800	800
Chargeable gains	900	0	200	0	2,000
	4,700	800	12,000	12,800	2,800
Less s393A(1)	2,350	200	10,800	11,600	2,800
	2,350	600	1,200	1,200	0
Less trade charges	1,200	600	1,200	1,200	0
non-trade charges	300	0	0	0	0
PCTCT	850	0	0	0	0

Loss memorandum

	£	£
Loss incurred in y/e 30.9.97		29,000
Less s393A(1): y/e 30.9.97	2,800	
y/e 30.9.96	11,600	
y/e 30.9.95	10,800	
p/e 30.9.94	200	
y/e 31.3.94	2,350	
		27,750
Loss unrelieved under s393A(1)		1,250
Add unrelieved trading charges y/e 30.9.97		1,200
Loss carried forward under s393(1) at 1.10.97		2,450

Note that losses are always dealt with on a FIFO basis, that is a loss from an earlier year is relieved before a loss from a later year is dealt with. If you think about this you will realise that in practice this would happen automatically but when working an example it is possible to make mistakes.

Until 1991 terminal loss relief was available to companies which ceased to trade. However, terminal loss relief was repealed by FA 1991 because relief under ICTA s393 was extended to periods which fall within three years of the beginning of the loss-making period. Any unrelieved trade charges can be added to the Schedule D Case I loss arising in the final period of trading which is carried back under s393 (ICTA s393A(7)).

Loss relief for surplus FII (ICTA 1988 s242)

Until now we have assumed that surplus franked investment income must be carried forward and relieved only when a dividend is paid. However, it is possible to claim relief for surplus franked investment income even if dividends are not paid.

Under ICTA 1988 s242(2) a company can claim for the surplus franked investment income to be treated as if it were profits chargeable to corporation tax for the purpose of:

- setting off trading losses against total profits under s393A(1)
- deducting unrelieved non-trading charges
- deducting management expenses of investment companies.

Investment companies in particular may have surplus franked investment income because dividends received are not subject to corporation tax. If a company's income is primarily dividends from UK companies there may be insufficient income which is subject to corporation tax to set management charges and other expenses against.

When a claim under this section is made the company is entitled to have paid to it the amount of the tax credit which is comprised in the amount of franked investment income by which the surplus is reduced (ICTA 1988 s242(1)(c)). Once the surplus franked investment income has been dealt with in this way it will not be available to set against franked payments in the future. This will lead to an increase in ACT payable when dividends are paid by the company in the future (ICTA 1988 s242(5)). In addition if a claim is made under this section a trading loss equal to the surplus franked investment income relieved is deemed to have also been relieved and so cannot be set against trading profits in the future (ICTA 1988 s242(5)).

If, in a later accounting period, franked payments made by the company exceed its franked investment income then, provided the company is carrying on the same trade, for the purpose of s393(1), the company shall be treated as having incurred a loss equal to the smaller of the amount by which the franked payments exceed the franked investment income and the amount of the relief which has been given under s242 (ICTA 1988 s242(5)). The loss thus released can be relieved against trading profits using any of the reliefs described above. This effectively partly or wholly reverses the s242 claim.

This section is complicated but once again an example may help you to understand it.

Don't do?

Activity

Norwich Ltd had the following results from its first four years of trading:

		Year ended		
	31.3.95 £	31.3.96 £	31.3.97 £	31.3.98 £
Trading profit/ (loss)	(11,000)	40,000	50,000	60,000
Franked investment income	25,000	0	0	6,000
Franked payments	12,000	10,000	2,000	10,000

Determine the profit chargeable to corporation tax and the ACT payable or recoverable by Norwich Ltd assuming that:
(a) a claim is made under s242.
(b) no claim is made under s242.

Feedback

(a) Section 242(2) claim

The s242(2) claim is made with respect of the year ended 31.3.95.

	Year ended			
	31.3.95	31.3.96	31.3.97	31.3.98
	£	£	£	£
Schedule D Case I	0	40,000	50,000	60,000
Less s393A(1)	0	(8,000)	(2,000)	(1,000)
PCTCT	0	32,000	48,000	59,000

Workings
Surplus (FP)/FII

	31.3.95	31.3.96	31.3.97	31.3.98
Balance b/f	0	2,000	0	0
FII	25,000			6,000
FP	(12,000)	(10,000)	(2,000)	(10,000)
	13,000	(8,000)	(2,000)	(4,000)
s242(2) claim	(11,000)	0	0	0
(Payable)/ Recoverable				
11,000 × 20%	2,200			
8,000 × 20%		(1,600)		
2,000 × 20%			(400)	
1,000 × 20%				(200)
3,000 × 20%				(600)

Loss memorandum

Trading loss for y/e 31.3.95	11,000
s242(2) claim for y/e 31.3.95	11,000
	0
Surplus FII treated as profit	11,000
s393(1) y/e 31.3.96 (surplus FP for y/e 31.3.96)	(8,000)
	3,000
s393(1) y/e 31.3.97 (surplus FP for y/e 31.3.97)	(2,000)
	1,000
s393(1) y/e 31.3.98 (surplus FP for y/e 31.3.98 limited to loss remaining unrelieved)	1,000

Total profits chargeable to corporation tax are £139,000. The net ACT paid over the four years is £600.

(b) No s242(2) claim

	Year ended			
	31.3.95	31.3.96	31.3.97	31.3.98
	£	£	£	£
Schedule D Case I	0	40,000	50,000	60,000
s393(1) claim	0	(11,000)	0	0
PCTCT	0	29,000	50,000	60,000

Workings

Surplus (FP)/FII

Balance b/f	0	13,000	3,000	1,000
FII	25,000			6,000
FP	(12,000)	(10,000)	(2,000)	(10,000)

(Payable)/				
Recoverable				
$3,000 \times 20\%$				(600)

Loss memorandum

Trading loss for y/e 31.3.93	11,000
s393(1) claim for y/e 31.3.94	11,000
	0

Total profits chargeable to corporation tax are £139,000. The net ACT paid over the four years is £600.

As you can see the total profits chargeable to corporation tax and the net ACT paid are unchanged by the s242(2) election.

Change of ownership

The legislation for the relief of trading losses outlined above may not apply if there is a change of ownership between the period in which the loss was incurred and the period in which the profits it is set against are earned. This rule applies to losses carried back under s393A(1) as well as losses carried forward under s393(1).

Specifically relief will not be available if there is a change of ownership between the two periods and there is either a major change in the nature or conduct of the trade within three years before or after the change of ownership or after the change of ownership there is a considerable increase in the level of the company's trading activities which had been small or negligible at the date of the change of ownership. If the change of ownership occurs during an accounting period the period is divided into two notional accounting periods, one before and one after the change. As usual if this is done profits and losses are time-apportioned.

If the company is a 75% subsidiary of the same company before and after the change of ownership it is deemed not to be a major change of ownership and can be disregarded for the purposes of loss relief (ICTA 1988 s768).

Basic tax planning of UK resident companies

Companies which are family owned and managed may have some flexibility when remunerating the owner/managers. Paying dividends or providing benefits in kind rather than high salaries may reduce the total national insurance contributions which must be paid. For example, when employees make contributions to a pension scheme the contributions are allowable deductions for tax purposes but not for national insurance contributions. But if the contributions are made by the employer they are fully deductible for tax purposes and do not give rise to a liability to either employee or employer national insurance contributions. Hence it may be tax efficient for small companies to operate non-contributory pension schemes.

Companies may have marginal rates of tax of 23%, 33% or 35.5% depending on the profits chargeable to corporation tax. Ideally companies should plan their affairs so as to avoid paying tax at a marginal rate of 35.5%. While this may not be possible a little thought may help a company to save tax at the highest possible rate. For example a company may reduce its profits chargeable to corporation tax by increasing its contribution to the company pension scheme in years in which the marginal rate of tax is relatively high. Similarly it may be possible to defer a chargeable gain to a period with a lower marginal tax rate. Many planning opportunities arise if a company is part of a group and these will be considered in the next chapter.

Summary

This chapter has provided you with the skills needed to calculate the corporation tax liability of companies which are resident in the UK. This chapter also lays the foundations for the next chapter in which you will learn how to deal with the taxation of groups of companies.

In order to calculate a company's tax liability it is necessary to undertake a number of steps:

- identify each source of income for a company
- determine the Schedule and Case which is used to calculate the taxable income for each source of income
- using the current year basis, which applies to the income and expenditure of companies, calculate the income which is assessable and determine any deductions from that income which are allowable for tax purposes
- determine details of any charges which are paid by the company
- this will enable you to calculate the profits chargeable to corporation tax
- calculate the advance corporation tax paid and the maximum advance corporation tax which can be relieved
- calculate the income tax paid
- using the small companies limits and the tapering relief equation if necessary determine the mainstream corporation tax liability.

You are also able to state the ways in which a loss can be calculated and calculate the mainstream corporation tax for periods in which a loss is incurred or relieved.

The imputation system was explained in detail in this chapter and the effect of recent changes in the system was discussed.

You have been able to compare and contrast the taxation of companies with the taxation of individuals. You might like to list the similarities and differences and decide if the differences between the two are sufficient for one business medium to be preferred to the other. However, it is important to remember that tax is just one aspect of the environment in which businesses operate. Other considerations are at least as important, for example the benefit of limited liability and the ability to raise extra finance.

Discussion questions

Question 1 (based on CIMA May 1987).

Compare and contrast the reliefs for trading loss in both UK unincorporated businesses and UK limited companies.

You are not required to deal with group relief.

Computational questions

Question 1 (based on ACCA June 1989).

Ultimate Upholsterers Ltd is a UK resident trading company which manufactures leather upholstered chairs. It has been trading for many years.

The company's results for the year ended 30th September 1997 are summarised as follows.

	£
Trading profits (as adjusted for taxation but before capital allowances)	375,000
Net dividend from UK company (29th May 1997)	18,000
Gross loan interest received (30th June 1997)	12,000
Gross debenture interest paid (31st December 1996)	10,000
Profit on sale of land	42,000
Writing down allowances on plant and machinery	49,000

The company operates from two factories, both of which meet the definition of 'industrial building' in the Capital Allowances Act. Neither building is situated in an enterprise zone.

Factory 1 was first occupied by Ultimate Upholsterers Ltd on 1st October 1977 under the terms of a 25-year lease which had been acquired for £50,000.

Factory 2 was purchased on 1st January 1997 for £300,000. The factory cost £150,000 on 1st January 1988 and had been used continuously as an industrial building by the previous owner until it was sold. An extension to Factory 2 was completed on 1st July 1997 at a cost of £125,000 to provide extra production facilities following increased demand for the company's products and was brought into use on 8th August 1997.

Notes
(a) The land had been purchased in March 1973 for £5,000 and sold in December 1996 for £47,000. The value in March 1982 was £10,000.
(b) The company paid a dividend of £50,000 on 17th February 1997.
(c) The company had no surplus of franked investment income, advance corporation tax or losses to carry forward on 1st October 1996.

Required
Calculate the mainstream corporation tax payable for the year ended 30 September 1997.

Question 2 (based on ACCA June 1990).
Unsurpassable Umbrellas Ltd is a UK resident trading company which began to trade in 1964. Accounts have always been prepared to 31st December and the summarised results for the year ended 31st December 1997 are as follows.

	£
Schedule D Case I adjusted profit	310,000
Income from property, after expenses (31.3.97)	4,000
Bank interest received (30.9.97)	1,900
Chargeable gain (17.3.97)	8,200
Patent royalties (30.6.97)	20,000
Gross debenture interest received (31.12.97)	28,200
Dividend from UK company (17.2.97)	14,000
Dividend from UK company (17.7.97)	18,000
Final dividend for 1996 (paid 31.3.97)	29,000
Interim dividend for 1997 (paid 19.9.97)	35,000

Notes
(a) Trading losses of £60,000 were brought forward from 1996.
(b) Income tax had been deducted from the debenture interest received.
(c) Dates in brackets are dates upon which the transactions occurred.

Required
(a) Calculate the advance corporation tax payable in respect of the dividends paid during the accounting period ended 31st December 1997, showing the dates when the tax is due.   (2 marks)
(b) Calculate the income tax payable to the Inland Revenue in respect of charges on income paid during the accounting period ended 31st December 1997, showing the dates when the tax is due.   (2 marks)

(c) Calculate the mainstream corporation tax payable for the year ended 31st December 1997. (19 marks)

Question 3 (based on ACCA June 1991).

Unstoppable Uniforms Ltd is a UK resident trading company which commenced in 1970. The company had always prepared accounts to 31st March but in 1996 moved to a 30th September accounting date. The company's results for the 30 months to 30 September 1997 were as follows.

	Year ended 31.3.96 £	6 months to 30.9.96 £	Year ended 30.9.97 £
Adjusted trading profit (loss)	80,000	(170,000)	900,000
Capital allowances	10,000	20,000	100,000
Building society interest received	4,500	5,000	2,200
Dividends from UK companies	5,000	8,000	39,000
Bank interest received	3,000	4,500	5,000
Profit on sale of shares	0	20,000	0
Patent royalties paid (gross)	2,500	5,000	5,000
Dividends paid	20,000	10,000	250,000
Deed of covenant to charity (gross)	500	500	500

Notes
(a) The book profit on the sale of shares resulted in an indexed chargeable gain of £15,000.
(b) Capital allowances were on plant and machinery.
(c) The company had no surplus franked investment income, surplus advance corporation tax or losses to carry forward on 1st April 1995.
(d) The company has claimed maximum set-off of advance corporation tax in periods down to 31st March 1995.

Required
(a) Calculate the loss relief available in respect of the trading loss for the period ended 30th September 1996 and show how this loss can be utilised assuming that claims are made against the earliest available profits.
(b) Calculate the mainstream corporation tax payable for all relevant periods after utilisation of any loss relief in respect of the loss sustained in the accounting period to 30th September 1996.

Question 4 (based on ACCA Paper 7th June 1994).

Unpretentious Undercurrents Limited (UUL) is a UK resident trading company which manufactures swimwear. It has no associated companies. The company's results for the year ended 31st December 1997 are summarised as follows:

	£
Trading profits (as adjusted for taxation but before capital allowances)	700,000
Dividends received from UK companies (note 1)	60,000
Bank interest received	1,700
Building society interest received	2,700
Dividends paid (note 2)	120,000
Chargeable gains	20,000

Capital acquisitions and disposals of plant and machinery during 1996 were:

	£
Acquisitions	
1. Machinery (not to be treated as a short-life asset) purchased on 1.5.97	65,000
2. Managing director's car (20% private use) purchased on 1.8.97	21,000
3. Four cars (costing £9,000 each) purchased on 1.8.97	36,000
Disposals	
1. Machinery (disposal proceeds less than original cost)	5,000
2. Managing director's previous car (cost £13,000)	4,000
3. Four cars (from car pool at less than original costs)	9,000

The written-down values at 1st January 1997 were:

	£
Main pool	80,000
Managing director's car	7,500
Car pool	12,000

The company purchased the factory, which it had previously rented, on 1st January 1997 for £350,000. The factory had cost £250,000 when new and was brought into use on 1st January 1991 by the first owner, whose accounting date was 31st December. The building had always been in industrial use and was not situated in an enterprise zone.

The following additional information is available:

1. Dividends were received from UK companies on the following dates:

   £
   30,000   30th June 1997
   30,000   31st December 1997
   60,000

2. Dividends were paid on the following dates:

   £
   85,000 (1996 Final)   30th April 1997
   35,000 (1997 Interim)   31st October 1997
   120,000

3. The company had no surplus of franked investment income, advance corporation tax or losses to carry forward on 1st January 1997.
4. There were capital losses brought forward of £25,000 on 1st January 1997.

Required
Calculate the mainstream corporation tax payable for the year ended 31st December 1997.

9

The taxation of close companies and groups

Introduction

Now that you are able to calculate the tax liability of a company you are ready to learn about the taxation of close companies and groups. Close companies are mainly family owned and managed companies. Special legislation applies to close companies in order to prevent the avoidance of tax.

In contrast many businesses take the legal form of a group rather than a single company. Sometimes a business may operate as a group for administrative purposes, for example an organisation might run its manufacturing, distribution and retailing operations through separate companies. Other businesses become groups by way of takeovers of other organisations. Sometimes companies agree to undertake joint ventures using a new company to administer the projects. Businesses may also have substantial shareholdings in other companies for a number of reasons.

At the end of this chapter you will be able to:

- identify a close company
- state the legislation which applies to close companies
- identify a close investment-holding company
- state the legislation which applies to close investment-holding companies
- identify an investment company
- state the legislation which applies to investment companies
- define the different groups which are recognised for tax purposes
- state the tax treatment of each of the group structures for the purposes of group income, the small companies rate, and loss reliefs
- state the treatment of capital gains when assets are transferred between members of a group
- determine the mainstream corporation tax liabilities of companies which are members of a group

- discuss some of the opportunities for tax planning which are available for the corporate members of a group.

Close companies

Definitions

A close company is a UK resident company which is under the control of five or fewer participators, or of participators who are directors (ICTA 1988 s414(1)). In addition UK resident companies are close companies if five or fewer participators who are directors, together possess or are entitled to acquire:

- the majority of the assets of the company which would be available for distribution among the participators on a winding-up of the company, or
- the majority of the assets of the company which would be available for distribution among the participators on a winding-up of the company if the rights of loan creditors were disregarded (ICTA 1988 s414(2)).

The following people are deemed to be directors of a company:

- any person occupying the position of director by whatever name called
- any person in accordance with whose directions or instructions the directors are accustomed to act
- any person who is a manager of the company, or otherwise concerned in the management of the company's trade or business, and is either on his or her own or with one or more associates, the beneficial owner of, or able, directly or through the medium of other companies or by any other indirect means, to control 20% or more of the ordinary share capital of the company (ICTA s417(5)).

Hence a director or manager is treated as owning or controlling what any associate owns or controls, even if he or she does not own or control share capital on their own (ICTA 1988 s417(6)).

If some of the participators are associated with each other they are grouped together in such a way as to produce the smallest possible number of participators.

A participator is a person who has a share or interest in the capital or income of the company and includes:

- any person who possesses, or is entitled to acquire, share capital or voting rights in the company
- any loan creditor of the company
- any person who possesses, or is entitled to acquire, a right to receive or participate in distributions of the company or any amounts payable by the company to loan creditors by way of premium on redemption and
- any person who is entitled to secure that income or assets (whether present or future) of the company will be applied directly or indirectly for his benefit (ICTA 1988 s417(1)).

An associate of a participator is any of the following:

- any relative or partner of the participator
- the trustees of any settlement for which the participator, or any relative, is a settlor
- the trustees of a trust in which the participator has an interest and the personal representatives of any estate in which the participator has an interest (ICTA 1988 s417(3)).

If the participator is a company then any other company with an interest in the shares or obligations of the participator is also an associate of the participator (ICTA 1988 s417(3)).

A relative is a husband or wife, parent or remoter forebear, child or remoter issue, or brother or sister (ICTA 1988 s417(4)).

A company is not treated as a close company if it is controlled by one or more companies which are not themselves close companies and it cannot be treated as a close company except by taking as one of the five or fewer participators requisite for its being so treated a company which is not a close company (ICTA 1988 s414(5)).

Activity

Enterprise Ltd is an unquoted company with an authorised and issued share capital of 120,000 ordinary shares of £1 each.
The shares in the company are currently owned as follows:

	Number of shares
Barbara	25,000
Trustees of a settlement made by Barbara for her two grandsons, Christopher and Peter	20,000
Rosemary, Barbara's niece	2,000
Mandy, who is not related to any of the above	6,000
Colin, Mandy's husband	6,000
Jennifer, Mandy's daughter	1,000
Jamie, Mandy's son	1,000
Sean, Mandy's nephew	2,000
Nigel, Sean's partner in a demolition business	2,000
Ian, who is not related to any of the above	15,000
Andy, Ian's brother	15,000
30 other shareholders who are not related to any of the above and none of whom owns more than 1,000 shares	25,000
	120,000

Is Enterprise Ltd a close company?

Feedback

A close company is one which is controlled by five or fewer participators together with their associates.

The five largest holdings are:

	Holding	Holding including associates
Barbara	25,000	
Trustees of settlement	20,000	45,000
Mandy	6,000	
Colin	6,000	
Jennifer	1,000	
Jamie	1,000	14,000
Sean	2,000	
Nigel	2,000	4,000
Ian	15,000	
Andy	15,000	30,000
Rosemary	2,000	2,000
		95,000
Others		25,000
		120,000

Since the five largest holdings control 95,000 shares Enterprise Ltd is deemed to be a close company.

Implications of close company status

A tax liability may arise if a close company makes a loan to a person with a material interest in the company. A liability may arise on both the company and the borrower. First you need to be able to identify which loans may give rise to a tax liability.

When a close company makes a loan to an individual who is either a participator in the company, or an associate of a participator which is not in the ordinary course of a business carried on by it, it must account for an amount equal to the advance corporation tax which would be payable nine months after the end of the accounting period unless the loan had been repaid by then. When the loan is repaid after the tax is due the tax will be repaid nine months after the end of the accounting period in which the loan was repaid.

A close company will also be regarded as making a loan to a person when that person incurs a debt to the close company or a debt due from that person to a third party is assigned to the close company (ICTA 1988 s419(2)). Tax shall be assessable whether or not the whole or any part of the loan or advance in question has been repaid at the time of the assessment and tax is due within 14 days after the issue of the notice of assessment (ICTA 1988 s419(3)). Where a close company has made a loan or advance which gave rise to a charge to tax on the company and the loan or advance or any part of it is repaid to the company, relief shall be given from that tax, or a proportionate part of it, by discharge or repayment (ICTA 1988 s419(4)).

Loans made to a director or employee of a close company which satisfy all of the following conditions are excluded from the legislation which relates to close companies:

- neither the amount of the loan, nor that amount when taken together with any other outstanding loans made by the close company or any of its associated companies to the borrower exceeds £15,000, and
- the borrower works full-time for the close company or any of its associated companies and
- the borrower does not have a material interest in the close company or any of its associated companies (ICTA 1988 s420(2)).

If a borrower does not have a material interest at the time the loan was made but subsequently acquires a material interest at a time when the whole or part of the loan remains outstanding the close company shall be regarded as making to him/her at that time a loan of an amount equal to the sum outstanding (ICTA 1988 s420(2)).

A person is treated as having a material interest in a company if that person, either on their own or with one or more associates, or if any associate of that person with or without such other associates possesses, or is entitled to acquire, such rights as would, in the event of the winding-up of the company or in any other circumstances, give an entitlement to receive more than 5% of the assets which would then be available for distribution among the participators (ICTA 1988 s168(11)).

The quarterly accounting system is not used to collect the tax because it is not, in fact, ACT. In addition because the tax is not ACT, it cannot be set against the company's corporation tax liability.

In addition to the potential tax consequences to the company of making a loan you need to be aware of the tax consequences to the borrower.

Where a company is assessed or liable to be assessed in respect of a loan or advance and releases or writes off the whole or part of the debt, then:

- for the purpose of computing the total income of the person to whom the loan or advance was made, a sum equal to the amount so released or written off shall be treated as income received by the person after deduction of income tax at the basic rate
- no repayment of income tax shall be made in respect of that income and no assessment shall be made on the individual in respect of income tax at the basic rate on that income. Hence the amount assessed cannot be used to cover charges paid thus avoiding an assessment on tax retained on charges which were not paid out of taxable income
- the amount of the loan written off and treated as income cannot be treated as income taxable at the lower rate
- for the purposes of determining whether any tax is to be taken into account as having been deducted from a gross amount in the case of an individual whose total income is reduced by any deductions so much only of that gross amount shall be taken into account as is part of his total income as so reduced (ICTA 1988 s421(1)).

Now that you are able to state the tax consequences of a close company making, or writing off a loan we can consider the definition of a distribution. This is important because if a sum is treated as a distribution it is necessary for the company to account for the related ACT.

When a close company incurs expenses in or in connection with the provision for any participator of living or other accommodation, of entertainment, of domestic or other services, or of other benefits or facilities of whatever nature, the company shall be treated as making a distribution to the person of an amount equal to so much of that expense as is not reimbursed to the company by the participator (ICTA 1988 s418(2)).

However, section 418(2) does not apply to the following expenses incurred in or in connection with the provision:

- for a person in employment for whom the expense is a benefit in kind
- for a person living in job-related accommodation (look back to Chapter 6 for a definition of job-related accommodation)
- for the spouse, children or dependants of a person employed by the company of any pension, annuity, lump sum, gratuity or other like benefit to be given on that person's death or retirement (ICTA 1988 s418(3)).

Close investment-holding companies

A close company is deemed to be a close investment-holding company for an accounting period unless throughout that period it exists wholly or mainly for any one or more of the following purposes:

- the purpose of carrying on a trade or trades on a commercial basis
- the purpose of making investments in land or estates or interests in land in cases where the land is, or is intended to be, let to persons other than any person, or persons connected to them, connected with the relevant company
- the purpose of holding shares in and securities of, or making loans to, one or more companies each of which is a qualifying company or a company which is under the control of the relevant company or of a company which has control of the relevant company and itself exists wholly or mainly for the purpose of holding shares in or securities of, or making loans to, one or more qualifying companies
- the purpose of coordinating the administration of two or more qualifying companies
- the purpose of a trade or trades carried on on a commercial basis by one or more qualifying companies or by a company which has control of the relevant company
- the purpose of making, by one or more qualifying companies or by a company which has control of the relevant company, investments in land or estates or interests in land in cases where the land is, or is intended to be, let to persons other than any person, or persons connected to them, connected with the relevant company (ICTA 1988 s13A(2)).

A company is a qualifying company in relation to the relevant company if it is under the control of the relevant company, or of a company which has control of the relevant company and exists wholly or mainly for the purpose of either:

- carrying on a trade or trades on a commercial basis, or
- making investments in land or estates or interests in land in cases where the land is, or is intended to be, let to persons other than any person, or

persons connected to them, connected with the relevant company (ICTA 1988 s13A(3)).

Inspectors have powers to restrict the repayment of tax credits on distributions made by a company if:

- the company is a close investment-holding company at the end of the accounting period in which the payment is made, and
- the inspector believe that one of the main purposes of making the distribution is to enable the eligible person to claim a repayment of the tax credit.

If an eligible person:

- receives a qualifying distribution consisting of a payment made by the company on the redemption, repayment or purchase of its own shares, or
- receives any other qualifying distribution in respect of shares in or securities of the company,

and the amount or value of the distribution is greater than might have been had there not been special arrangements in force then the inspector may restrict the tax credit which is repaid to the person to such an extent as appears to the inspector to be just and reasonable (ICTA 1988 s231(3A).

In determining whether any excess of tax credit paid to an eligible person should have the repayment restricted tax credits shall be set against income tax in the order that results in the greatest payment in respect of the excess (ICTA 1988 s231(3D)).

An eligible person, in relation to a qualifying distribution, is an individual, resident in the UK, who would be entitled to a repayment of part or all of the tax credit were it not restricted by the inspectors under section 231(3A) (ICTA 1988 s231(3C)).

This restriction will not apply in relation to a tax credit in respect of a dividend paid by a company in any accounting period in respect of its ordinary share capital if, throughout the period:

- the company's ordinary share capital consisted of only one class of shares, and
- no person waived his or her entitlement to any dividend which would have become payable by the company in the period or failed to receive any dividend which had become due and payable by the company in the period (ICTA 1988 s231(3B)).

The small companies relief is not available to companies which are close investment-holding companies at the end of the accounting period (ICTA 1988 s13(1)). However, for the purposes of the small companies relief the upper and lower limits are divided amongst all of the companies, including any close investment-holding companies (ICTA 1988 s13(4)).

Investment companies

An investment company is any company whose business consists wholly or mainly in the making of investments and the principal part of whose income is derived therefrom. The definition includes any savings banks (ICTA 1988 s130).

An investment company may or may not be a close investment-holding company.

An investment company is likely to receive most of its income in the form of taxed income and hence the management expenses which form the largest part of its expenditure cannot be set off against trading profits.

Remember that only expenses incurred wholly and exclusively for the purposes of the company's trade are deductible. If the inspectors consider that the management expenses are excessive they will disallow the amount deemed not to be wholly and exclusively for the purposes of trade.

To calculate the total profits for a UK investment company deduct any expenses of management which are not deductible apart from this section (ICTA 1988 s75(1)).

That is in effect there shall be deducted from the management expenses the amount of any income derived from sources not charged to tax other than franked investment income, group income and any regional development grant (ICTA 1988 s75(2)).

If, in an accounting period, the expenses of management together with any trade charges on income paid in the period exceed the amount of the profits from which they are deductible the excess shall be carried forward to the next accounting period and treated as if it had been an expense of management for that accounting period (ICTA 1988 s75(3)).

In addition any capital allowances which cannot be relieved are added to the unrelieved management expenses to be carried forward (ICTA 1988 s75(4)).

Investment companies are able to claim to set off the excess management expenses against surplus franked investment income under ICTA 1988 section 242. Look back to the section on losses in Chapter 8 for a full description and an example of how this relief operates.

When a claim made under section 242 relates exclusively to excess management expenses the inspectors may refuse to allow the claim in so far as it relates to excessive management expenses. Like close investment-holding companies investment companies cannot obtain the small companies relief.

Group structures for tax purposes

You are probably already familiar with the definitions of groups which are used by financial accountants. The Inland Revenue recognises groups using definitions which are slightly different from those used for the purposes of financial reporting. For tax purposes companies may be associated, 51% subsidiaries, 75% subsidiaries or consortia.

Associate companies

Two companies are associated with each other if one company is under the control of the other company or both the companies are under the control of a third party (ICTA 1988 s839(5)). To have control of a company it is necessary to have entitlement to more than 50% of one of:

- share capital
- votes
- income
- net assets on a winding-up.

When determining the percentage which is controlled the effective interest rather than the direct interest is used. For example, if A owns 40% of B and 75% of C and C owns 60% of B then A has effective control of 85% of B made up of 40% direct ownership and 45% (75% of 60%) indirect ownership.

Activity

Oxford Ltd owns 60% of Plymouth Ltd and 75% of Quin Ltd. Plymouth Ltd owns 60% of Ripon Ltd and Quin owns 20% of Ripon Ltd. What percentage of Ripon Ltd is owned indirectly by Oxford Ltd?

Feedback

Oxford Ltd owns 36% (60% of 60%) of Ripon Ltd indirectly through Plymouth Ltd. Oxford Ltd also owns 15% (75% of 20%) of Ripon Ltd indirectly through Quin Ltd. This gives Oxford Ltd ownership of 51% (36% + 15%) of Ripon Ltd.

Remember that the small companies limits are shared equally between associated companies. Look back to Chapter 8 for a detailed explanation of the small companies rate together with some examples.

If one or more companies which are associated with each other has very low taxable profits while other companies in the group have relatively high profits the group may have to pay more tax than if it has been organised as a single company.

Activity

Calculate the amount of tax paid in each of these situations:

(a) A company, which has no associated companies and taxable profits of £250,000.
(b) A group which consists of two associated companies, one with taxable profits of £25,000 and the other with taxable profits of £225,000.

Feedback

We will consider each of the situations:

(a) Tax will be levied at a rate of 23% on the entire taxable profits. Hence the tax paid by a company with no associated companies on profits of £250,000 is £57,500.
(b) In the case of the group the lower limit for the small companies relief will be shared equally between the two companies, that is each company will

receive £150,000. Hence the company with profits of only £25,000 will pay tax at 23% but the company with the higher profits will pay tax at a marginal rate of 35.5% because its profits exceed the lower limit. Hence the tax paid by the group is £66,875 (£25,000 × 23% + £150,000 × 23% + (£225,000 − £150,000) × 35.5%).

In this example then the tax paid depends on the organisational structure: the company without associates pays less tax than the group although both organisations earned the same taxable profits.

It is also possible for a company without associates to pay more tax than a group with the same profits. Consider a group with two companies, one with profits of £125,000 and the other with profits of £1 million. The first company will pay tax at a rate of 23% on its profits because its profits do not exceed one half of the small companies rate. The second company will pay tax at a rate of 33% on its profits because its profits exceed one half of the upper limit. The group will therefore pay less tax than a company without associates with profits of £1,250,000, all of which will be taxed at 33%.

Subsidiaries

As you have probably already guessed, a 51% subsidiary is a UK resident company in which the holding company, also a UK resident company, has beneficial ownership, directly or indirectly, of more than 50% of the share capital (ICTA 1988 s838(1)).

A company is a 75% subsidiary if the above definition applies but the percentage is 75% rather than 50% (ICTA 1988 s838(1)).

The definition of a 75% group is less restrictive for capital gains tax purposes than for group relief.

In order to obtain relief under the capital gains tax legislation each member of the group must be either a 75% subsidiary of one or more other companies in the group or the ultimate holding company. It is not necessary for each company to be a 75% subsidiary of the holding company.

For the purposes of group relief a more restrictive definition is used. It is necessary for the ultimate holding company to have beneficial ownership, directly or indirectly, of 75% of the other members of the group. For example, if a parent company has an 80% subsidiary, which also has an 80% subsidiary, the parent company will only have indirect control of 64% of the sub-subsidiary and hence the three companies form two groups for the purposes of group relief rather than one. When determining the percentage of beneficial ownership the holdings of non-UK resident companies are ignored. Hence if a group has a foreign parent it may be worthwhile to set up a UK holding company which is a wholly owned subsidiary of the foreign parent.

A company is a 90% subsidiary if the above definition applies but the percentage is 90% rather than 50% (ICTA 1988 s838(1)).

Consortia

A company is a consortium-owned company if at least 75% of its ordinary share capital is owned by UK resident companies, called the members of the consortium, each of whom owns at least 5% of the ordinary share capital and is entitled to at least 5% of any profits available for distribution and at least 5% of any assets available on a winding-up. However, a company which is a 75% subsidiary of another company cannot be considered to be a consortium-owned company for tax purposes.

An introduction to the taxation of groups

Now that you are able to identify a group for tax purposes we can discuss the taxation of groups. In this section we will consider the taxation of group income and group charges.

Group income

Group income comprises dividends which are paid by one member of a 51% group to another member of the same group.

In order to meet the conditions for group income both the companies must be UK resident and the paying company is either:

- associated with the recipient company, or
- owned by a consortium, and

the paying company is either:

- a trading company, or
- a holding company of 90% trading subsidiaries, but is not a 75% subsidiary, the members of which include the receiving company,

then the receiving company and the paying company may jointly make an election which applies to the dividends received from the paying company (ICTA 1988 s247(1)).

This means that if a consortium-owned company is also a 75% subsidiary it can only pay dividends without accounting for ACT to its holding company. The consortium-owned company must account for ACT on dividends paid to other members of the consortium who receive the dividend together with a tax credit.

As long as the election remains in force the dividends covered by the election are paid without paying advance corporation tax. These dividends are not franked payments made by the paying company, or franked investment income in the hands of the recipient company, but are termed group income (ICTA 1988 s247(2)). The main advantage of making the election is to improve the paying company's cash flow. It would also be advantageous if the recipient company was unable to use the ACT, perhaps because it has surplus ACT already.

Even with the election in force, if the paying company gives notice to the Inland Revenue stating that it does not wish for the election to apply to a particular dividend then that dividend will be treated as if the election had not been made (ICTA 1988 s247(3)).

Feedback

If a s247 election is in force Southend will pay a net dividend of £49,600 (200,000 × 80% × £0.31) to Tunstall as group income.

Southend will also pay a net dividend of £12,400 (200,000 × 20% × £0.31) to the minority interest on which it will account for ACT of £3,100 (£12,400 × 20/80) by 14th January 1998.

Tunstall makes a franked payment of £116,250 (£93,000 × 100/80) on 15th January 1998. Assuming that Tunstall has not received any franked investment income in the accounting year it will have to account for ACT of £23,250 (£116,250 × 20%) by 14th April 1998.

If no s247 election is in force Southend will pay a dividend of £62,000 (200,000 × £0.31) and ACT of £15,500 (£62,000 × 20/80). Tunstall will make the franked payment on 15th January 1998 but in this situation will only have to account for ACT of £10,850 (£93,000 × 20/80 − £15,500 × 80%).

Hence the total ACT paid by Southend and Tunstall is £26,350 (£3,100 + £23,250 or £15,500 + £10,850) whether or not a s247 election has been made. Note that the total amount of ACT paid is unchanged by the election. The advantages of making the election include:

- the cash flow of the group is likely to improve
- the group may be able to utilise its ACT more effectively
- the administrative burden may be reduced.

Group charges

Just as dividends can be paid without accounting for ACT charges can be paid by one member of a 51% group to another without deduction of income tax (ICTA 1988 s247(4)). In order to pay charges gross an election under ICTA 1988 s248 must be made. The election can be revoked in order to pay a charge net. Once revoked the election can be made again.

A consortium-owned company can also elect to pay charges gross to the consortium members but consortium members must deduct tax from charges paid to the consortium-owned company.

The small companies rate

Read the section in Chapter 8 which deals with the small companies rate to find out how the upper and lower limits are shared between companies which are members of a group.

Activity

Briefly describe the tax planning which should be undertaken by the managers of a group in the light of the legislation on the small companies rate.

Feedback

The upper and lower limits are shared equally between the associated companies regardless of the profits of each of the companies. If some members of the group do not fully utilise the small companies band available to them the group will have to pay more tax than a company, without associates, which had the same profits chargeable to corporation tax as the total for the group. A simple example may help to make the point.

Suppose that a group has two companies in it. One with profits chargeable to corporation tax of £500,000 and the other with profits chargeable to corporation tax of £Nil. Then the total tax paid by the group, assuming there is no franked investment income, is equal to £158,750 (£500,000 × 33% − 1/40 × (£1,500,000/2 − £500,000) × £500,000/£500,000).

However, if a company without associates had profits chargeable to corporation tax of £500,000 its tax bill is £140,000 (£500,000 × 33% − 1/40 × (£1,500,000 − £500,000) × £500,000/£500,000).

Hence the group will pay £18,750 more tax than a single company with the same profits.

It may therefore be possible for a group to reduce its total tax liability by organising the group structure carefully to maximise the small companies rate. Companies in a group are likely to have a number of strategies available to them to transfer funds and/or profits from one member of a group to another. These include:

- the level of dividends to be paid to the holding company
- the price at which goods or services, including management charges and overheads are transferred from one member to another
- leading and lagging payments between group members
- investment in one member of a group by another could take the form of debt or equity.

Other issues of group taxation

Now that you are able to determine the tax liabilities of groups with group income and group charges we can consider the surrender of ACT and the treatment of disposals of capital assets.

The surrender of ACT

Provided that the parent company owns more than 50% of the share capital and has a right to more than 50% of the income and the net assets on a winding up throughout the parent's accounting period, the parent may surrender any ACT paid to its subsidiary.

The subsidiary can use the surrendered ACT in the same way as it would use its own ACT. That is it can set it off against its corporation tax liability, up to the maximum set-off allowed. The subsidiary can use the surrendered ACT before it uses its own ACT. Any surplus of the surrendered ACT cannot be carried back, it can only be carried forward. Of course the subsidiary's own ACT can be carried back in the manner described in Chapter 8.

The subsidiary must be a 51% subsidiary of the company which surrendered the ACT throughout any period in which the surrendered ACT is used. Surrendered ACT can also be used if the group is reorganised even if it is not a 51% subsidiary of the surrendering company provided that both companies are 51% subsidiaries of a third company.

The subsidiary may pay the parent company an amount up to the value of the ACT surrendered without any corporation tax consequences.

Activity

Urlingford is a 100% subsidiary of Valencia throughout the accounting period ended on 31st March 1998. The companies have the following results for the year to 31st March 1998

	Valencia £'000	Urlingford £'000
Schedule D Case I	350	340
Chargeable gains	50	60
Group income	100	
Dividends paid	400	
Dividends paid under s247		100
FII	50	

Valencia has two other associated companies.

Assuming that surplus ACT is surrendered from Valencia to Urlingford calculate the mainstream corporation tax liability for both companies for the year ended 31st March 1998.

Feedback

The upper limit for tapering relief is £1,500,000/4 = £375,000.

The ACT paid by Valencia is £90,000 (£(400,000 × $^{100}/_{80}$ − 50,000) × 20%).

	Valencia £'000	Urlingford £'000
Schedule D Case I	350	340
Chargeable gains	50	60
PCTCT	400	400
FII	50	0
Small companies profits	450	400
Corporation tax on PCTCT		
£400,000 × 33%	132	
£400,000 × 33%		132
Less ACT limited to maximum set-off		
£400,000 × 20%	80	
ACT surrendered to Urlingford		10
MCT	52	122

Chargeable gains

The tax treatment of chargeable disposals depends on the structure of the group.

A group qualifies for special treatment if the group has a holding company which has control, both direct and indirect, of over 50% of the share capital of the group companies and all the other companies in the group are linked by a 75% share holding.

Transfers of chargeable assets between members of the group are deemed to be at a value which gives rise to neither a gain nor a loss (TCGA 1992 s171(1)). In practice this means that assets are transferred at their allowable cost plus an indexation allowance.

When the asset is finally disposed of, other than to another group member, the chargeable gain is calculated using the original cost to the group and the indexation allowance is based on the total period during which the asset was owned by members of the group.

If a company leaves the group within six years of receiving assets on this no gain and no loss basis and the assets are still held by the company on the date of its departure from the group it is deemed to have sold and immediately re-acquired the assets, at their market value, on the date on which the assets were transferred to the company.

Activity

Wakefield plc sold Yeovil Ltd, a wholly owned subsidiary, to Zelah plc in January 1998. The assets of Yeovil Ltd included an office block which was bought by Wakefield plc in May 1984 for £100,000. It was transferred to Yeovil Ltd at £110,000 in June 1995 which gave neither a gain nor a loss for capital gains tax purposes. Its market value in June 1995 was £350,000.

Calculate any capital gains tax liability, in respect of the office block, which arises from the sale of Yeovil Ltd.

Feedback

Since Yeovil Ltd left the group within six years of acquiring the offices from Wakefield plc it will be deemed to have sold, and immediately re-acquired, the building at its market value in June 1995.

	£
Proceeds	350,000
Less cost	100,000
Unindexed gain	250,000
Indexation allowance	
$\dfrac{149.8 - 89.0}{89.0} = 0.683$	
$0.683 \times £100,000$	68,300
Chargeable gain of Yeovil Ltd, in the accounting period which included June 1995	181,700

The relief available under TCGA 1992 s171(1) does not apply where the disposal is either:

- of a debt due from a member of a group of companies effected by satisfying the debt or part of it
- of redeemable shares in a company on the occasion of their redemption
- by or to an investment trust
- to a dual resident investing company
- to a company which, though resident in the UK, is regarded, for the purposes of any double taxation relief arrangements, as non-UK resident and by virtue of the arrangements would not be liable in the UK to tax on a gain arising on a disposal of the asset occurring immediately after its acquisition (TCGA 1992 s171(2)).

In addition the relief is not available to a disposal of an interest in shares in a company in consideration for a capital distribution from that company, whether or not involving a reduction of capital (TCGA 1992 s171(2)).

Where a member of a group of companies acquires an asset as trading stock from another member of the group, and the asset did not form part of the trading stock of any trade carried on by the other member, the member acquiring it shall be treated as having acquired the asset otherwise than as trading stock and immediately appropriated it for the purposes of the trade as trading stock (TCGA 1992 s173(1)).

Where a member of a group of companies disposes of an asset to another member of the group, and the asset formed part of the trading stock of a trade carried on by the member disposing of it but is acquired by the other member otherwise than as trading stock of a trade carried on by it, the member disposing of the asset shall be treated as having immediately before the disposal appropriated the asset for some purpose other than the purpose of use as trading stock (TCGA 1992 s173(2)).

For the purposes of rollover relief all the trades carried on by members of a group of companies shall be treated as a single trade, unless it is a case of one member of the group acquiring, or acquiring the interest in, the new assets from another or disposing of, or of the interest in, the old assets to another (TCGA 1992 s175(1)). Hence the acquisitions which take place between one year before the disposal and three years after the disposal may be matched with the disposal for the purposes of rollover relief.

Taxpayers can make an irrevocable election to use the market value on 31st March 1982 rather than the original cost in capital gains tax computations. Only the parent company can make such an election and the election applies to all of the companies in the group. Look back to Chapter 7 for details about the FA 1988 rebasing provisions.

In practice it is possible to transfer capital losses from one member of the group to another by the simple expedient of transferring the asset between the companies prior to its disposal outside the group. If this is to be done it is important that the transfer is completed before a buyer for the asset has been identified. Look back at the section on anti-avoidance in Chapter 1 to see why this is important. One way of maximising the use of any capital losses is to arrange for all disposals to go through one company.

Assets transferred between members of a group which do not meet the conditions described above are subject to capital gains tax in the normal way.

Group relief

Group relief enables trading losses to be surrendered by one member of a 75% group, the surrendering company, to another member of the group, the claimant company (ICTA 1988 s402(1)).

Group relief is also available to a consortium provided that one of them is a member of the consortium and the other is either:

- a trading company which is owned by the consortium and which is not a 75% subsidiary of any company
- a trading company which is a 90% subsidiary of a holding company which is owned by the consortium and which is not a 75% subsidiary of a company other than the holding company
- a holding company which is owned by the consortium and which is not a 75% subsidiary of any company (ICTA 1988 s402(3).

A payment for group relief is not taken into account either when computing profits or losses of either company for corporation tax purposes or for the purposes of ACT (ICTA 1988 s402(6)).

The loss of the surrendering company can be set against the total profits of the claimant for the corresponding accounting period (ICTA 1988 s403(1)). For the purposes of group relief an accounting period of the claimant company which falls wholly or partly within an accounting period of the surrendering company corresponds to that accounting period (ICTA 1988 s409(2)). If an accounting period of the surrendering company and a corresponding accounting period of the claimant company do not coincide the amount which may be set off against the total profits of the claimant company for the corresponding accounting period shall be reduced by applying the fraction A/B and the total profits of the claimant company for the corresponding accounting period shall be reduced by applying the fraction A/C where A is the length of the period common to the two accounting periods, B is the length of the accounting period of the surrendering company, and C is the length of the corresponding accounting period of the claimant company (ICTA 1988 408(2)).

Activity

Aston Ltd is a 90% subsidiary of Bakewell plc. In the year to 31st March 1997 Aston incurred a trading loss of £20,000. Bakewell had taxable profits of £24,000 for the year ended 30th June 1996 and £12,000 for the year ended 30th June 1997.
 Determine the maximum group relief that Bakewell can claim from Aston.

Feedback

Bakewell can claim the following group relief:

y/e 30th June 1996
The maximum loss which can be surrendered is £5,000 (3/12 × £20,000). This represents the period from 1st April 1996 to 30th June 1996.
 The maximum profits against which the loss can be relieved are £6,000 (3/12 × £24,000). Hence Bakewell can claim £5,000 of group relief.

y/e 30th June 1997
The maximum loss which can be surrendered is £15,000 (9/12 × £20,000). This represents the period from 1st July 1996 to 31st March 1997.
 The maximum profits against which the loss can be relieved are £9,000 (9/12 × £12,000). Hence Bakewell can claim £9,000 of group relief.

 If the surrendering company is an investment company it can surrender the excess of management expenses and charges over the profits of an accounting period to be set off against the total profits of the claimant company for its corresponding accounting period (ICTA 1988 s403(4)).

 If the surrendering company has paid charges on income during an accounting period which exceed its profits of the period the excess charges may be set off against the total profits of the claimant company for its corresponding accounting period (ICTA 1988 s403(7)). Both trade and non-trading charges can be relieved in this way.

 Before the claimant company can use any of the losses, capital allowances or charges which are surrendered to it, it must first relieve any of its own current year losses and losses brought forward from earlier years. However, the surrendering company does not have to relieve any loss against its own profits before it can be surrendered and is free to specify how much of its losses are to be surrendered. This enables losses to be used so as to maximise their value by relieving them against profits which would otherwise be taxed at a high marginal rate. Look back to Chapter 8 to find out what are the rates of corporation tax. The highest marginal rate is in the tapering relief band making these profits the preferred target for loss relief.

Now that you have read about group relief you should be ready to put what you have learned into practice. However, to complete the activity you will also need to deal with loss relief. So you may find it helpful to go back to Chapter 8 and re-read the section on loss relief before you attempt the next activity.

Activity

Castleton Ltd is a wholly owned subsidiary of Denby plc. The two companies reported the following results for the four years ended on 31st December 1997.

| | Year ended 31st December | | | |
	1994 £	1995 £	1996 £	1997 £
Castleton Ltd				
Trading profit (loss)	500	(2,800)	300	(5,000)
Rents receivable	1,800	1,800	1,800	1,800
Patent royalties paid	(200)	(300)	(100)	(200)
Denby plc				
Trading profit (loss)	(7,000)	4,800	(1,500)	5,000
Interest received gross	4,000	1,000	3,000	3,500
Debenture interest paid	(1,200)	(1,000)	(1,000)	(1,300)

Determine the profits chargeable to corporation tax for both companies for each of the four years. You should assume that all reliefs are claimed as early as possible.

Feedback

| | Year ended 31st December | | | |
	1994 £	1995 £	1996 £	1997 £
Castleton Ltd				
Schedule D Case I	500	0	300	0
Schedule A	1,800	1,800	1,800	1,800
	2,300	1,800	2,100	1,800
Less s393A(1)		1,800	2,100	1,800
		0	0	0
Less charges paid	200	300	100	200
	2,100	0	0	0
Less group relief	2,100	0	0	0
PCTCT	0	0	0	0

	Year ended 31st December			
	1994 £	1995 £	1996 £	1997 £
Loss memorandum				
Loss		2,800		5,000
s393A(1) claim:				
current year		1,800		1,800
		1,000		3,200
carry back		0		2,100
		1,000		1,100
Add excess trade charges		300	100	200
		1,300		1,300
Group relief surrender		1,300	100	1,300
		0	0	0
Denby plc				
Schedule D Case I	0	4,800	0	5,000
Less s393(1)(9) claim		2,100		
		2,700		
Schedule D Case III	4,000	1,000	3,000	3,500
	4,000	3,700	3,000	8,500
Less s393A(1) claim	4,000		1,500	
	0		1,500	
Less charges paid	1,200	1,000	1,000	1,300
	0	2,700	500	7,200
Less group relief claim		1,300	100	1,300
PCTCT	0	1,400	400	5,900
Loss memorandum				
Loss	7,000		1,500	
s393A(1) claim:				
current year	4,000		1,500	
	3,000		0	
Excess trade charges	1,200			
	4,200			
Surrender of group relief	2,100			
	2,100			
s393(1)(9)	2,100			
	0			

Note that Castleton Ltd does not carry back the loss incurred in 1995 because the profits can be used to relieve Denby's loss in 1994 by making a group relief claim.

Summary

In this chapter we have extended the material from Chapter 8 to include groups of companies. Companies may be associated, members of a 51% group, members of a 75% group or members of a consortium. Each structure operates within a slightly different tax framework.

Some of the tax consequences of forming a group are:

- the limits for the small companies rate and the tapering relief are divided equally between all the members of the group
- provided that an election is made, cash in the form of dividends and interest can be paid by one member of a group to other members of the group without the need to account for ACT or withholding taxes
- ACT can be surrendered from a holding company to its subsidiaries
- trading losses, excess charges, capital allowances and excess management expenses can be surrendered from one member of a group to another using group relief
- assets can be transferred from one member of a group to another without a liability for capital gains tax arising.

There are opportunities for tax planning in a group but there are also potential pitfalls. In order to undertake effective tax planning a group must probably plan years ahead. Tax planning should include considerations about residency, particularly of the holding company, and the form of intra-group transfers. For example, if the holding company needs to transfer funds to a subsidiary it is worth considering whether equity should be issued or loans should be made.

Computational questions

Question 1 (based on ACCA June 1991).

H Ltd owns 76% of the ordinary share capital of A Ltd and 40% of the ordinary share capital of D Ltd. The remaining ordinary shares in A Ltd are owned by individual members of the general public. The remaining ordinary shares in D Ltd are owned equally by P Ltd and Q Ltd, both of which are unconnected with H Ltd or with each other. A Ltd owns 80% of the ordinary share capital of B Ltd which in turn owns 75% of the ordinary share capital of C Ltd. H Ltd owns 5% of the ordinary shares in B Ltd and 0.1% of the ordinary shares in C Ltd. The remaining ordinary shares in B Ltd and C Ltd are owned by individual members of the general public. All of the companies concerned are trading companies resident in the UK. The issued share capital of each company consists of ordinary shares only.

Required

(a) (i) State, giving reasons, which set (or sets) of the above companies form a group (or groups) for capital gains purposes.

(ii) Describe the general tax treatment of a transfer of an asset from one group company to another where the asset was a fixed asset of the first company but forms part of the trading stock of the second company.

(iii) Describe the second company's right of election in these circumstances and indicate when such an election would be likely to be favourable.

(b) (i) State, giving reasons, which of the above companies can surrender trading losses to other companies, in each case identifying those other companies concerned.

(ii) Explain the rules regulating the amount of the loss which can be surrendered in each case.

(iii) Would your answer to (b)(i) have been different if firstly Q Ltd was not resident in the UK or secondly A Ltd was not resident in the UK?

(c) (i) State, giving reasons, which of the above companies can elect to pay dividends to other companies without accounting for ACT.

(ii) Explain the possible benefits of such an election.

Question 2 (based on ACCA June 1988).

H Ltd has owned 60% of the issued ordinary share capital of S Ltd since its incorporation, the remaining 40% being held by Mr S. Both companies have always prepared accounts to 30th June, their most recent accounts showing the following:

	H Ltd		S Ltd	
	y/e 30.6.96 £	y/e 30.6.97 £	y/e 30.6.96 £	y/e 30.6.97 £
Adjusted trading profit	2,000		10,000	40,000
Adjusted trading loss		(28,000)		
Dividend received from a 12% holding in Foreign Ltd (net)			13,500	40,500
Charges paid (gross)			12,000	12,000

On 1st January 1996, H Ltd acquired 80% of the issued ordinary share capital of N Ltd, a company which had always prepared accounts to 31st December.

N Ltd's accounts for the period 1st January 1996 to 30th June 1997 show the following:

	£
Adjusted trading profit, before capital allowances	32,625
Chargeable gain, after indexation allowance on land bought in 1979 and sold in February 1997	12,000

N Ltd had a written down value on plant at 1st January 1996 of £9,000 and had incurred expenditure as follows:

	£
3rd February 1996: new car to be used by the managing director of N Ltd 80% for business, 20% for private use	16,000
4th January 1997: new plant	32,000
20th March 1997: secondhand plant bought on hire purchase, the cash price being £8,000, a deposit of £2,000 being paid on the above date followed by 24 monthly instalments of £300, commencing 20 May 1997.	

Dividends were paid and received as follows:

	H Ltd £	S Ltd £	N Ltd £
Dividends paid			
20th June 1996		15,000	
3rd December 1996	7,000		
15th March 1997			20,000
17th September 1997	8,000		
Dividends received			
From S Ltd 20th June 1996	9,000		
From N Ltd 15th March 1997	16,000		

Dividends received by H Ltd, where possible, were covered by valid group elections.

The dividend from Foreign Ltd was net of a 10% withholding tax. Foreign Ltd had suffered overseas tax on its profits at a rate of 25%.

Required
Compute the mainstream corporation tax payable by H Ltd, S Ltd and N Ltd for the above periods of account, assuming all available claims and surrenders are made to minimise the mainstream corporation tax payable by the group.

Question 3 (based on ACCA December 1989).
Xerxes Ltd is a manufacturing company which owns all of the issued share capital of its two manufacturing subsidiaries, Bella Ltd and Donna Ltd. The accounting profits of the group of companies are as follows:

	Year ended 31st December 1997 Profit/(loss) £
Xerxes Ltd	(71,000)
Bella Ltd	649,000
Donna Ltd	617,000

Donna Ltd paid dividends to Xerxes Ltd as follows: £250,000 on 6th February 1997 and £230,000 on 1st July 1997. Xerxes Ltd paid a dividend of £560,000 to its shareholders on 15th March 1997. Xerxes Ltd made a loan of £450,000 to Bella Ltd on 1st July 1997, with interest payable at 10% a year on a monthly basis. The loan was used for trading purposes. No elections were made in respect of any of the above intra-group payments. The interest payments are not included in the calculation of the accounting profits set out above.

On 9 August 1997, Bella Ltd sold part of an office building for £100,000 less solicitors' fees of £3,000. It had acquired the entire building in June 1980 for £20,000 plus legal fees of £2,000. In May 1985, the part of the building which was sold had been extended at a cost of £9,000. The value of the entire building on 31st March 1982 was £40,000 and the current value of the part retained was £33,000. The gain is not included in the accounting profits set out above.

In all cases, depreciation charges in the accounts and capital allowances claimed are identical in amount, except in respect of the purchase of a freehold factory for £120,000 by Xerxes Ltd from an unconnected manufacturing company, Nugent Ltd, on 1st August 1997. Nugent Ltd had acquired the factory new on 1st May 1984 from a builder at a cost of £50,000, of which £15,000 related to land. The current value of the land in August 1997 was estimated at £25,000 and the estimated useful life of the building at the time of Xerxes Ltd's purchase was 50 years. No other tax adjustments to the accounting profits are required.

It has been suggested that the staff of Xerxes Ltd should in future undertake market research for Bella Ltd, and that a management charge of £10,000 a year should be made for this service.

Required
Calculate the tax position of each of the group companies for the year ended 31st December 1997 on the basis that all claims for relief are made in the most favourable manner. Assume that no relief can be claimed for periods before 1993. Explain briefly your reasons for selecting the claims actually made.

Question 4 (based on ACCA June 1993 Advanced Taxation).
You are the tax advisor to Albion plc, the holding company for a group of companies involved in the retail food trade. Albion plc has recently completed the purchase of Rundown Ltd, buying 100% of its share capital. This company was purchased because of the large number of freehold shops that it owns in desirable locations. However, Rundown Ltd has been badly managed, and currently has substantial unutilised trading losses and a small amount of surplus ACT.

Over a five-year period Albion plc plans to wind down the trade of Rundown Ltd as follows:
(i)   Those shops that are in desirable locations will be transferred to various other group companies, and used by them.
(ii) Those shops that are no longer required will be sold by Rundown Ltd, with the proceeds being used to finance the purchase of new shops by other group companies. These new shops will consist of both freehold properties and leasehold properties on leases of between 25 and 75

years. The sale of Rundown Ltd's shops will result in substantial capital gains.

Albion plc recently adopted the same policy with another purchased company, although the shops sold in that instance mostly resulted in capital losses.

The other companies in the group are varyingly owned between 51% and 100% by Albion plc.

Required

Draft a report to Albion plc covering the tax implications arising from:

(a) its proposed treatment of Rundown Ltd
(b) its proposed treatment of Rundown Ltd's shops
(c) the proposed purchase of new freehold and leasehold shops by other group companies.

You should include tax planning advice as appropriate.

10 Value added tax

Introduction

VAT (value added tax) has become an increasingly important source of income for the government since it was introduced in 1973. The Treasury expects to raise £50 billion from VAT in the fiscal year 1997/98. In the months before the budget statement receipts from VAT were lower than anticipated. It was generally thought that this was largely due to tax avoidance. As a result a number of measures intended to increase the revenue raised by VAT were included in the budget statement. A three-year limit on refunds of VAT together with a three-year limit on Customs and Excise's powers to recover underdeclared indirect taxes and duties will be introduced. Changes have also been made to bad debt relief and business splitting in order to increase VAT receipts. These, and other measures, will be discussed in this chapter.

At the end of this chapter you will be able to:

- state the broad principles of VAT
- state the criteria for compulsory registration and deregistration
- state the advantages and disadvantages of registration
- identify taxable supplies
- list the occasions on which input tax is irrecoverable
- state which goods are standard rated, zero rated and exempt from VAT
- state the differences in the treatment of standard rated, zero rated and exempt supplies
- describe the main characteristics of the administration of VAT including the special schemes
- state the VAT consequences of imports and exports
- describe the system for administering VAT which is operating within the EU
- discuss the difficulties of harmonisation of VAT within the EU.

Background

VAT was introduced in April 1973 as a consequence of the UK joining the European Union. It replaced purchase tax, which had many anomalies and introduced three classifications of goods. Goods and services were taxed in accordance with their classification. When VAT was first introduced it was seen to be a relatively simple tax which was not amenable to tax planning. However, in recent years VAT has been the focus of a considerable amount of attention.

The legal basis for VAT is contained in the Value Added Tax Act (VATA 1994) and subsequent Finance Acts. VAT is administered by HM Customs and Excise who have extensive enforcement powers. The legislation covering the administration of VAT is contained in the Customs and Excise Management Act 1979 (CEMA 1979). The Commissioners of Customs and Excise are responsible to the Treasury but are appointed by the Crown (CEMA 1979 s6(1)). The Commissioners are responsible for collecting and accounting for, and otherwise managing, the revenues of Customs and Excise (CEMA 1979 s6(2)).

Principles of VAT

VAT is an indirect or expenditure tax which is borne by the final consumer although it is charged whenever a taxable person makes a taxable supply of goods and services in the course of his business (VATA 1994 s4(1)).

A taxable person

A person is a taxable person for the purposes of VAT while he is, or is required to be, registered under the Value Added Tax Act 1994 (VATA 1994 s3(1)).

A taxable supply

A taxable supply includes all forms of supply made for consideration (VATA 1994 s5(2)). The following transfers are taxable supplies:

- Any transfer of the whole property is a supply of goods. The transfer of any undivided share of the property or the possession of goods is a supply of services. If the possession of goods is transferred either under an agreement for the sale of goods or under agreements which expressly contemplate that the property will also pass at some time in the future, which is not later than when the goods are fully paid for, it is a supply of goods (VATA 1994 Sch 4 s1(1))
- a treatment or process applied by one person to another person's goods (VATA 1994 Sch 4 s2)
- the supply of any form of power, heat, refrigeration or ventilation (VATA 1994 Sch 4 s3)
- the grant, assignment or surrender of a major interest in land (VATA 1994 Sch 4 s4)

- the transfer of fixed assets or current assets, including transfers to the registered trader whether or not for a consideration (VATA 1994 Sch 4 s5(1) & (4))
- business gifts are taxable supplies unless the transfer or disposal is either a gift of goods made in the course or furtherance of the business which cost the donor not more than £15 or a gift to an actual or potential customer of the business of an industrial sample in a form not ordinarily available for sale to the public (VATA 1994 Sch 4 s5(2))
- goods which were owned by the business and are put to any private use or are used, or made available to any person, including the registered trader, to use for a private purpose (VATA 1994 Sch 4 s5 (6)).

Input and output tax

A taxable person's input tax is the VAT:

- on the supply to him or her of any goods or services
- on the acquisition by him of any goods from another member state
- paid or payable by him on the importation of any goods from a place outside the EU

provided that the goods or services are, or will be, used for the purposes of a business carried on by the taxable person (VATA 1994 s24(1)).

A taxable person's output tax is the VAT on supplies he makes or on the acquisition by him of goods from another member state (VATA 1994 s24(2)).

The tax point

The basic tax point is the date on which a supply of goods or services is treated as taking place. A supply of goods shall be treated as taking place if the goods are:

- to be removed, at the time of the removal
- not to be removed, at the time when they are made available to the person to whom they are supplied
- removed before it is known whether a supply will take place, at the time when it becomes certain that the supply has taken place, or, if sooner, 12 months after the removal (VATA 1994 s6(2)).

A supply of services is any taxable supply which is not a supply of goods. A supply of services shall be treated as taking place at the time when the services are performed (VATA 1994 s6(3)). A trader can elect to use the basic tax point. However, if a tax invoice is issued within 14 days of the date on which the supply is deemed to have taken place the supply will be treated as taking place at the time the invoice is issued (VATA 1994 s6(5)). The Commissioners can, at the taxpayer's request, substitute a period longer than the 14 days specified in s6(6) (VATA 1994 s6(6)). For example, some companies generate all invoices at the end of the month; if this is the case then it is likely that this date will be treated as the date of supply. The deemed date of supply is termed the tax point.

The impact of VAT on registered traders and final consumers

One of the most powerful ways of demonstrating the impact of VAT on registered traders and consumers is to use an example. The following activity illustrates the cascade effect of VAT where traders effectively account for VAT on their value added.

Susan runs a small farm on which she keeps some rare breed sheep. She sells the fleeces for £200 to a local manufacturer, Country Crafts Ltd, who employs spinners and knitters to produce garments which are sold for a total of £600 to a shop, Country Clothes Ltd, who sells the clothes to members of the public for £1,000. Both Susan and Country Crafts Ltd are registered for VAT purposes. None of the above amounts include VAT which is levied at the standard rate of 17.5% on each of the transactions. Output tax is the VAT charged on the business's supplies while input tax is the VAT suffered on supplies bought by the business.

Complete the following table which shows the impact of VAT on the transactions described above.

Taxable person	Cost £	Input tax £	Net sales price £	Output tax £	VAT payable to C&E £

Feedback

Taxable person	Cost £	Input tax £	Net sales price £	Output tax £	VAT payable to C&E £
Susan	0	0	200	35	35
Country Crafts	200	35	600	105	70
Country Clothes	600	105	1,000	175	70

Note that the VAT suffered by the final consumer is £175 which is exactly the amount payable to Customs and Excise (£35 + £70 + £70).

Hence the tax is charged by each registered person in the chain of production. Each person is charged input tax on taxable supplies received and charges output tax on taxable supplies by him. If there is an excess of input tax over output tax the excess can be reclaimed (VATA 1994 s25(3)). An excess of output tax over input tax must be paid to the Customs and Excise (VATA 1994 s25(2)). The person making the supply is liable for any tax which becomes due at the time of supply (VATA 1994 s1(2)).

The value of a taxable supply

If the supply is for a consideration in money the consideration is taken to be the VAT inclusive price. If the supply is for a consideration which is not wholly in money the money value of the consideration is also taken to be the VAT inclusive price (VATA 1994 s19(3)).

If consideration in money is received for more than just a supply of goods or services a proportion of the consideration which is properly attributable to the supply shall be attributed to it (VATA 1994 s19(4)).

The open market value of a supply of goods or services is deemed to be the amount which would be payable by a person in an arms's length transaction (VATA 1994 s19(5)). Note then that the value of the supply is taken to include VAT. Since the standard rate of VAT is 17.5% the VAT proportion of the consideration is $17.5/(100 + 17.5) = 7/47$. This proportion is called the VAT fraction.

In theory then businesses are not affected by VAT except in so far as they have to administer the tax and suffer a loss of cash flow. However, as you will see, in practice VAT does affect the operation of business.

Accounting for VAT

Before you can study the special schemes for VAT later in this chapter you need to understand the principles of accounting for VAT and you need to know the basic legislation which deals with the accounting for VAT.

VAT returns

Registered traders must submit a VAT return, together with any VAT payable, within one month of the end of a tax period.

A tax period is a period covered by a VAT return. It is normally three months long and ends on the last day of the month. The Customs and Excise have classified trades and businesses and allocated tax periods by reference to the type of trade that is being carried on. This enables HM Customs and Excise to spread their work evenly throughout the year. However, variations on this are allowed. For example, a trader who operates four-week periods can apply to use this basis for VAT periods rather than using month ends. Some businesses also prefer to have one of the tax periods ending on the same date as the accounting year end and this is likely to be acceptable to the Customs and

Excise. It is even possible to shorten the length of the tax periods to one month. This would be attractive to traders who regularly receive a repayment of VAT, and so could improve their cash flow, but carries the penalty of having to complete 12 VAT returns a year. Indeed small businesses can elect to complete only one tax return a year although they must still pay VAT throughout the year.

A transaction must be accounted for in the tax period in which the tax point occurs. The transaction is subject to the rate of VAT which prevails on the date of the tax point.

A VAT return, called VAT 100, includes the following information:

- output tax
- input tax
- net amount payable or repayable
- value of supplies to other EU countries
- value of acquisitions from other EU countries
- input VAT due on acquisitions from other EU countries.

Tax invoices

Once a trader is registered for VAT the trader must supply a tax invoice to other registered traders (VATA 1994 Sch 11 s2(1)). He or she must also retain a copy of the tax invoice.

A tax invoice must include:

- supplier's name, address and registration number
- tax point
- invoice number
- name and address of the customer
- description of the goods or services including, for each type of goods or services supplied:
    — quantity purchased
    — rate of tax
    — tax exclusive amount
    — type of supply, for example sale or hire
    — rate of any cash discount available and separate totals of the cash discounts which applies to zero rated and exempt supplies.

Retailers may issue less detailed invoices when the VAT inclusive total is less than £100. They need only disclose:

- supplier's name, address and registration number
- date of the supply
- a description of the goods or services supplied
- rate of tax
- the total amount chargeable including VAT.

If a less detailed invoice is used it must not include supplies which are taxable at different rates.

Cash operated machines, for example in car parks, do not need to provide a tax invoice provided that the total value of the invoice is less than £25.

Purchasers can still reclaim the input tax even though they do not have a tax invoice.

Sometimes goods and services are sold as a unit but are, in fact, made up of a mixture of standard rated, zero rated and exempt supplies. For example if a book and cassette tape are sold together, perhaps as a foreign language course, the book is zero rated and the tape is standard rated. In this case the supplier must apportion the value of the supply between the different components using an equitable basis. VAT is then levied on each part at the appropriate rate. The legislation does not offer one method to be used to apportion the value but acceptable methods are likely to include apportionment by reference to the cost to the supplier of the components and apportionment by reference to the open market value of each component. Sometimes it is not possible to apportion the value in this way and then it is necessary to consider the sale as a composite supply and one rate will be applied to the whole of the supply.

Cash discounts

With the exception of imports from non-EU-member states, if a cash discount is offered for early settlement of the invoice the VAT is levied on the value of the supply net of the cash discount (Sixth VAT Directive 77/388 art11 s11(A)). For imports from outside the EU the discount offered is ignored for the purposes of VAT unless it is actually taken up.

Input tax

So far we have simply suggested that registered traders can reclaim input tax provided that they have a VAT invoice. In principle this is certainly correct but there are a number of special situations which you need to know about.

We will start by considering capital expenditure and then list the occasions on which input tax cannot be reclaimed.

Capital expenditure

Capital expenditure is not differentiated from revenue expenditure for VAT purposes. Hence input tax is fully recoverable and when the asset is disposed of VAT is charged as for any other taxable supply. The exception is the treatment of cars. Generally, input tax on cars cannot be reclaimed. Equally, registered traders need not account for output tax when the car is subsequently sold, unless it is sold at a profit, when output tax must be levied on the profit element. However, there are a number of exceptions to the rule. VAT can be reclaimed on cars:

- acquired new and intended to be sold
- intended to be leased to or used in a taxi business, a self-drive hire business or a driving school
- bought after 1st August 1995 wholly for business purposes, primarily leasing. If there is any use of the car for private motoring only 50% of the input VAT can be recovered.

Where input VAT is recoverable output VAT must be accounted for when the car is eventually disposed of.

Accessories bought at the same time as the car suffer the same treatment but if they are acquired and fitted after the car was acquired, the input VAT can be reclaimed provided that the expenditure is for business use.

Bad debts

Where a person has supplied goods or services for a consideration in money and has accounted for and paid tax on the supply, and the whole or any part of the consideration for the supply has been written off in his or her accounts as a bad debt, and a period of six months from the date on which payment was due has elapsed, the person shall be entitled to a refund of the amount of tax chargeable by reference to the outstanding amount (VATA 1994 s36(1) & (2)). A refund can be claimed only if the value of the supply is less than or equal to its open market value and, in the case of goods, title to the goods has passed from the trader to either the purchaser or a person deriving title from, through or under that person (VATA 1994 s36(4)). If payments on account are made they are treated as meeting the earliest liabilities first for the purposes of this legislation. If the debtor subsequently repays all or part of the debt a corresponding proportion of the VAT repaid must be reimbursed to Customs and Excise.

The Chancellor introduced a new measure in the budget in November 1996 which was intended to enable Customs and Excise to claw back bad debt relief. Registered traders must now repay any VAT which they reclaimed on supplies for which they have not paid and on which bad debt relief was claimed by the supplier.

A number of other measures were introduced in the 1996 budget which were intended to make it easier for suppliers to claim bad debt relief. From the date on which the Finance Bill receives Royal Assent it will not be necessary for title to the goods to have passed to the debtor for the supplier to be able to claim the relief. From the same date the buyer of a business will be able to claim bad debt relief on supplies made by the business before the transfer provided that the business was transferred as a going concern and the buyer took over the VAT registration number. Additionally, from the date of Royal Assent, registered traders who use the annual accounting scheme and hence only complete one VAT return a year will be able to account for output tax and claim bad debt relief on the same return.

Input tax specifically disallowed

In addition to unrecoverable input tax on the acquisition of cars discussed above even a registered trader cannot reclaim input tax on expenditure on:

- business entertaining unless the expense is allowable for either income tax or corporation tax purposes
- living accommodation for directors
- non-business items which have been recorded in the business accounts. If the taxable supply is acquired partly for a business use and partly for private use the registered trader may either reclaim all of the input tax and then account for output tax on the value of the supply taken for private use or

reclaim only the business element of the input tax. If the taxable supply is a service only the second method can be used.

Note that non-deductible input tax is deductible for income tax, corporation tax and capital gains tax purposes if the related expenditure is deductible for Schedule D Cases I and II or capital gains tax purposes.

Mixed output

Input tax is only recoverable by a registered trader if it has been paid on supplies which are attributable to taxable supplies made by the trader.

If a trader's outputs consist of both taxable and exempt supplies the basic rule is that only input tax which relates to taxable outputs is recoverable.

This matching is achieved by firstly determining how much input tax can be related directly to taxable outputs and exempt outputs. The input tax which relates to taxable outputs is fully reclaimable and that which relates to exempt supplies is not deductible. The remaining input tax is apportioned between taxable supplies and exempt supplies by using the percentage (taxable turnover excluding VAT/total turnover excluding VAT) × 100% rounded up to the next whole percentage point. The following items are omitted from the calculation:

● tax on goods acquired and sold without any work being carried out on them
● tax on self-supplies. A self-supply occurs when a trader produces a marketable output and then uses it during the course of the business. For example, a business may own a printing operation which produces stationery which is used by the business
● tax on capital goods acquired for use within the business.

The Customs and Excise may be willing to allow an alternative basis to be used to allocate input tax between taxable and exempt supplies.

If the amount of input tax which is deemed to relate to exempt supplies is less than an average of £600 a month the above apportionment is ignored and all of the input tax is reclaimable.

Cars and travelling costs

As you have already seen the VAT on the acquisition of a new car is generally not recoverable although the VAT on accessories bought at a later date is recoverable provided that the accessories are acquired for a business purpose. In this section we will concentrate on the VAT on petrol and maintenance costs.

By concession, provided that the car is used for business purposes, the VAT on the full cost of any repair and maintenance costs is reclaimable even if the car is also used for private purposes.

VAT on fuel used for business purposes is deductible even if the fuel is bought by an employee who is then reimbursed, either through a mileage allowance or by repayment of the cost of the fuel.

If a business provides its employees with petrol for private use and the employee does not fully reimburse the company for the cost of the fuel the business is considered to have made a taxable supply. Consequently the business can reclaim the input tax on the petrol but must also account for output tax using a scale charge. However, if the business chooses not to reclaim the input tax on the fuel they do not have to account for output tax. The scale charge is approximately equal to a quarter of the fuel scale charge rounded up to the nearest pound. If the employee does fully reimburse the company for the cost of the fuel used privately VAT must be accounted for on the amount reimbursed as if it were VAT inclusive.

VAT on fuel for private use is also deductible unless the employee fully reimburses the cost of the fuel. However, the business must also account for output tax using the scale charges per quarter, or per month.

If an employee reimburses an employer for the cost of either the use of the car or any private fuel used the payment is treated as if it were VAT inclusive provided that the payment is equal to or exceeds the cost of the private fuel.

Self-supply

If a registered person either takes possession of, or produces, goods in the course or furtherance of a business carried on by him or her and which are neither supplies to another person nor incorporated in other goods produced in the course or furtherance of that business but are used by him for the purpose of a business carried on by him or her the goods are treated as being both supplied to him or her for the purpose of that business and supplied by him or her in the course or furtherance of it (VATA 1994 s5(5)).

If a person makes a supply to themselves, the input tax on the supply shall not be allowable (Statutory Instrument Value Added Tax (General) Regulations 1985 s32A).

If a registered trader made a self-supply of a motor car the input tax cannot be reclaimed (SI VAT (Cars) Order 1992 s5). This legislation also applies if the trader originally acquired a car and used it for a purpose which enabled the input tax to be reclaimed, specifically as a taxi, a self-drive hire car or a driving school car and subsequently the car was used for other purposes (SI VAT (Cars) Order 1992 s6).

Where a person produces printed matter in the course of their business and the printed matter is not supplied to another person or incorporated in other goods produced in the course or furtherance of that business, but is used by that person for the purpose of a business carried on by them then the printed matter shall be treated as a self-supply provided the value of the self-supply exceeds £46,000 a year (Statutory Instrument Value Added Tax (Special Provisions) Order 1992 s7(1)).

Registration and deregistration

A registered trader is a sole trader, partnership or company who is registered for VAT. It is important that a trader who is liable to register does notify the Customs and Excise because failure to register carries severe penalties as well as a liability to pay the VAT which should have been accounted for.

Initial registration

A person who makes taxable supplies, but is not registered for VAT, becomes liable to be registered:

- at the end of any month, if the value of taxable supplies in the period of one year then ending has exceeded £48,000, or
- at any time, if there are reasonable grounds for believing that the value of taxable supplies in the period of 30 days then beginning will exceed £48,000 (VATA 1994 Sch 1 s1(1)).

In determining the value of a person's supplies for this purpose supplies of goods or services that are capital assets of the business are ignored (VATA 1994 Sch 1 s1(7)).

The trader will then be registered for VAT from the end of the month following the 12-month period in which he exceeded the limit. If the Customs and Excise and the trader agree to an earlier date this will be used instead.

Registration must also take place if there are reasonable grounds for believing that the taxable supplies will exceed the annual limit in the next 30 days.

However, if the Commissioners are satisfied that the value of a trader's taxable supplies in the period of one year from the date on which he would be required to register under section 1(1) will not exceed £46,000 the trader is not liable to register (VATA 1994 Sch 1 s1(3)).

There is legislation to prevent the avoidance of registration by dividing the business between a number of persons each of whom would not be liable to register under the turnover rule contained in Schedule 1 section 1(1).

The Commissioners can make a direction under which all the persons named in the direction are treated as a single taxable person carrying on the activities of the business described in the direction. The traders named in the direction are liable to be registered for VAT from the date of the direction, unless a later date is specified in the direction (VATA 1994 Sch 1 s2(1)). The Commissioners shall not make such a direction unless they are satisfied that:

- the trader is making, or has made taxable supplies, and
- the trader's activities in making those taxable supplies form only part of the total activities which can be considered to be the business that is described in the direction. The other activities are carried on by one or more other persons, and
- if all the taxable supplies of that business were taken into account, a person carrying on that business would at the time of the direction be liable to be registered under Schedule 1 section 1(1), and
- the main reason or one of the main reasons for the person concerned carrying on the activities described in the direction in the way he or she does is the avoidance of a liability to be registered, whether that liability would be his, another person's or that of two or more persons jointly (VATA 1994 Sch 1 s2(2)).

The November 1996 budget contained further measures to reduce the scope for splitting businesses artificially so that each of the separate parts can avoid registering for VAT. From the date of Royal Assent of the Finance Bill connected businesses which have avoided registration by artificially separating will be liable to be treated as one business regardless of the reason for the separation. Until now Customs and Excise have been required to prove that the main reason for the separation was the avoidance of registration. However, the new legislation will not enable Customs and Excise to treat independent businesses which are conducted at arm's length as one business. As a result most franchised businesses will not be affected by these changes.

As soon as it becomes known that a trader is required to register they should keep VAT records and charge VAT on his taxable outputs although they cannot issue VAT invoices until a VAT registration number is received. During this period the trader should notify customers that the price charged is VAT inclusive and a full tax invoice should be sent within 30 days of receiving the registration number.

Traders who fail to register will be liable for VAT on taxable supplies from the date on which they should have registered. If it is not possible to collect the VAT due from customers they will still be liable for the tax due.

Traders making only zero-rated supplies can request exemption from registration. Traders with this exemption are responsible for notifying Customs and Excise if there is any change in the nature of their supplies.

Voluntary registration

Where a person who is not liable to be registered under the Act and is not already so registered satisfies the Commissioners that he or she either makes taxable supplies or is carrying on a business and intends to make such supplies in the course of that business, they shall, if he or she so requests, register them with effect from the day on which the request is made or from such earlier date as may be agreed between them (VATA 1994 Sch 1 s9).

There are a number of benefits and disadvantages of voluntary registration.

Activity

List some of the advantages and disadvantages of voluntary registration.

Feedback

The following are advantages of voluntary registration:

- the input tax can be reclaimed
- customers who are VAT registered can reclaim the output tax charged to them
- the trader may appear to be a larger business than he or she actually is which may increase his or her status with customers.

The following are disadvantages of voluntary registration:

- customers who are not VAT registered cannot reclaim the output tax and so the trader may lose his competitive edge with non-registered customers
- the administrative burden of registration should not be overlooked.

It appears then that the tax status of a trader's customers are an important factor when deciding whether voluntary registration is likely to be beneficial. Let's consider this in a little more detail.

Feedback

Sales to public	Registered £	Not registered £
Value of supply		
40 × £500	20,000	20,000
Less output VAT	2,979	
Net sales	17,021	20,000
Less costs 40 × £100 excluding VAT	4,000	4,000
Non-reclaimable VAT		700
Net costs	4,000	4,700
Profit	13,021	15,300

If Elaine chooses to sell her quilts directly to the public she should not register for VAT.

Sales to retail outlet	Registered £	Not registered £
Value of supply		
40 × £500		20,000
20,000 × 117.5%	23,500	
Less output VAT	3,500	
Net sales	20,000	20,000
Less costs as above: net costs	4,000	4,700
Profit	16,000	15,300

If Elaine chooses to sell her quilts to the retailer she should register for VAT. Of the four options the most profitable is to register for VAT and sell her quilts to the retailer.

Deregistration

Deregistration may be voluntary or compulsory.

A person who has become liable to be registered for VAT purposes shall cease to be so liable, and become compulsorily deregistered, if the Commissioners are satisfied that he or she has ceased to make taxable supplies and is not included in a directive under Schedule 1 section 1A(1) (VATA 1994 Sch 1 s3).

A person who has become liable to be registered for VAT purposes shall cease to be so liable if the Commissioners are satisfied that the value of his or her taxable supplies in the next 12 months will not exceed £46,000 (VATA 1994 Sch 1 s4(1)).

A person cannot be registered under two or more different provisions under the Act. A registered trader who ceases to make or have the intention of making taxable supplies shall notify the Commissioners within 30 days unless, when he or she so ceases, he or she would still be liable or entitled to be registered under the VATA 1994 (VATA 1994 Sch 1 s11).

A trader may claim to be voluntarily deregistered if Customs and Excise are satisfied that the traders taxable supplies, net of VAT, in the following 12 months will not exceed £46,000. Note that traders will not be able to claim to be voluntarily deregistered if they intend to cease to trade or if there will be a suspension of taxable supplies for a continuous period of 30 days or more in the next 12 months.

The date of a voluntary deregistration is the later of the date on which the request is made or an agreed date.

If a trader who is voluntarily registered ceases to make or have the intention of making taxable supplies he or she shall notify the Commissioners within 30 days unless, when he or she so ceases, they would still be liable or entitled to be registered under the VATA 1994 (VATA 1994 Sch 1 s12).

When a registered trader takes goods or services from the business for non-business purposes, for example a retailer taking goods for self-consumption, VAT is chargeable on their cost rather than the selling price.

Taxable supplies and exempt supplies

Now that you are able to discuss the need for and consequence of registration for VAT purposes we can turn our attention to identifying taxable and exempt supplies. Unless a supply is specifically exempt or zero rated it is taxable at the standard rate of 17.5%. At the beginning of this chapter there is a list of taxable supplies. Go back and re-read that section before reading the lists of exempt and zero-rated supplies.

Exempt supplies

The exemptions to VAT are contained in Schedule 9 of the VATA 1994. The Schedule contains a number of groups, which are listed here, together with some important examples of exempt goods and services.

Group 1 — land.
  Including:

- granting of any interest in or right over land
- holiday accommodation
- mooring fees including anchoring and berthing.

Group 2 — insurance.
Group 3 — postal services.
Group 4 — betting, gaming and lotteries.
Group 5 — finance.
  Including:

- provision of credit
- issue, transfer or receipt of, or any dealing with, any security or secondary security.

Group 6 — education.
  Including:

- provision of education or research by a school, eligible institution or university
- supply of any goods or services incidental to the provision of any education, training or re-training.

Group 7 — health and welfare.
  Including:

- supply of services by registered medical practitioners, ophthalmic opticians and dentists
- provision of spiritual welfare by a religious institution as part of a course of instruction or a retreat.

Group 8 — burial and cremation.
Group 9 — trade unions and professional bodies.
Group 10 — sports competitions.
Group 11 — works of art.
Group 12 — fund-raising events by charities and other qualifying bodies.

Zero-rated supplies

The goods and services which are zero rated are contained in Schedule 8 of the VATA 1983. The Schedule contains a number of groups, which are listed here, together with some important examples of zero-rated goods and services.

Group 1 — food.
  Including:

- food of a kind used for human consumption
- animal feeding stuffs.

  Exceptions include:

- supply in the course of catering, including all food which is consumed on the premises and all hot food

- ice cream, confectionery and chocolate biscuits
- spirits, beer and wine
- pet food.

Group 2 — sewerage services and water.
Group 3 — books.
  Including:

- books, booklets, brochures, pamphlets and leaflets
- newspapers, journals and periodicals.

Individual knitting patterns are taxable supplies but booklets containing more than one pattern are zero rated.
Group 4 — talking books for the blind and handicapped and wireless sets for the blind.
Group 5 — construction of buildings, etc.
Group 6 — protected buildings.
Group 7 — international services.
Group 8 — transport.
Group 9 — caravans and houseboats
Group 10 — gold.
Group 11 — bank notes.
Group 12 — drugs, medicines, aids for the handicapped.
Group 13 — imports, exports, etc.
Group 14 — tax-free shops.
Group 15 — charities, etc.
Group 16 — clothing and footwear.

Special schemes

You need to be aware of the special schemes which are available to registered traders. The payments on account scheme is compulsory for large organisations but other schemes are offered to taxpayers on a voluntary basis. None of the schemes alters the amount of VAT which must be paid; they merely affect either the date of payments to Custom and Excise or the administration of VAT. In practice the take-up of these voluntary schemes is very low despite the apparent attractiveness of some of them. This may be partly due to the stringent conditions for joining the schemes.

The payments on account scheme

Companies which have to pay over £2 million a year to the Customs and Excise complete their VAT returns in the normal way but are required to make two payments on account in each quarter, the first payment is made a month before the end of the quarter, the second payment is made at the end of the tax period and the final payment, which is sufficient to extinguish the VAT liability for the tax period, is made at the usual time.

This means that the trader will make a payment to the Customs and Excise at the end of each month of the year.

Registered traders with a VAT liability of over £2 million for the last accounting period are required to operate the payments on account scheme. The Customs and Excise will use current information in order to determine the monthly payments of the members of the scheme (Statutory Instrument 1993/2001 as amended by Statutory Instrument 1995/291).

The cash accounting scheme

The cash accounting scheme uses the following tax points:

- for output tax, the day on which payment or other consideration is received, or the date of any cheque, if later
- for input tax, the date on which payment is made or other consideration is given, or the date of any cheque, if later (Statutory Instrument VAT (Cash Accounting) Regulations 1987 s3).

Taxable persons are eligible for admission to the scheme if:

- they have reasonable grounds for believing that the value of taxable supplies made by them in the period of one year beginning at the date of their application for authorisation will not exceed £300,000
- they have made all the returns which they are required to make and all VAT payments are up to date
- they have not, in the three years preceding the date of application for authorisation, been convicted of any offence in connection with VAT (SI VAT (Cash Accounting) Regulations 1987 s4(1)).

The scheme does not apply to hire purchase agreements, conditional sale agreements or credit sale agreements (SI VAT (Cash Accounting) Regulations 1987 s4(3)).

Authorised persons may remain in the scheme unless:

- at the end of any quarter or prescribed accounting period the value of taxable supplies made in the year then ended has exceeded £375,000 and in the year then beginning is expected to exceed the figure of £300,000, in which case they shall within 30 days notify the Commissioners and cease to operate the scheme at the anniversary of joining, or
- at any time there is reason to believe that the value of taxable supplies made by them in the year then beginning will exceed £375,000 in which case they shall within 30 days notify the Commissioners who may terminate authorisation at the end of the next prescribed accounting period (SI VAT (Cash Accounting) Regulations 1987 s6(2)).

Authorised persons may withdraw from the scheme if:

- they derive no benefit from remaining in the scheme
- they are unable, by reason of accounting systems, to comply with the requirements of the scheme

and following written notification of that fact by them to the Commissioners they shall terminate authorisation at the end of the prescribed accounting period in which such notification is received by them (SI VAT (Cash Accounting) Regulations 1987 s6(3)).

The Commissioners may terminate an authorisation if:

- a false statement has been made by or on behalf of an authorised person in relation to the application for authorisation
- an authorised person has, while admitted to the scheme, been convicted of an offence in connection with VAT
- an authorised person has failed to leave the scheme despite having a turnover which exceeds £375,000 a year
- an authorised person has claimed input tax as though he or she had not been admitted to the scheme (SI VAT (Cash Accounting) Regulations 1987 s10(1)).

A person whose authorisation has been terminated shall account for and pay on a return made in respect of his or her current prescribed accounting period all tax which has not been accounted for and paid in accordance with the scheme, subject to any adjustment for credit for input tax (SI VAT (Cash Accounting Regulations 1987 s10(2)).

The annual accounting scheme

The Commissioners may authorise taxable persons to account for tax in accordance with a scheme by which they:

- pay, by direct debit on their bank account in nine equal monthly instalments commencing on the last day of the fourth month of their current accounting year, 90% of tax liability as estimated by the Commissioners for that current accounting year
- furnishes by the last day of the second month following the end of that current accounting year a return in respect of that year, together with any outstanding payment due to the Commissioners in respect of their liability for tax declared on that return (SI VAT (Annual Accounting) Regulations 1988 s3).

Taxable persons shall be eligible to apply for authorisation under the scheme if:

- they have been registered for at least one year at the date of application for authorisation
- they have reasonable grounds for believing that the value of taxable supplies in the period of one year beginning at the date of application for authorisation will not exceed £300,000
- they have made all the returns which they are required to make
- total credits for input tax did not exceed total output tax in the year prior to application for authorisation
- registration is not in the name of a group or a division
- they have not, in the three years preceding the date of application for authorisation, had authorisation terminated (SI VAT (Annual Accounting) Regulations 1988 s4(1)).

An authorised person may start to use the scheme at the beginning of the accounting year stated in the notification of the authorisation (ST VAT (Annual Accounting) Regulations 1988 s5(1)).
  Authorised persons may remain in the scheme unless:

- at the end of any current accounting year the value of the taxable supplies made by them in that year has exceeded £375,000, in which case their authorisation shall be terminated immediately
- at any time there is reason to believe that the value of taxable supplies made in the current accounting year will exceed £375,000 in which case they shall within 30 days notify the Commissioners who may terminate authorisation
- they are expelled from the scheme (SI VAT (Annual Accounting) Regulations 1988 s5(2)).

Authorised persons who cease to operate the scheme either of their own volition or because the value of taxable supplies made by them exceeds £375,000 a year shall account for and pay tax as provided for, by or under the Act (SI VAT (Annual Accounting) Regulations 1988 s6).

The Commissioners may terminate an authorisation in any case where:

- a false statement has been made by or on behalf of an authorised person in relation to the application for authorisation
- an authorised person fails to furnish by the due date a return in respect of the current accounting year
- an authorised person fails to make any payment due under the scheme
- an authorised person has failed to leave the scheme although his or her taxable supplies exceed £375,000 (SI VAT (Annual Accounting) Regulations 1988 s8(1)).

Retail schemes

There are 12 schemes which are used by about 270,000 retailers and which are legislated for by the VAT (Supplies by Retailers) Regulations 1972. The normal VAT legislation requires registered traders to maintain detailed records of every transaction. Retailers who make a mixture of standard rated, zero rated and exempt supplies face particular problems. Retailers are able to keep less detailed records by using one of the schemes and calculate output tax in a way which suits their circumstances. Some of the schemes require totals for different sorts of supply rather than details of individual transactions while others allow the VAT liability to be estimated using purchases and mark-up percentages. However, the November 1996 budget contained a number of measures to restrict the use of the retail schemes. In the future the retail schemes will only be available to retailers who cannot reasonably be expected to account for VAT in the normal way. Customs and Excise will discuss arrangements for transferring to normal methods of accounting for VAT with retailers individually.

In addition no business with a taxable retail turnover of over £1 million per annum will be eligible to join Retail Scheme B after 26th November 1996 and such businesses already using the scheme will have to change to a different method of accounting by 1st April 1997.

From 1st March 1997 the tax point on self-financed credit sales will be based on the time of supply rather than on the date of payment as in the past.

A periodic review of the retail schemes which are available to small businesses has recently been carried out and the changes, intended to simplify the range of schemes, will be introduced from 1st April 1997. At the same time individually agreed schemes for businesses with taxable retail turnover in excess of £10 million per annum will be introduced.

The secondhand goods scheme

The secondhand goods scheme is available to traders who buy secondhand goods from individuals who are not registered traders. The Commissioners can make an order allowing a reduction on the supply of such secondhand goods (VATA 1994 s32(1)).

The maximum reduction available is equal to the amount of tax which would have been due had the acquisition of the goods been a taxable supply (VATA 1994 s32(2)).

This means that VAT is due only on the trader's margin rather than on the sales price of the goods. Hence the trader has to account for 7/47 of the difference between his purchase price and his selling price (VATA 1994 s50A).

A registered trader who buys goods from a trader who is using the secondhand goods scheme will not be able to reclaim the input tax because he will not have received a tax invoice.

Orders under this scheme can apply to all secondhand goods, works of art, antiques and collectors' items. The scheme cannot be applied to precious metals and gemstones.

A system of global accounting for VAT on secondhand goods is currently being introduced. Under the global accounting system registered traders will only need to account for VAT on the difference between the total purchases and the total sales of eligible goods in a tax period rather than on an item by item basis.

Tax planning points

We have already seen that it is possible for a trader to register voluntarily for VAT, but there are some more options when registering which we should consider.

Groups of companies under common control can elect to register as a group. One company must be appointed as the representative member who deals with all VAT matters for the group. For the purposes of VAT a VAT group is deemed to be a single taxable person. That is although each company within the group has a separate legal identity for VAT purposes they are not considered to have a discrete identity (*Commissioners of Customs and Excise v Kingfisher plc* (1994)). Intra-group transfers are ignored for VAT purposes and all taxable supplies to and from any member of the group are treated as a taxable supply by or to the representative member.

If a group registration is made it is not necessary for all members of the group to participate. This may be useful if one member of the group is making exempt supplies.

In order to be eligible for group registration all companies in the group must be resident in the UK or have an established place of business in the UK. In addition either one company must control each of the others, or one person, an individual or a company, must control all of the companies, or two or more persons who are partners in business must control them all.

From 26th November 1996 any special status attributed to the representative member of the group will not be capable of being used to obtain relief from VAT by other members of the group who are not otherwise entitled to the relief. Examples of special status companies include:

- companies providing insurance and reinsurance who are permitted to carry on insurance business in accordance with section 2 of the Insurance Companies Act 1982 (VATA 1994, Sch 9 Group 2)
- eligible bodies providing education, research or vocational training. An eligible body is a school, including state schools, independent schools and grant-maintained schools, Colleges of Further and Higher Education, UK universities and youth clubs (VATA 1994, Sch 9 Group 6)
- charities supplying goods and services in connection with a fund-raising event organised for charitable purposes (VATA 1994, Sch 9 Group 12).

Customs and Excise retain the right to refuse any application for group registration if they deem that it is necessary in order to protect the revenue.

In contrast to group registration it is possible for a company to apply for divisional registration. Provided that the Commissioners see fit registration is in the names of the divisions (VATA 1994 s46(1)). This would be advantageous if the organisation of the company is divisional and it is simpler administratively to operate as divisions for VAT purposes. However, the company is still liable for any VAT liability. In order to obtain divisional registration it is necessary to fulfil the following conditions:

- all divisions must register regardless of the size of their turnover
- each division must be distinct from the other divisions in terms of their accounting function and business activities
- the input tax which relates to exempt supplies must be, on average, less than £600 a month for the whole company
- each division must use the same tax periods
- supplies from one division to another are not supplies for VAT purposes and so tax invoices should not be issued.

Imports and exports

With the creation of a Europe without trade barriers on 1st January 1993 it has become necessary to differentiate between transactions with traders resident in other countries in the European Union and those resident in countries outside the European Union.

Imports

Imports may come from other EU member states or from countries which are not members of the EU. The tax treatment of imports depends on the source of the goods.

On 1st January 1993 the fiscal frontiers inside the EU were abolished and the single market was created. We will discuss the detail of the arrangements which are in force within the EU member states in the next section. In this section we will consider imports from countries from outside the EU.

Tax on the importation of goods from places outside the member states shall be charged and payable as if it were a duty of customs (VATA 1994 s16(1)). The rate of the duty is the same as the rate which would apply if the same goods were supplied in the home market by a registered trader. The person who is to be treated as importing any goods from outside the member states is the person who would be liable to discharge any such EU customs debt (VATA 1994 s15(2)). The registered trader is then able to reclaim the duty on the goods which are used for the purposes of a business carried on by him or her as input tax in the normal way (VATA 1994 s24(6)). A registered trader may apply for approval under the Customs Duties (Deferred Payment) Regulations 1976 in order to make deferred payments. The Commissioners shall grant an approved person deferment of customs duty until payment day (Statutory Instrument Customs Duties (Deferred Payment) Regulations 1976 s5). Payment day is the 15th day of the month next following that in which the amount of duty deferred is entered into the Commissioners' accounts, or in the case of import entries scheduled periodically, the 15th day of the period following that in which deferment is granted. A period commences on the 16th day of any month and ends on the 15th day of the month next following (SI Customs Duties (Deferred Payment) Regulations 1976 s2(1)). On each payment day an approved person shall pay to the Commissioners the total amount of customs duty of which he has been granted deferment (SI Customs Duties (Deferred Payment) Regulations 1976 s6).

If relevant services are supplied to a registered trader who is UK resident by a person resident overseas, either within the EU or a place outside the EU, the reverse charge system will be used. Relevant services include:

- transfers and assignments of copyright, patents, licences, trademarks and similar rights
- advertising services
- services of consultants, engineers, consultancy bureaux, lawyers, accountants and other similar services; data processing and provision of information
- banking, financial and insurance services including re-insurance
- any other service supplied to a registered trader provided that it is not exempt under VATA 1994 Sch 9 (VATA 1994 Sch 5).

VAT will be accounted for as if the registered trader had supplied the services in the UK in the course of business and that supply were a taxable supply (VATA 1994 s8 (1)). If the recipient is not VAT registered and the supply is only a relevant supply because it is not exempt under VATA 1994 Sch 9 the supplier, if registered, will be required to account for VAT in the normal way.

From 26th November 1996 multinational groups which are registered as a group for VAT purposes will be prevented from obtaining services from overseas without accounting for VAT. The reverse charge system only allows a business to recover tax due as input tax to the extent that it relates to the business's taxable supplies. Hence, where the reverse charge relates to exempt supplies the tax due cannot be recovered. Prior to the 1996 budget a number of VAT registered groups were using an overseas branch of one of the group companies to provide relevant services thus avoiding tax because the reverse charge procedure could not apply. Under the new legislation announced in the budget such a supply within a VAT registered group will be taxed so as to produce broadly the same consequences as the reverse charge system.

The Finance Act 1997 will also contain legislation whichwill lead to telecommunication services supplied to UK businesses from outside the EU being liable to VAT.

Imports of works of art, antiques and collectors' pieces from outside the EU are subject to VAT at a reduced rate of 2.5%.

Exports

A supply of goods is zero-rated if the Commissioners are satisfied that the person supplying the goods has:

- exported them to a place outside the member states
- shipped them for use as stores on a voyage or flight to an eventual destination outside the UK, or as merchandise for sale by retail to persons carried on such a voyage or flight in a ship or aircraft (VATA 1994 s30(6)).

The Finance Act 1997 will contain legislation which will enable a supply of telecommunication services to businesses registered either in non-EU countries or other EU member states to be free of VAT.

The EU harmonisation proposals for VAT

On the 1st January 1993 a single market was created within the EU. The single market was intended to lead to the free movement of goods, services, capital and people. To achieve this it was necessary to abolish the tax frontiers and for imports into the UK from member states to be charged to VAT in the same way as acquisitions in the UK (F(No 2)A 1992 s14(1)).

Schedule 3 of Finance Act (No 2) 1992 entitled 'Value Added Tax: Abolition of Fiscal Frontiers etc.' contains the detailed legislation necessary to establish the single market.

Until the creation of the single market, VAT was collected and charged using the destination principle, that is goods and services were taxed on entry into the country of consumption. Hence exports were zero rated and VAT was charged on imports at countries' borders at the rate which would be applied to the supply of the equivalent domestic goods in order to avoid discrimination between domestic and imported goods. However, with the abolition of internal frontiers it will not be possible to charge VAT on imports. In fact a taxable supply from one member state to another is no longer regarded as an import or an export.

The European Commissioners proposed the use of the origin principle. Under this system goods would be chargeable to VAT at the rate prevailing in the member state in which the exporter operates and the tax would be remitted to the exporter's national tax authority. It would then be necessary to operate a centralised clearing house system in order to transfer the revenues to the member state of final consumption. This system would remove the need for any border adjustments and so there would be a system of free trade regulated only by the country of origin. Member states concluded that there were too many problems with the origin system to enable it to be introduced on 1st January 1993. The central clearing house would be expensive to run and might be prone to error and fraud. Until the introduction of the single market goods were checked at borders to ensure that zero rated exports did, in fact, leave the country. In addition the VAT on imports was calculated, and sometimes paid, at the border. However, the borders are expensive to operate and some believe they have led to a decline in the economic strength of the Community when compared to the United States and Japan. There was also some doubt as to whether the central clearing house could be protected from fraud.

The second difficulty about implementing the origin principle was that tax rates differ between member states. This would affect competition in the country of destination.

Consider two manufacturers of children's clothing, one based in the UK where children's clothes are zero rated and the other in a member state where children's clothes are liable to VAT at 9%. If both companies sell their clothes in the UK the UK manufacturer will be at an advantage caused by the disparity in their VAT liabilities. The UK company would not have to charge VAT while the other company would have to charge VAT at 9%. Hence businesses operating in low tax areas would have a competitive advantage over producers in high tax areas. In the long term this might influence the location of production, encouraging businesses to operate in low tax countries.

Not all VAT is recoverable, for example, VAT on cars in the UK is normally irrecoverable. Businesses might choose to pay their non-deductible input tax in member states with low rates of tax. This could be achieved by buying assets in countries with low rates of VAT. This might also encourage businesses to locate in low tax countries.

The Commission decided, in 1987, that before a system using the origin system could be introduced it would be necessary to achieve a degree of convergence of the tax rates throughout the Community. It was believed that a difference of around 5% across a border between neighbouring states was the maximum which could be tolerated. Differences of more than this were thought likely to lead to distortions in the market. Individuals might undertake personal importation of goods, such as cars, and undertake cross-border shopping. First the Commission proposed that the three rates of tax operating in many countries should be reduced to two, a standard rate and a reduced rate to be applied to items of basic necessity such as food, energy for heating, water, books and passenger transport. It was proposed that the standard rate of tax should lie between 14% and 20% with a reduced rate of between 4% and 9%. Achieving this convergence has proved to be difficult. For some governments, adopting these bands may be seen as a restriction of what is a major tool of their economic policy. The UK has been reluctant to accept the loss of parliamentary sovereignty that agreeing to the legislation is seen to bring. In the end the government accepted the regulations for a limited number of years. However, the UK has refused to abolish its zero rating in favour of a reduced rate band because of the political unpopularity such a move would bring. The UK government believes that market forces should be allowed to operate and that this will lead to VAT rates moving closer together. However, the UK operates among the lowest rates in Europe and so is unlikely to be disadvantaged if the origin principle operates. Firms based in other countries are likely to operate with a significant disadvantage compared to UK companies and the UK government is unlikely to suffer a loss of revenue.

Some economists believe that exchange rates will adjust to compensate for the differences, under a theory called purchasing power parity. Briefly this theory states that exchange rates will adjust so that the purchasing power of the two currencies is maintained. Hence if a country suffers 10% inflation during a year in which another country enjoys zero inflation purchasing power parity predicts a 10% devaluation for the first currency in order to maintain purchasing power parity. The empirical evidence is that purchasing power parity holds but only in the long term. Many other factors affect exchange rates and so it seems unlikely that currency exchange rates will completely compensate for differences in the rate of VAT, at least in the short term.

It is thought that the single market may create opportunities for fraud because the border checks will no longer exist and the system will depend on purchasers and sellers disclosing all their transactions. It may also be difficult to verify that input tax reclaimed was in fact paid.

There are also competitive distortions created by the classification of goods in different ways by member states. Some goods are exempt in one country and standard rated in another. As a consequence of all these difficulties a transitional period, running until 31st December 1996, has been introduced. At the end of this time a system, as yet uncertain, using the origin principle should be introduced.

However, an HM Customs and Excise business brief issued in September 1995 expressed doubts that an origin system could be implemented in 1997 and suggested that 1st January 1999 was more likely, although there are doubts about whether an origin system will ever be introduced.

During the transitional period the destination system will be used, under which suppliers are taxed at the rate in force in the country of acquisition apart from supplies of goods to individuals, unregistered traders and exempt traders under the 'de minimis limits', which are lower limits set by the European Commissioners and which are taxed under the origin system.

The destination system allows registered traders in a member state to supply goods to registered traders in other member states at zero rate. The acquiring trader will be required to account for VAT as both a taxable supply and input tax at the rate in force in his own country.

In order to use the destination system the supplier must have documentary evidence that the goods have left the UK and have been supplied to a registered trader in another member state. The sales invoice must include the customer's VAT registration number as well as his country prefix code. If these conditions are not met the origin system must be used. This means that supplies to unregistered traders must be made using the origin system.

During the transitional period tax shall be charged on any acquisition from another member state of any goods where:

- the acquisition is taxable and takes place in the UK
- the acquisition is otherwise than in pursuance of a taxable supply
- the person who makes the acquisition is a taxable person or the goods are subject to a duty or excise or consists in a new means of transport (F(No 2)A 1992 Sch 3 s3(2A(1))).

A means of transport is any of the following:

- any ship over 7.5 metres long
- any aircraft with a take-off weight of over 1,550 kilograms

- any motorised land vehicle which either has an engine of over 48cc or is electrically propelled using more than 7.2 kilowatts (VATA 1994 s95(1)).

A new means of transport is a means of transport which:

- first entered into service less than three months ago
- has travelled, under its own power, less than 100 hours for a ship, 40 hours for an aircraft and 3,000 kilometres for a land vehicle since its first entry into service (VATA 1994 s95(3)).

An acquisition of goods from another member state is a taxable acquisition if it is not an exempt acquisition and:

- the goods consist in a new means of transport
- the goods are acquired in the course or furtherance of business carried on by any person or any activities carried on otherwise than by way of business by a body corporate or by any club, association, organisation or other unincorporated body
- it is the person who carries on that business, or those activities, who acquires the goods
- the supplier is taxable in another member state at the time of the transaction in pursuance of which goods are acquired and in participating in that transaction, acts in the course or furtherance of a business carried on by him or her (F(No 2)A 1992 Sch 3 s3(2A(2) & (3))).

The tax point is the earlier of the date of issue of a tax invoice and the 15th of the month following removal of the goods.

Tax on any acquisition of goods from another member state is a liability of the person who acquires the goods and, subject to provisions about accounting and payment, becomes due at the time of acquisition (F(No 2)A 1992 Sch 3 s3(2A(4))).

Summary

In this chapter you have read about the operation of VAT, one of our most important taxes.

VAT has to be paid whenever a taxable person makes a taxable supply of goods or services in the course of business. Unless a supply of goods or services is specifically exempt in the legislation it is a taxable supply. With the exception of domestic fuel, which is taxable at 8%, taxable supplies are either standard rated or zero rated. The standard rate of VAT is 17.5% in 1997/98.

A trader must register if turnover exceeds certain limits, for 1997/98 the limit is £48,000 a year. A trader whose turnover is lower than the registration limit may elect to register voluntarily.

A registered trader is able to reclaim allowable input tax but must account for output tax on taxable supplies.

VAT is paid quarterly to Customs and Excise on the invoices received and issued in the quarter. However, there are a considerable number of special schemes, some of which are compulsory, which require VAT to be accounted for on a different basis.

There is debate about the acceptability of further increases in the amount of revenue which is raised using indirect taxation. This debate is considered in the first three chapters.

We have suggested that with the exception of non-deductible input tax VAT is merely a cash flow and administrative issue for registered traders. However, in Chapter 3 we discussed the nature of VAT and concluded that the burden of VAT fell on traders as well as final consumers. In the budget of 1991 the standard rate of VAT was increased from 15% to 17.5% to fund a reduction in the community charge. At the time the economy of the UK was in recession and a large number of retailers including Marks and Spencer announced that they would absorb the increase in VAT themselves rather than pass it on to their customers. The retailers recognised that increases in prices would lead to a decrease in demand which would reduce their profits.

Project areas

The harmonisation of VAT within the EU provides considerable scope for dissertation titles.

There are also opportunities for comparative studies, for example the special schemes on offer to small businesses in EU member states.

Since 1979 there has been a significant shift in taxation in the UK from direct taxation to indirect taxation. A number of titles suggest themselves, for example, is it possible for there to be further shifts from direct taxes to indirect taxes? Alternatively would a shift back towards direct taxation be possible or desirable?

Computational questions

Question 1 (based on CIMA May 1988).

(a) A trader started in business, selling mainly foodstuffs which are zero rated for VAT purposes, on 1st January 1997 and the following information was extracted from his records for the year ended 31st December 1997.

The purchases (but not the sales) are inclusive of VAT.

	£
Fixed assets purchased (all standard rated)	7,000
Other standard rated purchases and expenses	3,000
Sales of zero rated foodstuffs	42,000
Sales of standard rated items	8,000

He approaches you shortly after the end of the year and informs you that he does not intend to register for VAT since 'the sales liable to VAT were well below the threshold'.

Required
Advise him on the position regarding registration for VAT, and show the final value added tax position which would have applied for the above year if the trader had registered voluntarily at the start of the year.

Question 2 (based on CIMA November 1992).

You are the chief accountant of Z Ltd, a UK resident company, whose activities to date have been confined wholly to the UK.

The company is about to acquire three UK resident subsidiaries, and the members of the newly-formed group will engage, for the first time, in import and export activities.

Required
Draft a brief report to the board on the VAT implications of the above changes.

Question 3 (based on ACCA Paper 3.3. December 1993).
Part c
Alison Able, the senior partner in Able, Keane and Ready, is planning to set up a new business venture in the near future that she will run herself, rather than as part of the partnership. None of the partnership assets or staff will be involved in the new business. The income from the new business is expected to be £50,000 p.a., net of VAT. All the income is in respect of standard-rated supplies, 80% of which will be made to VAT-registered persons. Because of the highly competitive nature of the business, it will not be possible to pass on the additional cost of VAT to the 20% of customers who are not VAT registered.

The business is to be run from Alison's home, so the only expenses of the new business will be:

	£
Leased office equipment	2,820 p.a.
Telephone (40% private)	1,175 p.a.
Entertaining clients	705 p.a.
Insurance	470 p.a.

Alison also plans to spend £5,875 on a pre-launch advertising campaign. All the above figures include VAT where applicable.

Required

(i)   Will Alison automatically have to account for VAT on the income of her new business as a result of the partnership being registered for VAT?

(ii) Assuming that the answer to (i) is that Alison does not automatically have to account for VAT on her income, would it be beneficial for her to register voluntarily for VAT in any case?

(iii) Would it be beneficial for Alison to defer the pre-launch advertising expenditure until after she has commenced trading? Your answer should consider both the VAT and the income tax implications.

Question 4 (based on ACCA Paper 11 June 1994).

Part b

Skunk Ltd owns 70% of the ordinary share capital of both Zebra Ltd and Emu Ltd. All three companies are involved in the construction industry. Skunk Ltd's sales are all standard rated, whilst Zebra Ltd's and Emu Ltd's are zero-rated and exempt respectively. The companies' sales and purchases for the year ended 31st March 1998 are as follows:

	Sales £	Purchases £
Skunk Ltd	1,170,000	480,000
Zebra Ltd	540,000	270,000
Emu Ltd	390,000	150,000

The purchases for all three companies are standard rated. In addition Skunk Ltd incurred standard rated overhead expenditure of £300,000 which cannot be directly attributed to any of the three companies' sales. Skunk Ltd charges both its subsidiary companies a management charge of £40,000 p.a. each in respect of the services of its accountancy department. All the above figures are exclusive of VAT where applicable. Skunk Ltd and its two subsidiaries are not registered as a group for VAT purposes.

Required

(i) Calculate the VAT position of Skunk Ltd, Zebra Ltd and Emu Ltd for the year ended 31st March 1998.
(ii) Advise Skunk Ltd of the conditions that must be met for itself and its two subsidiaries to register as a group for VAT purposes, and the consequences of being so registered.
(iii) Advise Skunk Ltd of whether or not it would have been beneficial for itself and both its subsidiaries to have been registered as a group for VAT purposes throughout the year ended 31st March 1998. Your answer should be supported by appropriate calculations.

11 ▷ Inheritance tax

Introduction

Inheritance tax was introduced in 1986. It replaced Capital Transfer Tax which itself replaced Estate Duty. Look back to Chapter 1 for a brief history of the taxation of capital. As you will see taxes have been levied on wealth, particularly the value of a citizen's estate on his death, since Roman times. Inheritance tax is intended to tax an individual's estate on death and some lifetime gifts and transfers to trust funds. Look back to Chapter 3 for a discussion of the use of wealth as a tax base. Inheritance tax is sometimes referred to as an avoidable tax and certainly with some judicious planning and a little luck it is possible for an individual to transfer substantial wealth to the next generation without incurring an inheritance tax liability. Ironically such transfers are much more likely to attract a capital gains tax liability.

The Conservative government has made it clear that it intends to abolish inheritance tax, together with capital gains tax, at some time in the future. As part of this policy the threshold for inheritance tax was increased by £15,000 to £215,000 from 6th April 1997. This represents an increase of nearly 40% over two years and it is estimated that only 14,000 estates will be liable to inheritance tax in 1997/98, about 1,500 fewer than would have been the case if the threshold had risen in line with the increase in the retail price index. It is estimated that inheritance tax will raise £1,550 million in 1997/98.

At the end of this chapter you will be able to:

- state the broad principles of inheritance tax, including their relevance to trusts
- calculate any inheritance tax consequences of making lifetime gifts
- calculate any inheritance tax liability on death including the taxation of lifetime gifts made within seven years of the donor's death
- discuss the uses of quick succession relief, business property relief and agricultural property relief
- state the main factors to be considered when planning for inheritance tax.

Principles of inheritance tax

Inheritance tax is levied on some lifetime gifts and the value of estates at death net of reliefs and exemptions. A lifetime gift may be exempt, potentially exempt or chargeable. A potentially exempt transfer becomes an exempt transfer if the transferrer lives for at least seven years after the date of the transfer. A cumulative total of chargeable lifetime transfers made in the previous seven years is maintained and the tax liability will be determined by reference to the cumulative total as well as the value of the transfer and the date of death of the donor if it is within seven years of the date of the transfer.

In practice, as you will see later, few lifetime transfers are chargeable.

In the next section we will concentrate on lifetime transfers before turning our attention to the inheritance tax computation on death.

Occasion of the charge

Inheritance tax is charged on the value transferred by a chargeable transfer (IHTA 1984 s1).

In addition inheritance tax is levied on property held in discretionary settlements on each ten-year anniversary of the trust being set up (IHTA 1984 s64).

A chargeable transfer is a transfer of value, made by an individual, which is not an exempt transfer (IHTA 1984 s2(1)). In fact the only lifetime transfers which are not potentially exempt are transfers to a discretionary trust, other than an accumulation and maintenance trust or a trust for the disabled, and some transfers involving companies. We will consider trusts later in this chapter.

Transfers of value

A transfer of value is a disposition made by a person, the transferrer, as a result of which the value of his estate immediately after the disposition is less than it would be but for the disposition. The value transferred is equal to the reduction in value of the estate of the transferrer (IHTA 1984 s3(1)). That is, the amount which is chargeable to tax is the reduction in the wealth of the taxpayer rather than the value of the gift in the hands of the recipient. Hence for a charge to inheritance tax to arise there must be a transfer of value which results in a reduction in the value of the transferrer's wealth.

A liability to inheritance tax can only arise if the donor intended to confer a gratuitous benefit. If an arm's length transaction is entered into it is not taken to be a chargeable transfer. A transfer between connected people can still be exempt if the transaction was one which might be expected to be made between persons not connected with each other (IHTA 1984, s10). The definitions of connected persons are the same for inheritance tax purposes as for capital gains tax purposes. You will find a list of connected persons in Chapter 7.

Chargeable property

All property is chargeable property unless it is designated excluded property by the legislation. Transfers of excluded property do not give rise to an inheritance tax liability unless, by making the transfer, the value of other property is affected. If this happens a liability to inheritance tax may arise.

The following property is excluded:

- property which is situated outside the UK provided that the person who is beneficially entitled to it is an individual who is not domiciled in the UK (IHTA 1984 s6(1))
- securities issued by the Treasury for exemption from taxation so long as the securities are in the beneficial ownership of persons neither domiciled nor ordinarily resident in the UK (IHTA 1984 s6(2))
- war savings certificates, national savings certificates, premium savings bonds, deposits with the National Savings Bank and certified contractual savings schemes providing that the person beneficially entitled to the rights is domiciled in the Channel Islands or the Isle of Man (IHTA 1984 s6(3))
- settled property which is situated outside the UK provided that the settlor was domiciled outside the UK on the date on which the settlement was made
- the emoluments paid by the government of any designated country to a member of a visiting force of that country, not being a British citizen, a British Dependent Territories citizen or a British Overseas citizen, and
- any tangible movable property the presence of which in the UK is due solely to the presence in the UK of such a person while serving as a member of the force (IHTA 1984 s155(1))
- a reversionary interest unless:
    — it has at any time been acquired, whether by the person entitled to it or by a person previously entitled to it, for a consideration in money or money's worth, or
    — it is one to which either the settlor or his spouse is or has been beneficially entitled, or
    — it is the interest expectant on the determination of a lease treated as a settlement (IHTA 1984 s48(1)).

A reversionary interest means a future interest under a settlement, whether it is vested or contingent, including an interest expectant on the termination of an interest in possession which is treated as subsisting in part of any property (IHTA 1984 s47).

Exceptions to the inheritance tax charge

There are a number of transfers which are excepted from a charge to inheritance tax.

A disposition is not a transfer of value if it is shown that it was not intended, and was not made in a transaction intended, to confer any gratuitous benefit on any person and either:

- that it was made in a transaction at arm's length between persons not connected with each other, or
- that it was such as might be expected to be made in a transaction at arm's length between persons not connected with each other (IHTA 1984 s10(1)).

A disposition made by any person is not a transfer of value if it is allowable in computing that person's profits or gains for the purposes of income tax or corporation tax or would be so allowable if those profits or gains were sufficient and fell to be so computed (IHTA 1984 s12(1)).

The waiver or repayment of remuneration is not deemed to be a transfer of value provided that, if it had not been waived, it would have been subject to income tax under Schedule E (IHTA 1984, s14).

Finally the waiver of dividends is not a chargeable transfer provided that the waiver is made within the 12 months before the date on which the right to the dividend accrues (IHTA 1984, s15).

The order in which the exemptions are applied is laid down in the legislation. First exclude those transfers which are not chargeable because they fall within small gifts, spouse, marriage, charity, political party, national purposes and out of income exemptions. Then use the annual exemptions available to reduce the remaining transfers.

Exempt transfers

The following lifetime gifts are totally exempt from tax:

- Transfers of capital for family maintenance. The transfer will be exempt if it is intended to make reasonable provision for a dependent relative (IHTA 1984, ss11, 51). This would include expenditure such as payment of school fees.
- Transfers between spouses are exempt unless the donee spouse is foreign domiciled when transfers are only exempt up to £55,000 (IHTA 1984, s18).
- The first £3,000 of gifts in the tax year are exempt. If the allowance is not used in full in a tax year it can be carried forward for one year. In that year it is deemed to be used after the limit that applies to that year has been used (IHTA 1984, s19).
- Any gifts to the same person provided that they have a total value of less than £250 in the tax year (IHTA 1984, s20).
- Any gift which is part of the donor's normal expenditure during the year. The gift or gifts must not be so large that the donor's residual income is inadequate to maintain his usual standard of living (IHTA 1984, s21).
- Gifts in consideration of marriage. Parents may make gifts of up to £5,000, grandparents gifts of up to £2,500 and other people gifts of up to £1,000. The gift must be in consideration of marriage and so if the marriage does not take place the gift must fail. The gift must be either an outright gift to the people getting married or it must be a gift into a marriage settlement which will be for the benefit of the couple, their children or their children's spouses (IHTA 1984, s22).
- Gifts to charities and transfers to charitable trusts (IHTA 1984, s23).

- Gifts to political parties with at least two members of parliament, or at least one member of parliament and at least 150,000 votes in the most recent general election (IHTA 1984, s24).
- Gifts for national purposes (IHTA 1984, s25).
- Transfers of property which is deemed to be of special interest. For instance, historical buildings are exempt provided that a number of conditions are met, for example that the public should have access. If any of the conditions cease to be met the donee will become liable to inheritance tax (IHTA 1984, s26).
- Transfers into a maintenance fund for heritage property for which a Treasury direction has been made (IHTA 1984, s27).

Chargeable persons

Only individuals and trustees of settled properties are deemed to be chargeable persons for inheritance tax purposes. Companies are not subject to inheritance tax although the participators in a close company may become liable if the company makes a transfer of value.

All transfers of value, both lifetime and on death, made by a person who is domiciled in the UK fall within the scope of inheritance tax. Individuals not domiciled in the UK are only liable for inheritance tax on transfers of UK assets.

The term domicile is defined in Chapter 4. The definition is extended for inheritance tax purposes to include individuals resident in the UK on or after 10th December 1974 and who were so resident for at least 17 of the 20 years immediately prior to the date in which the transfer was made. In addition anyone domiciled in the UK on 10th December 1974 will be deemed to continue to be domiciled for inheritance tax purposes for three years after he ceases to be domiciled for any other purpose (IHTA 1984 s267(1)).

The inheritance legislation does not contain guidance on the location of assets so the general law rules apply. These are:

- physical assets including tangible property and land and buildings, whether freehold or leasehold, are located in the country in which they are physically situated
- debts are usually located in the country of residence of the debtor
- life policies are located in the country where the proceeds from the policy are payable
- bank accounts are located in the country in which the branch where the account is kept is situated
- shares and securities are located in the country in which they are registered or normally traded
- an interest in a business, be it in a partnership or the goodwill of a business, is located where the business is resident.

If assets are held in trust the above rules apply regardless of the rules of the trust or the residency of the trustees.

Before we can consider the inheritance tax treatment of trusts you will need to know something about trusts, and in particular the different types of trust which may be created.

A trust is created when an individual, called the settlor, transfers assets to trustees who hold the assets for the benefit of one or more persons. The beneficiaries may receive income and/or capital from the trust. A trust can be created either during an individual's lifetime or under the terms of his will. Lifetime transfers into a trust are potentially exempt, apart from transfers to a discretionary trust, while in the case of transfers on death any inheritance tax due on the deceased's estate will be calculated before assets are transferred into a trust fund.

A trust may be:

- A *trust with an interest in possession*
  An individual, called the life tenant, has a right to receive the income from the trust for a period of time. The trustees are charged basic rate tax on the income from the assets in the trust. No personal allowances are available and the trustee's expenses are not tax deductible. In addition the beneficiaries are also liable to income tax on the income from the trust regardless of whether they draw it or not. However, the beneficiaries do receive a tax credit equal to the amount of tax paid by the trustees. If the beneficiaries' tax liability is lower than the tax credit the difference is reclaimable. The trustees are also liable to capital gains tax at 24% on the chargeable gains on the trust. An annual exemption of £3,250 for 1997/98 is available but must be shared between all the trusts created by the same settlor. After the life tenant's death a beneficiary becomes absolutely entitled to the trust property. Although the trustees are regarded as having disposed of the property, at its then market value, no capital gains tax liability arises, hence the gain is free of tax. If the trust terminates before the life tenant dies, for instance if a widow remarries, a capital gains tax liability may arise. A life tenant is deemed to own the underlying assets which provide their income for inheritance tax purposes. Hence when the life tenant dies the assets in the trust fund are included in their estate and the inheritance liability is calculated on the resulting value.

- A *discretionary trust*
  Nobody has an absolute right to the income from a discretionary trust. The trustees are liable to tax in the same way as for trusts with an interest in possession but the rate of tax is the basic rate of tax plus 10% (ICTA 1988 s686(1A)). However, the trustees' expenses are an allowable deduction against the additional 10% of tax only. Beneficiaries must pay tax on the income they receive. They also receive a tax credit which is equivalent to the amount of tax which the trustees have paid. Hence if a beneficiary receives £67 from the trust he or she is deemed to have received £100 (£67 × 100/67) of income together with a tax credit of £33 (£100 × 33/100). This tax credit is reclaimable. Hence there is a tax incentive for trustees to pay out all of the trust's income to beneficiaries who are basic rate taxpayers. For capital gains tax purposes the exemption limit is as for trusts with an interest in possession but tax is payable at 33% rather than 23%. Unless the trustee and beneficiary jointly elect to effectively defer the capital gains tax liability by transferring the asset at original cost, capital gains tax is payable when a beneficiary becomes absolutely entitled to trust assets. Inheritance tax is not payable on the trust funds. However, there is a charge of 15% of the inheritance scale rate on the value of the trust every ten years. The same percentage is also charged when funds leave the trust. Fifteen percent of the inheritance scale rate gives a maximum rate of 6% on the current scale.

- *An accumulation and maintenance trust*
  Income is accumulated for minor children until they reach a specified age. Income which arose from capital provided by parents and used for the education or maintenance of unmarried children under 18 years old is treated as the income of the parents. Other income arising in the trust is taxed at 33% because the trust is discretionary. Once again the 33% can be used as a tax credit by the beneficiaries. When the beneficiaries reach the specified age the trust funds are transferred without any further income tax liability arising. However, capital gains tax is payable when a beneficiary becomes absolutely entitled to the trust's assets because the trust is a discretionary trust. Provided that the trust satisfies certain conditions no inheritance tax liability will arise either ten yearly or when the assets are transferred to the beneficiaries. To qualify for this preferential treatment the trust must terminate before the earlier of 25 years after its creation and 25 years from 15th April 1976. In addition at least one of the beneficiaries must be 25 years old or younger when becoming either absolutely entitled to the property or gaining an interest in possession.

Potentially exempt transfers

Remember that most lifetime transfers are potentially exempt transfers (PET) and provided that the donor survives for seven years following the date of the transfer no inheritance tax liability will arise. However, if the donor dies within seven years of making a potentially exempt transfer it becomes a chargeable transfer.

Gifts to an individual or to an accumulation and maintenance trust or to a trust for disabled persons made on or after 18th March 1986 are potentially exempt transfers.

Transfers on or after 17th March 1987 are potentially exempt if they create or supplement a trust fund in which someone has an interest in possession. An interest in possession entitles an individual to the income from the trust for life. In addition when the interest in possession is terminated during the lifetime of the person who has the interest, perhaps on the remarriage of a widow, and is followed either by another life interest or by someone becoming absolutely entitled to the trust property, the transfer is treated as being potentially exempt. They are included in the donor's inheritance computation at their value at the time of the transfer rather than their value at the date of death.

If potentially exempt transfers are made which later become chargeable the amount of tax due may be much less than if the assets had been transferred on death if the assets have increased in value since the transfer. However, if the donor continues to enjoy any sort of benefit from the assets transferred at the time of his death the assets are treated as having belonged to him on the date of death.

If potentially exempt transfers become chargeable they are reduced by any annual exemptions which may be available. You will find a list of annual exemptions later in the chapter. If two or more potentially exempt transfers become chargeable within a year they will be deemed to be made in the same order as that in which they were made.

Husbands and wives

Husbands and wives enjoy much the same treatment under the legislation for inheritance tax as they do under the legislation for capital gains tax.

Each spouse is taxed separately and generally transfers between spouses are exempt (IHTA 1984 s18(1)). Each spouse has the nil rate band, exemptions and reliefs which are available to a single person. However, if immediately before the transfer, the transferrer, but not the transferrer's spouse, is domiciled in the UK the value in respect of which the transfer is exempt shall not exceed £55,000 less any amount previously taken into account for the purposes of this exemption (IHTA 1984 s18(3)). This includes the occasion when an interest in possession comes to an end and the settlor's spouse or the settlor's widow or widower, if the settlor had died less than two years earlier, becomes beneficially entitled to the settled property and is domiciled in the UK (IHTA 1984 s53(4)).

Where on the death of a person entitled to an interest in possession in settled property the settlor's spouse, or if the settlor has died less than two years earlier, the settlor's widow or widower, becomes beneficially entitled to the settled property and is domiciled in the UK, the value of the settled property shall be left out of account in determining for the purposes of inheritance tax the value of the deceased's estate immediately before his death (IHTA 1984 s54(2)).

The basic inheritance tax computation

A record is kept of chargeable transfers made and the amount of tax due is calculated with respect to the aggregate value of the transfers made in the previous seven years (IHTA 1984 s7(1)). Hence, once seven years have passed, a transfer ceases to be included in any inheritance tax computation.

For the purposes of determining the rate at which the tax should be charged potentially exempt transfers will be ignored for lifetime transfers but included when determining the rate which should apply to an estate on the death of the individual.

A liability to inheritance tax can arise during the lifetime of the donor if the total value of the chargeable transfers within seven years exceeds the 'nil rate' threshold which is £215,000 in 1997/98 (£200,000 in 1996/97). Tax is charged at a flat rate of 40% but lifetime transfers are charged at half the full rate, that is 20%.

As you have seen the value transferred is measured by reference to the donor's estate rather than the donee's. That is the value transferred is equal to the diminution in the value of the donor's estate rather than the increase in the value of the donee's estate. Of course in most cases these two measures will be the same. However, there are some circumstances when they may be different. This may happen when shares in family companies are transferred from one generation to the next over a number of years. This will usually take the form of majority shareholders transferring shares to minority shareholders. Shares are worth more if they are part of a majority shareholding because of the voting rights they confer. A majority shareholder who transfers shares may reduce his or her estate not only by the value of the shares transferred but also by the loss of value of the remaining shares.

Roland owns 11,000 shares in his family company which has an issued share capital of 20,000 shares. His daughter, Gail, has worked for the company for a number of years and already owns 1,000 shares. Roland intends to transfer 2,000 of his shares to Gail.

Currently Roland's shares are worth £50 each but Gail's are worth only £10 each. After the transfer Roland's shares will fall to a value of £35 each and Gail's will be worth £15 each. The large fall in the value of Roland's shares is caused by his loss of control of the company.

Calculate the value transferred.

Feedback

To calculate the value transferred:

	£
Before the transfer 11,000 × £50	550,000
After the transfer 9,000 × £35	315,000
Reduction in value	135,000

The value transferred is £135,000.

In order to calculate the tax which is due to be paid on a chargeable transfer it is necessary to refer to all the chargeable transfers made within the seven years prior to it. It is also important to establish whether the transferrer or the transferee will pay any inheritance tax liability which may arise on the transfer of value. If no explicit arrangements for paying the tax have been made it is the transferrer who is deemed to be liable.

The amount of tax which is payable will vary according to who is liable for the tax. Remember that the amount of tax payable is dependent on the loss in value in the transferrer's estate. Hence if the transferrer pays the tax the loss in value of his estate is equal to the aggregate of the gift and the related tax payment. However, if the recipient of the gift agrees to pay the tax the tax is calculated on the loss of value due to the transfer only.

Activity

Within the last seven years Joe has had a balance on his inheritance computation account of £300,000. Joe is making a transfer of value of £100,000.

Calculate the value transferred if:
(a) the transferee agrees to pay the tax
(b) Joe agrees to pay the tax.

Feedback

The balance on Joe's inheritance computation account exceeds £200,000. So long as this is the case any further lifetime chargeable transfers are assessable to tax at the lifetime rate of 20%.

(a) If the transferee agrees to pay the tax the tax due is £100,000 × 20% = £20,000.

(b) If the transferrer agrees to pay the tax the tax due is £100,000 × 20/80 = £25,000.

The inheritance computation on death

On the death of an individual an inheritance tax liability may arise in respect of the following:

- the estate of the deceased person
- chargeable transfers made within the seven years preceding the death of the transferrer
- potentially exempt transfers made within the seven years preceding the death of the transferrer.

In order to calculate the inheritance tax on death you will first need to determine the value of the deceased estate and any transfers made within seven years of his death. You will then need to deduct any reliefs which are available. Finally you will need to determine the rate of tax which is applicable to each transfer in order to calculate the inheritance tax liability. It will be simpler to start by considering the rates of inheritance tax before determining the value of the estate and the value of any chargeable lifetime transfers made within seven years of the death of the transferrer. Finally we will consider the reliefs which may be available on the death of a taxpayer.

The rates of inheritance tax

The rate of inheritance tax charged on transfers on death is:

Value of transfer	Rate
£1–£215,000	0%
over £215,000	40%

The inheritance tax threshold was £154,000 before 5th April 1996 and £200,000 for 1996/97.

Lifetime transfers are charged at a rate which is half the death rate (IHTA 1984 s7(2)). Hence for 1997/98 the lifetime rate is nil for the first £215,000 and 20% for transfers in excess of this. Chargeable lifetime transfers made between three and seven years before death are charged at the following percentage of the rate charged on transfers on death:

Years between gift and death	Percentage of rate charged on transfers on death
Before death but not more than 3	100
More than 3 but not more than 4	80
More than 4 but not more than 5	60
More than 5 but not more than 6	40
More than 6 but not more than 7	20 (IHTA 1984 s7(4))

Remember that the tax due is calculated with respect to the aggregate value of the transfers made in the previous seven years.

The rate of inheritance tax is likely to change over time. The rate used when the taxpayer has died is always the rate prevailing at the date of death, even on lifetime transfers which took place in the seven years before death. However, the gross values of chargeable lifetime transfers are not recalculated using the rates in force on the date of death.

If the rate of inheritance tax changes and an individual's chargeable transfers during a seven-year period straddle the change the following steps must be carried out to calculate the inheritance liability:

Step 1

Determine the individual's gross cumulative total of transfers, within the previous seven years, at the date of the change of the rates.

Step 2

Calculate the inheritance tax attributable to the cumulative total using the new rates.

Step 3

Deduct the inheritance tax calculated in Step 2 from the cumulative total to find the net total.

These restated totals of inheritance tax and the net total are used when dealing with future transfers.

Activity

Bob gives £300,000 to a discretionary trust on 1st June 1995 and a further £300,000 on 1st June 1997. The nil rate band was £154,000 at the time of the first transfer on which the trustees agreed to pay the tax. Bob has agreed to pay the tax on the second transfer. Calculate the inheritance tax liabilities on each of the transfers. You may ignore the annual exemption.

Feedback

	Gross £	Inheritance tax £	Net £
1.6.95			
Transfer	300,000	29,200 (1)	270,800
5.4.97 Restate	300,000	17,000 (2)	283,000
1.6.97			
Transfer	375,000 (6)	75,000 (5)	300,000
	675,000 (3)	92,000 (4)	583,000

Notes

(1) The inheritance tax on the transfer of £300,000 is £29,200 ((£300,000 − £154,000) × 20%).

(2) The restated inheritance tax on the transfer of £300,000 is £17,000 ((£300,000 − £215,000) × 20%).

(3) The cumulative net transfer of £583,000 is the equivalent of a gross transfer of £675,000 ((£583,000 − £215,000) × 100/80 + £215,000).

(4) The inheritance tax is the difference between the net transfer and the gross transfer which is £92,000 (£675,000 − £583,000).

(5) The inheritance tax payable is equal to the difference between the inheritance tax on the new cumulative total and the restated inheritance tax brought forward. That is the inheritance tax payable is £75,000 (£92,000 − £17,000).

(6) The gross transfer is equal to the actual transfer made and the inheritance tax payable and is £375,000 (£300,000 + £75,000).

Calculation of the inheritance tax payable on lifetime transfers within seven years of the death of the donor

Now that you can determine the value that is transferred and the rate at which tax is levied you need to know how to maintain the cumulative total and calculate the tax payable on death if the individual made lifetime transfers within seven years of his death.

The inheritance tax liability on death can be calculated by undertaking the following steps:

Step 1

Calculate the cumulative total of transfers, including potentially exempt transfers, made in the last seven years of the deceased's life.

Step 2

Calculate the inheritance tax on each lifetime transfer which falls in the seven year period, including potentially exempt transfers, using the full rate in force at the time of death.

Step 3

Reduce the tax calculated in Step 2 according to the time between the date of the gift and the date of death by using the table on p. 307. Note that a transfer exactly seven years before the transferrer's death is excluded from the calculation (IHTA 1984 s7(5)).

Step 4

Deduct any inheritance tax which has already been paid on the transfers. If the result of Step 3 is less than the result of Step 4 no tax is repaid by the Inland Revenue. However, if the result of Step 3 is greater than the result of Step 4 the difference is the inheritance tax liability that arose on death.

Activity

Nesta made the following transfers.

31st July 1997   Cash of £300,000 to her daughter.

31st July 2001   Cash of £300,000 to a discretionary trust with the trust
                  paying any tax due.

8th July 2003   On death she left her estate of £400,000 to her daughter.

Determine the inheritance tax arising on each of these disposals. Note that the gift to her daughter is a potentially exempt transfer (PET). Remember that no inheritance tax liability arises on a potentially exempt transfer unless the transferrer dies within seven years of the gift. We will deal with the taxation of potentially exempt transfers made within seven years of death later in this chapter.

Feedback

31st July 1997
The cash paid to her daughter is a potentially exempt transfer and so no inheritance liability arises in 1997/98.

31st July 2001
The transfer of cash to a discretionary trust is a chargeable lifetime transfer and hence tax is levied at half the death rate. The inheritance tax payable is £17,000 (£(300,000 − 215,000) × 20%).

8th July 2003
Nesta died within seven years of making a potentially exempt transfer which consequently becomes chargeable.

Following the steps described above:

Value of gift £	Cumulative total £	Rate of tax %	Inheritance tax at full rate £
300,000	85,000	40	34,000
300,000	385,000	40	154,000
400,000	785,000	40	314,000

The full rate of tax due on the first transfer is £34,000. The full rate of tax due on the second transfer is £120,000 (£154,000 – £34,000). The full rate of tax due on the third transfer is £160,000 (£314,000 – £154,000).

Use the tapering relief to calculate the inheritance tax payable on each transaction.

31st July 1997
The tax due at the full rate is £34,000. The gift was made more than five years but less than six years before the death and so only 40% of the tax at the full rate is payable. Hence inheritance tax payable is £13,600 (£34,000 × 40%).

31st July 2001
The tax due at the full rate is £120,000. The transfer was made less than three years before the date of death and so no tapering relief is available. The inheritance tax payable is £106,400 which is equal to the tax due at the full rate less the tax already paid.

8th July 2003
The tax due is £160,000.

Now that you can calculate the inheritance tax which is payable on a chargeable lifetime transfer, maintain the cumulative totals of chargeable transfers and tax due and calculate the inheritance tax liability on death, we can consider what happens when a chargeable transfer drops out of an inheritance computation because it was made more than seven years before the latest chargeable transfer.

When a transfer was made more than seven years ago the gross value of the transfer is deducted from the cumulative total but no adjustment is made to the tax payable.

Activity

George died on 30th December 1997. His chargeable estate was valued at £400,000. George made a chargeable lifetime transfer of £300,000 on 30th September 1988 and a potentially exempt transfer of £100,000 on 31st August 1993.

Compute the inheritance tax liabilities which arise on George's death. Assume that the rates and allowances for all years are the same as for 1997/98. You may ignore the annual exemption.

Feedback

Inheritance tax computation on death	Gross value of transfer tax £	Inheritance payable £
30.9.88		
Transfer	300,000	17,000 (1)
31.8.93		
Transfer	100,000	40,000 (3)
	400,000	57,000 (2)
30.9.95		
Transfer on 30.9.88 drops out as seven years have elapsed	(300,000)	
30.12.97		
Estate at death	400,000	114,000
	500,000	114,000 (4)

The tax liabilities arising on George's death are:

	£
30.9.88 transfer over seven years before death	nil
31.8.93 tax at full rate £40,000 × 60% (tapering relief)	24,000
30.12.97 estate at death	114,000

Notes

(1) Tax payable equals £17,000 ((£300,000 − 215,000) × 20%).
(2) Tax payable equals £57,000 (£40,000 + 17,000).
(3) Tax due on the PET at the full rate of 40% is £40,000 (£100,000 × 40%).
(4) Tax due on the estate at death is £114,000 ((£500,000 − 215,000) × 40%).

Gifts with reservation

If an individual disposes of any property by way of gift and either:

- possession and enjoyment of the property is not *bona fide* assumed by the donee at or before the beginning of the relevant period, or
- at any time in the relevant period the property is not enjoyed to the entire exclusion, or virtually to the entire exclusion, of the donor and of any benefit to him by contract or otherwise

then the property is referred to as property subject to a reservation (FA 1986 s102(2)). The relevant period means a period ending on the date of the donor's death and beginning seven years before that date, or, if it is later, on the date of the gift (FA 1986 s102(1)).

If, immediately before the death of the donor, there is any property which, in relation to him, is property subject to a reservation then the property shall be treated, for the purposes of inheritance tax, as property to which he was beneficially entitled immediately before his death (FA 1986 s102(4)).

In determining whether any property which is disposed of by way of gift is enjoyed to the entire exclusion, or virtually to the entire exclusion, of the donor and of any benefit to him by contract or otherwise:

- in the case of property which is an interest in land or a chattel, retention or assumption by the donor of actual occupation of the land or actual enjoyment of an incorporeal right over the land, or actual possession of the chattel shall be disregarded if it is for full consideration in money or money's worth
- in the case of property which is an interest in land, any occupation by the donor of the whole or any part of the land shall be disregarded if:
  - it results from a change in the circumstances of the donor since the time of the gift, being a change which was unforeseen at that time and was not brought about by a donor to receive the benefit of this provision, and
  - it occurs at a time when the donor has become unable to maintain himself through old age, infirmity or otherwise, and
  - it represents a reasonable provision by the donee for the care and maintenance of the donor, and
  - the donee is a relative of the donor or his spouse (FA 1986 Sch 20 s6(1)).

Associated operations

Two or more operations are associated operations if:

- they are operations which affect the same property, or one of which affects some property and the other or others of which affect property which represents, whether directly or indirectly, that property, or income arising from that property, or any property representing accumulations of any such income
- one operation is effected with reference to the other, or with a view to enabling the other to be effected or facilitating its being effected, and any further operation having a like relation to any of those two, and so on,

whether those operations are effected by the same person or different persons, and whether or not they are simultaneous. The term operation includes an omission (IHTA 1984 s268(1)).

Where a transfer of value is made by associated operations carried out at different times it shall be treated as made at the time of the last of them.

Special rules apply when any one or more of the earlier operations is a transfer of value made by the same transferrer as the present operation. The value transferred by the earlier operations is deemed to reduce the value transferred by all of the operations taken together. This rule is not applied to the extent that the transfer constituted by the earlier operations, but not that made by all the operations taken together, is exempt under the rules for transfers between spouses (IHTA 1984 s268(3)).

Inheritance tax on death

On death an individual is deemed to make a final transfer of the whole of his estate. Any transfers made to an individual's spouse are exempt and so are excluded from the estate.

Remember that there are three ways in which a liability to inheritance tax can arise on the death of an individual:

- the value of the estate may give rise to an inheritance tax liability
- potentially exempt transfers made within seven years of death become chargeable transfers and may give rise to an inheritance tax liability
- chargeable lifetime transfers made within seven years of death may also give rise to a further inheritance tax liability.

We will consider each of these in turn.

The estate at death

The value of an individual's estate is calculated by valuing all the assets owned together with any interest he or she has as a joint tenant and any capital held by a trust fund in which he or she has an interest in possession.

When a joint tenant dies the property automatically transfers to the other joint tenants. This is not the case for tenants in common where each tenant can dispose of their share as they choose in their will.

The tax on assets which were owned outright by the deceased immediately before death is payable by the executors or personal representatives.

If the estate includes an interest in possession the trustees are responsible for paying the inheritance tax due but the capital is included in the deceased estate for the purposes of determining how much tax is due.

The tax due on any property which is subject to a reservation which is included in the estate is payable by the person who is in possession of the property.

Some property is excluded from an inheritance tax computation.

Liabilities which have been incurred for money, or money's worth, or have been imposed by law such as tax liabilities, are allowable deductions from the estate of the deceased before the inheritance tax liability is calculated. Similarly reasonable funeral expenses, including the cost of a tombstone, may be deducted from the value of the deceased estate before the inheritance tax liability is calculated.

There are also reliefs available if assets are disposed of within a given period after death for less than their value at the date of death.

If quoted securities are disposed of within one year of the date of death and the value of the securities is less when they are disposed of than it was immediately before the death the value of the investments shall be treated as reduced by an amount equal to the loss on sale (IHTA 1984 s179). If this happens it will be necessary to recalculate the inheritance tax liability on the entire estate.

Similarly if land is sold within three years of the date of death and the value of the land on the date of disposal is less than its value immediately before the death the value at the date of disposal shall be substituted for the value at the date of death in the inheritance tax computation (IHTA 1984 s191).

Potentially exempt transfers

If the transferrer dies within seven years of making a potentially exempt transfer it will become chargeable to inheritance tax. The rate of tax which is used is the one in force on the date of the transferrer's death. However, potentially exempt transfers which are made more than three years before the death of the transferrer are not taxed at the full rate. Go back and re-read the section on rates of inheritance tax to find out how much tapering relief is available.

Chargeable lifetime transfers

Remember that chargeable lifetime transfers are subject to inheritance tax at half of the death rates. However, if the transferrer dies within seven years of the transfer being made a further liability to tax may arise. Like potentially exempt transfers some relief is available if the transfer was made more than three years before the death of the transferrer. Once again the section on the rates of inheritance tax contains the detail of the relief available.

Principles of valuation

Remember that the general rule concerning valuations is that it is the loss to the donor's estate which is used to calculate the tax rather than the gain to the recipient. This may not be the same as using an open market price to value the transfer. However, there is some guidance which can be used to value a transfer.

Quoted securities

The valuation for inheritance tax purposes is the same as for capital gains tax purposes. That is the value transferred will be the lower of:

- one quarter up from the lower of the two prices quoted in the stock exchange daily official list
- the midpoint of the recorded bargains.

The date for which the prices are taken is either the date of the transfer for a lifetime transfer or the date of death. If there are no quotes for the relevant day whichever of the previous or the next day gives the lower value will be used instead.

If the subject of the transfer is unit trusts then the lower of the two published prices will be used.

Unquoted securities

The open market value should still be used although the difficulty lies in calculating the open market value of the holdings, a problem which is beyond the scope of this book.

Joint tenancy

If property is held by joint tenants a proportion of the open market value assuming vacant possession reduced by 15% is used to value the joint tenant's share of the property. The proportion applied to the open market value is equal to the share of the house which the joint tenant was entitled to.

Related property

Property which is held in the estates of spouses is related property. In addition property held at any time within the last five years by a charity, political party or national body which was transferred by one of the spouses by way of an exempt transfer is also deemed to be related property. Property held by children is not taken to be related property. This provision might have the effect of significantly increasing the value of property. For example, in the case of unquoted shares an individual might hold only 30% of the shares of a company giving a relatively low value for any shares transferred. However, if his wife also holds 30% of the shares the related property provision requires that the shares transferred are treated as being transferred from a majority holding of 60% (30% + 30%). Formally the transferrer's related property before the transfer is valued by reference to the value of all of the related property apportioned on the basis of the respective values. Then the transferrer's value retained is calculated on the same basis in order to calculate the value lost.

Activity

John held 300 of the 1,000 issued share capital of Craft Ltd, a non-quoted company. His wife Janice held 600 of the remaining shares. Their daughter Julie held the final 100 shares of Craft Ltd. John transfers 100 of his shares to Julie. One share in a holding of 85% or more of the share capital is valued at £10. One share in a holding of 80% to 85% or more of the share capital is valued at £9. Any share in a minority holding is valued at £2. Calculate the value transferred by John.

Feedback

Prior to the transfer, John's holding of 300 shares together with the 600 held by his wife gives a related holding of 90% of the shares with a value per share of £10. Hence John's holding was worth £10 × 300 = £3,000.

After the transfer John's holding of 200 shares is part of a related holding of 800 shares, or 80% of the share capital with a value per share of £9. Hence John's holding is worth £9 × 200 = £1,800.

The value transferred was £3,000 − £1,800 = £1,200.

The administration of inheritance tax

Excepted estates

An estate is an excepted estate if immediately before the person's death:

- the value of the estate is attributable wholly to property passing under that person's will or intestacy or under a nomination of an asset taking effect on death or by survivorship in beneficial joint tenancy
- the total gross value of that property did not exceed £125,000, and
- of that property not more than £15,000 represented value attributable to property then situated outside the UK, and
- that person was domiciled in the UK and had not made any chargeable transfers during his lifetime (Capital Transfer Tax (Delivery of Accounts) Regulations 1981 s3).

No person shall be required to deliver to the Board an account of the property comprised in an excepted estate (CTT (Delivery of Accounts) Regulations 1981 s4). If any person who has not delivered an account in reliance on Regulation 4 discovers at any time that the estate is not an excepted estate, the delivery to the Board within six months of that time of an account of the property comprised in that estate shall satisfy any requirement to deliver an account imposed on that person (CTT (Delivery of Accounts) Regulations 1981 s5).

Payment of inheritance tax

Unless specifically stated otherwise the tax on the value transferred by a chargeable transfer shall be due six months after the end of the month in which the chargeable transfer is made or, in the case of a transfer made after 5th April and before 1st October in any year otherwise than on death, at the end of April in the next year (IHTA 1984 s226(1)).

Personal representatives shall, on delivery of their account, pay all the tax for which they are liable and may, on delivery of that account, also pay any part of the tax chargeable on the death for which they are not liable, if the persons liable for it request them to make the payment (IHTA 1984 s226(2)).

So much of the tax chargeable on the value transferred by a chargeable transfer made within seven years of the death of the transferrer as exceeds what it would have been had the transferrer died more than seven years after the transfer shall be due six months after the end of the month in which the death occurs (IHTA 1984 s226(3)).

The tax chargeable on the value transferred by a potentially exempt transfer which proves to be a chargeable transfer shall be due six months after the end of the month in which the transferrer's death occurs (IHTA 1984 s226(3A)).

Where any of the tax payable on the value transferred by a chargeable transfer is attributable to the value of qualifying property and:

- the transfer is made on death, or
- the tax so attributable is borne by the person benefiting from the transfer, or

- the transfer is settled property and the property concerned continues to be comprised in the settlement

the tax so attributable may, if the person paying it by notice in writing to the Board so elects, be paid by ten equal yearly instalments (IHTA 1984 s227(1)).

Reliefs for inheritance tax purposes

There are three main reliefs for inheritance tax purposes: business property relief, agricultural property relief and quick succession relief. These reliefs are intended to reduce the risk that a business would have to be sold in order to satisfy an inheritance tax liability. We will look at each of the reliefs in turn.

Business property relief

Business property relief is available, on both lifetime transfers and transfers on death, of relevant business property at two rates, 100% and 50%, provided that certain conditions are met (IHTA 1984 s104). Relief is available at 100% on the following transfers of property:

- property consisting of a business or interest in a business. This will include both sole traders and partners regardless of the size of any partner's holding
- shares or securities, in an unquoted company, which gave the transferrer control of the company immediately before the transfer takes place. The transferrer is deemed to have control if he has a majority of votes on all questions affecting the company as a whole. It is not necessary for control to be transferred in order to obtain the relief. When determining the size of the holding it is the related property which is considered rather than the size of the transferrer's holding.
- shares in an unquoted company which gave the transferrer at least 25% of the votes capable of being cast on all questions affecting the company as a whole provided that the transferrer has maintained at least a 25% holding throughout the two years immediately preceding the transfer. Once again it is the related property which is used to determine the size of the transferrer's holding (IHTA 1984 s105).

Relief is available at 100% on the transfer of shares in an unquoted company. Relief is available at 50% on the following transfers of property:

- shares in or securities of a quoted company which gave the transferrer control of the company immediately before the transfer took place. A company is quoted if it is listed on a recognised stock exchange or dealt in on the Unlisted Securities Market (IHTA 1984 s272)
- any land or buildings, plant and machinery which, immediately before the transfer, was used wholly or mainly for the purposes of a business carried on by a company of which the transferrer had control or by a partnership of which he was then a partner. The relief is also available if the assets used by the business were settled property in which the transferrer was beneficially entitled to an interest in possession immediately prior to the transfer. There is a difference here then between the treatment of assets owned by the transferrer and those used by a company or an unincorporated

business. If they are used by a company the transferrer must own a majority shareholding in order to claim the relief but a mere share in a partnership is enough to enable the relief to be claimed if the asset is used by an unincorporated business (IHTA 1984 s105(1)).

Holdings in businesses which consist wholly or mainly of dealing in stocks and shares and securities or land and buildings or making or holding of investments, other than as a holding company, are not eligible for business property relief (IHTA 1984 s105(3)).

Property is not relevant business property if a binding contract for its sale has been entered into at the time of the transfer unless:

- the property is a business or interest in a business and the sale is to a company which is to carry on the business and is made in consideration wholly or mainly of shares or securities of that company, or
- the property is shares in or securities of a company and the sale is made for the purpose of reconstruction or amalgamation (IHTA 1984 s113).

In order to obtain business property relief the relevant business property must:

- have been owned by the transferrer for at least two years immediately preceding the transfer (IHTA 1984 s106) or
- have replaced other property, which was owned by the transferrer for periods which together comprised at least two years falling within the five years immediately preceding the transfer of value and had the transfer of value been made immediately before it was replaced, it would, apart from section 106, have been relevant business property (IHTA 1984 s107).

If the first condition is not satisfied the relief will still be available if when the transferrer acquired the property it was eligible for business property relief and either the previous or the current transfer was made on death (IHTA 1984 s109).

If either a potentially exempt transfer becomes chargeable or a chargeable lifetime transfer attracts an additional inheritance tax liability on the death of the transferrer within seven years of the transfer of value then in order to claim business property relief:

- the property must be owned by the transferee from the date of the transfer of value to the date of the transferrer's death and
- the property must comprise relevant business property, disregarding the two-year rule, at the date of the transferrer's death, unless the asset transferred consists of quoted shares or securities, or all or part of a controlling holding of unquoted shares or securities which were unquoted throughout the period of ownership by the transferee (IHTA 1984 s113A(3)).

Business property relief is applied before all other reliefs are claimed.

Julian is a partner in the firm of Smith and Jones. He owns the offices from which the partnership operates. He settles the following property on his son Jason for life:

- his interest in the partnership, currently valued at £600,000
- the offices currently valued at £200,000.

Calculate the value of transfers after accounting for business property relief.

Feedback

Business property relief is available on the transfer of Julian's interest in the partnership at the rate of 100%. Relief is available on the offices at a rate of 50%.

Hence the value transferred after the business property relief is 50% of £200,000 which is £100,000.

Agricultural property relief

Agricultural property relief is available on the agricultural value of agricultural property in the UK, the Channel Islands or the Isle of Man. Like the business property relief agricultural property relief is given by way of a deduction from the value transferred. Provided the transferrer had the right to vacant possession, or the right to obtain it within 12 months, a deduction of 100% is available. In all other cases a deduction of 50% is available (IHTA 1984 s116).

Agricultural property is defined as agricultural land or pasture including woodland and any building used in connection with the intensive rearing of livestock or fish provided the woodland or building is occupied with agricultural land or pasture and the occupation is ancillary to that of the agricultural land or pasture. It also includes such cottages, farm buildings and farmhouses, together with the land occupied with them, as are of a character appropriate to the property (IHTA 1984 s115(2)).

The agricultural value of any agricultural property is the value which would be the value of the property if it were subject to a perpetual covenant prohibiting its use otherwise than as agricultural property (IHTA 1984 s115(3)).

In order to claim the relief a number of conditions must be satisfied:

- the property must have been occupied by the transferrer for the purposes of agriculture throughout the period of two years ending with the date of the transfer, or
- it must have been owned by him throughout the period of seven years ending with the date of transfer and was throughout that period occupied, by him or another, for the purpose of agriculture (IHTA 1984 s117).

Even if the agricultural property occupied by the transferrer on the date of the transfer replaced other agricultural property the conditions stated in s117 will be deemed to be satisfied if:

- the transferrer has occupied the other property for at least two years out of the five years ending with the date of transfer (IHTA 1984 s118(1)) or

- the transferrer has owned agricultural property which was occupied, by the transferrer, for the purposes of agriculture for at least seven years out of the ten years ending with the date of transfer (IHTA 1984 s118(2)).

For the purposes of ss117 and 118 occupation by a company which is controlled by the transferrer shall be treated as occupation by the transferrer (IHTA 1984 s119).

If the transferrer acquired the property on the death of another person he or she shall be deemed to have owned and (provided that he subsequently occupied it) occupied it from the date of the death unless the other person is his or her spouse, in which case he or she will also be deemed to have owned it for any period for which his or her spouse owned and occupied it for the purposes of agriculture (IHTA 1984 s120(1)).

Quick succession relief

Where the value of a person's estate was increased by a chargeable transfer made not more than five years before:

- the person's death, or
- a chargeable transfer which is made by the person otherwise than on death and as to which the conditions specified below are satisfied

the tax chargeable on the value transferred by the transfer made on death or, as the case may be, referred to above shall be reduced by an amount calculated in accordance with the rules specified below (IHTA 1984 s141(1)).

The conditions which must be satisfied are:

- the value transferred by the later transfer falls to be determined by reference to the value of settled property in which there subsists an interest in possession to which the transferrer is entitled, and
- the value transferred by the first transfer also fell to be determined by reference to the value of that property, and
- the first transfer either was or included the making of the settlement or was made after the making of the settlement (IHTA 1984 s141(2)).

The amount by which the value transferred is reduced is a percentage of the tax charged on so much of the value transferred by the first transfer as is attributable to the increase. The percentage is:

Time between two transfers	Percentage
Not more than one year	100
Over one and up to two years	80
Over two and up to three years	60
Over three years and up to four years	40
Over four years	20 (IHTA 1984 s141(3)).

Where, in relation to the first transfer, there is more than one later transfer, the quick succession relief shall only be available for the first of them unless the reduction represents less than the whole of the tax charged under sub-section 3 and in that case a reduction may be made in respect of subsequent transfers, in chronological order, until reductions representing the whole of that tax have been made (IHTA 1984 s141(4)).

A reduction is equal to the amount by which the tax liability is reduced under sub-section 3 above (IHTA 1984 s141(5)).

Activity

Ernie died on 14th January 1995. His estate, valued at £300,000 gross, was left to his son Maurice who died on 20th January 1998 leaving an estate of £500,000. Inheritance tax of £58,400 had been paid on the death of Ernie.

Calculate the inheritance tax liability which arises on Maurice's death assuming that Maurice had made no lifetime transfers.

Feedback

	£
Inheritance tax on £500,000	114,000
Less QSR 40% × (£58,400 × $\dfrac{300,000 - 58,400}{300,000}$	18,813
Inheritance tax due on Maurice's estate	95,187

Summary

An inheritance tax liability may arise when there is a chargeable transfer of value, that is there is a transfer of value of chargeable property by a chargeable person. However, some property is excluded from the charge and some transfers are exempt. Most lifetime transfers are either exempt or potentially exempt. A potentially exempt transfer becomes chargeable if the transferrer dies within seven years of the date of the transfer. Tax on lifetime transfers over £215,000 in a seven-year period is levied at a rate of 20% while the inheritance tax is levied at a rate of 40% on the value of the transferrer's estate at death.

A cumulative total of transfers made in the previous seven years is maintained. The tax due on a chargeable transfer depends on the cumulative total and the loss in value of the transferrer's estate due to the transfer as well as any exemptions and reliefs which may be available.

On the death of an individual inheritance tax may be levied on the estate at death. In addition a liability to inheritance tax may arise due to lifetime transfers, including potentially exempt transfers, made during the seven years before death.

The exemptions and reliefs available can be used to minimise a liability to inheritance tax. Inheritance tax is often avoidable if good use is made of lifetime transfers. However, the planning process may need to span decades. Life assurance policies offer scope for tax planning. If an individual takes out a policy and pays premiums then on death the maturity value will be included in the deceased person's estate. However, if the policy is transferred to the beneficiary during the policyholder's lifetime the transfer of value is the greater of the surrender value and the premiums paid. If the policy is transferred then future premiums paid will be transfers of value. However, they are likely to be exempt as a gift out of income.

Computational questions

In order to answer the first question you will need to have read this chapter. However, the second question requires a knowledge of both income tax and capital gains tax and before you attempt it you may want to go back and re-read Chapters 4 and 7.

Question 1 (based on ACCA December 1990).

You have been asked to provide tax advice at today's date (which you should assume to be 1st February 1998) to the personal representative of Richard. Richard was aged 65 and died on 2nd November 1997, leaving the following assets.

	Probate value £	Current value £
1,000 shares in Bluechip plc (a quoted company with a share capital of 2 million shares)	22,000	17,000
2,500 shares in Giltedge plc (a quoted company with a share capital of 3 million shares)	15,000	20,000
6,000 shares in Nobody Ltd (a private investment company with a share capital of 100,000 shares)	39,000	30,000
Private residence	190,000	230,000
Holiday home	55,000	40,000
	321,000	337,000

Potential selling costs are estimated at 2% of sale price in respect of each asset.

Richard had made the following transfers prior to his death.

(a) Annual gifts of £3,000 made out of capital to his nephew Oscar on 6th April of each year.

(b) A gift of £110,000 cash to a discretionary trust on 3rd September 1989. All taxes on the gift were borne by the trustees.

(c) A gift of £80,000 cash to his son Boris on his marriage on 1st September 1994.

(d) A gift of ten acres of farmland to his son Christian on 1st July 1995. The land was valued at £200,000 and was subject to a mortgage of £30,000. Richard had occupied the land and farmed it since January 1987. Christian sold the land to an unconnected third party on 11th October 1997 for £180,000. He used the proceeds to pay off the mortgage and also to buy himself a yacht.

In his will Richard left all his assets to his sons Boris and Christian. He appointed his brother Nigel as his executor. He was confident that his sons would look after his widow Maria, who is aged 73 and owns no assets in her own right. Maria is in very poor health and is not expected to live much longer.

Required

(a) Calculate the inheritance tax arising as a result of Richard's death.

(b) Explain whether the inheritance tax arising could be reduced by disposing of all or any of Richard's assets before winding up his estate. Indicate any possible disadvantage of such a course of action.

(c) Explain whether it would be advisable from an inheritance tax view-point to alter the terms of Richard's will. Outline the conditions which must be satisfied for such an alteration to be valid for inheritance tax purposes.

(d) Describe briefly Nigel's responsibilities as executor for making returns in respect of inheritance tax on his brother's estate. State when any inheritance tax due should be paid in order to avoid interest charges, bearing in mind the availability of instalment relief. Explain who becomes liable if Nigel fails to account for the inheritance tax due to the Inland Revenue.

Question 2 (based on ACCA June 1991).

Mr Gog, who was born in Ruritania in 1937 came to live and work in Scotland in May 1983. Mr Gog, whose wife has died, hopes to return to Ruritania when he is 70. Mr Gog is in good health.

Details of Mr Gog's assets and liabilities at today's date (which you should assume is 5th April 1998), together with their current market values, are as follows:

	£
Deposit account with National Bank of Ruritania (held with branch in Glob, the capital of Ruritania)	60,000
Current account with UK bank held in Glasgow	23,000
Private residence (located in Scotland)	127,000
10,000 shares in Bah plc, an investment company quoted on the UK Stock Exchange with a total issued share capital of 5,000,000 shares	150,000
3.5% War Loan Government Stock, nominal value £80,000	27,000
Ruritanian antique kept in private residence	6,000
Scottish farm acquired in January 1987 and occupied since that date by farming tenants. Mr Gog has the right to obtain vacant possession on two years' notice if he so wishes	165,000
	558,000
Less building society mortgage loan on private residence (12% fixed rate)	(40,000)
	518,000

Further information is available as follows.

(a) On 1st June 1997 Mr Gog disposed of an investment property located in Ruritania. The disposal gave rise to a nil gain/nil loss position for capital gains tax purposes.

(b) Mr Gog had let out the property continuously for many years at a rent of £300 per month (gross) payable at the end of each month. The rents were subject to Ruritanian tax at a rate of 20%. Ruritania does not have a double tax treaty with the UK. Mr Gog transferred £200 of his rental income each month to Scotland, any balance remaining being lodged to his Ruritanian bank account.

(c) Mr Gog acquired his shares in Bah plc for £20,000 in August 1992. Mr Gog has not received any dividends from Bah plc since he acquired the shares.

(d) Mr Gog acquired the 3.5% War Loan Stock for £25,400 in January 1996.

(e) Mr Gog acquired the antique for £5,000 in April 1996.

(f) Due to the availability of previous year losses, no taxable income has arisen from the farmland for several years. The farmland was acquired in January 1987 at a cost of £95,000.

(g) Interest credited to the Ruritanian bank deposit account has been as follows:

Year ended 5.4.97   £2,000
Year ended 5.4.98   £1,500

These amounts are net of Ruritanian tax of 10%. No amounts of this interest were brought back into the UK.

(h) Mr Gog's gross salary for the year ended 5th April 1997 was £29,350, which was subject to PAYE of £6,700.

(i) Mr Gog is anxious to transfer some assets, other than his private residence, to his son Enrico. Enrico, who is 23, was born in Scotland and intends to remain there for the rest of his life. Enrico is keen to manage the farm in Scotland. Mr Gog would like to transfer assets to Enrico as quickly as possible. However, Mr Gog is not prepared to make transfers which could give rise to inheritance tax liabilities if he were to die within the next seven years. He understands that he may be able to avoid such liabilities by making transfers of excluded property as well as using his nil rate band. Mr Gog is also not prepared to make transfers of assets which would give rise to capital gains tax liabilities. He intends to leave the balance of assets retained by him to a charity under his will.

(j)   Mr Gog has made no previous transfers of assets.

Required

(a)   Compute Mr Gog's income tax liability for 1997/98.

(b)   Explain to Mr Gog his likely present domicile status for inheritance tax purposes, and why this may alter in future years.

(c)   Advise Mr Gog as to which of his assets he should transfer on 5th April 1998. Show all supporting calculations. You should assume that Mr Gog is non-UK domiciled for inheritance purposes at 5th April 1998.

(d)   Assuming that Mr Gog follows your advice under (c), describe the inheritance consequences of his dying before 6th April 2005.

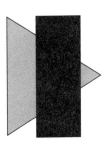

Appendix: Tables of tax rates and allowances

Income tax rates

Year	Bands £	Rates %
1997/98	1–4,100	20
	4,101–26,100	23
	Over 26,100	40
1996/97	1–3,900	20
	3,900–25,500	24
	Over 25,500	40

Personal allowances and reliefs

	1997/98 £	1996/97 £
Personal allowance	4,045	3,765
Married couple's allowance	1,830	1,790
Age allowance		
Single person		
— aged 65–74	5,220	4,910
— aged 75 and over	5,400	5,090
Married couple's allowance		
— aged 65–74	3,185	3,115
— aged 75 and over	3,225	3,155
Income limit	15,600	15,200
Additional personal allowance	1,830	1,790
Widow's bereavement allowance	1,830	1,790
Blind person's allowance	1,280	1,250

Car benefits
Car scale benefit from 6th April 1994

Age at end of tax year	Under 4 years	4 years and over
Business mileage		Percentage of list price
First car		
1 – 2,499 p.a.	35	$\frac{2}{3} \times 35$
2,500 – 17,999 p.a.	$35 - (\frac{1}{3} \times 35)$	$(\frac{2}{3} \times 35) - (\frac{1}{3} \times \frac{2}{3} \times 35)$
18,000 and over p.a.	$35 - (\frac{2}{3} \times 35)$	$(\frac{2}{3} \times 35) - (\frac{2}{3} \times \frac{2}{3} \times 35)$
Second car		
less than 18,000 p.a.	35	$\frac{2}{3} \times 35$
18,000 p.a. and over	$\frac{2}{3} \times 35$	$\frac{2}{3} \times 35 - (\frac{1}{3} \times \frac{2}{3} \times 35)$

Car fuel benefit

	1997/98		1995/96	
	Petrol £	Diesel £	Petrol £	Diesel £
Cylinder capacity				
Up to 1400cc	800	740	710	640
1401 – 2000cc	1,010	740	890	640
Over 2000cc	1,490	940	1,320	820

Retail price index

	Jan	Feb	Mar	Apr	May	Jun	Jul	Aug	Sep	Oct	Nov	Dec
1982			79.4	81.0	81.6	81.9	81.9	81.9	81.9	82.3	82.7	82.5
1983	82.6	83.0	83.1	84.3	84.6	84.8	85.3	85.7	86.1	86.4	86.7	86.9
1984	86.8	87.2	87.5	88.6	89.0	89.2	89.1	89.9	90.1	90.7	91.0	90.9
1985	91.2	91.9	92.8	94.8	95.2	95.4	95.2	95.5	95.4	95.6	95.9	96.0
1986	96.2	96.6	96.7	97.7	97.8	97.8	97.5	97.8	98.3	98.5	99.3	99.6
1987	100.0	100.4	100.6	101.8	101.9	101.9	101.8	102.1	102.4	102.9	103.4	103.3
1988	103.3	103.7	104.1	105.8	106.2	106.6	106.7	107.9	108.4	109.5	110.0	110.3
1989	111.0	111.8	112.3	114.3	115.0	115.4	115.5	115.8	116.6	117.5	118.5	118.8
1990	119.5	120.2	121.4	125.1	126.2	126.7	126.8	128.1	129.3	130.3	130.0	129.9
1991	130.2	130.9	131.4	133.1	133.5	134.1	133.8	134.1	134.6	135.1	135.6	135.7
1992	135.6	136.3	136.7	138.8	139.3	139.3	138.8	138.9	139.4	139.9	139.7	139.2
1993	137.9	138.8	139.3	140.6	141.1	141.0	140.7	141.3	141.9	141.8	141.6	141.9
1994	141.3	142.1	142.5	144.2	144.7	144.7	144.0	144.7	145.0	145.2	145.2	146.0
1995	146.0	146.9	147.5	149.0	149.6	149.8	149.1	149.9	150.6	149.8	149.8	150.7
1996	150.2	150.9	151.5	152.6	152.9	153.0	152.4	153.1	153.8	153.8	153.9	154.4
1997	154.6	154.9	155.0	155.2	155.5	155.8	156.0	156.2	156.5	156.9	157.2	157.6
1998	158.0	158.2	158.5									

The figures from January 1997 to March 1998 are estimates.

Capital gains tax

	1997/98 £	1996/97 £
Annual exemption	6,500	6,300

Corporation tax

Financial year	1997	1996
Full rate	33%	33%
Small companies rate	23%	24%
Lower limit	£300,000	£300,000
Upper limit	£1,500,000	£1,500,000
Small companies fraction	1/40	9/400

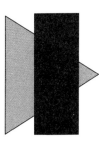

Glossary

1982-holding A pool of identical securities acquired between 6th April 1965 and 5th April 1982 used for capital gains tax matching purposes.

Ability to pay A system of taxation under which tax is levied on a taxpayer according to his economic ability to pay tax. *See also* Benefit principle.

Accounting period The interval for which corporation tax is assessed and charged on the profits arising during the interval.

Accruals basis Under the accruals basis profits for an accounting period equal revenue earned in the period less expenses incurred in earning that revenue.

Accumulation and maintenance trust A trust in which income is accumulated for minor children until they reach a specified age.

Additional personal allowance (APA) An allowance given to any single person with a child living with them.

Additional voluntary contributions Payments made by an employee to increase retirement benefits due from the approved pension scheme run by his employer.

Advance corporation tax A payment which is made to the Inland Revenue whenever a UK company pays a dividend.

Age allowance An allowance available to individuals over 65 years of age instead of the ordinary personal allowance.

Agricultural buildings allowance An allowance, for income tax and corporation tax purposes, available for capital expenditure on farmhouses, farm buildings cottages, fences, drainage and similar works.

Agricultural property relief Relief from inheritance tax available on the agricultural value of agricultural property in the UK, the Channel Islands or the Isle of Man.

Annual accounting scheme A method of accounting for VAT which only requires the registered trader to complete one VAT return each year.

Annual exemption The amount of capital gains that an individual may make each year that is not subjected to capital gains tax. Also the amount which an individual may transfer each year which is not subjected to inheritance tax.

Annuity An amount of money paid annually or at other regular intervals.

Arising basis   Income, which is taxed as it arises regardless of if or when it is remitted to the UK.

Artificial scheme   A self-cancelling scheme used to avoid tax which is made up of a series of preordained steps which leaves taxpayers in the same position at the end as they were at the beginning.

Associated companies   Companies who are either under common control or where one company controls the other.

Associated disposal   One of a series of linked disposals of related assets to connected persons.

Associated operations   Two or more operations which are related are deemed to take place at the time of the last of the operations for inheritance tax purposes.

Average rate of tax   Equal to the total tax paid in the tax period, usually one year, divided by the total income received in the period.

Avoidance   The legal manipulation of a taxpayer's affairs in order to reduce the taxpayer's tax liability.

Bad debt relief   Relief for VAT paid on a taxable supply made by a registered trader who has subsequently written off all or part of the debt in his accounts.

Badges of trade   The six elements which the Royal Commission identified as helping to determine whether or not trading is taking place.

Balancing allowances and charges   Relief for capital expenditure, or the claw back of relief already given, given in the year in which an asset is disposed of or the business ceases to trade.

Basic rate of tax   The main rate at which income and capital gains taxes are levied at. For 1997/98 the rate is 23%.

Basis period   The time period whose profits are taxed in the fiscal year.

Beneficial loan   A loan given to an employee who derived the benefit of the loan because of their employment.

Beneficiary   Individual who may derive benefit from a trust.

Benefit principle   In contrast to the ability to pay principle, under the benefit principle tax is raised by reference to the amount of benefit a taxpayer is deemed to receive from the public sector. *See also* Ability to pay.

Benefits in kind   A benefit received by an employee or members of his or her family or household due to their employment.

Blind person's allowance   An allowance given to taxpayers that are registered blind.

Board of Inland Revenue   Civil servants appointed by the Treasury who administer income tax, corporation tax and capital gains tax.

Bonus issue   An issue of additional shares in proportion to existing holdings to shareholders.

Budget   An annual statement by the Chancellor of the Exchequer setting out proposals for taxation and government expenditure in the following fiscal year.

Burden of tax   The amount by which a taxpayer's income is reduced because of taxation.

Business property relief   Relief from inheritance tax on transfers of relevant business property.

Capital allowances   Relief from income tax and corporation tax on capital expenditure on eligible assets.

Capital Allowances Act 1990 (CAA 1990)   The Act that governs capital allowances for income tax and corporation tax purposes.

Capital distribution   A repayment of capital by a company to its shareholders.

Capital gains   The net increase in the value of an asset after the indexation allowance on its disposal by an individual.

Capital gains tax   The tax levied on capital gains. The liability to tax only arises when the asset is disposed of.

Capitalisation of future tax benefits   Future tax benefits are capitalised when the current value of an asset includes an allowance for the increased expected yield from the asset due to future tax benefits.

Cash accounting scheme   A method of accounting for VAT which depends on payments and receipts rather than invoices for identifying tax points.

Cash voucher   A voucher, stamp or similar document capable of being exchanged for a sum of money.

Cash-flow tax base   Under a cash-flow tax based system cash flows rather than profits are taxed.

Certificate of tax deposit   A payment to the Inland Revenue which can be used to met a tax liability.

Charge on income   A recurring, legally enforceable, liability which income tax law allows as a deduction from the payer's total income.

Chargeable asset   All assets are chargeable assets unless they are specifically exempted from capital gains tax.

Chargeable business asset   The whole or part of a business or assets used in a business until it ceased to trade or shares or securities of a company.

Chargeable lifetime transfer   A transfer of value made by an individual during their lifetime that is not an exempt or potentially exempt transfer. In practice, only transfers into a discretionary trust are chargeable lifetime transfers.

Chargeable transfer   A transfer of value made by an individual who intended to confer a gratuitous benefit that is not an exempt transfer.

Chattel   Tangible movable property.

Class 1 national insurance contributions   Payments made by employees, primary contributions, and employers, secondary contributions.

Class 1A national insurance contributions   Payments made by employers when employees are provided with cars or fuel for private use.

Class 2 national insurance contributions   Flat rate payments made by the self-employed.

Class 3 national insurance contributions   Voluntary payments made to individuals in order to maintain rights to some state benefits.

Class 4 national insurance contributions   Payments made by the self-employed based on a percentage of taxable profits.

Close company   A UK resident company which is under the control of five or fewer participators or of participators who are directors.

Close investment-holding company   A close company which is a non-trading company.

Collector of taxes   Civil servants appointed by the Board of Inland Revenue to collect the tax which is assessed to be payable.

Commissioners of Customs and Excise   Civil servants appointed by the Crown who are responsible for collecting and accounting for, and otherwise managing, the revenues of Customs and Excise.

Commissioners of Inland Revenue Individuals appointed by the Lord Chancellor to hear taxpayers' appeals against the assessment of the inspectors.

Compliance costs Costs which are incurred by a taxpayer in order to enable him to comply with a tax.

Composite supply A taxable supply for VAT purposes made up of a mix of standard rated, zero rated or exempt supplies where it is not possible to apportion the value of the supply to each of the rates. One rate is applied to the whole of the supply.

Comprehensive income tax A tax which is levied on an individual's comprehensive income. An individual's comprehensive income is the amount which an individual could consume without diminishing the value of their wealth. *See also* Economic income.

Connected persons Persons who are defined as having a special relationship for tax purposes and transactions between them are sometimes accorded special treatment.

Consortium A group of companies in which one company is at least 75% owned by UK resident companies who are called members of the consortium.

Consortium relief Allows trading losses to be surrendered from a member of a consortium to a consortium held company and vice versa.

Consumption taxes Also called expenditure taxes, a consumption tax taxes the resources which an individual has consumed during a set period of time.

Corporate PEP A single company personal equity plan which invests in the securities of only one company.

Corporation tax The tax that is levied on the profits of companies and unincorporated associations such as clubs and political associations but not partnerships.

Corrective taxes A tax which is intended to affect the behaviour of taxpayers. Tax relief on pension contributions is intended to encourage individuals to provide for a private pension.

Corresponding accounting period An accounting period of a company claiming group relief which falls wholly or partly within an accounting period of the surrendering company.

Crowding out This is the effect which may occur when public expenditure increases and causes a reduction in size of the private sector, thus reducing the tax base.

Cum div A quoted security which carries the right to an imminent dividend.

Cum int A quoted security which carries the right to an imminent interest payment.

De minimis limit Expenditure on long life assets below this figure will not be subject to a writing down allowance of only 4%.

De-pooling An election made by taxpayers for nominated items of plant and machinery with a short life to be maintained outside the pool so that balancing allowances may be claimed on their disposal.

Deed of covenant A payment made under a covenant made otherwise than for consideration in money or money's worth in favour of a person or charity whereby the annual payments are payable for a period which may exceed three years and is not capable of earlier termination without the consent of the beneficiary.

Depreciating asset   An asset which is, or within the next ten years will become, a wasting asset. Wasting assets have a useful life of 50 years or less thus a depreciating asset has a useful life of less than 60 years.

Deregistration   The process by which a registered trader voluntarily or otherwise ceases to be registered for VAT.

Diminution in value   The loss in value of the donor's estate when a transfer of value for inheritance tax purposes occurs.

Direct taxes   A tax which is levied on the taxpayer who is intended to bear the final burden of paying tax. Examples include income tax and employee national insurance contributions.

Discovery assessment   An assessment made by the Inland Revenue based on evidence they discover after a self-assessment return became final.

Discretionary trust   A trust in which no beneficiary has an absolute right to the income.

Disincentive effect of taxation   Where a transaction, such as employment, is subject to tax there is a gap between the selling price and the purchase price which is equal to the tax levied. This gap may act as a disincentive to the transaction. For example an employee may be unwilling to undertake overtime at the rate offered if he is subject to a high marginal rate of tax.

District inspector   Each district is headed by a district inspector who has other inspectors working for them.

Divisional registration   Registration by a company so that each division is registered separately for VAT purposes.

Domicile   A domicile is the place that an individual thinks of as home. He or she may not live in the place of domicile but he or she is likely to retain some links with it.

Duality test   When expenditure has both a business and a private purpose the expenditure is likely to fail the 'wholly and exclusively' text and be disallowable for tax purposes because of a duality of purpose.

Due date   The date on which tax is due to be paid.

Earnings cap   The upper limit on the earnings on which an approved pension scheme can be based.

Economic efficiency   A tax is economically efficient if it does not distort the economic decisions which are made by individuals.

Economic income   The maximum value which an individual can consume during a period and still expect to be as well off at the end of the period as at the beginning. *See also* Comprehensive income tax.

Economic rent   The amount that a factor of production, such as land, earns over and above what could be earned if it was put to its next best use.

Effective incidence of tax   The effective incidence of tax falls on those individuals whose wealth is reduced by the tax. This may not be the same as the formal incidence of tax.

Eligible interest   Either mortgage interest paid under the MIRAS scheme or interest paid on loans to purchase annuities or other qualifying loan interest payments.

Emoluments   Income, not necessary money, from an office or employment.

Employee   An individual with a contract of services.

Employee share ownership plan (ESOP)   A trust into which a UK resident company transfers funds for the benefit of some or all of its employees.

Enhancement expenditure   Capital expenditure incurred to enhancing an asset.

Enterprise zone   An area designated as benefiting from tax and other incentives in order to encourage investment.

Error or mistake relief   Relief for tax overstated due to some error or mistake on the part of the taxpayer.

Estate at death   The value of all the assets owned on the date of death together with any interest held as a joint tenant and capital held by a trust in which the deceased had an interest in possession.

Evasion   The illegal manipulation of a taxpayer's affairs so as to reduce the taxpayer's tax liability.

Ex div   A quoted security which does not carry a right to the imminent dividend.

Ex int   A quoted security which does not carry a right to the imminent interest payment.

Excepted estate   An estate in respect of which it is not necessary to deliver an account of the property for inheritance tax purposes.

Excess burden of tax   Where a tax is not economically efficient the loss to the economy caused by the distortion is termed the excess burden of tax.

Excluded property   Property which is specifically excluded from an estate at death for the purposes of inheritance tax.

Exempt income   Income which is specifically exempt from income tax.

Exempt supply   A supply of goods or services which is specifically exempt from VAT.

Exit charge   An inheritance charge levied when funds leave a discretionary trust.

Expenditure taxes   A tax on the amount consumed by an individual in a given period of time.

Extra-statutory concession   A series of statements made by the Inland Revenue or Customs and Excise which give concessions to taxpayers over and above those allowed by legislation.

FA 1985 pool   A pool of shares of the same class in the same company acquired on or after 6th April 1982 and held on 6th April 1985 and those acquired on or after 6th April 1985, maintained for capital gains tax purposes.

Fall in value relief   An inheritance tax relief available if assets are disposed of within a given period after death for less than their value at the date of death.

Finance Act   Usually an annual Act of Parliament which contains the fiscal legislation needed to implement the budget.

Financial year   Runs from 1st April to the following 31st March. The rate of corporation tax is set for financial years.

First year allowance   A capital allowance which may be available in the year in which an asset is acquired.

Fiscal neutrality   A fiscally neutral tax system does not discriminate between economic choices.

Fiscal year   A tax year which runs from 6th April until the following 5th April.

Follow-up account   A TESSA which was set up using some of the proceeds of an earlier TESSA on its maturation.

Foreign emoluments   The emoluments of a person, not domiciled in the UK, from an office or employment with an employer not resident in the UK.

Franked investment income (FII)   Dividends together with the related tax credit received by a UK company from another UK company which are not treated as group income.

Franked payment (FP)   Dividends together with the related tax credit paid by a UK company to another UK company which are not treated as group income.

Free estate   The value of all the assets owned outright by an individual at his death.

Free-standing additional voluntary contributions   Payments made by an employee who is a member of an occupational pension scheme in order to increase retirement benefits.

Full rent   A rent paid under a lease which is sufficient, taking one year with another to defray the cost to the lessor of any expenses which are borne by him.

Functional test   A test to identify assets which are actively used in the business and thus are eligible for capital allowances as opposed to those which form part of the setting in which the business was carried on.

Furnished holiday letting   Holiday lettings taxed under Schedule A using the regulations for Schedule D Case I. The income is treated as earned income for tax purposes.

Furnished letting   A letting of furnished property which is taxed under Schedule D Case VI.

General Commissioners   Part time and unpaid individuals who hear taxpayers' appeals against the assessments of the inspectors.

Gift relief   A relief from capital gains tax when a qualifying asset is disposed of and both the transferor and transferee elect for the transferor's gain to be reduced to nil.

Gift with reservation   A gift which the donator is not able to benefit from to the exclusion of the donor during the period.

Gratuitous disposition   A disposal of an asset which was intended to confer some benefit to the recipient.

Gross amount of tax   The aggregate of the input tax and output tax included in the VAT return for a period.

Grossing up   The process of adding the inheritance tax liability to the net value of the gift made when the donor agrees to pay any inheritance tax due.

Group charge   A charge paid under an election by one member of a 51% group to another without deduction of income tax.

Group   Companies which are either associated, 51% subsidiaries, 75% subsidiaries or consortia.

Group income   Dividends paid under an election by one member of a 51% group to another member of the same group.

Group interest   Interest paid under an election by one member of a 51% group to another without deduction of income tax.

Group registration   Registration for VAT purposes by a group of companies under common control.

Group relief   Trading losses incurred by one member of a 75% group can be surrendered to another member of the same group.

Higher rate tax   Taxable income of an individual in excess of £26,100 is taxed at the higher rate of 40%.

HM Customs and Excise   A government department which is responsible to the Treasury and administers VAT.

Holdover relief   Relief from capital gains tax which can be claimed when a business asset is replaced by a depreciable asset.

Horizontal equity   A hypothecated tax is one which is raised to provide a particular benefit.

Imputation system   A system under which shareholders are given a tax credit for the advance corporation tax paid by a company on the payment of a dividend.

Incidence of taxation   The formal incidence of tax falls on those who must actually pay the tax while the effective incidence of tax falls on those whose wealth is reduced by the tax. *See also* Indirect taxes; Regressive taxes.

Incidental costs of acquisition   Costs incurred when an asset was acquired which are allowed when calculating a chargeable gain for capital gains tax purposes.

Incidental costs of disposal   Costs incurred when an asset was disposed of which are allowed when calculating a chargeable gain for capital gains tax purposes.

Incidental expenses   Small payments to employees to cover expenses.

Income and Corporation Taxes Act 1988 (ICTA 1988)   Act of Parliament which contains the majority of the legislation dealing with the taxation of individuals and companies.

Income distortion   This is the transfer of wealth from the taxpayer to the government.

Income tax   A tax levied on all income, earned and unearned, attributed to an individual in a given period.

Income taxed at source   Income paid net of tax at the rate of 20% or 23%.

Income taxed by assessment   Income paid gross on which income tax is levied.

Income   Valuable consideration received in exchange for the provision of goods or services.

Incorporation   Creation of a company from a business run by a sole trader or partnership.

Independent taxation   The taxation of spouses as individuals rather than as a family unit.

Indexation allowance   An allowance intended to compensate for the effect of inflation on the value of capital assets when determining a capital gains tax liability.

Indirect taxes   A tax which is ultimately borne by someone other than the taxpayer on whom it is levied. However, it is not always possible to identify the effective incidence of an indirect tax. VAT is an example of an indirect tax which is intended to be suffered by the final consumer. However, market forces might lead to manufacturers absorbing some of the VAT themselves, rather than passing it on to the final consumer. *See also* Incidence of taxation.

Industrial buildings allowances (IBA)   Capital allowance available on expenditure on industrial buildings and hotels.

Inheritance tax   Tax levied on certain lifetime transfers and estates on the death of individuals.

Inheritance Tax Act 1984 (IHTA 1984)   Act of Parliament containing the majority legislation dealing with inheritance tax.

Inland Revenue   The government department responsible for income tax, corporation tax, capital gains tax and inheritance tax.

Input VAT   VAT levied on the purchases of goods and services by a registered trader.

Inspector of taxes   Civil Servants who assess individuals, companies and other organisations liability to tax.

Instalment option   Facility, which allows some capital, gains tax and inheritance tax to be paid in instalments.

Intending trader registration   Registration for VAT by an individual or organisation which has not yet begun to trade.

Interest in possession trust   A trust in which the beneficiaries, the life tenants, have a right to receive the income from the trust for a period of time.

Interim payments   Payments of income tax on account on 31st January in the fiscal year and 31st July following the end of the fiscal year.

Intra-group transfer   A transfer of assets between two members of a group which would in other circumstances give rise to a capital gains tax charge.

Irrecoverable VAT   VAT levied on the purchases of goods or services that cannot be recovered as input tax.

Job-related accommodation   Accommodation provided to an employee which is eligible for some tax relief.

Landlord repairing lease   A lease of property at a full rent. That is the rent paid under the lease is sufficient taking one year with another, to defray the cost to the lessor of any expenses subject to the lease which fall to be borne by him.

Lease   The granting of a right to the use of an asset for a specified period.

Less detailed VAT invoice   May be issued by retailers when the VAT inclusive total is less than £100.

Letting exemption   Relief from capital gains tax available when part or all of a property, which was at some time the taxpayer's principal private residence, is let.

Life interest trust   A trust in which beneficiaries have an interest in possession throughout their life.

Life tenant   An individual who has a right to receive the income from a trust for a period of time.

Linked transactions   A series of transactions to connected persons where the disposal proceeds of each disposal are taken to be a proportion of the value of the aggregate of the assets transferred for capital gains tax purposes.

Loss relief   Tax relief for trading or capital losses given by setting losses against taxable income or chargeable gains.

Lower rate of tax   The lowest rate of tax, currently 20%, levied on the income and chargeable gains of individuals.

Lump sum taxes   A fixed amount of tax paid by an individual regardless of his or her income.

Maintenance payments   Payments to a spouse, former spouse or children.

Management expenses   Expenses incurred in managing an investment company.

Marginal rate of tax   This is the rate at which a taxpayer would be taxed if his income increased by a small amount.

Marginal relief   Relief given to companies with taxable profits lying within given limits.

Marriage exemption   Relief from inheritance tax on gifts made in consideration of marriage.

Married couple's allowance   An allowance available to a married man whose wife lives with him.

Matching rules   The rules used to match acquisitions and disposals of quoted securities for capital gains tax purposes.

Minor   An unmarried child under the age of 18.

MIRAS   The mechanism used to give individuals tax relief on the interest paid on their mortgages called Mortgage Interest Relief At Source.

Mixed supply   A supply of goods and services by a registered trader which is made up of a separable mix of elements. The appropriate VAT rate to be applied to each part.

National insurance contributions   A tax paid by individuals and employers to secure certain benefits such as a state pension.

National Savings Bank   A government owned bank in which individuals can invest in order to obtain interest.

National Savings Certificate   Certificates issued by the Government which offers tax-free returns.

Negligible value claim   A capital gains tax relief that can be claimed by a taxpayer when an asset becomes effectively worthless.

Net Relevant Earnings   Schedule D Case I and II, Schedule E and income from furnished holiday lettings taxed under Schedule D Case VI net of loss relief and excess of trade charges over other income.

Nil rate band   The band of transfers for which the rate of inheritance tax is nil.

No gain/no loss transfer   Disposal of an asset without a gain or loss for capital gains tax purposes regardless of the actual costs and the value of any proceeds.

Nominal rent lease   A lease which is not expected to generate a profit over a number of years.

Non-cash voucher   A voucher which can only be exchanged for goods or services.

Non-savings income   Income other than interest and dividends.

Normal expenditure out of income exemption   Exemption from inheritance tax where the gift or gifts are not so large that the donor's residual income is inadequate to maintain his or her usual standard of living.

Occupational pension scheme   Pension schemes available for employees set up by their employers.

Ordinary residence   A taxpayer is ordinarily resident if the UK is a regular choice of abode which forms part of the regular order of an individual's life.

Output VAT   The VAT on supplies made by a registered trader or on the acquisition by a registered trader of goods from another member state.

Overlap losses   Losses incurred by a trader in a period which forms all or part of the basis period of more than one fiscal year.

Overlap profits   Profits earned by a trader in a period which forms all or part of the basis period of more than one fiscal year.

Part disposal   The disposal of part of an asset for capital gains tax purposes.

Partial exemption   Where a trader makes some taxable supplies and some exempt supplies he may be unable to recover all of his input tax.

Participator   A person who has a share or interest in the capital or income of a close company.

Partnership Two or more individuals carrying on a business.

Pay and file The system used to collect corporation tax.

Pay As You Earn (PAYE) The system used to collect income tax and national insurance contributions from employees.

Payment basis Charges are recognised for tax purposes when they are paid.

Payroll deduction scheme Payments to charity from an employee's gross income under the PAYE scheme.

Period of account The period for which a business prepares accounts.

Personal allowance An allowance which can be claimed by individuals and is not taxable.

Personal company A company is an individual's personal company if he exercises at least 5% of the voting rights in the company.

Personal equity plan (PEP) A plan which enables individuals to invest in equities either directly or using unit trusts free of income tax or capital gains tax.

Personal pension scheme A pension scheme which employees can invest in provided that they are not a member of their employer's occupational pension scheme.

Plant and machinery Apparatus used by a business person for carrying on business not their own stock-in-trade which they buy or make for resale. Capital expenditure on plant and machinery may qualify for capital allowances.

Political accountability Tax raising bodies should be accountable to those they raise taxes from. This usually takes the form of requirement to obtain a mandate from the electorate in regular elections.

Potentially exempt transfer (PET) A lifetime transfer of value, other than one to a discretionary trust, made by an individual which is not an exempt transfer for inheritance tax purposes. A potentially exempt transfer becomes a chargeable transfer if the donor dies within seven years of making the transfer.

Premium A payment in return for the granting of a lease on land or property.

Principal charge A charge of 15% of the inheritance scale rate on the value of a discretionary trust every ten years.

Principal private residence The main residence of an individual or a married couple. An individual who owns more than one residence may nominate one as his or her main residence.

Profit sharing scheme A scheme for employees which enables shares in their employer company to be distributed to them.

Profits chargeable to corporation tax (PCTCT) Tax adjusted profits of a company excluding franked investment income after deducting charges and loss relief.

Profits for small companies rate purposes Profits chargeable to corporation tax plus franked investment income.

Progressive taxes A tax is progressive if individuals with a larger taxable capacity pay proportionately more of their income in tax than individuals with a lower taxable capacity.

Proportional taxes A tax is proportional if tax paid is a fixed proportion of taxable capacity.

Qualifying corporate bond A sterling bond which is a normal commercial loan which is exempt from capital gains tax.

Quarter days   25th March, 24th June, 29th September and 25th December. Often rents are due on the quarter days.

Quarter up rule   A valuation rule for quoted securities for capital gains tax purposes. The valuation is equal to the lower of the two prices quoted in the Daily Official List plus a quarter of the difference between the two prices.

Quarterly accounting   The system used by companies to account for ACT when they pay dividends.

Quick succession relief   Relief from inheritance tax when a chargeable transfer increased the value of a person's estate within the previous five years.

Ramsay principle   A principle that if an artificial scheme is used to avoid or delay a tax liability the courts can set aside the scheme and instead compare the position of the taxpayer in real terms at the start and finish of the scheme.

Rate applicable to trusts   The 34% rate for income tax and capital gains tax applied to discretionary trusts.

Rebasing   The procedure under which capital gains are calculated by assuming that assets owned on 31st March 1982 were bought on that date at their market value on that date.

Receipts basis   A way of allocating income to fiscal years on the basis of when it is received.

Receivable basis   A way of allocating income to fiscal years on the basis of when it was due to be received. This basis is used for assessing companies' Schedule A income.

Regressive taxes   A tax is regressive if the proportion of tax paid increases as income falls. *See also* Incidence of tax.

Reinvestment relief   Relief from capital gains tax available to individuals or trustees, but not companies, when some or all of the proceeds from the disposal of an asset or a material disposal of shares in a qualifying company are reinvested in a qualifying investment.

Related property   Property held in the estates of spouses.

Relevant supplies   Supplies to a non-taxable person in the UK from another EU member state. The supplier may be liable to register for VAT in the UK.

Remittance basis   A way of determining taxable income on the basis of amounts remitted to the UK.

Remoteness test   A test for determining whether an expense is deductible. An expense which is considered to be too remote from the trade will not be deductible.

Renewals basis   An allowable deduction from income from furnished letting for the replacement of furniture.

Rent a room scheme   A scheme under which if an individual lets one or more furnished rooms in their main residence rents received up to £4,250 a year are exempt from tax under Schedule A.

Residence   An individual is deemed to be resident in the UK for a fiscal year if he or she spends more than 183 days in the UK during the tax year.

Retail prices index (RPI)   An index used to calculate the indexation allowance for capital gains tax purposes.

Retail schemes   Schemes for accounting for VAT which are available to some retailers.

Retirement relief   Relief from capital gains tax is given in any case where a material disposal of business assets is made by an individual who at the time of the disposal, has attained the age of 50 or has retired on the grounds of ill-health below the age of 50.

Reverse charge   A system of accounting for VAT on supplies made to a UK resident registered trader by a person resident overseas.

Reversionary interest   An interest in a trust which will depend on the termination of another interest in the trust.

Rollover relief   Relief from capital gains tax available if the proceeds from the disposal of certain classes of assets are reinvested in other qualifying assets.

Savings income   Income, primarily interest and dividends, which is taxed at 20% unless the taxpayer is a higher rate taxpayer.

Schedular system of taxation   Income is taxed under the schedular system in the UK. The income to be taxed, the deductible expenses and the date of the payment of tax is laid down in the schedular system.

Secondhand goods scheme   A VAT scheme available to traders who buy second-hand goods from individuals who are not registered traders.

Self-assessment   A system of administration of taxation in which taxpayers are responsible for assessing their own liability to tax.

Self-employed person   An individual who has a contract for services. An employee has a contract of service.

Self-supply   A supply of goods or services by a registered person which is used by themselves in the course of their business.

Settled property   Assets held within a trust.

Settlement   A trust.

Seven year cumulation   An inheritance computation depends on the transfers of value which have occurred in the seven years prior to the most recent transfer.

Share option scheme   A scheme open to employees and directors which grants them share options.

Short-life asset   Plant or machinery which is kept separate from the general pool for the purposes of calculating capital allowances.

Single company PEP   A personal equity plan which only holds shares in one company.

Small companies rate   The rate at which profits chargeable to corporation tax are taxed provided the profits for small companies rate purposes lie below a given limit.

Small gifts exemption   An inheritance tax exemption for gifts to the same person provided that they have a total value of less than £250 in the fiscal year.

Special Commissioners   Full-time paid individuals who have been legally qualified for at least ten years who hear complex appeals of taxpayers against the assessment of the inspectors.

Standard rated supply   A supply of goods or services by a registered trader which are not exempt or zero rated.

Statement of practice   A statement issued by the Inland Revenue in order to clarify the application of some aspect of the legislation.

Statutory total income   An individual's total income before deduction of allowances.

Substitution effect of tax   A substitution distortion occurs when individuals consume one item rather than another because of the effect of taxation.

Surplus ACT ACT paid by a company which cannot be set against its corporation tax liability for the period in which the ACT was paid.

Tapering relief Relief given to companies with taxable profits lying within given limits. Also called marginal relief.

Tax avoidance The use of legal means to reduce tax liabilities.

Tax base All taxable items form the tax base. Tax may be levied on income, wealth or expenditure.

Tax borne The tax on an individual's taxable income less tax relief on tax reducers other than those paid net.

Tax credit A credit received with dividends from UK companies which is equal to the amount of tax deemed to have been suffered by the taxpayer.

Tax evasion The use of illegal means to reduce tax liabilities.

Tax exempt special savings account (TESSA) Savings accounts which give tax free returns provided that they are held for five years.

Tax liability Tax borne plus income tax retained on charges paid net.

Tax life The deemed life of an industrial or agricultural building. The life is currently 25 years.

Tax payable Tax liability less tax already suffered and tax credits.

Tax point The date on which a supply of goods or services is treated as taking place for VAT purposes.

Tax reducer An allowance or relief which has the effect of reducing the tax due on taxable income.

Tax wedges In the case of an indirect tax the tax wedge is the difference between the marginal cost of producing a good or service and the marginal benefit of consumption.

Tax year Also called a fiscal year or a year of assessment. A tax year runs from 6th April to the following 5th April.

Taxable capacity This is the capacity of an individual to pay tax and may be measured by reference to the individuals income, expenditure, wealth or even ability to generate income.

Taxable income Statutory total income less allowances.

Taxable person A person who is, or should be, registered for VAT.

Taxable supply A supply of goods or services by a registered trader which is not an exempt supply.

Taxable turnover The turnover of a business which is subject to VAT at any rate.

Taxation of Chargeable Gains Act 1992 (TCGA 1992) The Act which provides the majority of the legislation for capital gains tax.

Taxed income Income received net of basic rate or lower rate tax.

Taxpayer's Charter A statement setting out what a taxpayer is entitled to expect from the Inland Revenue.

Tenant's repairing lease A lease where the tenant is obliged to maintain or repair the whole or substantially the whole, of the premises which are the subject of the lease.

Terminal loss relief An income tax relief available to individuals for losses incurred in the final 12 months of trading.

Transfer of value A disposition by an individual which reduces the value of their estate.

Treasury A government department responsible to the Chancellor of the Exchequer which is responsible for the Inland Revenue and HM Customs and Excise.

Trust A trust is created when a settler transfers assets to trustees who hold the assets for the benefit of one or more persons.

Trustees Hold assets within a trust for the benefit of one or more persons.

Unfranked investment income (UFII) Taxed income received by a UK resident company.

Value Added Tax Act 1994 (VATA 1994) The Act containing the principal legislation for VAT.

Value added tax (VAT) An indirect or expenditure tax borne by the final consumer which is charged whenever a taxable person makes a taxable supply of goods or services in the course of his or her business.

VAT invoice An invoice which must be supplied by registered traders to other registered traders.

VAT period The period of time, usually three months, which is covered by a VAT return.

VAT return Form VAT 199 which must be submitted to HM Customs and Excise together with any VAT payable within one month of the end of the VAT period.

Vertical equity A tax system has vertical equity if those whose need is greater suffer less tax.

Void period A period in which there is no tenant leasing property and the property is not occupied by the owner.

Wasting asset Assets with an estimated remaining useful life of 50 years or less.

Wealth taxes A wealth tax is levied on a taxpayer's assets at a particular date. The primary difficulty with a wealth tax comes from valuing assets, especially intangibles like pension funds.

Wear and tear allowance A deduction from the income from furnished lettings to give relief for the wear and tear of furniture and equipment provided.

Widow's bereavement allowance An allowance given to a widow in the fiscal year in which her husband dies and the following fiscal year provided that she has not remarried by the beginning of that year.

Withholding taxes Some income, such as debenture interest, has tax deducted at source regardless of the personal circumstances of the recipient. The tax so deducted is termed a withholding tax.

Work effort and taxes There is a potentially complicated relationship between work effort and taxes. If marginal rates of tax are too high they may act as a disincentive to work.

Writing down allowance A capital allowance which is given as a deduction from profits to determine the Schedule D Case I or II assessment.

Year of assessment A fiscal or tax year which runs from 6th April to the following 5th April.

Zero rated supply A supply of goods or services made by a registered trader which is subjected to a nil rate of VAT.

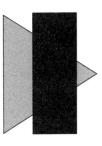

Suggested solutions to questions

Chapter 4

Question 1

(a) The general strategy to be adopted in order to maximise the benefits of the system of independent taxation should aim to:

- ensure that each spouse has sufficient income to fully utilise their personal allowances. The married couple's allowance should be claimed in such a way as to ensure that it is fully utilised.
- ensure that, if possible, each spouse fully utilises their lower and basic rate bands. The situation where one spouse pays tax at 40% while the other is a lower or basic rate taxpayer should be avoided if possible.
- chargeable disposals should be made by the spouse with the lowest marginal rate of tax. Wherever possible each spouse should fully utilise their exemption limit.
- chargeable disposals should be made in such a way as to fully utilise any allowable losses.

(b) This strategy can be achieved by:

- transferring income generating investments to the spouse with the lowest marginal rate of tax.
- taking the spouse of a self-employed taxpayer into partnership or providing employment in the business in order to generate income for the spouse with the lower marginal rate of tax.
- using charges and other tax deductible payments to reduce the taxable income of the spouse with the highest marginal rate of tax. Remember that the spouse who wishes to claim such reliefs must actually make the relevant payment.
- transferring chargeable assets between spouses on a no gain/no loss basis in order to ensure that:
- annual exemption limits are fully used

- chargeable gains are realised by the spouse with the lowest marginal rate of tax
- allowable losses are not wasted by being relieved against chargeable gains which would otherwise have been relieved by the annual exemption limit.

Question 2

Personal tax computation for 1997/98

	Janet £	£	Dave £	£
Earned income				
Schedule E: Salary	26,000			16,000
Bonus	3,000	29,000		
Less pension contribution				
£2,002 × 100/77		2,600		
		26,400		
Investment income				
Taxed income £3,000 × 100/80			3,750	
Schedule A				
Income £8,000 × 6/12	4,000			
Less expenses	1,000	3,000		
Less deed of covenant				
£308 × 100/77			400	3,350
Statutory total income		29,400		19,350
Less personal allowance		4,045		4,045
Taxable income		25,355		15,305
Lower rate band				
£4,100 × 20%		820		
£(4,100 + 3,750) × 20%				1,570
Basic rate band				
£21,255 × 23%		4,889		
£ 7,455 × 23%				1,715
		5,709		
Less tax reduction				
Additional personal				
allowance £1,830 × 15%		275		
Tax borne		5,434		3,285
Add tax retained on charges paid net				
£2,600 × 23%		598		
£400 × 23%				92
Tax liability		6,032		3,377
Less tax deducted at source		–		750
Tax payable		6,032		2,627

Chapter 5

Question 1

The treatment of each of the items, for tax purposes, is as follows:

(a) *Reconstruction of the roof*

The expenditure was incurred to renovate an asset soon after it was acquired and the asset, a building, was not in a usable condition immediately after acquisition. Following the decision in *Law Shipping Co Ltd v CIR (1923)* the expenditure will be deemed to be capital and hence will be disallowable for tax purposes. If the use of the warehouse qualifies the building for an industrial buildings allowance the expenditure will qualify for capital allowances.

The expenditure on the roof should be added back to the net profit in order to determine the Schedule D Case I profit.

(b) *Embezzlement by the sales director*

Defalcations by directors are not allowable deductions for Schedule D Case I purposes (*Curtis v J & G Oldfield 1933*). Hence the expense should be added back to the net profit in order to determine the Schedule D Case I profit.

(c) *Redundancy payment to a works manager*

Redundancy payments made wholly and exclusively for the purpose of trade are allowed without limit, provided that the business continues to trade. If Q plc ceases to trade there is a limit on the amount of any redundancy payment of the statutory amount plus up to three times the statutory amount. In the case of the works manager the maximum deductible is £48,000 (£12,000 × 3 + £12,000). Since the actual payment is lower than this it will be an allowable expense even if Q plc ceases to trade.

Hence no adjustment needs to be made in order to determine the Schedule D Case I profit.

(d) *Salary of senior manager seconded to a charity*

Such a payment is specifically allowable for tax purposes and hence no adjustment needs to be made in order to determine the Schedule D Case I profit.

Salary of manager working entirely for the subsidiary

Salaries are only deductible for tax purposes if they are incurred for the purposes of trade. Hence the manager's salary will only be deductible if Q plc's trade benefits from his work. It is not enough to argue that his work will benefit the subsidiary and thus increase the value of Q plc's shareholding in the subsidiary.

Provided that Q plc does benefit from the manager's work, by for example, charging the subsidiary for his work, no adjustment needs to be made in order to determine the Schedule D Case I profit. Otherwise the expense should be added back to the net profit in order to determine the Schedule D Case I profit.

(e) *Costs of the crèche*

The construction costs are capital expenditure and as such are not allowable for tax purposes although if Q plc's trade is a qualifying trade it may be eligible for industrial buildings allowance.

The running costs of the crèche are incurred in order to provide a benefit in kind for employees and as such are allowable deductions for tax purposes.

Hence the construction costs should be added back to the net profit in order to determine the Schedule D Case I profit while no adjustment is required for the running costs.

(f) *Receipt from insurance company*

The cost of repairing the asset is an allowable expense. The receipt from the insurance company will reduce the allowable expenditure by £18,000 because the company has been reimbursed for its costs.

The receipt of £6,000 in compensation for loss of profits is taxable.

Since the company has reduced the balance on the repairs account by £18,000 and increased the balance on the profits and loss account by £6,000 no adjustments in respect of these items are necessary.

(g) *Gain on the sale of investments*

Although companies pay corporation tax on their capital gains they are not taxed under Schedule D Case I. Hence the gain of £30,000 should be deducted in order to calculate the Schedule D Case I profits.

(h) *Sales to X Ltd*

Drawings in the form of goods or services made by sole traders or partners have to be dealt with at market prices. There is no such requirement for companies and hence no adjustment needs to be made in order to calculate the Schedule D Case I profits.

However, were X Ltd and Q plc under common control and X Ltd were not a UK resident trading company, the proceeds would be deemed to be £80,000 and hence the profits would need to be increased by £30,000 in order to calculate the Schedule D Case I profits.

Question 2

(i) Bill and Ben make a joint election for industrial buildings legislation to apply

Period	Computation £	Allowances claimed £
Bill		
y/e 31.3.99		
Cost	30,000	
Less WDA	(1,200)	1,200
WDV c/f	28,800	
y/e 31.3.00		
Less WDA	(1,200)	1,200
WDV c/f	27,600	
y/e 31.3.01		
Proceeds	(20,000)	
Balance allowance	7,600	7,600
Ben		
y/e 30.6.01		
Residue before sale	27,600	
Balancing allowance	(7,600)	
Residue after sale	20,000	

The total tax life of the poultry house is 25 years. Bill owned the house for two years so the remaining tax life is 23 years.

The writing down allowance which Ben can claim for each of the next 23 years is £870 (£20,000/23).

(ii)   No election is made

Period	Computation	Allowances claimed
	£	£
Bill		
y/e 31.3.99		
Cost	30,000	
Less WDA	(1,200)	1,200
WDV c/f	28,800	
y/e 31.3.00		
Less WDA	(1,200)	1,200
WDV c/f	27,600	
y/e 31.3.01		
Less WDA	(900) (Note 1)	900
	26,700	
Ben		
y/e 30.6.01		
Allowable cost	26,700	
Less WDA	(600) (Note 2)	600
WDV c/f	26,100	

For the accounting periods from y/e 30th June 2002 to y/e 30th June 2022 the writing down allowance of £1,200 can be claimed and in the accounting period ended 30th June 2023 Ben will be able to claim an allowance of £900 which is simply the difference between the original cost of the building and the total allowances given to date. Thus by the 30th June 2023 the total allowances given will equal the original cost of the building.

Note 1
Without an election Bill is entitled to the writing down allowance in the year of disposal restricted by reference to the proportion of the period of account during which he owned the asset. Bill owned the asset for nine months and hence the writing down allowance is £1,200 × 9/12.

Note 2
Similarly Ben's writing down allowance will be restricted by reference to the proportion of the period of account during which he owned the asset. Ben owned the asset for six months and hence the writing down allowance is £1,200 × 6/12.

Question 3

Accounting period	Pool	Car (1)	Car (2)	Allowance
	£	£	£	£
15 months to 31.12.96				
Additions	10,000	12,200		
WDA × 15/12 (Note 1)	(3,125)	(3,750) × 80%		6,125
WDV c/f	6,875	8,450		
y/e 31.12.97				
Disposals	(2,000)	(7,000)		
	4,875	1,450		
Additions			13,000	
WDA	(1,219)		(3,000) × 80%	3,619
Balancing allowance		(1,450) × 80%		1,160
WDV c/f	3,656		10,000	4,779
y/e 31.12.98				
WDA	(914)		(2,500) × 80%	2,914
WDV c/f	2,742		7,500	

The Industrial Buildings Allowance for the y/e 31.12.98 is £800 (£20,000 × 4%).

Accounting period	Profits	Capital allowances	Net profits
	£	£	£
15 months to 31.12.96	35,000	6,125	28,875
y/e 31.12.97	24,000	4,779	19,221
y/e 31.12.98	42,000	2,914	39,086

Fiscal year	Basis period		Taxable profits £
1995/96	1.10.95–5.4.96	(Note 2)	11,815
1996/97	1.1.96–31.12.96	(Note 3)	23,062
1997/98	1.1.97–31.12.97		19,221
1998/99	1.1.98–31.12.98		39,086

The overlap period is 1st January 1996 to 5th April 1996 a period of 95 days. Hence the overlap profits carried forward are £6,002 (£28,875 × 95/457).

Note 1
The first period of account is 15 months long and so the writing down allowance is increased by 15/12.

Note 2
The basis period is 187 days long and the accounting period is 457 days long. Hence the taxable profits are £28,875 × 187/457.

Note 3
The basis period is 365 days long and the accounting period is 457 days long. Hence the taxable profits are £28,875× 365/457.

Chapter 6

Tax computation for Mr and Mrs Thistlethwaite for 1997/98

	Maurice £	Maurice £	Marjorie £	Marjorie £
Earned income				
Schedule E				
Salary	24,407			17,000
Less pension contributions	1,220		1,020	
AVCs			1,169	2,189
	23,187			14,811
Private health insurance	275			
Car £14,500 × 35% × 5/12	1,856			
Fuel 1,010 × 5/12	420			
	25,738			
Less professional subs	100			60
		25,638		14,751
Schedule D Case I	3,000			
Less pension contributions	600	2,400		
		28,038		
Investment income				
Bank interest £600 × 100/80	375		375	
BSI £4,000 × 100/80	2,500		2,500	
UK dividends £3,500 × 100/80	2,187		2,188	5,063
	5,062			
Less deed of covenant to				
charity £250 × 100/77	325	4,737		
Statutory total income		32,775		19,814
Less personal allowance		4,045		4,045
Taxable income		28,730		15,769
Income tax				
£4,100 × 20%		820		820
Interest and dividends				
£5,062/£5,063 × 20%		1,012		1,013
£19,568/£6,606 × 23%		4,501		1,519
		6,333		
Less tax reductions				
Married couple's allowance		275		
£1,830 × 15%				
Tax borne		6,058		3,352
Add: tax retained on charge £325 × 23%		75		
tax retained on AVC £1,169 × 23%				269
Tax liability		6,133		3,621

Capital gains tax computation for Mr and Mrs Thistlethwaite for 1997/98

	Maurice £	Marjorie £
Capital gains	8,550	8,550
Less annual exemption	6,500	6,500
Taxable gains	2,050	2,050
Capital gains tax £2,050 × 23%	472	471

Notes: Maurice had the car for only five months. The lower limit for the car benefit is thus reduced to 1,042 (2,500 × 5/12) business miles.

Question 3

Schedule E assessment for Martin for 1997/98

	£
Salary £30,000 × 9/12	22,500
Commission (none paid in fiscal year)	—
Car £30,000 × (35 − 2/3 × 35)% × 9/12 − £50 × 9/12	2,625
Fuel (Note 1)	—
Clothing allowance £600 × 10/12	500
Medical health insurance £600 × 10/12	500
Flat £1,200 × 9/12 + £(120,000 − 75,000) × 9/12 × 10%	4,275
Furniture £10,000 × 9/12 × 20%	1,500
Schedule E assessment	32,312

Note 1

The cost of private fuel was £76.67 (1,000/30 × £2.30). This is less than the amount reimbursed by Martin of £180 (£20 × 9) and hence no benefit exists.

Chapter 7

Question 1

(a) Adrienne
The FA 1985 pool

	Number of shares	Cost £	Indexed pool £
Acquisition May 88	1,500	5,000	5,000
Indexed rise $\dfrac{156.2 - 106.2}{106.2} \times £5,000$			2,354
			7,354
Disposal	1,500	5,000	7,354

Disposal from FA 1985 pool

	£
Proceeds £18,000 × 1,500/2,000	13,500
Less cost	5,000
	8,500
Less indexation allowance £(7,354 − 5,000)	2,354
Indexed gain	6,146

Disposal from 1982 holding

	Cost £	31 March 1982 value £
Proceeds £18,000 × 500/2,000	4,500	4,500
Less—cost 500/1,500 × £4,000	1,333	
—31.3.1982 value £4 × 500		2,000
	3,167	2,500

Less indexation allowance
$\dfrac{156.2 - 79.4}{79.4}$

	Cost	31 March 1982 value
0.967 × £2,000	1,934	1,934
Indexed gain	1,233	566

The chargeable gain is £566

Adrienne's chargeable gain is £6,712 (£6,146 + £566).

(b) James

Dates	Commentary	Exempt months	Chargeable months
July 83–Dec 83	(i)	6	—
Jan 84–Jun 86	(ii)	30	
Jul 86–Jun 87	(iii)		12
Jul 87–Jun 94	(iv)		84
Jul 94–Jun 96	(v)	36	—
Total		72	96

Commentary

(i)   The property was occupied as a principal private residence.
(ii) James was working overseas. It was not necessary for James to return to the property on his return to the UK because he was required by his employers to live elsewhere in the UK.
(iii) James did not return to the property after working elsewhere in the UK although not required to live elsewhere by his employers. Hence the period is chargeable.
(iv) James did not occupy the property as his principal private residence.
(v)   The final 36 months of ownership are exempt.

Capital gains tax computation	£
Proceeds	200,000
Less cost	50,000
Unindexed gain	150,000
Less indexation allowance	
$\dfrac{155.8 - 85.3}{85.3} = 0.826$	
0.826 × £50,000	41,300
Indexed gain	108,700
Less exempt proportion 72/(72 + 96)	46,586
Chargeable gain	62,114

Question 2
(a) Arthur

Capital gains tax computation	£
Proceeds	40,000
Less allowable cost	
$£120,000 \times \dfrac{40,000}{40,000 + 187,500}$	21,099
Unindexed gain	18,901
Less indexation allowance	
$\dfrac{156.0 - 103.7}{103.7} = 0.504$	
$0.504 \times £21,099$	10,634
Indexed gain	8,267

(b) Margaret

	£	£
Proceeds		65,000
Less allowable costs:		
—31.3.82 market value (Note 1)	25,000	
—enhancement expenditure	4,000	29,000
Unindexed gain		36,000
Indexation allowance		
$\dfrac{155.2 - 79.4}{79.4} = 0.955$		
$0.955 \times £25,000$	23,875	
$\dfrac{155.2 - 95.2}{95.2} = 0.630$		
$0.630 \times £4,000$	2,520	26,395
Indexed gain		9,605

Note 1
It is not necessary to calculate the indexed gain using the original cost because it will clearly give rise to a larger gain.

(c) Anne
The following reliefs may be claimed by Anne and Jocelyn:

● retirement relief
● gift relief.

The effect of claiming the reliefs is as follows:

- where both gift relief and retirement relief are available retirement relief must be claimed first. Then gift relief is calculated without reference to retirement relief. Gift relief cannot exceed the gain after retirement relief
- the maximum retirement relief available to Anne on the disposal of this business is £200,000, the chargeable gain before reliefs. Retirement relief is only available on the disposal of chargeable business assets. Chargeable business assets are all chargeable assets which are used for the purposes of trade. Assets which are held for investment purposes only are not chargeable business assets
- gift relief can be claimed when business assets are transferred provided that both the transferrer and the transferee make an election. Once the election has been made the transferrer's gain is reduced to nil and the base cost to the transferee will be taken to be the market value on the date of transfer less the amount of the gift relief.

Chapter 8

Question 1

1. Because the small companies rate of tax changed from 24% to 23% on 1st April 1997 it will be necessary to undertake two separate computations, each covering a period of six months, in order to calculate the mainstream corporation tax.

Ultimate Upholsterers Ltd
Corporation Tax Computation for the 6 months to

	31st March 1997 £	30th September 1997 £
Schedule D Case I (Note 1)	155,568	155,568
Taxed income	6,000	6,000
Chargeable gain (Note 2)	13,775	13,775
	175,343	175,343
Less charges on income	5,000	5,000
Profits chargeable to corporation tax	170,343	170,343
Franked investment income ((£18,000 × 100/80)/2)	11,250	11,250
Profits for small companies rate purposes	181,593	181,593
Corporation tax £170,343 × 33%	56,213	56,213
Less tapering relief		
9/400 × £(750,000 − 181,593) × 170,343/181,593	11,997	
1/40 × £(750,000 − 181,593) × 170,343/181,593		13,330
	44,216	42,883

Calculation of the Mainstream Corporation Tax

	£
Corporation tax for year to 30th September 1997	87,099

Less ACT: Maximum relief (20% × 340,686)	£68,137	
ACT paid		
(£(50,000 − 18,000) × 20/80)	£8,000	
ACT set off		8,000
		79,099
Less income tax suffered		
£12,000 × 23% − £10,000 × 24%		360
Mainstream corporation tax		78,739

Note 1: calculation of Schedule D Case I assessment
In order to calculate the Schedule D Case I assessment we need to calculate the capital allowances. The writing down allowance is given in the question. Ultimate Upholsterers cannot claim capital allowances on Factory 1 because the right to capital allowances on a lease of less than 50 years rests with the lessor. However, tax relief will be available on the lease premium paid. The landlord will be assessed on £24,000 (£50,000 × (25 − 1) × 2%). Ultimate Upholsterers will be able to claim relief of £1,040 (£26,000/25).

Factory 2 is eligible for an industrial buildings allowance. The remaining tax life of Factory 2 is 17 years (25 years − 8 years) because it was eight years old when Ultimate Upholsterers Ltd acquired it. The writing down allowance on Factory 2 is calculated as follows:

	£	£
Original cost (lower than purchase price)	150,000	
Annual writing down allowance		
(£150,000/17)		8,824
Extension cost	125,000	
Writing down allowance	(5,000)	5,000
Written down value carried forward	120,000	
Total allowances available		13,824
Trading profit		375,000
Less: Capital allowances		
plant and machinery	49,000	
industrial building	13,824	
Relief on lease premium paid	1,040	
		63,864
Schedule D Case I		311,136

Note 2: calculation of chargeable gain on land

	£
Proceeds (£42,000 + £5,000)	47,000
Less 31st March 1982 value	10,000
Unindexed gain	37,000
Less indexation allowance	
$\dfrac{154.4 - 79.4}{79.4} = 0.945$	
0.945 × £10,000	9,450
Indexed gain	27,550

There is no need to undertake a computation based on the original cost because it will clearly give a higher gain than using the March 82 valuation.

Chapter 9

Question 1

(a) (i) In order to be a member of a group for capital gains tax purposes a company must be either a 75% subsidiary of one or more other companies in the group, or the ultimate holding company. It is not necessary for each company to be a 75% subsidiary of the holding company but the holding company must have direct or indirect control of at least 51% of each member of the group. H Ltd holds 76% of A Ltd directly and A Ltd holds 80% of B Ltd. While B Ltd holds 75% of C Ltd H Ltd itself only controls 49.45% (76% × 80% × 75% + 75% + 0.1%) and so C Ltd cannot be a member of the group. Hence H Ltd, A Ltd and B Ltd form a group for capital gains tax purposes.

Note that B Ltd and C Ltd cannot form a separate group because a company can only be a member of one group for capital gains tax purposes.

(ii) Transfers of chargeable assets between members of the group are deemed to be at a value which gives rise to neither a gain nor a loss. The transferee company will then be deemed to appropriate the fixed asset into its trading stock. This appropriation will be treated as a chargeable disposal. The proceeds will be deemed to be the market value on the date of appropriation, the allowable cost will be the transfer value and any further indexation allowance between the date of the transfer and the date of appropriation will be available. The cost of sales of the asset will be deemed to be the market value at the date of appropriation for the purposes of Schedule D Case I.

(iii) The transferee company can elect to use the market value at the date of appropriation less the chargeable gain as the proceeds for capital gains tax purposes and as the cost of sales. This will have the effect of reducing the chargeable gains and increasing the Schedule D Case I profits. This may be beneficial if the company has unrelieved trading losses brought forward.

(b) (i) Trading losses can be surrendered by one member of a 75% group, the surrendering company, to another member of the group, the claimant company. In order to form a 75% group the ultimate holding company must have beneficial ownership, directly or indirectly, of 75% of the other members of the group. Hence H Ltd and A Ltd are members of one 75% group while B Ltd and C Ltd are members of a separate 75% group. There is no restriction on the number of groups a company can be a member of for group relief purposes. In addition D Ltd is a consortium owned company because H Ltd, P Ltd and Q Ltd each own more than 5% and less than 75% of the share capital of D Ltd and together they own more than 75% of the share capital of D Ltd.

(ii) In the case of a 75% group a loss making company can surrender any amount of its loss but the maximum surrendered loss that the claimant company can utilise is equal to its profits chargeable to corporation tax net of any of its own losses apart from losses carried back.

In the case of a consortium, the maximum that a member of the consortium can surrender to the consortium owned company is the consortium owned company's profits chargeable to corporation tax times the percentage of the ordinary share capital owned by the member. The maximum that the consortium owned company can surrender to a member of the consortium is its loss after making any s393A claim times the percentage of the ordinary share capital owned by the member.

(iii) If Q Ltd was not resident in the UK, D Ltd would not be a consortium owned company because 75% of its share capital would no longer be owned by UK resident companies. As a result D Ltd would not be able to use the provisions of group relief to surrender or claim losses from other companies.

If A Ltd was not resident in the UK it could no longer be a member of a 75% group and so could not benefit from the provisions for surrendering trading losses or claim relief for capital gains tax. B Ltd and C Ltd would still form a group.

Chapter 10

Question 1

A person who makes taxable supplies becomes liable to be registered for VAT:

- at the end of any month, if the value of his or her taxable supplies in the period of one year then ending has exceeded £48,000, or
- at any time, if there are reasonable grounds for believing that the value of his or her taxable supplies in the period of thirty days then beginning will exceed £48,000

Taxable supplies are made up of both standard rated and zero rated supplies. Since the trader's taxable supplies total £50,000 (£42,000 + £8,000) does exceed the annual limit of £48,000 the trader is liable to register for VAT. The trader must notify the Customs and Excise within 30 days of the end of the 12 months in which the limits were exceeded. The trader will then be registered from the first day of the following month.

Had the trader voluntarily registered from the beginning of the accounting period his VAT position would have been:

	£
Output tax:	
—standard rated supplies £8,000 × 17.5%	1,400
Less input tax:	
—(7,000 + 3,000) × 7/47	1,489
VAT recoverable	89

Question 2

REPORT

To: The Board of Directors
From: D Hancock
Date: 12 June 1997
Subject: VAT implications of forming a group and trading overseas

Group Position
Groups of UK registered companies under common control can elect to register for VAT as a group. Either one company must control each of the others, or one person, an individual, two or more persons in partnership, or a company, must control all the companies. It is not necessary for all members of the group to participate in the scheme. One company must be appointed as the representative member who deals with all VAT matters for the group. All members of the group are jointly and severally liable for any tax due from the representative member.

Intra-group transfers are ignored for VAT purposes and all taxable supplies to and from any member of the group are treated as a taxable supply by or to the representative member.

Imports
Tax on goods imported from outside the EU is charged and payable as if it were a duty of customs and the rate which would apply if the same goods were supplied in the home market by a registered trader. The registered trader is then able to reclaim the duty on the goods which are used for the purposes of a business carried on by him as input tax in the normal way.

Goods supplied by a registered trader resident in another EU country are zero rated. The importing trader will be required to account for VAT as both a taxable supply and input tax at the rate in force in his own country.

Exports
A supply of goods is zero rated if the Commissioners are satisfied that the person supplying the goods will be exporting to a place outside the EU.

Goods supplied to registered traders in other member states are zero rated.

Chapter 11

Question 2

(a) Mr Gog's income tax computation for 1997/98

	£	£
Earned income		29,350
Schedule E		
Investment income		
Schedule D Case III (£80,000 × 3.5%)	2,800	
Schedule D Case V (£200 × 12 × 100/80)	3,000	
		5,800
Statutory total income		35,150
Less personal allowance		4,045
Taxable income		31,105
Income tax		
(£4,100) × 20%	820	
£22,000 × 23%	5,060	
£5,005 × 40%	2,002	
£31,105		
Tax borne		7,882
Less double taxation relief (£500 × 20%)		100
Tax liability		7,782
Less tax paid under PAYE		6,700
Tax payable		1,082

Commentary

Because Mr Gog is domiciled (see part (b)) in Ruritania he is assessable on income arising outside the UK only if it is remitted to the UK. Hence interest on the account with the National Bank of Ruritania and rent from the property in Ruritania are not subject to UK tax unless income from either source is remitted to the UK.

Although Ruritania does not have a double tax treaty with the UK the Inland Revenue will give full credit for tax withheld by the country in which the income arose provided that the tax withheld does not exceed the UK tax which would have been payable if the income had arisen in the UK.

(b) Mr Gog acquired a domicile of origin when he was born in Ruritania. Because he intends to return to Ruritania eventually he has not acquired a new domicile and hence during the fiscal year 1997/98 Mr Gog is domiciled in Ruritania. However for inheritance tax purposes individuals who were resident in the UK on or after 10th December 1974 and who were so resident for at least 17 of the 20 years immediately prior to the fiscal year will be deemed to be UK domiciled for that year. Mr Gog became UK resident in 1982/83 and will be deemed to be UK domiciled got inheritance tax purposes from the fiscal year (1998/99).

(c) Transferring the foreign deposit account will not have any inheritance tax implications because it is excluded property.

Any other transfer of Mr Gog's assets to his son will be potentially exempt transfers. A potentially exempt transfer will become chargeable to inheritance tax if Mr Gog dies within seven years of making the transfer.

If all the assets are transferred the total of potentially exempt transfers will be calculated as follows:

	£
UK current account	23,000
10,000 shares in Bah plc (Note 1)	7,666
3.5% War Loan	27,000
Ruritanian antique (Note 2)	6,000
Scottish farm (Note 3)	82,500
Total	145,618
Less annual exemptions (Note 4)	6,000
Total of potentially exempt transfers	139,618

Note 1: a capital gains tax liability may arise on the transfer of the shares.

	£
Proceeds	150,000
Less cost	20,000
Unindexed gain	130,000
Less indexation allowance	
$\dfrac{158.5 - 138.9}{138.9} \times £20,000$	2,822
Indexed gain	127,178

In order to avoid a capital gains tax liability Mr Gog would have to transfer only £7,666 (£150,000 × 6,500/127,178) of shares in Bah plc.

Note 2: the transfer of the antique qualifies for the relief for chattels with a market value of £6,000 or less.

Note 3: the capital gains tax implications of disposing of the farm are:

	£
Deemed proceeds	165,000
Less cost	95,000
Unindexed gain	70,000
Less indexation allowance	
$\dfrac{158.5 - 100.0}{100.0} = 0.585$	
0.585 × £95,000	55,575
Indexed gain	14,425

If the farm is transferred a small liability to capital gains tax will arise. If Mr Gog is still unwilling to transfer the asset he could elect jointly with his son for gift relief. In this case the gain will be deferred and ultimately will be paid by Mr Gog's son when he disposes of the farm. The potentially exempt computation is made on the basis that such an election is indeed made.

The transfer of the farm gives rise to eligibility to agricultural property relief at 50%. Hence the net potentially exempt transfer is £82,500 (£165,000 – 0.5 × £165,000).

Note 4: Mr Gog can claim the annual exemption of £3,000 for both the current fiscal year and the preceding one giving a total exemption of £6,000.

(d) If Mr Gog dies before 6th April 2005 the transfers will become chargeable. However the total value transferred is less than the nil rate band of £215,000. There will be no further inheritance tax liability arising from the transfer of Mr Gog's estate on death because it will all be donated to charity. Hence the above transfers will not give rise to an inheritance tax liability if Mr Gog dies within seven years of the transfers.

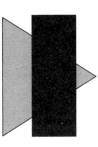

Index of cases

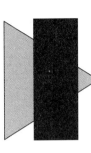

Subject index

Economic rent 43–4, 332
  taxation of 43
Effective incidence of tax 332
Eligible interest 72–3
Emoluments 132–41
Employees
  approved share option schemes 142–3
  profit sharing schemes 143–4
  share ownership plans 144
Equitable taxes 13
Estate duty 8, 10, 297
Estates
  excepted 316
  valuation at death 313, 314
European Union (EU), VAT 267, 268, 273,
  289–92
Evasion *see* Tax evasion
Excepted estates 316
Excess burden of tax 24, 41–2, 332
Excise duties 6
Excluded property 299
Exempt income, income tax 59–60
Exempt supplies, VAT 275, 280–1
Exit charge 302
Expenditure, recognition 91
Expenditure renovating assets 96
Expenditure taxes 52–3, 332
  income tax comparison 54–5
Expenses, close companies 246
Exports, VAT 289

FA 1985 pool 172–4
Fairness 47–9
Fall in value relief 313
FII *see* Franked investment income
Finance Act 1944, capital allowances 105
Finance Act 1985, shares pool 172–4
Finance Act 1988, share options 142
Finance Act 1989 146
  insurance premiums 74
  share ownership 144
Finance Act 1990 73, 74
Finance Act 1991 23
Finance Act 1994 155
Finance Acts (FA) 13, 16
Financial investment instruments 24
First year allowance 95
Fiscal neutrality 14–15, 23–4, 33–6, 38, 332
  test for 35
Fiscal year 11
Flexibility 45–6
Foreign emoluments 63
Form CT61 219, 223
Franked investment income (FII) 214, 218–20, 223
  loss relief 230–3

Franked payments 218–20
Free-standing additional voluntary contributions
  146
Furnished holiday letting 131
Furnished lettings 131, 207, 209, 211

General Aid system 6
General Commissioners
  duties 11
  introduction 7–8
Gift relief, CGT 192–3
Gifts
  IHT exemptions 300–1
  with reservation 307
Gladstone, William 8
Government borrowing, effect of 41
Gross amount of tax 269
Grossing up 305
Group charges 252
Group income 251–2
Group registration 286–7
Group relief 248, 257–60
Groups 241–2, 248–61
  associate companies 248–50
  chargeable gains 255–7
  consortia 250–1
  group relief 257–60
  rollover relief 257
  structure, tax consequences 252–3
  subsidiaries 250
  surrender of ACT 254–5
  VAT planning 286–7

Harcourt, Sir William 8–9
Hearth tax 6
Highest rate, UK/USA 14
Historical perspective 1–10
  current administration 10–16
  Roman period 2–3
  twentieth century 9–10
  UK, introduction of 3–9
HM Customs and Excise 268
HM Inspectors of Taxes 10–11
Holdover relief 190–2
Holiday lettings 131, 207, 211
Home ownership 33
  government intervention 32–3
  tax advantages 32
  tax incentives 32–3
Horizontal equity 47, 332
Housing 43–4
  tax incentives 32–3
Howe, Geoffrey 156
Hypothecated taxes 13–14, 332

Political accountability 46–7, 332
   1995 consultative document 46
Poll tax 3
   origins 5, 6
Positive cash flow 36
Potentially exempt transfers (PET), IHT 303,
   310–11, 314
Preceding year basis 87–8
Premiums on leases 131–2
Principal charge 302
Principal private residence 181–3
Profit sharing schemes 143–5
Profit-related pay relief 18
Profits chargeable to corporation tax (PCTCT)
   205
Progressive tax system 15, 20
Progressive taxes 333
Progressivity 20
Property, schedule A 130–2
Proportional taxes 333
Purchase tax 10

Qualifying child 69–70
Qualifying corporate bond 159
Qualifying loans 94
Quarter-up rule 160
Quarterly accounting 218
Quick succession relief IHT 320–1
Quoted securities 171–80
   bonus issues 175–7
   capital distributions 180
   FA 1985 pool 172–4
   1982 holding 174–5
   IHT 314
   matching 171–2
   reorganisations 180
   rights issues 177–80
   share splits 175–7
   takeovers and mergers 180

Ramsay principle 17
Rate applicable to trusts 302
Rates of tax
   CGT 162–3, 329
   corporation tax 214–18, 329
   IHT 306–7
   income tax 60, 327
Rebasing 168
Recession 46
Registered traders [VAT], definition 276
Registration, VAT 276–80
Regressionary taxation 75
Regressive taxes 333
Reinvestment relief, CGT 186–9
Related property, IHT 315

Relative, definition 243
Relevant supplies 291
Relief against income 118–20
Reliefs, personal 327
Renewals basis 130
Rent
   allowable deductions 207–8
   assessment, Schedule A 206–7
   economic 332
'Rent a room' scheme 131
Reorganisations 180
Residence 60–1, 62, 63
   definition 333
   see also Principal private residence
*Residents and Non-Residents – liability to tax in the
   UK (IR20, 1986)* 62
Retail price index 328
Retail schemes, VAT 285–6
Retirement relief, CGT 184–6, 188–9
Revenue expenditure 95
Revenue income 95
Reverse charge 288
Reversionary interest 299
Rights issues 177–80
Road fund licences see Vehicle excise duties
Road pricing, motorways 14
Rollover relief 189, 257
   CGT 189–90
Royal Commission on the Taxation of Profits and
   Income (1955:Cmd 9474) 88

Savings income 58–9
Schedular system of tax 58, 333
   introduction 7
   summary 12
Schedule A 60, 130–2
   allowable deductions 207–8
   basis of assessment 206
   holiday lettings 207, 211
   loss relief 208–9
   taxable receipts 206–7
Schedule B, abolition 7
Schedule C 62
Schedule D 12, 60–1
   Case I 12, 38, 57, 61, 87–8, 131, 204–5
   Case II 61, 87–8
   Case III 61, 205
   Case IV 62
   Case V 62
   Case VI 12, 62, 132, 207, 211
Schedule E 12, 62, 133
   allowable expenses 133–4
   basis of assessment 133–4
   benefits in kind 134–41
   Case I 63

Unquoted securities, IHT 314

Valuation, IHT purpose, guidance 314–15
Value Added Tax Act 1994 (VATA 1994) 13, 268, 277
Value added tax (VAT) 2, 8, 15, 267–95
   accounting for 271–6
   annual accounting scheme 284–5
   background 267–8
   bad debts 274
   capital expenditure 273–4
   cars 273–4, 275–6
   cash accounting scheme 283–4
   cash discounts 273–4
   definition 333
   deregistration 280
   domestic fuel 41–2, 47, 49
   double glazing 41–2
   EU harmonisation 289–92
   exempt supplies 275, 280–1
   exports 289
   fiscal neutrality 24
   impact of 270–1
   imports 287–9
   input tax 269, 273–6
   newspapers 39–40
   output tax 269
   payments on account scheme 282–3
   registration 276–9
   retail schemes 285–6
   returns 271–2
   secondhand goods scheme 286
   self-supply 274
   tax invoices 272–3
   tax planning 286–7
   tax point 269
   taxable person 268
   taxable supplies 268–9, 271, 280
   travelling costs 275–6
   voluntary registration 278–9
   zero rated supplies 281–2
VAT invoice 272
VAT period 271
Vehicle excise duties 13, 14
Vertical equity 47, 47–8, 333
Void period 207–8

Wasting asset 166
Wealth taxes 50–2, 333
Wear and tear allowance 130
Widow's bereavement allowance (WBA) 68, 327
Window tax 6
Withholding taxes 7, 333
   income tax, companies 223–5
Work effort, tax relationship 333
Work and leisure options 25–8

Zero rated supplies, VAT 281–2